ECONOMICS AND SOCIETY

LEONARD W. WEISS

UNIVERSITY OF WISCONSIN

JOHN WILEY & SONS, INC.
NEW YORK   LONDON   SYDNEY   TORONTO

This book was set in Melior by Graphic Arts Composition.
It was printed and bound by Halliday Lithograph Corporation.
The designer was Edward A. Butler. The drawings were
designed and executed by John Balbalis with the assistance of
the Wiley Illustration Department. Thomas Hitchings was the
in-depth editor. Marion Palen was the production manager.

Library of Congress Cataloging in Publication Data

Weiss, Leonard W.
  Economics and society.

  Includes bibliographies.
  1. Economics. I. Title.

HB171.5.W393   330   74-18054
ISBN 0-471-92704-X

Printed in the United States of America

10 9 8 7 6 5 4 3 2

PREFACE

This book is meant primarily for the basic, one-term principles of economics course that exists at an increasing number of colleges and universities. I feel that a solid one-term course should be a valuable part of the undergraduate program of virtually all college students. This book is an attempt to facilitate the development of such courses.

The essential features of a good one-term course are (1) that it have a solid theoretical core, and (2) that it cover the major economic policy issues in a sophisticated way. How can this be accomplished in a single term? My solution is to build the analysis around supply and demand and to avoid most marginalism. My experience is that at least a month, and more likely six weeks, are required to get across the theories of consumer choice, of the firm, and of various types of markets. Moreover, these are subjects that many general students resist and never really grasp. And a large number of general, liberal arts students who are quite capable of economics at the "informed citizen" level are turned away by them. I believe that the marginal analysis is essential for a thorough grasp of economics, but I also feel that it can reasonably be postponed until a second course.

The trick that permits me to present much of the elementary core of economic theory with hardly any reference to marginalism is the assumpton of constant costs in the long run. This, of course, makes average and marginal cost identical. I do not feel that this is a very extreme assumption. It permits a surprisingly rigorous analysis of short- and long-run competitive equilibrium, of monopoly and oligopoly, of price discrimination, and of public goods. The one place where marginal concepts seem unavoidable is in the analysis of factor markets, but, even there, the main points can be made more simple than is commonly the case. My experience is that students can grasp the elements of economic analysis at the level used in this book in quite short order.

Although I feel that theory should be the core of the one-term principles course, I am opposed to the mere development of theoretical tools for their own sake. I feel that to be interesting and to produce informed citizens, the analysis should be applied to the major policy problems of our day. I have tried to economize on the tools introduced, but to apply them again and again in many different settings. Concepts like opportunity cost, short- and long-run competitive equilibrium, and externalities appear regularly in the book after they are introduced. I try to say *opportunity cost* in every chapter but never to say *marginal cost*. I have included a few appendices containing concepts such as elasticity or the multiplier for those who feel these are essential, but they are self-contained. No other part of the book depends on them.

It would probably be a struggle to present everything in this book in one term. I have covered many policy areas, to allow for varying tastes within the profession. I feel that a good course should cover some of these topics but need not cover all of them.

The essential core of the course, to my mind, consists of Chapters 2, 3, 5, 7, 10, 12, 13, the last half of 14, and 15 and 16. A course confined to this core would be a pretty limited one, however. Users should surely pick and choose among the other chapters and appendices. In my own courses I have left out or given little emphasis to the material in Chapters 1 and 19. I have also skipped the subjects dealt with in the appendices to Chapters 5, 6, and 13: elasticity, marginal revenue, and the multiplier, respectively. I have tried to teach something about corporate and national income accounting, but here they are presented in appendices to Chapters 4 and 12, and they are also unnecessary for understanding the rest of the book.

I would expect that for a majority, or at least a large minority, of readers this book will be the only formal economics they will see at the college level. However, I hope that many students taking the course will want to go further. I can see three main routes for them. One possibility is to provide a second term at an elementary level for such students. I have taught such a course with some success. It is long on marginal analysis, micro-policy, and empirical illustrations. A second possibility is to put economics and business majors into a two-term sequence in intermediate micro and macro theory after their completion of the one-term course. I feel that they would be prepared for such courses after working through this book. Finally, with this book as background, students should be able to handle quite a large range of upper-division courses in economics. My own experience is largely in industrial organization and public control of business. I find that most of the points I cover, including quite complex discussions of price discrimination and of peak load pricing, can be presented on the basis of the simple theory developed in this book. Surely a major should have more theory than is presented here, but he can handle a surprising number of important policy issues starting at this level.

Like most of my undertakings, this book has depended heavily on the contributions of others. I was helped by many of my colleagues at Wisconsin, especially by Eugene Smolensky, Robert Haveman, and Peter Lindert. I owe a great debt of thanks to Ernest Nadel and James Sinclair for their extensive and insightful comments. Tom Hitchings did the most thorough and helpful job of editing I have ever experienced. Linda Bielski typed and typed and typed.

Leonard W. Weiss
University of Wisconsin
Madison, Wisconsin
October 1974

CONTENTS

UNIT ONE
AN
INTRODUCTION
TO
ECONOMICS

1
WHAT ECONOMICS IS

ECONOMIC ISSUES

Economics is a *social* science. It is *not* primarily concerned with how to handle personal business affairs, though a good deal of what will be said should help in that enterprise also. It *is* concerned with social issues of many sorts that are of great importance to the nation and the world. The following list comes from this morning's paper. It will be out of date by the time you read it. In a few minutes, though, you can find a similar list of topics from your paper that are equally relevant and equally economic.

☐ Consumer groups are exercised about high oil prices and the spectacular oil company profits that have accompanied them. Some are demanding that oil prices be rolled back. Others object that a rollback would cause shortages and discourage expansion by the oil companies.

☐ The Department of Justice has initiated an antitrust suit against the Oregon state bar association, charging that the attorney fee schedule that it maintains is an illegal restraint of trade.

☐ Environmentalists are challenging proposed new power plants in several states. As a result, the completion of a number of plants has been delayed. Some of our largest cities face brownouts during the peak demand periods this summer.

☐ Rapidly rising interest rates have led to a drastic slump in home construction activity. The Federal Reserve Board is still resisting pressure for easier credit, however, because it believes that lower interest rates would make inflation worse.

☐ The simultaneous problems of unemployment and inflation have led many congressmen to call for tax cuts and price and wage controls. The Administration argues that such a policy would hinder rather than help in the solution of these problems.

☐ After rising in value for six months, the dollar came under pressure on international money markets and declined moderately in value. Observers said this was due to a deterioration in the American balance of payments.

All these subjects and more are matters of economic study. The economist does not always offer a complete solution, but he can usually contribute a good deal of understanding for those who must deal with these issues.

ECONOMICS AND COMMON SENSE

Any study of economics is bound to have a lot to say about consumption, employment, prices, and wages. These subjects are all parts of our ordinary lives. Many people feel pretty expert on such subjects already and doubt that an economist can teach them much. But they are in for a surprise. Everyday experience and common sense can lead a person far astray in economics.

One major reason is that the way things look from the point of view of society as a whole is often different from the way they look from the viewpoint of an individual. A trap that students fall into repeatedly is what the logicians call the "fallacy of composition": the belief that what is true for each part must be true of the whole of those parts. Often it is not so:

☐ If your house were smaller you'd pay less property tax, but if all the houses in town were smaller, homeowners as a group would pay just about as much money in property taxes as they do now.

☐ If you drive downtown instead of taking the bus you'll probably get there sooner, but if everyone drives instead of taking the bus, most of them are likely to get there later.

☐ If a new machine is introduced that makes shoes automatically, many shoe company employees will be worse off, but the country as a whole will be better off.

☐ If a farmer has a bad crop he will be poorer, but if all farmers have bad crops, they may well earn more than they do when crops are good.

Things aren't always turned on their ears like this when seen from the point of view of society as a whole, but they often look different in the big picture.

That big picture is worth having. Once you get it, you'll see the little picture—of the world as it affects you—more clearly. Your views on many public issues are likely to change. And you may be a little more skeptical about the "obvious" conclusions of common sense.

ECONOMICS AND SCIENCE

Economics claims to be a science. At the risk of repeating a familiar tale, we will look for a minute at what the **scientific method** is.

Basically, it consists of developing theories about the world and testing them against the facts. The purpose is to be able to predict events accurately. This process, in turn, will permit us to control events more effectively.

An example will help. For centuries, diseases were explained by various environmental theories. Some diseases were attributed to bad water or bad air (including "miasmas," or swamp gas). Some were blamed on exposure to sick people, or on spontaneous generation. These theories were not empty. They reflected the accumulated experience of some of the best-educated people of each century: the doctors. By the early 1800s, some quite systematic knowledge of the spread of disease was available. It was clear by then that certain diseases that had once been thought to be spontaneous were, in fact, infectious. Experience told us to quarantine persons with certain diseases, to stay out of swamps to avoid malaria, to move to dry climates to get over tuberculosis, and to stay out of cities in the summertime. It led people to pipe water into, and sewage out of, cities. By the middle of the nineteenth century, the big cities were already developing water and sanitation systems and were somewhat less unhealthful than before.

Bacteria had been known ever since the invention of the microscope around 1590. Still, their connection with disease had not been made. Then, in the late 1850s, Louis Pasteur demonstrated that bacteria caused fermentation and the souring of milk. His discovery led a number of people to investigate the connection of bacteria to disease. During the 1870s, Pasteur identified the bacteria associated with certain diseases of silkworms, chickens, and cattle by exposing healthy animals to various germs and seeing which ones got sick—something he could hardly have done with humans. Vaccines that immunized cattle from anthrax were developed by Pasteur and Robert Koch in the early 1880s. With that step, the germ theory of disease became generally accepted. Knowing what to look for, scientists soon tracked down the major bacteria that caused human diseases. Hospitals adopted sterile techniques, and it became safe to drink the water in most of the cities of the Western world.

This story has several lessons. First, note how one theory replaced another. The old environmental theory wasn't so much wrong as it was limited. Knowing the conditions that produced malaria or measles told us little about typhus and cholera. The new theory could explain more things than the old one, and in a more general way. But the findings of the environmental studies were not discarded. Indeed, research on similar topics continues today under the title of epidemiology.

The second major lesson is that both theories were tested **empirically**—that is, tested against experience. As a theory passed more tests, it became widely accepted. Other theories along the way that didn't hold up empirically were discarded. (For instance, at one time in the 1800s, many scientists thought that oxygen caused infections.)

Third, both theories made it possible to predict the conditions that would lead to disease. Under the old environmental theories these conditions had to be searched out anew for each disease. But with the germ theory, investigators had a good idea of where to look for the cause of infectious diseases.

Fourth, with the ability to predict came the ability to control. The environmental theories led to quarantines, escape to the country during epidemics (for the wealthy), and a start on public sanitation. The germ theory led to antiseptics, vaccines, and chlorinated water.

Finally, it should be said that the germ theory wasn't the end of the matter. In this century scientists have become aware of viruses. This amendment to the germ theory finally accounted for smallpox, measles, polio, and our old adversary, the common cold. Viruses may yet provide an explanation for some cancers and for multiple sclerosis. Currently, a large amount of research is devoted to the mechanisms by which the body develops immunities to bacteria and viruses. This research could lead to theories that would partially replace the germ and virus theories. It would replace them, though, not by showing them wrong, but by offering more fruitful predictions about disease, cure, and immunity.

Economics has some similar stories. Periodic depressions were scourges almost as serious as contagious diseases in the nineteenth century. They were even worse in the first third of the twentieth century. Many economists worked on the problem and developed a number of theories. Quite a few of these theories are still valid, though limited.

In 1936 an English economist, John Maynard Keynes (pronounced "canes"), published a theory that seemed to account for depressions in a more general way. Many of his ideas depended on the previous work, but Keynes's theory was richer in predictions than its predecessors. It was subject to more empirical tests during the next twenty years than any previous theory in the history of economics.

By the late 1940s, Keynes's theory was widely accepted. It provided governments around the world with a means of predicting the effects that their actions would have on the level of economic activity. Many countries have based their economic policies firmly on this theory since the end of World War II. The United States made tentative moves in that direction in the 1940s and 1950s. Finally, it adopted a thoroughly Keynesian ("canezian") policy in the early 1960s. No major country has had a serious depression since World War II.

Yet economic research on the subject has continued. The Keynesian theory does not deal very well with inflation, and many economists feel that it understates the role of money in the economy. Many economists are working on both points. The new theories that are emerging do not so much contradict Keynes as they go beyond him. (The content of Keynesian theory and subsequent additions to it are discussed in Chapters 12–17.)

THEORY VERSUS FACT

It is the theory part of these stories that bothers many students. You regularly hear the statement, "That's all right in theory, but not in fact." It is often taken to mean that theory is unreliable and that only facts count. What it really means, if it is correct, is that the theory involved doesn't hold up very well. In that case, we need a new theory.

Actually, some sort of theory is essential if we are to understand anything at all. If someone were to set out to understand the weather in Chicago using only facts and avoiding all theory, he would be in for a tedious and unproductive chore. He could fill volumes with the detailed history of the temperature, humidity, air pressure, and precipitation in Chicago. He could do the same for other cities. Still he would have no basis for prediction. What would almost certainly happen is that he would develop theories in spite of himself. He would soon conclude that temperature rises with the length of the day and with the steepness of the angle of the sun; that storms generally move from the west to the east in the Midwest; that falling air pressure tends to precede rain, and so forth. Our investigator may not acknowledge it, but if he doesn't use some sort of theory, he won't even be able to predict that the weather will be cold in January.

We all use theory all the time. It is best to make our theory explicit, so that it can be examined for internal consistency and tested systematically against the facts.

A good theory is one that yields many predictions. For one thing, such a theory provides the basis for many tests. In addition, it generally provides a deeper understanding of its subject matter and a better means of control. The old environmental theories of disease were of some value, but most of them were special to particular diseases. The germ theory was a big improvement because it explained many diseases at once. It also provided a better understanding of how disease was transmitted. As a result, we learned to control communicable diseases of all sorts.

The development of predictions from a theory involves the use of logic to derive the theory's implications. Using logic and some unexplained observations, scientists were able to predict the existence of viruses as early as 1898—even though viruses remained invisible until the invention of the electron microscope almost half a century later.

All theories begin with assumptions, and assumptions always involve simplifications. Theories almost always assume that "all other things are equal." The higher the angle of the sun, the warmer it will be—*given* the *same* location, and the *same* cloud cover, air pressure, wind, and so forth. Likewise, a certain microbe will have a predictable effect, *given* the proper genetic background and environment of the organism affected.

Most theories simplify the world even more than these examples do. Physicists assume a perfect vacuum or no friction for many purposes, even though neither condition can be attained on this earth. Biologists often assume that organisms have identical genetic backgrounds, something that occurs only in identical twins. Similarly, at various points in this book we will assume that there are only two countries in the world or that our country produces only two goods.

Simplifying assumptions like these do not make a theory invalid. In fact, they must often be made if we are to get anywhere at all. What count are the number and significance of the predictions that we can derive from a theory and how well these predictions hold up when tested. It is true that different assumptions may result in different predictions. Some of the great leaps in human thought have occurred when new theories were constructed on the basis of new assumptions. But what made the new theories important—instead of mere exercises in logic—was that they yielded a richer set of predictions about the world than theories that had gone before, and that those predictions held up when tested.

THE FORM OF ECONOMIC THEORIES

The theories of economics are often expressed in mathematical form, but you don't need to be a mathematician to read economics. Neither this book nor the ones listed at the ends of the chapters will require skills

TABLE 1.1 A hypothetical altitude-temperature function

ALTITUDE	TEMPERATURE
Sea level	70°
2,000 ft.	65°
4,000 ft.	60°
6,000 ft.	55°
8,000 ft.	50°

beyond simple arithmetic and enough elementary algebra to solve for x in the expression $5 + 4x = 25$. In other words, everyone who made it past junior high school should be able to understand all the mathematics in this book.[1]

Our analysis *will* make regular use of graphs, however. It may be useful to introduce them right here. We will speak a good deal about **functions**, a technical term that merely means relationships. For instance, the relationship between altitude and temperature can be thought of as an altitude–temperature function.

Functions can be expressed in various ways: as **schedules** (that is, tables), as graphs, or as equations. The schedule in Table 1.1 might show the relationship between altitude and temperature at 8:00 on a summer morning at a particular location. The numbers are hypothetical, but the relationship seems to be right, in that the temperature drops as altitude increases.

The same function can be expressed equally well as a **curve** in a graph or diagram such as that shown in Figure 1.1. ("Curve" is a general term for any function expressed as a graph. Even straight lines are called curves in economics.) Each dot represents a combination of altitude and temperature from Table 1.1. The lines connecting the dots provide us with estimates for altitudes not shown in the schedule. For instance, we would expect the temperature at 5,000 feet to be 57½ degrees. Note that the curve in this graph slopes downward to the right, meaning that the temperature is a *decreasing function* of altitude. That is, temperature falls as altitude rises.

This temperature function can also be expressed as an equation. In this

[1] It is only fair to add that professional economists use considerably more sophisticated mathematics today. Persons thinking of doing graduate work in the field should take a year of calculus and probably a term of matrix algebra before they get out of college. But you can understand everything in elementary economics, and for that matter in most undergraduate economics at any level, even if you are completely innocent of either subject.

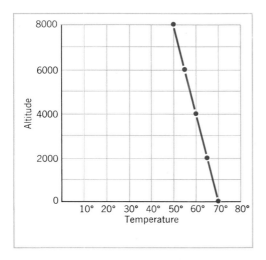

FIGURE 1.1 A graph of air temperature against altitude at 8:00 A.M. The dots represent the values from Table 1.1. From the curve it is easy to estimate temperatures at other altitudes.

case the equation is: $T = 70° - (.0025°A)$, where T stands for temperature and A for altitude. At zero altitude, the temperature is 70 degrees. At 2,000 feet, the temperature is

$$70° - (.0025° \times 2,000) = 70° - 5° = 65°$$

and so forth. This book will try to keep such equations to a minimum, however. Most functions will be expressed as schedules or curves.

Now consider what happens when a function changes. Let's wait until noon and measure air temperatures again. There will still be a systematic relationship between altitude and temperature, but this time the temperatures will be higher than before at each altitude. Table 1.2 reproduces Table 1.1 and adds a third column for noontime temperatures. Each number in the third column is greater than its counterpart in the 8:00 column. Similarly, Figure 1.2 shows the two altitude–temperature

TABLE 1.2   The altitude-temperature function as time changes

ALTITUDE	TEMPERATURE AT 8:00 AM	TEMPERATURE AT NOON
Sea level	70°	80°
2,000 ft.	65°	75°
4,000 ft.	60°	70°
6,000 ft.	55°	65°
8,000 ft.	50°	60°

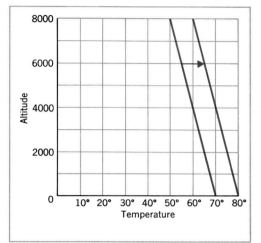

**FIGURE 1.2   The altitude-temper-
ature function later in the day. At
noon the air at all levels is warmer,
and the curve shifts over to the right.**

functions as curves. At noon the entire curve is shifted over to the
right—that is, toward higher temperatures. However, it still has the same
shape, sloping downward to the right, because temperature still falls as
altitude rises. As a result of the shift, the temperature is higher at each
altitude than before. We will see relationships expressed as schedules
and curves like these again and again throughout the book.

The function used here was intentionally simple. Only one variable,
altitude, was used to explain temperature. In fact, many other factors are
also relevant. A complete explanation of temperature would have to
consider the time of day, the season, the longitude, and the amount of
cloud cover as well as the altitude. Human minds are limited, however.
They cannot easily juggle a half dozen variables at once. We can say how
temperature changes as altitude increases, but who can say what will
happen if the altitude increases, we move 500 miles to the south, and it
rains? Actually, it is possible to take many different variables into
account at once using modern computer techniques, but that isn't feasible here. Instead we assume that *all other things are equal*. We see how
temperature changes when only the altitude increases. The functions
described showed how temperature changes with altitude, *given the*
time of day, the season, the location, and the cloud cover. A change in
any one of the variables that we were holding constant will shift the
altitude–temperature curve, as it did when the time of day changed in
Figure 1.2.

EMPIRICAL TESTS IN ECONOMICS

Relationships that are worked out in theory are not the end of the story. The largest part of economic research consists of testing our theories.

Most of the natural sciences depend primarily on experiments for their empirical work (though this is not true of astronomy or meteorology). But economics, as we have said, is a *social* science. It has some disadvantages in empirical testing as a result. Biologists really can come close to keeping the genetic backgrounds of animals in their experiments constant by inbreeding many generations. Chemists can keep conditions almost constant by using pure chemicals and clean test tubes. But even when economists do run experiments—for instance, trying different health insurance or welfare programs on different people—they can't keep the genetic backgrounds and previous experience of their subjects the same. Moreover, people read the newspapers and learn from experience, unlike molecules. As a result, economic experiments must be ingeniously planned. They must be interpreted keeping in mind all the other factors that affect people's decisions. Most of the time experiments of any sort are impossible.

The leading method of empirical testing in economics today is statistical. As an example, let's go back to the altitude–temperature relationship. Meteorologists can test it by releasing balloons and reading temperatures as the balloons rise. The result might be a series of observations like those in Table 1.3, reproduced as the dots in Figure 1.3. The observations do not fall into a perfectly straight line. Perhaps there are differ-

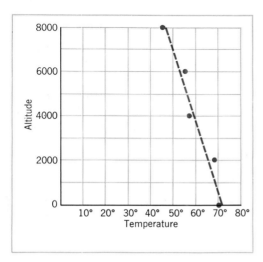

FIGURE 1.3   Actual measurements would probably not fall in a perfect straight line because of differing local conditions or measurement errors. The broken curve is an attempt to estimate the underlying relationship. If the fitted curves are similar in repeated tests, we can have confidence in our attitude –temperature function.

TABLE 1.3   Altitude-temperature measurements

ALTITUDE	TEMPERATURE
Sea level	70°
2,000 ft.	68°
4,000 ft.	57°
6,000 ft.	55°
8,000 ft.	52°

ences in local conditions or errors in our measurements. But there is still a systematic tendency for temperature to fall as altitude rises. Functions like the ones represented in Figures 1.1 and 1.2 would be based on many such experiments.

Statisticians have developed methods by which they can find the curve that best "fits" a set of observations like those in Figure 1.3. They can also estimate the range within which the true relationship is likely to lie. We will not examine these statistical methods here, but they underlie much of what will be said in this book.

Of course, having made an empirical study, we have not actually proven the rule that we set out to test. In fact, we can *never* prove it empirically. We merely don't *dis*prove it.

Repeated tests that all support a theory may give us enough confidence in it to use it in our work. For instance, repeated balloon flights may help us to predict the temperature. But we could still be surprised. For instance, there are such things as temperature inversions, in which a cool air mass is trapped under a warmer one. Similarly, the conclusions of economic analysis, no matter how often they are confirmed in empirical tests, are still only generalizations. They are useful, but they may not hold universally. A pot of gold (or at least a tenure appointment at a leading university) waits for the person who proves one of the major economic principles false in some important way. It has been done before.

POSITIVE AND NORMATIVE ECONOMICS

Economic knowledge, then, consists of a body of theory, often expressed in schedules or curves, that can be confirmed or disproved by observations of the real world and that has held up under testing. But there is more to economics. The whole point of the discipline is to give us the background for important policy decisions. Such decisions require more than a knowledge about what the world is like. We also have to decide where we want to go.

Economists often draw the distinction between *positive* and *normative* economics. **Positive economics** has to do with questions about what the world is like. The relationship of temperature to altitude could be described as a simple bit of "positive meteorology." In economics, statements about how income is actually distributed, or how consumers respond to changes in income or price, are positive economic statements. Both theoretical and empirical studies are directed toward making such statements. There may be initial disagreements about some aspect of the world, but reasonable people can ultimately be convinced by logic or evidence or both that positive statements in meteorology or economics are true or false.

Normative economics has to do with whether particular conditions or trends in the economy are desirable or not. Their desirability is a matter of individual values. It is not susceptible to logical or empirical proofs. If you feel that greater equality of income is a bad thing, I cannot prove to you that it is not. I *can* perhaps show you what effect greater equality will have, and I may bring to your attention effects that you had not considered. This information may even convince you that your initial judgment was wrong. But if you do change your mind, it will be because your first judgment was in conflict with another one of your values. You must weigh your own values and decide for yourself what is desirable and undesirable in economic life.

This is not to say that we can ignore normative economics. On every policy issue some value judgments are necessary. However, the individual and not the text must make them.

Fortunately, there seems to be considerable agreement in our society on what is good or bad in many areas of economic life. At various points in this book we will discuss the policies that probably best fit particular widely held value judgments. When we do, we will try to point out the value judgments involved. You have every right to draw different normative conclusions to the extent that your own values differ.

A few of the value judgments that are widely held in mid-twentieth century American society are worth spelling out. You can look over the list and see if you agree. There is no way to make these judgments binding on you if you do not.

☐ An increase in income per person is a good thing, though not the only goal in life.

☐ Clean air and water are good things, though, again, not the only goals in life.

☐ If one person gains at the expense of another, it would be desirable if the winner would compensate the loser.

☐ It would be bad for someone to gain at the expense of the rest of us just because he is in a powerful position.

☐ Greater equality of income is a good thing.

☐ Poverty is a bad thing.

☐ Unemployment is undesirable.

☐ Inflation is undesirable.

☐ An increase in your own economic welfare is a really good thing.

You may or may not agree with some or all of these statements. Probably you would support most of them by themselves. It is when there is some tradeoff between two or more of these values that differences of opinion arise. For instance, you may oppose both inflation and unemployment. But what happens if you had to suffer inflation to attain low levels of unemployment? How much unemployment would you be willing to permit to prevent inflation? You and your neighbor are quite likely to differ on questions like this one. Since the issues are normative, you won't be able to prove him wrong, and vice versa.

The last item on the list, personal self-interest, is bound to play a role in most public policy decisions. People who stand to be seriously hurt by a decision usually oppose it. Those who will be significantly helped by it usually support it, regardless of their other values. When the welfare of a powerful group is at stake we often adopt policies that run counter to widely supported values. It is not rare to have policies that slow economic growth or harm the environment or make for greater inequality or do all three at once. We can't prove them "wrong," but we can show how they affect widely held values.

SUMMARY

Economics is a social science. It is mainly oriented toward public policy, though it has something to say about business decisions as well. The method of science is to develop theories and to test them against experience. All theories involve simplifying assumptions. The usefulness of a theory depends not on the correctness of its assumptions, but on the number of predictions that it yields and on how well those predictions hold up.

Economic theories are often expressed as functions, which may be presented as schedules, curves, or equations. When there are changes in the things we have assumed to be constant, the precise values of a function may change. The basic relationship usually remains. Experiments are seldom possible in economics, though. The most common way to test economic theories is with statistics.

Positive economics consists of theories about the way the economic world behaves. It is subject to logical discussion and empirical tests. Normative economics consists of value judgments about what is desirable in economic life. Each person must decide normative questions for himself. There seems to be widespread agreement about many economic values taken one at a time. The disagreements arise when we must trade off one goal against another. Conflicts are especially likely when one of the values involved is personal self-interest.

STUDY QUESTIONS

1 If you study harder, you will learn more and you will get better grades. If everyone in class studies harder, will the class as a whole learn more? Will the average grade in the class as a whole necessarily be better? You could commit the "fallacy of composition" here. Would it hurt in answering the first question? The second question?

2 The following numbers represent the heights and weights of eight persons, all of ages eighteen to 21:

HEIGHT	WEIGHT	HEIGHT	WEIGHT
5'2"	135 lbs.	5'10"	137 lbs.
5'8"	166 lbs.	5'4"	122 lbs.
5'10"	160 lbs.	5'0"	105 lbs.
5'7"	146 lbs.	5'9"	150 lbs.

Try estimating a height–weight function based on these observations. First plot each observation as a point on a piece of graph paper, with height on the vertical axis and weight along the horizontal axis. Then move a ruler around until it comes closest to passing through the eight points and draw a line. Next, read off the estimated weights along the line at 5'0", 5'2", 5'4", and so forth. Record those weights in a new height–weight schedule.

Now add one more bit of information. The four persons listed on the left above are of a different sex from those on the right. Go back to your graph and turn the dots representing one group into **x**'s. Draw a new height–weight curve for each sex separately. Which is men and which is women?

3 Which of the following disciplines is most similar to economics in method? Explain.

☐ Geometry

☐ Chemistry

☐ Meteorology

☐ Ethics

4   Can you explain why your breath is short at high altitudes *without using theory?*

5   Are the following statements positive or normative?

☐ A person who goes into debt to cover current expenses is making a mistake.

☐ A tax that falls more heavily on the poor than on the rich is unfair.

☐ The lower the unemployment level is, the more severe inflation is.

☐ The moon is made of green cheese.

6   How can you tell if a positive economic statement is correct? How can you tell if a normative economic statement is correct?

2
THE
SOURCES
AND
PROBLEMS
OF
ECONOMIC
GROWTH

STANDARDS OF LIVING AND RATES OF GROWTH

Most Americans are rich. Our standards of living in the 1970s are roughly twice those of our parents at the start of World War II. Our parents, in turn, were living about twice as well as our grandparents at the turn of the century, and so forth back at least to the Civil War. Americans, Canadians, and the peoples of northwestern Europe have average incomes many times those of most of the rest of the world. Many of the people of Asia, Africa, and Latin America earn incomes at which we would *literally* starve.

This state of affairs is perhaps the most important fact about the economic world today. How did the West attain its wealth? Can our economic growth continue? Should it? And can the rest of the world get on the same gravy train, or are the low-income countries doomed to perpetual poverty?

These issues will be the main concern of this chapter. The reader should be warned, though, that the discussion will also be used as a hook on which to hang many basic concepts that are essential to the understanding of economics in general. When you see them, stop and examine them carefully. They will reappear throughout the book.

A good way to start is to spell out our evidence about economic growth in a little more detail. We will measure it in terms of the **gross national product**, or **GNP**. The GNP is the total output of final goods and services of a country. Except for a few accounting quibbles, GNP is also equivalent to the total income earned by the people of the country involved.[1] Since we are mainly concerned about individual standards of living, we will usually be interested in GNP per person (that is, GNP ÷ Population).

Figure 2.1 shows how GNP per capita varies across the world today. The red and pink patches that mean near-subsistence standards of living are the typical lot of mankind. But the black and grey areas have now reached across the temperate zones of the world. These countries have standards of living that were just not available to any but the aristocracy over most of history. Jesus said, "For the poor you have always with you." That has certainly been the case to date. Starvation was a feature of every civilization that ever existed until about two centuries ago. It still threatens in the poorest half of the world. There were famines during the lives of Aristotle, St. Thomas Aquinas, and Shakespeare. Those writers didn't dwell on them because they thought such events were normal. For most people in history, life has always been brutal and short. Nevertheless, some countries did get out of this eternal rut. How did they do it, and what are the chances for the rest of the world?

OUTPUT POTENTIAL AND PRODUCTIVE RESOURCES
SCARCITY

Although we are the richest people who have ever lived, all of us still have unfulfilled wants. If someone came to class and started handing out dollar bills, just about all of us would accept them; we would undoubtedly have very good uses for them. This reaction illustrates the fundamental fact of economics: **scarcity.** We don't have enough resources to satisfy every want of every person. No society ever has in the past or does now. There simply isn't enough to go around.

Scarcity underlies everything that will be said in this book. Because the things we consume and the resources that produce them are scarce, it is worthwhile to worry about how efficiently our resources are used, how these resources can be increased, and how our output is distributed

---

[1] The definition of GNP and the quibbles that distinguish it from national income will be explored in Chapter 12.

FIGURE 2.1   Per capita gross national product around the world.

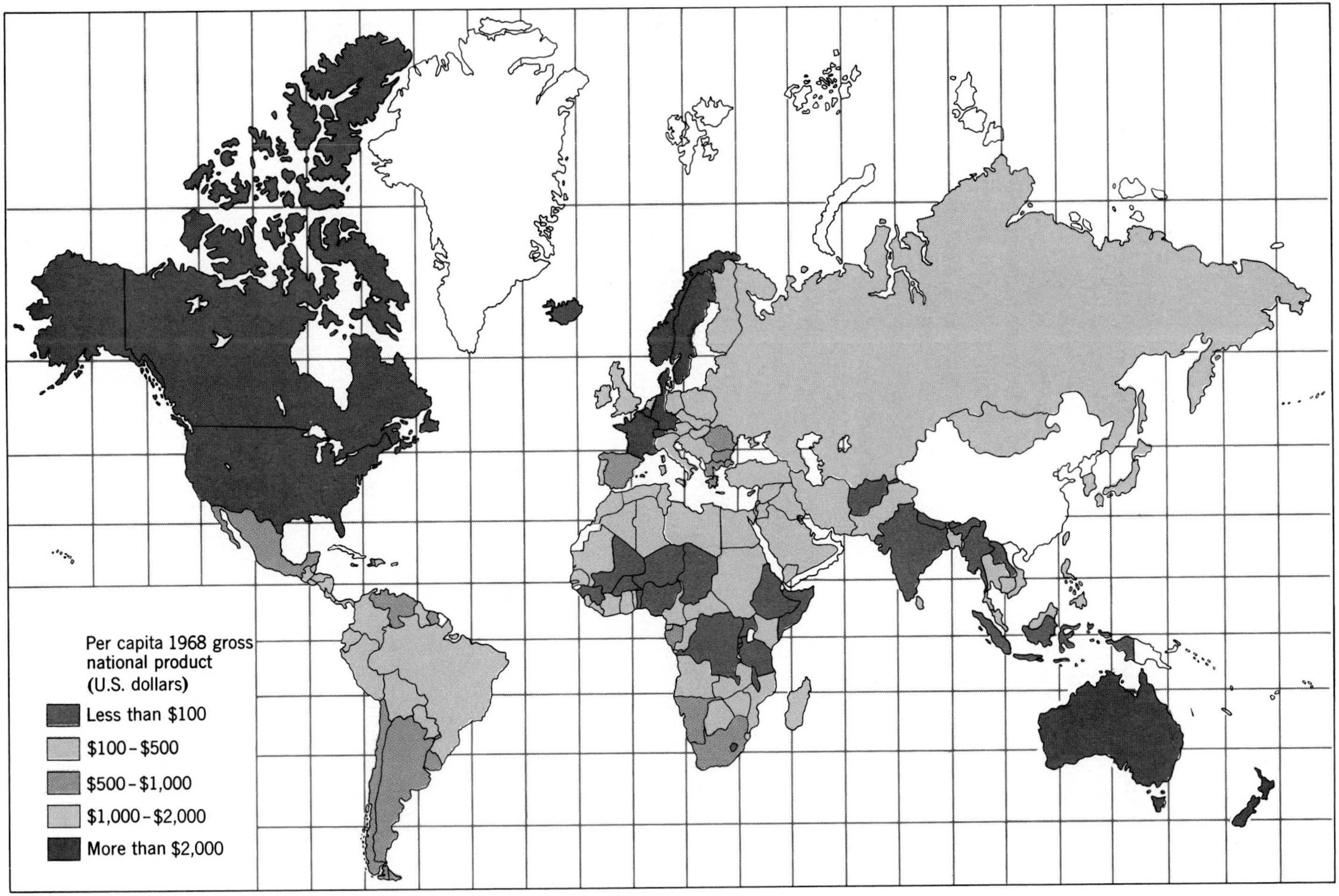

Per capita 1968 gross
national product
(U.S. dollars)

Less than $100

$100–$500

$500–$1,000

$1,000–$2,000

More than $2,000

TABLE 2.1   An alternative product function

FOOD	CLOTHING
200	0
150	50
100	80
50	95
0	100

among various wants and various persons. These questions will be our concern throughout the book. In the broadest sense, economics can be thought of as the study of how society allocates its scarce resources among alternative ends.

ALTERNATIVE PRODUCT CURVES

This basic problem of scarcity and its relationship to economic growth can be illustrated with a new concept, the **alternative product function.** Such a function shows the maximum possible output of a hypothetical country that produces only two different products, say clothing and food. For any level of food output, it shows the amount of clothing that the country will also be able to produce, and vice versa. The reason we have limited it to just two products is simple: it allows us to graph the function on a sheet of two-dimensional paper, the only kind we have.

Table 2.1 shows several alternative combinations of food and clothing that an economy could produce if it utilized its resources fully. The relationship is plotted in Figure 2.2.

If the country put all of its resources into producing food, it would turn out 200 units per year at most. Instead, it could divert some of its resources to producing clothing. At first it would not have to give up much food to do so, because the resources diverted (maybe old ladies with knitting needles) wouldn't be producing much food anyway. But these gains could not go on forever. Even if our hypothetical economy were to put all of its resources into clothing, it could produce only so much—only 100 units per year according to Figure 2.2. The last steps would be very costly in terms of food. This time the country would be diverting resources that are highly effective in producing food but that can't produce much clothing (perhaps Iowa land).

The diagram in Figure 2.2 is called an **alternative product curve,**

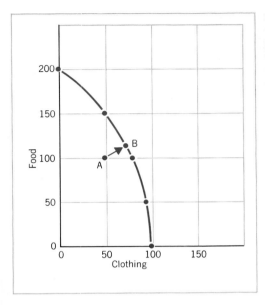

FIGURE 2.2   An alternative product curve. This one shows all the possible combinations of food and clothing that a hypothetical country could produce. If it is producing at lower levels, as at point A, it is not using its resources fully.

because it shows the various alternative combinations of products available to society.[2]

If the country in Figure 2.2 happened to be operating at point A, producing 100 bushels of food and 50 suits of clothing, its problem of economic growth would be comparatively easy. It could just increase the output of either food or clothing or both, perhaps to point B. The reason is that at point A, the country was not employing its resources fully. Once it gets to a point such as B, however, the problem gets harder. Now the country is making full use of its resources. Any further increase in the output of clothing can be accomplished only by giving up some food. And any overall economic growth requires an increase in the nation's total capacity. Somehow the whole curve must be shifted outward.

When a country starts out in a depression, growth like that from A to B is possible. However, most of the rising standards of living that have characterized Western experience have been due to repeated outward shifts in the output frontiers. These shifts can occur only if a nation's

[2] Such curves are sometimes referred to as "production possibilities curves" or as "transformation curves." The last term is used because they show the rate at which resources of a country can be diverted from one product to another and thus, in effect, the rate at which one product can be transformed into another. Given a little time, economies are much more flexible than they often appear to be. For instance, the United States "transformed" almost half its output from civilian goods to military goods between 1941 and 1945 and back again from 1945 to 1948.

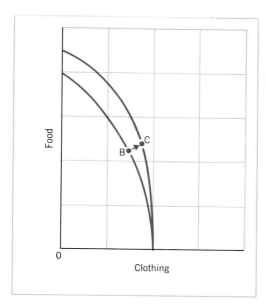

FIGURE 2.3 If some development makes possible more food production, the whole curve pivots. Most likely, the country will produce more of both food and clothing than before.

resources are increased or if they are used with more efficiency.

Figure 2.3 shows the case of a country that has just completed a dam. It can now irrigate a great deal more land and thus grow more food. The dam affects only food production directly. But in practice there is a good chance that production of both food and clothing will increase. The citizens of that country are apt to reflect their good fortune in increased consumption of all sorts. The country will be able to shift some workers from food to clothing production and still have more food than before.

Next, try a new development in the clothing industry, such as the invention of a power loom. The output frontier pivots again, this time along the clothing axis, as in Figure 2.4. Finally, a rise in the number of workers due to growing population can raise the nation's capacity in both dimensions at once. This is what happens in Figure 2.5.

FACTORS OF PRODUCTION

The economic resources of a country are commonly referred to as **factors of production**. They could be classified in any number of ways, but traditionally they have been assigned to three basic categories: land, labor, and capital. These terms need careful definition, because in each case economists have adopted words in common parlance and given them their own, peculiar meanings.

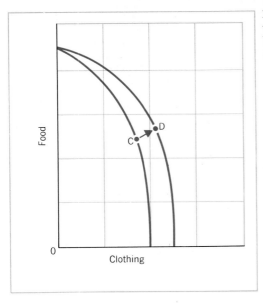

FIGURE 2.4 A new technique in the clothing industry makes possible greater production of both food and clothing.

Land means all the natural resources used in production. This category includes what the real estate agent means by land (mainly location) and what the farmer means by land (mainly topography, climate, and natural fertility) and all other useful natural endowments as well. It includes all natural mineral resources, virgin forests, and such invaluable geographic features as the Great Lakes, San Francisco Bay, and the Strait of Gibraltar. In one sense there is only so much land in the world. However, more of it can be made available for use. Land is increased through discovery (as when we strike oil) or through development (as when the Dutch reclaim another polder from the North Sea) or through improved transportation (as when we complete a pipeline to the North Slope of Alaska).

Labor refers to all the human effort expended on production. It includes the efforts of self-employed farmers and merchants as well as of those with paying jobs. It includes white-collar labor as well as blue; managers as well as those managed; and union members, free riders, and those who are never blessed by unions one way or another. As long as we are human and we are willing to work, we contribute to the nation's supply of labor.

Capital as a factor of production includes all man-made resources. It is a particularly tricky concept, because in other contexts capital sometimes has a quite different meaning, even to economists. Some elements

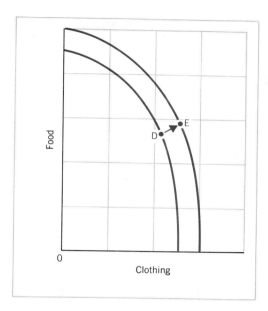

FIGURE 2.5 A rise in the number of workers through population growth can expand the country's production capacity for both goods at once.

of capital are straightforward enough. Buildings and equipment fall into this category in everyone's book. It may be worth mentioning, though, that a house occupied by its owner is just as much a part of the nation's capital stock as a house that is rented.

Inventories are also capital. They include stocks of seed in the ground, materials in process, and final products ready for sale. If these inventories didn't exist, our farms, factories, and stores couldn't produce much of anything. Up to a point, our productive capacity will increase as the size of such inventories grows. Much of the spectacular economic growth in Europe and Japan after World War II was due to the replacement of inventories. Right after the war, inventories were down almost to zero. To produce a car, a manufacturer had to scrounge all over Europe for steel, the steel producers had to struggle to find coal, and so forth. But just a few years later, the same steel mills and auto plants were producing at full blast—and often with little more labor, plant, and equipment than before. The reason was merely that they now had full stockpiles of materials.

The main difficulty with the term "capital," however, is what it does *not* include. In many contexts, capital means financial instruments, such as stocks, bonds, mortgages, and even bank accounts. However, these items are *distinctly not* included in capital as a factor of production. To see the reason, compare what happens when we build a new plant or machine with what happens when we issue a new stock or bond or mortgage.

A new machine means that we can produce more. (In other words, the alternative product curve shifts outward, as it did when we went from B to C in Figure 2.3.) But we do not gain any more productive capacity just because we have more stocks or bonds. Stocks and bonds are often issued in order to *finance* new equipment. But it is the equipment itself that increases our productive resources, not the bonds. It would be double counting to include both the financial instruments and the machines as capital. Similarly, I own my house. The bank owns a mortgage against my house. That mortgage is a claim against my property. We can't count both the house and the mortgage as parts of the country's stock of capital.

To look at it another way, whenever we issue new stock or bonds some of us own more—but others of us owe more by the same amount. The country as a whole, including both parties, is neither richer nor poorer. But when we build new plant or equipment the country *is* richer. Stocks and bonds by themselves do not produce anything. Capital as a factor of production is defined to exclude financial instruments. Otherwise, it would appear that we could increase our productive resources just by running the printing presses.

INCREASING EFFICIENCY

A nation can increase its GNP either by increasing its factors of production or by using them more efficiently. Both methods were important in the growth of the Western world.

TECHNOLOGICAL PROGRESS

Technological change has always been an important means of increasing efficiency. If asked how and when Western man got out of the eternal rut, most people would certainly point to the Industrial Revolution. That development was basically the adoption of new techniques on a large scale in a wide variety of fields. Actually, economic historians feel that technological change in agriculture was at least as important as the obvious changes in industry. In England, where it all began, a widespread "enclosure" movement converted the Medieval open fields into modern farms. Enclosure reached its peak in the 1700s. This development permitted the systematic breeding of stock and the cultivation of root crops in larger fields. These and other changes greatly increased the productivity of agriculture. The result was the release of a large number of farm workers, who supplied the labor for the new factories. The flow of new techniques, once begun, has never stopped. It still shows up in continuously increasing productivity.

The importance of these changes is probably obvious. However, a few qualifications are in order. First, technological change is often very disruptive. It leaves behind it a trail of obsolete equipment and workers with useless skills. When the enclosure movement was under way, many people considered it an unmitigated evil. One morose soul declaimed, "Inclosure, thou'rt a curse upon the land." Enclosure swamped England with displaced peasants. While the absorption of these poor people into factory jobs eventually turned out to be the Industrial Revolution, it meant many years of misery for many people while the process was under way.

Modern Americans can get some idea of the costs involved by considering a much smaller "enclosure movement" that occurred in the South after World War II. In those years, the cotton industry was mechanized. The old sharecropping system, in which tenant farmers produced cotton by hand- and mule-power on small acreages, was largely phased out. The change has released millions of black workers with virtually no urban skills into our cities. Eventually they will almost certainly be better off than in their former, miserable existence, but the cost of the transition during the first generation or two has been terrible.

In the long run, society as a whole benefits from technological progress through lower prices or higher incomes. However, there are often victims along the way. Society could protect these people by preventing the changes. But a better solution for all concerned is to help the losers fit into the new world by training them in new skills and helping them move to new locations.

The process of technological change itself uses resources that could otherwise go into consumer goods. Most of the changes in agriculture and industry involved large investments in new capital. They also required the learning of new skills. You could produce textiles more efficiently with power looms than with hand looms. In order to do so, however, you had to invest in a water mill or a steam engine to drive the looms, and you had to train workers to tend them.

For all its costs and disruptions, technological change must be one of the main hopes for raising living standards in the low-income countries today. It is also a major hope for any further improvements in the West as well. The prospects are fairly bright. The pace of research and development seems to be accelerating, if anything. The prospects for the low-income countries are particularly good, because they have examples to follow. They can often adapt well-developed techniques to their own uses. Certainly one of the great events of human history was the spread of the new technology from its birthplace in England. It carried to Europe and North America in the nineteenth century, and to the other temperate-zone countries of the world in this century. Today it is well advanced in a few of the tropical countries: Mexico, Brazil, and Malaysia, for instance. Most of the remaining low-income countries are eager to join the parade.

SPECIALIZATION

Another source of increased efficiency is increased specialization. Specialization has always been closely linked with industrialization. Compare a typical seventeenth-century peasant or frontier farmer with almost any modern Westerner. One of the most striking differences is that the peasants were generally jacks-of-all-trades, while we are practically all specialists. They produced most of what they consumed, aside from a little iron, sugar, and tea, which had to be traded for on the outside. You and I produce almost exclusively for the market, and most of us would starve if we had to depend on our own output. Even the modern farmer goes to the store for most of his necessities.

Specialization offers several sources of efficiency. First, it permits a great deal of economy in training. Each of us has to learn only one trade instead of all the skills needed in production. Second (and really part of the first), we can be much more thoroughly trained in what we do undertake. Instead of learning a little bit about everything, we can learn all there is to know about one occupation. Third, we are much more likely to conceive of new improvements if we are thoroughly trained in one job than if we know only a little bit about a hundred. And finally, specialization permits us to make full use of the differences in abilities that were built into us at birth. We are much better supplied with both operas and economics lectures if I give the lectures and Joan Sutherland sings in the operas.

Specialization among regions is just as important. By letting North Carolina produce shirts and cigarettes while Wisconsin produces cheese and beer, we can have more of all four items than if each state insisted on producing everything it needed for itself. Such gains from specialization seem obvious to almost everyone. Still, many people seem to get off the track when we reach international boundaries. They are wrong. It pays the countries of the world to specialize just as it pays regions of the country to do so. We will expand on this point in Chapter 18.

Specialization has its costs, just as technical progress does. For specialization to work we must become interdependent, and that means

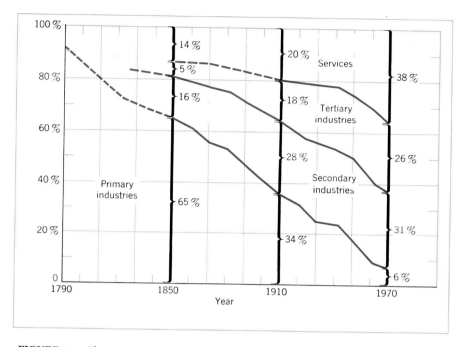

FIGURE 2.6   **The percentage of total employment in the various sectors of the American economy since 1790. Primary industry's share has continuously declined, while that of the services has steadily grown.**

a lot of resources must be devoted to distribution and exchange. Somehow the Wisconsin cheese and beer must get to North Carolina, and the shirts and cigarettes have to get back.

All the nations of the world that have set out on the route to industrialization have had to put a large part of their resources into transportation, wholesaling, and retailing. Figure 2.6 shows the share of the United States labor force employed in the main branches of industry at various stages in its history. In the beginning we were mostly in **primary industries**—that is, industries devoted to extracting goods from nature.[3] This group includes mining, forestry, fishing, and agriculture.

The primary share of the total labor force has declined continuously. By 1970 only six percent of the American labor force was in primary

---

[3] Actually, the first census that asked about occupations was in 1820. Before that date we have to guess about occupations by place of residence. In 1790 more than 90 percent of the American population was on the farm.

industries. At first, the main gainers were the **secondary industries**. These industries take raw materials produced in primary industries and convert them into manufactured goods or buildings. This development is pretty much what one would expect in a country undergoing an *industrial* revolution. But the secondary share itself just about stopped growing about World War I and is, if anything, declining now.

The continuous gainers have been the **tertiary industries**—those that aid in the exchange of goods, such as transport, wholesaling, and retailing. This transition is almost inevitable with the growth of specialization and interdependence. The remaining sector of the economy is the **services**. They include finance, law, medicine, education, entertainment, and government, as well as the personal services. This sector has grown even faster in recent decades.

Some people express a certain concern about a country in which a quarter of the population is shopkeepers. They can see something productive about a farmer starting with seed and winding up with wheat, or a manufacturer starting with wheat and ending up with flour or bread. But what do all those merchants produce when all they do is push the same goods back and forth? Actually, they produce quite a lot. Wheat in Kansas is no more useful to me than wheat that has never been grown. Even bread in gross lots at the bakery doesn't help me any. The man who provides it in quantities I can use at the time and place that I need it is adding to its value just as much as the farmer, the miller, and the baker were. He won't provide those services unless I pay him for them.

The growth of distribution, and the specialization that it allowed, has undoubtedly contributed a lot to the economic progress of the West over the last two centuries. However, it is not so clear that we have much more to gain along these lines. In fact, trade's share of total employment has been about the same since World War II. We are still becoming more interdependent, but the supermarket and the drive-in have reduced the amount of resources needed to distribute a given amount of goods. The low-income countries still have a great deal to gain from greater specialization and trade. For them, of course, specialization has to come first. Just setting up a lot of shops won't accomplish much by itself.

INCREASING THE RESOURCE BASE

Every country that has attained rapid economic growth has done much of it by using its resources more efficiently. But ordinarily there has been some increase in the resources in use as well. We should look at the various factors of production to see how much more development can be expected along these lines.

NATURAL RESOURCES

In one sense, of course, we can't have any more land—just what God gave us to start with. But this answer is inadequate. Almost anyone looking at the growth of the West has to acknowledge that one of its advantages has been the enormous increase in the amount of land available to it over the last two centuries. Westerners in 1775 had access to most of Europe, a strip along the east coast of America, and a few Caribbean Islands. That was about all. We had hardly touched the mineral reserves of any of these areas. But in the two centuries since, we have added the rest of the Americas, Australia, and a good part of Africa. We have found ways of using many—though by no means all—of the minerals of those continents. We've added to our stock of land by several hundred percent. This growth has come at the expense of the American Indians, the Australian aborigines, and the Africans. Probably nothing like this expansion has ever happened before, and it doesn't seem likely to happen again.

The low-income countries can't hope for the sort of lift that we got from having a continent full of natural resources practically asking to be exploited. On the other hand, it is plain that most of them have more natural resources than they are using now. One reason that North America seems so rich in resources is that it has been more thoroughly explored than most of the world. There is no reason to suppose that other continents should be any less well endowed, on the average. A thorough search for minerals has gone on over the last two centuries in both the United States and Europe. Yet we continue to find new resources. One of the most striking finds in recent years was the discovery of large deposits of oil and gas under the North Sea, some of it within sight of the birthplace of the Industrial Revolution.

So far, at least, the ultimate limits on our supplies of natural resources have not been a drag on economic growth. The role of the primary industries has steadily declined in all developed countries. This change suggests that the production of food and raw materials has become relatively easier over the last two centuries, rather than harder. The decline shows up in the prices of primary products. With a few exceptions (mainly lumber), their prices have fallen, or at least risen more slowly than the prices of finished products and services. We will discuss this change further at the end of this chapter.

CAPITAL FORMATION

By definition, capital *can* be created. Indeed, some capital formation is essential just to keep us where we are. One of the features of capital is

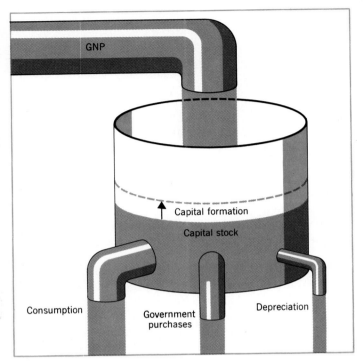

FIGURE 2.7   Capital formation. If the GNP exceeds the sum of consumption, government purchases, and depreciation, the nation's capital stock increases.

that it **depreciates**. That is, it wears out or becomes obsolete. This capital must be replaced. Moreover, capital formation is essential for most growth. To adopt new techniques we must install new equipment. To specialize we must build both railroads and inventories. And to exploit new natural resources we must first invest in finding them. Then we must invest further in the pipelines and mines needed to make them useful, once found. All these requirements imply that, to keep growing, a country must find some way to create more capital each generation.

Capital formation is a tricky business. Figure 2.7 may help you to understand the process. Think of the economy as a big spigot. It spews forth a continuous stream, the GNP, which drops into a barrel. The water in the barrel is the nation's stock of capital. Increasing the GNP, therefore, will increase the level of capital in the barrel. But that's only a part of the story. The barrel has leaks. The biggest one is the outflow into **consumption**, the use of goods and services to satisfy current wants. A second hole is government purchases. We consume goods just as thoroughly when the Air Force explodes a bomb as when we consume goods at home. And finally, some of the contents of the barrel are continuously draining away in the form of depreciation, the loss of capital through wear and obsolescence. The only way to raise the level in the barrel is for the GNP to exceed the sum of consumption, government spending, and depreciation. In short, we must do some **saving**. Saving is producing and not consuming.

The story is still only half told, however. If all we did was save, we would be poorer, not richer. If John Calvin returned to earth and convinced us that to get into heaven we should all be more frugal, and if nothing else happened, the result would be a drop in the demand for goods and services. The GNP would fall. In order to have the level of the capital stock rise, someone must also invest.

Investing means buying goods and services to add to the capital stock. "Investment" in this sense includes the addition of new buildings, equipment, and inventories. But it *excludes* the purchase of paper claims (stocks and so forth), just as "capital" as a factor of production excludes stocks, bonds, and mortgages. Both saving and investment are required for capital formation. Someone must decide to invest at the same time that you and I decide to save.

Back in the days of self-sufficient farmers the decisions to save and to invest went together automatically. When the farmer decided to build a barn, he was deciding in the process not to use the results of his effort for current consumption. But today, you and I are apt to be the savers, while General Motors does the investing. We have specialized in this important area just as we have in production. One result has been the growth of a large group of financial intermediaries. One of the most rapidly growing parts of the service sector consists of bankers, insurance companies, and stockbrokers. Their business is to link up saving and investment decisions efficiently. They take in money supplied by savers and lend it to finance investment, just as wholesalers and retailers link up producers and consumers in our specialized society.

SOURCES OF SAVING

The saving process is easy enough for us. Rich people can save quite a bit and still eat well. But how do you get saving out of a country where the GNP per person is $100 a year? It sounds like getting blood out of turnips. Yet our ancestors did it.

Part of the reason is that even poor farmers have extra *time* that can be invested. The frontier farmer who built that barn and the Indian peasant who worked on the irrigation system in the off-season were both saving and investing.

Another answer lies in inequality. Even poor countries have some people who have sufficient incomes to save quite a bit. The question is, will they? In many countries the rich disdain to dirty their hands in the business of saving and investment. They prefer to put their resources into pyramids and cathedrals. But one of the West's great advantages was that much of the wealth of the seventeenth and eighteenth centuries was in the hands of businessmen whose value system gave high marks for thrift. Many historians, in fact, explain the start of the West's takeoff by the rise of Protestantism. Most Americans have been sufficiently trained in the Protestant ethic to recognize it easily. We must work hard but be frugal, it says. It follows simply that we must save *and* invest. Some historians have asked whether this ethic wasn't, in fact, older than Protestantism. In any case, the Protestant middle class of Northern Europe did a lot of saving and investing. Their savings financed much of the Industrial Revolution and made many of them rich.

If not enough is saved voluntarily, there are means by which a country can exact saving from its people. Taxes are, in effect, public decisions that some part of the GNP will not go into consumption. A government can require its citizens to save by raising taxes. It can then invest the proceeds itself. Through loan programs, it can also turn them over to private firms to invest. Such subsidized investments played a large role in the development of the West. The biggest investment project in the nineteenth-century United States was the construction of the railroads. They were financed in good part by large public grants of land and money.

Another way to build railroads is to let someone else save and then to import the capital. We did that too. In the nineteenth century the United States was the world's leading borrower, depending in large part on loans raised in England.

Investment can also be financed by inflation. The government prints some new money and uses it to build, say, a railroad. The people who worked on the railroad, along with everyone else, go out to spend what they earned. However, not enough consumer goods were produced to meet all this demand, because some of our resources were diverted to railroad construction. Prices are bid up as a result. When a person who earned $100 goes out to spend his money, he gets goods worth only $90 at the old price level. In effect, a tax has been imposed on people who hold money. We have created new capital (the railroad) regardless of whether anyone planned to save or not.

The United States also engaged in this sort of sleight of hand in the nineteenth century. One of the great reforms of Andrew Jackson's presidency (1829–1837) was "free banking." Under this policy, banks were established all over the West with the right to print money. They did so and lent it out to land developers. The result was an inflation, *and also* the most rapid development of new land in our history. Economists are generally unenthusiastic about this method of accumulating capital, but it will work if nothing else is possible.

Finally, the Communist countries have developed a marvelously simple machine for both saving and investing. Their governments own most of their economic enterprises. They can simply pay their workers less than the value of what is produced and divert the rest into capital goods. In this effective (if painful) way, they have been able to accumulate huge quantities of capital very rapidly.

Much of the investment that is needed in a low-income country is in such facilities as roads, sewers, power plants, railroads, and schools. These works are public undertakings in most non-Communist countries. Large-scale government investment is natural. There may not be enough incentives for private saving and investment. This is often the case in countries that have unstable governments. For them, public investment financed by taxation, foreign borrowing, or inflation may be the only means by which they can attain economic development.

POPULATION AND THE LABOR FORCE

Another way a country can add to its productive resources is to increase its labor supply. The result will usually be more output. However, it will often mean more mouths to feed as well. Is the country any better off? The answer is sometimes, but by no means always.

There are two ways to increase the amount of labor available. One is to increase the population. The other is to increase the amount of labor *potential* in a given population. Let's look at labor potential first.

INVESTING IN HUMAN CAPITAL

By putting resources into such public needs as health and education a country can improve its labor force. At the turn of the century a third of the American population was fourteen years old or younger. The average life expectancy at birth was only 47 years. Since then, by improving our health standards, we have been able to keep a much larger proportion of our people alive through their working years. Today only 28 percent of the population is fourteen or younger. Life expectancy is up to 70 years.

Again, we have undoubtedly increased our productivity by educating our people more intensively. At the turn of the century the average American had completed only seven rather short years of school. Now more than half of us have completed twelve much longer school years. Our economic growth in this century owes much to these two developments: the increase in the proportion of our population that is of working age, and the improvement in the health and skills of our labor force.

Expenditures on health and education are a form of investment. Like other investments, they require resources that must be diverted from other uses. And they also yield a return—quite a good one, in fact. For instance, on the average, a person who finishes college earns several hundred thousand dollars more over his lifetime than a person who stops after high school. It has been estimated that this extra earning power means a return of ten to fifteen percent on the original investment. (The investment consists of tuition, books, and also the income that the student foregoes while attending school.) This monetary return is supplemented by a better quality of life for the person in whom the investment is made. Many people also believe that we get a more stable society and a more effective democracy with an educated population.

However, human capital also depreciates. The investment in a person is obviously extinguished at death. But even during that person's lifetime, what he learned in school is becoming obsolete. Similarly, continuing expenditures are needed to maintain his health. For this reason a country must continually spend money on education and health just to keep its stock of human capital intact.

Investments in human capital may be either public or private. Primary and (usually) secondary education and urban sanitation are publicly financed all over the world. Yet a large part of the investment in human capital in the United States is private. This is true of the largest part of our expenditures on higher education and health.

DIMINISHING RETURNS

We've left the hardest question for last. What if we add to the actual numbers of people, and not just to their life spans and education? The answer is that we can add to our GNP per person *only* if greater population brings with it greater productivity as a result.

To understand the population problem we need to introduce a crucial economic concept, the principle of **diminishing returns**. Take any productive process, keep at least one input fixed, and then see what happens when any of the other inputs increase. For instance, say we want to

TABLE 2.2 Output of a hypothetical potato patch

LABOR (workers)	OUTPUT (bushels)	OUTPUT PER WORKER (bushels)
0	0	0
1	20	20
2	50	25
3	81	27
4	100	25
5	115	23
6	120	20
7	120	17
8	112	14

grow potatoes on 40 acres of land. The land is the fixed input here. Now try using different amounts of labor in the potato-growing process. The first two columns of Table 2.2 work out some of the possibilities.

With one worker, our piece of land will yield twenty bushels of potatoes. But with two workers it produces more than twice as many. The two have time to cultivate as well as to plant and harvest. With a third worker, the output jumps even more. The three have time to fertilize also. With crews of four or five or six workers, output continues to grow. But it is growing at a slower and slower rate. The extra workers are now doing less important tasks, such as cultivating a second and third time and plowing and planting in the corners of the fields. The seventh worker doesn't add anything at all, and the eighth actually detracts. By now all those people are getting in each other's way. They are trampling potato plants and talking too much during coffee breaks. Diminishing returns set in well before the eighth worker, however. A good farm manager would never let the situation get that far. He'd do better to let the last couple of men stay home.

Diminishing returns showed up some time earlier. Look at the last column of Table 2.2. It shows the total potato output divided by the number of workers who produced it. This figure increases at first, as we would expect. After the third worker, however, it goes into a continuous decline. Output per worker begins to decline as more workers are added—even while the total output is still going up. This tendency is known as diminishing returns. More generally, the principle of diminishing returns holds that in any productive process, if some inputs are held fixed while other inputs are increased, then sooner or later the output per variable input will decline.[4] Beyond that point the output per variable input will go on declining indefinitely.

No one should take the particular figures in Table 2.2 very seriously; I am no expert in growing potatoes. But the general principle is important. Our 40 acres had a finite capacity, and as we approached that capacity, the output per variable factor had to decline.

This is a very general statement about the world, and it is one that you can check for yourself. Suppose that there were no diminishing returns, so that each additional man added 25 more bushels to the harvest indefinitely. Then four men would produce 100 bushels. Eight men would produce 200, twelve would produce 300, 1,000 would produce 25,000, and so forth—all on the same 40 acres. Obviously this is not the way potato farming works. If it were, we could grow all the potatoes in the world on just that one little plot of ground. You can do the same sort of mental experiment with any process, not just agriculture. Try putting two, three, four, five, and more men on a lathe. Up to a point you'll add to output. Still, there is a limit. With 500 times as many laborers hovering over the machine you won't get 500 times as much output.

Diminishing returns is not just a matter of varying the labor inputs, either. Try keeping the number of workers constant instead, while increasing the amount of our potato land. Try 80 acres, then 160, then a square mile, two square miles, and so forth. At some acreage, the output per acre just has to start falling. Our few workers simply can't work a huge farm as intensively as they could 40 acres.

This principle holds in all areas of life. You can earn higher grades by studying two hours a day rather than one, and higher yet by studying three or four. But these gains won't go on forever. Studying 24 hours a day, every day, is not recommended. You—the fixed factor—have a limited capacity no matter how much you study. Similarly, one can sell more soap with two TV ads per day than with one, and more yet with three, but at some point the number of sales per ad will begin to decline. Here the potential TV audience is the fixed factor.

This idea is so important that it is worth driving into the ground. Figures 2.8 and 2.9 reproduce the numbers in Table 2.2. The number of workers is plotted along the horizontal axis. In Figure 2.8 we show the

---

[4] Diminishing returns also implies that after some point each additional unit of a variable input adds less to output than the previous unit did. For instance, in Table 2.1, the third man adds 31 units to output; the fourth adds 19; the fifth adds 15; the sixth adds 5; and the seventh adds nothing at all. Diminishing returns are usually thought of as beginning where these additions to output begin to decline. Both the additions to output and the output per variable factor must ultimately decline if diminishing returns are present. This aspect of diminishing returns will be explained further and used in Chapter 7.

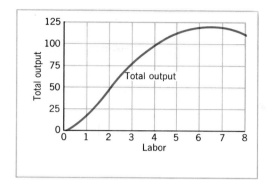

FIGURE 2.8 Total output from a fixed plot of land as the number of workers is increased.

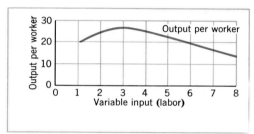

FIGURE 2.9 Output per worker as the number of workers is increased. The output per worker drops off long before the total output begins to decline.

total output of our potato farm. It increases at first, but not so fast after a point. Figure 2.9 shows the output per worker. It rises at first but finally stabilizes and declines. We can expect to find such a pattern in *any* productive process.

POPULATION

Now back to population. A country represents a fixed set of resources at any one time. With more population and the same land, capital, and techniques, we can expect a set of outputs like those in Figures 2.8 and 2.9. Let the country involved be fairly small and let it produce just one good—potatoes again. As the labor force grows we will find the output per worker rising at first. But ultimately it falls, just as it did in our small potato patch.

Now enters a famous economist, Thomas Malthus, who lived at the turn of the nineteenth century. Malthus studied population very carefully. He came up with the conclusion that regardless of where you start, most people in most countries will ultimately be living close to starvation most of the time. Armed with the principle of diminishing returns, it is quite easy to see how Malthus reached this conclusion. Just assume that people tend to *more* than reproduce their own numbers—and over

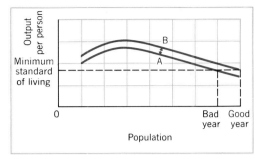

FIGURE 2.10 According to Malthus, human numbers would eventually grow until the whole population was at the subsistence level. Population would then expand in a good year (B) and drop, through famine, when the output per worker curve shifted down to A in a bad year.

history this has certainly been the rule. Even if a country had only one or two workers per 40 acres to start with, its population would continue to grow. And when the population reached four workers per 40 acres the same thing would happen that happened in our potato patch. Diminishing returns would set in. The population would keep on growing, with fewer and fewer potatoes per person, until there was just enough food to go around. Say the minimum feasible standard of living is twenty bushels per person per year. The country's population would grow, then, until it reached the highest level that was still able to produce that much. We see from Table 2.2 that that level is six workers for each 40 acres. At that point the whole population would be at the subsistence level, and famine would become common. Population growth beyond six workers per 40 acres would be checked by starvation.

Of course, this model is too simple. A plot of land will produce more in some years than in others, depending on how much it rains. In Figure 2.10, curve B shows a good year and curve A shows a bad one. A series of good years would just mean more mouths to feed. Then a bad year would mean famine. Since we are bound to have bad years from time to time, it follows that population size is dictated by the area and fertility of the country. Most people will face the threat of starvation periodically.

This dismal idea played a major role in nineteenth-century thought. It implied that there would usually be poverty. It meant that philanthropy was useless, because it just was squandered by the poor on more babies. Charles Darwin, after absorbing this idea, came to the conclusion that life was a continuous struggle for survival and that the best adapted would inherit the earth. Others concluded that the wage rate would hover close to the bare survival level, and that the only issue was how to split up the output in excess of wage payments among the owners of land and capital.

The argument seemed watertight, and the evidence in various countries of the world at that time all seemed to support the predictions. We

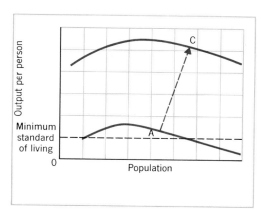

FIGURE 2.11 **What actually happened in the agricultural and industrial revolution was an enormous upward shift in the output per worker curve (as from A to C) so that a country could support far more people.**

now know by hindsight, however, that the Malthusian prediction missed the mark. We have had *both* rising populations *and* rising standards of living. Why?

One reason was the agricultural and industrial revolution, once again. Productivity in the nineteenth century increased not just by a small amount but by many times over. The shift was more like the jump from curve *A* to curve *C* in Figure 2.11. This solution isn't enough, however. The output per worker might be high enough to put off the bitter day for a few generations, but the population would eventually just grow all the more as a result. The population of England and Wales went from eight million in 1800 to 40 million by 1900. In the wide-open spaces of the United States it grew from five million to 75 million in the same years. The Malthusian devil seemed still to be lurking in the wings.

But something else was happening. The population growth in the nineteenth century was caused largely by falling death rates. They can fall only so far. It is fairly easy to save lives when the problem is malaria or smallpox, but much harder after that, when what is left is cancer and heart disease. At the same time, the birth rate was dropping. In 1800 the American birth rate was 55 babies per year for every 1,000 persons. By 1900 it was down to 32, and today it is only 17. We are now near the point where, ultimately, our population will not grow at all. "Ultimately" is still pretty far off, because the number of women of childbearing age is still growing. But the population explosion is definitely over in the United States.

Why did it end? There are many reasons. Religious taboos against birth control have weakened, of course, and the means of birth control have improved. But it takes more than birth control: couples have to *want* fewer children. One reason we did was the falling death rate among children. A couple who wants a family of a given size needs to have fewer babies today to attain its goal. But more important, the most popular family size has also fallen. A major reason for this change has been the movement of population to the cities. Back on the farm, another child meant one more free worker and someone else to take care of you in old age. But in the city, these days, children are mostly luxuries. You might get them to do the dishes if you are lucky, but in general they require more work than they offer. They certainly will not support you when you are old. In this situation two children are as good as twenty —better!

This pattern of population growth has been repeated in country after country as they have industrialized and become more urban: England, France, Germany, Russia, and Japan, to name a few. If we can count on these new fashions in family size to continue, we can keep the Malthusian disaster away indefinitely.

The situation is less optimistic in largely rural countries such as India and Brazil. Their birth rates show little sign of slowing down. In those countries the increase in productivity that comes with new technology and new crops will be largely wasted unless they can learn to check their flood of babies.

Now back to people as factors of production. Can a country add to GNP per person by increasing its population? The answer depends on how much population it already has. If a country is still pretty empty, so that output per person is still rising, then an increase in population will make everyone better off. This was surely true of the United States a century ago, and there are countries that are still in this situation. They probably include Canada, Australia, and Argentina. For them, more people means greater opportunities for specialization and better roads. But for most of the world, diminishing returns seem much more likely. This is certainly the case for the low-income countries of Asia. More people there is the route to disaster.

ECONOMIC GROWTH IN THE FUTURE

We started out with the questions of how the West got so rich, whether we could keep it up, and what the chances were for the low-income countries. Now we can put together some answers.

THE PROSPECTS FOR FURTHER GROWTH

The West did well partly because it was lucky—there was lots of new land to work with—and partly because of new techniques, the accumulation of capital, and heavy spending on health and education. In this setting, the population explosion that accompanied our early growth probably did little harm. But further growth will depend largely on yet more technical advances and more capital. The prospects are probably bright, but from now on most Western countries would do well to keep the size of their populations under control. Most of them seem to be doing so.

The low-income countries generally do not have the bountiful natural resources per capita that we did in 1800. This lack shouldn't prevent their economic progress, however. Even such poorly endowed countries as Japan have made it out of the ancient rut. Capital accumulation will be hard for them, but others have done it. And technological change is likely to be easier now, if anything, because emerging countries can adapt processes from the West. In fact, practically every low-income country has experienced some increase in GNP per person in the last two decades. It is absolutely essential that they control their birth rates, however. If they do not, their prospects are dim.

WORLD POPULATION GROWTH

The growth in world population that is already assured is startling. The world's population was about 1.6 billion in 1900. In 1970 it was about 3.6 billion. If present birth and death rates are maintained, this number will be doubled by the year 2000. And the process wouldn't stop even if birth rates were to fall *immediately* to levels that would ultimately assure a stable population (about 2.2 children per couple in the United States). The world population would still double in just a few more years. The reason is the number of children already born who will become parents in the meanwhile. Even if we reached zero-growth levels right now, world population would reach about ten billion before it stopped growing. If birth rates do not fall, and *if* death rates do not rise, our population could reach astronomical numbers—maybe 30 billion a century from now. Somewhere out there death rates will certainly rise if births remain unchecked.

Most of the world's population growth today is in the low-income countries. Though world population will double in the next thirty years, the United States population will grow by only about 40 percent, if present patterns continue. And in fact, our birth rates are still falling. The populations of most countries in both Western and Eastern Europe are growing more slowly than ours. Those of the Soviet Union and Japan are growing at about the same rate as ours. Nine tenths of the growth we can expect by 2000 will be in the low-income countries of Asia, Africa, and Latin America.

The flood of births in low-income countries can be checked. Japan had galloping growth through the 1920s but has now cut its birth rate almost to the zero-growth level. Birth rates have fallen by as much as half in a number of low-income countries and territories since World War II. They include Hong Kong, Singapore, Taiwan, South Korea, Malaysia, Cuba, Puerto Rico, and Jamaica. In other, less urban lands, however, birth control may be harder to accomplish. The task seems urgent for many of them.

In the developed countries the problem of population growth is primarily a question of the quality of life, rather than any threat of economic disaster. The population growth foreseeable in our lifetimes may mean more cars on the roads, bigger suburbs, and less open space, but it will hardly mean starvation. A further drop in birth rates to levels that would stabilize our populations would change the quality of life, too. A stable population with our present life expectancies would leave us with as many people over 60 as under fifteen. (Right now there are about half as many.) The labor force would be a smaller part of the population than it is now. Voting patterns would probably be a good deal more conservative.

IS GROWTH WORTH IT?

There is one more question. Should incomes continue to grow? Until recently the answer was a resounding "yes" from almost everyone, but now some people have doubts. A recent study attempted to predict what would happen with various patterns of growth. One projection let the population and capital stock increase at the same percentage rates that they have in the past. The result was an exhaustion of the world's natural resources, followed by a disastrous loss of life, in less than a century. Even assuming a much greater resource base, the crisis came in only a few more years because of drastic increases in pollution. So far, pollution has been only an annoyance for most people. But the study predicts that if pollution continues to increase in proportion to the GNP, and if GNP doubles and redoubles throughout the world, the holding capacity of our atmosphere and waters will be exhausted in less than a century. Pollution will become a major cause of deaths. Even if there were universal and effective birth control, the remaining growth in population and a continued increase in production would seem to bring disaster within the twenty-first century. The authors of the study conclude that only with a worldwide policy aimed at zero economic growth can we avoid a crisis as we approach the limits set by our natural resources and environment.

THE CASE FOR GROWTH

There is still much to be said for economic growth. It is by far our most promising prospect for improving the condition of the poor. For the majority of the world's population a stop to economic growth would mean mass starvation in a very short time. Perhaps large-scale and continuing assistance from the high-income countries could forestall it, but that does not seem likely.

Even in the advanced countries, economic growth is the main hope for the poor. During the 1960s the United States cut the percentage of its population with incomes below the officially-defined poverty line almost in half (from 22 percent to twelve percent). This progress was almost entirely due to our increasing GNP. The share of our total income earned by the poorest fifth of our population rose only from 4.9 percent to 5.5 percent in the same years. In other words, only a small part of the gains of the poor has resulted from their receiving a larger slice of the pie. Most of their progress has always been due to a bigger pie.

We could conceivably redistribute more of our income in favor of the poor in the future, but even this task will be much easier if growth continues than if the GNP is stopped in its tracks. Poor people get ahead by getting better jobs. These advances come at little sacrifice on the part of the rest of us if there are more good jobs each year. However, in a no-growth economy, better jobs for the poor would mean worse jobs for others, a change that the middle-class losers can be counted on to resist. Another way to help the poor is to increase the amount of government cash payments that they receive. These payments doubled in the 1960s, but so did the GNP; the assistance involved little increase in tax rates. But if the GNP were to stop growing, a further doubling of such payments would require that taxes rise from 33 to 38 percent of the GNP, a change that taxpayers would not accept without a fight. And finally, stopping the growth in GNP would almost certainly mean large-scale unemployment during the decades in which we adjusted to the no-growth state. Unemployment falls most heavily on the poor.

A second argument for economic growth is, surprisingly, that it is probably necessary if we are to improve our environment materially. The cost of attaining acceptably clean air and water and of keeping it that way is going to be large. The government itself is already spending six billion dollars a year on it. The special equipment, fuels, and processes needed to meet current pollution-control requirements will be at least that much again. Those costs will fall on industry and consumers together. Yet it is difficult to sense much improvement in our environment as yet. To meet the air- and water-quality goals set by Congress will cost many times what we are now spending. The figure may run as high as $40 billion a year. That figure is easily attainable if we continue to grow. We could reach that level of expenditure by 1980 by just cutting our annual *increase* in consumption per person by one fourth. In a no-growth economy, however, those costs would mean a permanent *reduction* in consumption by about $200 per person a year (or about $800 per family). There is a good chance that a majority of people would accept mildly *slower increases* in their material standards of living to clean up the environment. But how many would vote for it if it meant a significant *drop* in their standards of living from now on?

Of course, the main gain from growth is in improved standards of living. It would be hard to sell a majority of the public on a policy that would bring these improvements to an end. Left to their own devices, people will go right on saving and investing and trying to find easier ways to produce. Of course, the government could stop growth in spite of the public's desire to get ahead by bringing about a deep and continuing depression. But hardly anyone wants that. In a democracy a government that attempted such a policy would soon be out of office.

On the other hand, we might try reducing the work week. But the cuts would have to be pretty drastic. The growth in our labor force down to the end of this century is already pretty much determined by births over the past twenty years. Meanwhile, our output per man-hour is steadily growing. If those trends keep on, then to keep our GNP stable the work week would have to drop by about a third each decade to avoid general unemployment. That would mean a work week of about 27 hours in the early 1980s, one of eighteen hours in the early 1990s, and one of twelve hours at the turn of the next century. Half-year vacations or four-day weekends may have a lot of appeal to some people, but others would probably want to work longer hours by taking more than one job or by becoming self-employed. Altogether, a deliberate policy aimed at stopping economic growth would be enormously disruptive. It may not even be feasible.

RESOURCES AND POLLUTION

Many economists are unconvinced about predictions of disaster associated with further growth. The exhaustion of our resources has been regularly expected for the past hundred years. What has happened instead is that as growth has produced shortages of specific raw materials, their prices have gone up. The rising prices have induced a search for alternatives. So far, we have always been able to find them. Sometimes they took the form of new reserves, but often they were new techniques that permitted the exploitation of reserves we already knew about. We also substituted new products for scarce old ones. There is every reason to expect this process to continue.

To be more specific, our most important mineral resource has been energy. We can foresee the future sources of power. Known reserves of fossil fuels are remarkably large. The world has several hundreds of years' reserves of coal at our present rates of use. Proved reserves of gas and oil in the United States have not been growing as rapidly as demand in recent years. However, they are abundant in other parts of the world. Some major Middle-Eastern producers have 50 years' reserves. Some of the most likely geological formations, such as those in Siberia and under the waters of the Persian Gulf and around Indonesia, are just now being explored. Beyond these reserves, there are oil shale and tar sands that are said to contain more oil than the total of all the presently known liquid petroleum reserves.

Perhaps more important, nuclear energy is just beginning to be used. By the 1980s we will have the fast breeder reactor, which produces more fuel than it consumes (though it may result in tough environmental problems). And further off, some scientists expect workable fusion reactors that will use deuterium, or "heavy water," of which almost limitless amounts exist in the oceans. The exhaust, helium, is inert and harmless. As far as metals go, the soils of the tropics are, in good part, low-grade iron and aluminum ores. Enormous amounts of metals are dissolved in the oceans.

The limits on growth imposed by our resources are certainly not perfectly elastic, of course. There are only so many resources in the earth's crust. But the ultimate limit is still probably far off. During the 1960s a group of careful scholars employed by an organization called Resources for the Future studied the prospects for each of our main resources. They consistently came to the conclusion that economic growth in the foreseeable future would not be slowed by the depletion of these resources.

If, in spite of everything, natural resources do become much scarcer than they have been, their prices will rise. As a result, the prices of goods with large resource content will rise compared with the prices of services and highly fabricated goods. (These last are goods that use lots of labor and technology and relatively few natural resources, such as computers.) Consumers will be induced to take a greater share of their standards of living in such low-resource goods and services. They will tend to buy more durable products. And at the same time, the high price of materials should make recycling more profitable. It should also induce research into ways of increasing the efficiency with which materials are used.

But what about pollution? Here the problem is to make the polluters take into account the costs that they impose on the public. From the beginning of time we have been dumping our waste in the air and water. Now these receptables are becoming noticeably full. So far, polluters have had little incentive to limit their discharges. We have only begun attempts to control them. There are several possible ways we can make auto drivers and power plants responsive to the costs of the junk they are spewing into our atmosphere and waters. These methods will be discussed in Chapter 11. If properly applied, they should increase the cost of pollution to the persons responsible for it. Here again, the higher costs should induce a search for less dirty methods, and rising prices should induce consumers to shift to goods and services that cause less pollution. Of course, these strategies may not work. We can hardly tell that they won't at this time, however. We have only just begun to try to deal with the problem.

If our problems with natural resources or pollution or both should turn out to be unsolvable, growth in the GNP will slow automatically. If we arrange for the costs of pollution to be assumed by the polluters, the rising costs of materials and of pollution will simply make it impossible for us to expand our output further. In other words, we don't need to turn off the growth machine in advance. The slowdown would happen of its own accord. It probably wouldn't come abruptly, though. The prices of materials with a large natural-resource content would rise gradually as reserves became scarcer. This is what happened to timber, the one major resource whose supplies have become distinctly shorter in the last century. If we do succeed in imposing the cost of pollution on those who create it, then the prices of pollution-causing goods will rise gradually as the carrying capacity of our environment is more and more taxed. It's not likely that the joyride will come to a sudden end without warning.[5] A

[5] An obvious way the world could end with a bang would be an all-out war. Another would be some form of pollution that we didn't understand. Few people worried much about the small amounts of mercury being emitted into the environment until people in Japan started dying from it. Similarly, some seemingly harmless substance that is going into the oceans might reach a critical level and kill all the plankton before we knew what was happening. That event would turn off much of the process by which carbon dioxide is converted into oxygen and fixed carbon. We'd face suffocation. It's essential that we put lots of resources into the study of the effects of new substances as they come along. We should monitor the crucial life-support systems on earth continuously.

gradual slowdown is much more probable.

These considerations do not mean that we can simply ignore the problem of growth. Most economists would probably urge further effort to check population growth, even in the high-income countries. They certainly would support it in the low-income countries. And almost all economists support policies that will force polluters to take the effects of their discharges into account. But only a minority feel that a deliberate policy of checking growth in the GNP per person is called for at this point.

After all this argument, it must be acknowledged that the questions of whether we should grow, and, if so, how fast, call for value judgments. The economist can lay out the alternatives and suggest some new solutions to the more pressing problems, but ultimately it is up to the public to decide.

SUMMARY

The economically advanced countries today are the first ones in history to have raised the bulk of their populations much above bare subsistence standards of living. They did so through huge increases in resources and in the efficiency with which they were used. These increases in efficiency were caused by both technological progress and specialization. Specialization has led to increasing interdependence and exchange.

The factors of production are often divided into land, labor, and capital. Though the amount of land (natural resources) in the world is fixed, that available for use has been increased greatly through exploration and development. Increases in capital (man-made factors of production) require both saving and investment. Saving is possible, even in poor countries, if the values of the rich encourage it. Taxation, inflation, and the central decisions of Communist countries are all ways of imposing more saving on society.

Labor (all human effort used in production) increases with improved education and health and with rising population. The effect of population growth depends on diminishing returns. Thomas Malthus assumed that population would always grow until people were near bare subsistence levels. His forecast has not held up in Western countries. One reason was the increase in their land, capital, and technology. More important, their birth rates fell as they became more urban. The populations of low-income countries are still growing rapidly, however. Prospects for permanently higher incomes in those countries are dim if their birth rates are not reduced.

The problems of further economic growth are real but probably not disastrous. As resources get scarce, shortages will force their prices up. Industry will have to use them sparingly and search for substitutes. The rise in price will also induce consumers to shift to goods with a lower resource content. If we impose the costs of pollution on the polluters, similar changes will limit the environmental effects of growth. If we ever do approach the limits to our resources, growth will slow automatically.

STUDY QUESTIONS

1   Try working out a budget as though you had an income of $100 per year. You'll find it impossible to live in an area with severe winters. Just providing enough heat to keep you alive would take most of your income. Assume that there is no winter, as in tropical countries, and see how far your hundred dollars would go at the supermarket. Stick to dried beans and flour. "Luxuries" such as peanut butter would take several days' income. How often would you buy shoes with that income? How often would you see the doctor? Would you let your sixteen-year-old son stay in school if he could earn another $100 a year by working instead?

2   Why do secondary industries grow faster than the GNP in the early stages of economic growth? (Hint: We surely had processed meats, bread, clothing, furniture, heat, and transportation equipment before the Industrial Revolution. Where did these things come from when secondary industries were less than ten percent of total employment?)

3   Why do tertiary industries grow faster than the GNP over both the early and middle stages of economic growth?

4   Which of the following items are included in the "capital" as a factor of production?

☐ Iron ore in the ground in northern Minnesota

☐ Iron ore in a pile beside a blast furnace

☐ Iron ore inside the blast furnace being converted into pig iron

☐ The blast furnace itself

☐ Stock in the company that owns the blast furnace

5   Your house has just burned down, but you are fully compensated by insurance. Are you any poorer as a result? Is the country as a whole any poorer as a result?

6   Which of the following is saving, which is investment, which is both, and which is neither?

☐ I use a third of this month's pay to pay off a debt

☐ I spend most of my spare time for a month building a garage onto my house

☐ I take money out of the bank and use it to buy stock in a new oil refinery

☐ You borrow money and build a house with it

☐ You forego a trip to Europe so that you can pay college tuition this term

7   The Civil War was disastrous for the South. More than half of its wealth was destroyed. Some of this loss was in the form of cities and railroads that were destroyed, and some was confederate money and bonds that became worthless after the war. But the greatest loss by far was the freeing of the slaves without compensation. Was the South as a whole poorer for this change? Did it have less capital? The blacks who were freed were still there, but their former owners were clearly poorer. Who, if anyone, was richer?

8   Would Malthus's population predictions work out the same way if there were no diminishing returns?

FURTHER READING

A good, brief elementary summary of economic growth is Robert Baldwin's *Economic Development and Growth*, 2nd ed. (New York: John Wiley, 1972). A longer (3-volume) book on the subject that is still aimed at the general reader is Gunnar Myrdal's *Asian Drama* (New York: Pantheon, 1972). Edward F. Dennison has attempted to measure the impact of increased capital, increased education, improved technology, and the like on American economic growth in *The Sources of Economic Growth and the Alternatives Before Us* (New York: Committee for Economic Development, 1962). A similar study by the same author attempts to account for differences in the level of GNP per person between the United States and Europe. It appears in *Why Growth Rates Differ* (Washington, D.C.: Brookings Inst., 1967). Robert Heilbroner's *The Making of Economic Society* (Englewood Cliffs, N.J.: Prentice–Hall, 1962) is a readable introduction to the history of the Western economy.

The classic on population was Thomas Malthus, *An Essay on Population* (New York: Augustus M. Kelley, 1971). It is full of eighteenth-century language but otherwise within the reach of general readers, though it is pretty long. For a fascinating, brief examination of world population growth, going all the way back to Neolithic times, see Carlo M. Cipolla, *An Economic History of World Population* (Baltimore: Penguin, 1964). The controversial attempt to project the effect of further economic growth into the future appears in D. H. Meadows, D. L. Meadows, J. Randers, and W. W. Behrens III, *The Limits to Growth* (New York: Universal Books, 1972).

3
HOW ECONOMIES ARE ORGANIZED

So far, we have been ignoring one crucial area: how the economy is organized. Every society that has ever existed has had to settle three basic economic questions. They are:

☐ What to produce

☐ How to produce it

☐ How to distribute the output

Each of these questions calls for some explanation.

What to produce. We can produce shoes or ships or sealing wax, but we cannot produce all we could possibly use of each. We must choose among the alternatives. Usually the real question comes down to how much of each good we should produce.

How to produce it. Again, there are almost always alternatives. Some can be ruled out as obviously inefficient or immoral. But there are plenty left. Consider the following alternative ways of digging a given ditch:

☐ *Process 1*   A hundred men and a hundred $10 shovels

☐ *Process 2*   Ten men and two $20,000 trenching machines

☐ *Process 3*   120 men and 120 $10 shovels

☐ *Process 4*   50 men, 49 shovels, and one whip

Process 3 can immediately be dropped as clearly less efficient than Process 1 on all counts. Process 4 might seem more efficient, but it won't work short of slavery, and moralists have fortunately ruled that out. But

TABLE 3.1   Alternative ways of digging a ditch

	PROCESS 1 (100 men and 100 shovels)	PROCESS 2 (10 men and 2 machines)
(1) Rental per day on capital used	$10	$400
(2) Labor at a wage of $20 per day	$2,000	$200
(3) Total cost at a wage of $20 per day	$2,010	$600
(4) Labor at a wage of $1 per day	$100	$10
(5) Total cost at a wage of $1 per day	$110	$410

how do we choose between 1 and 2? We can't tell until we know how much both the labor and the capital cost.

Let's say that capital—the equipment needed for digging the ditch —rents for ten dollars per $1,000-worth per day. The hundred shovels are worth $1,000, so they will cost us ten dollars a day. The two machines are worth $20,000 apiece, so they will cost us $400 a day. A big difference. But we still haven't solved our problem until we know the cost of the labor involved. It depends on the wages we pay. Table 3.1 works the problem out.

Say the wage is twenty dollars a day, as in lines (2) and (3). In that case, using the trenching machines is clearly cheaper. But twenty dollars a day would be unheard of in much of the world. In India the going wage would more likely be a dollar a day. The result is shown in lines (4) and (5). In India the shovels win. Clearly the decision of which to use depends on the relative costs of the factors employed. This example isn't frivolous, either. Builders in India do find that earth moving is best done by a swarm of human ants.

How to distribute the output. This problem breaks down into two related subquestions. The first is, given the output of each individual product, how should it be allocated among members of society? That is, how many pairs of shoes should each person get? How many potatoes? And so forth for each commodity produced. The second question is, What should each person's income be? What should be his share of the total pie?

WAYS OF ORGANIZING THE ECONOMY

No society can leave these basic questions unanswered, but there are many ways of settling them. Some of the answers that have been given in the past are instructive.

TRADITIONAL ECONOMIES

In many societies the answers are deeply imbedded in the family, religious, and legal mores of the culture. We traditionally planted wheat in one field and another grain in a second and left a third fallow. We always plowed on Good Friday and planted when the oak leaf was as big as a mouse's ear. Parents were obliged to support minor children. Adult children had to work to support their incompetent parents. Women raised the children, and their husbands worked in the fields. And on and on, in myriad customs. A substantial part of every economy is organized this way, but in most primitive societies such customary rules are generally predominant. Only a small part of total output is sold in markets, and almost nothing is done for profit.

Such rules work passably well in slowly-changing traditional societies. We have a fair number of these rules even now—for instance, that wives raise the children while husbands work. But, as in this example, such rules are more likely to produce frictions in our rapidly changing world.

COMMAND ECONOMIES

A second basic plan is the **command economy**, in which a dictator or a bureaucracy simply tells its members what and how to produce and how to split up the proceeds. Historians tell us that the story of Joseph in Egypt is a fair representation of how ancient Egypt was organized over much of its history. The pharaoh owned the land, and bureaucrats gathered its entire output into central warehouses and doled it back out to the people. The contemporary Communist countries determine most of what and how to produce by means of central decisions, though individuals are still free to make consumption decisions and, to a large extent, to choose where to work. The medieval manor, though heavily laced by customary rules, was essentially a small command economy in which the lord and his representative called the shots. Output for sale at a profit on markets was a very minor part of total economic activity. Most of what was produced went to the lord or the church or was kept for consumption by the producer.

MEDIEVAL CITIES AND MERCANTILISM

The (somewhat later) medieval city had more familiar-looking institutions. However, appearances can be deceiving. People did specialize and produce for sale, and they had absolutely voracious profit motives, but they were regulated within an inch of their lives by **guilds**. Modern Americans tend to identify guilds with labor unions. Actually, they were more of a cross between industrial trade associations and fraternal organizations. They commonly ran the city governments, which were largely free from higher authority. The guildhall *was* the city hall in medieval England. The guilds had rules to determine the output, quality, and price of each good. They had more rules about what could be imported into and exported from the city when, and by whom. There were yet more rules about who could enter each trade and on what terms. Of course, the rules tended to be made in the interests of the guild members.

When nation states developed in early modern times they adopted an economic system known as **mercantilism**, which resembled the older city system at a national level. Now Queen Elizabeth I and Louis XIII made the rules. They kept the old privileged guilds and created new ones that had exclusive rights to trade with particular nations. They made national laws specifying wage rates and the terms of apprenticeships. They controlled all imports and exports and the trade and industries of their colonies. They made laws reserving certain lines of commerce to favored persons. In general, they tried to regulate all the conditions of national economic life as the cities had controlled the local economies before them. Of course, this time the rules tended to be made in the interest of Queen Elizabeth and Louis XIII and their counterparts in other countries. To be fair, though, mercantilism, for all its controls, represented a move toward a freer national economy, because it broke down many purely local restrictions.

LAISSEZ FAIRE CAPITALISM

By the 1700s, mercantilism had fallen into disrepute. The centralized rules lent themselves to corruption. The special privileges often went to the highest bidder. Time after time, the regulations turned out to be obstacles to economic progress. Actually, the rules were often violated, but in the process honest businessmen were made into uneasy, systematic lawbreakers.

In France a group of thinkers known as the physiocrats attacked mercantilism and called for a new economic policy.[1] One of them is supposed to have responded to a royal request for advice on the economy with the words, *"Laissez faire, laissez passer,"* meaning that the King should let the people do whatever they liked and go wherever they liked. At any rate, the new policy came to be knows as **laissez faire** (''less-ay fair''). The leading advocate of laissez faire turned out to be a Scot named Adam Smith, who has a reasonable claim to being the founder of modern economics. He published a now-famous book in 1776[2] entitled *An Enquiry into the Nature and Causes of the Wealth of Nations*, or *The Wealth of Nations* for short. This book set the course for the economic organization of England in the nineteenth century. It became the bible of the advocates of unregulated private enterprise.

In the early 1800s the major countries of the Western world, led by Great Britain, moved a long way toward a laissez faire policy, though no country ever adopted it completely. In the latter part of that century, and much more in this century, governments began to intervene in economic decisions again.

THE RATIONALE OF LAISSEZ FAIRE

No country has a purely laissez faire economy today, but individuals still make the largest share of economic decisions in most non-Communist countries. It is worthwhile to see how a laissez faire economy is supposed to work.

THE ECONOMIC PROBLEM IN THE REAL WORLD

In a modern economy, the questions of what, how, and for whom to produce are not three questions but millions. Imagine the job of a commissar (that is, a bureaucrat) who is put in charge of the shoe industry and instructed to make all the necessary decisions to maximize human satisfaction. He would have to decide how many shoes of each size, style, and color to produce; how much of each type of labor and of capital to use in each shoe factory; how much leather, thread, glue, nails, and electricity to use for each pair of shoes; and how many shoes of each size, color, and style each consumer should get. It sounds like an almost impossible job. Yet it has to do with only one small piece of the economy.

---

[1] A physiocrat familiar to most Americans was Eugène I. Du Pont de Nemours, who later came to America and built a gunpowder factory in Wilmington, Delaware. His descendants are still the primary owners of the DuPont chemical company.

[2] The notable date is not quite a coincidence. Many of the colonial complaints that led to the American Revolution were against mercantilist restrictions.

The commissars of meat, furniture, medicine, and automobiles would have problems at least as difficult. And all of these commissars would have to be coordinated by a super-commissar if the economy as a whole were to make any sense.

Altogether, the job of managing such an economy seems just short of impossible. The Communist countries have tried to do part, but not all, of the job on a centralized basis. Even they have left most consumption and employment choices to the individual. Yet, even limiting themselves to the questions of what and how to produce, they have had a hard time. The selection of the right mix of consumer goods has not been a strength of the Communist economies. Nor have they starred in the development of efficient methods of production. Communist department stores are famous for having the wrong size, color, and style of shoes and other consumer goods. And the "self-criticism" in the Communist press is full of complaints about wrong-headed production decisions. The main accomplishments of the Communist economies are elsewhere. They have been able to divert amazingly large parts of their GNPs into investment and defense, and they have attained remarkably equal income distributions.

If Commissars have so much trouble making economic decisions in a modern industrial economy, then how can we have anything but chaos from a system in which everyone makes whatever decisions he likes? How can such a system possibly work?

WHAT, HOW, AND FOR WHOM TO PRODUCE

Adam Smith's answer was that prices on markets were supposed to lead consumers, producers, and workers to make correct decisions. A **market** is the place where sellers compete for the business of a common group of buyers and within which prices are determined. Some are strictly local, such as the market for fish or houses. But some are worldwide, like the markets for coffee or copper. It is worth examining how such markets control economic decisions.

Take first the basic question of what to produce. In a laissez faire economy, this decision is made by individual businessmen on the basis of what would yield them maximum profits. They obviously would choose to produce goods and services whose selling price was the highest relative to the costs of production. In other words, they would produce those things on which people put the highest value relative to the costs of the factors used in production. And they would avoid producing things that people didn't want badly enough to pay much for. The quest for profit would lead businessmen to produce just those things that our commissar would want them to produce if he were trying to get the greatest value out of our limited resources. Of course, the business-men could make mistakes. When they did, however, they would take losses. They would be forced either to change their ways or to get out of business.

Now consider the question of how to produce. Again, the businessmen would make their decisions with the goal of maximizing profits. In other words, they would try to minimize their costs by using as few resources as possible. Faced with our ditch-digging problem, for instance, Ameri-can businessmen would use trenching machines. Capital is cheap in America, and labor is expensive, precisely because capital is plentiful here and labor is scarce. So American businessmen economize on scarce labor resources, using them only for the most essential tasks—like push-ing the "on" button. They substitute capital wherever possible. Again, this is just what our commissar would want them to do. For the same reason, businessmen in India would use the shovel method, saving on relatively expensive and scarce capital by substituting plentiful and cheap labor wherever possible. They would save capital for jobs where it was essential. It is better to have everyone using shovels than to have a few workers running big machines while the rest must use their finger-nails. Of course, businessmen can make mistakes in these decisions, too. But again, when they do, they turn out to be high-cost producers. They take losses until they switch to the low-cost methods or they go out of business completely.

When it comes to rationing the goods produced, each person is simply free to buy whatever he wants. His decisions depend on the prices of the various goods available. If the price of sirloin steak were $1.50 a pound, then the steak would go to people who valued it at least that much. The people who didn't think it was worth that much to them wouldn't get any, but they wouldn't go away empty-handed. They would spend their money on things that were worth more to them—maybe lamb chops. As a result, the sirloin steak would go to those who put the highest dollar value on it. So would the lamb chops. And so would every other com-modity. Given the goods that we have produced, this system of rationing would distribute those goods so that they yield the largest possible dollar value to consumers.

Finally, when it comes to distributing income, each person could take whatever job he wanted. He would choose the job that offered him the greatest rewards. The rewards, of course, would depend on what the employer thought he was worth. Employers seeking maximum profits would hire only those persons who added at least as much to the value of output as they cost. As a result, each person would earn as much as he added to production in his best possible employment. The result is that people would be employed where they were most useful. They would have an incentive to work hard, but they would also have an incentive *not* to work beyond the point where the extra income (the value of the extra goods produced) was not worth the extra leisure given up. Workers could make mistakes, of course, just like businessmen. But when they did they would wind up spending their time doing things that yielded less well-being than they could attain elsewhere. In the long run they would be apt to switch jobs.

All in all, unregulated private enterprise is far from chaos. Instead, it would seem to lead us to produce just the right things, in just the right ways, and to distribute them to just those persons who put the highest dollar value on them. You should be warned right away, though, that this is a greatly oversimplified picture of the world and even of what Adam Smith had to say. But at least the ideal of laissez faire private enterprise has a plausible rationale.

ASSUMPTIONS OF LAISSEZ FAIRE CAPITALISM

The picture of a laissez faire economy that has just been drawn is based on a set of assumptions. These assumptions may or may not hold in practice. For one thing, it assumes a government that plays a special role. Although it was supposed to keep out of business decisions, the government was still expected to keep the peace, enforce contracts, prevent fraud and violence, and define property rights so that the owners of productive resources can use them effectively.

Such conditions do not always hold. Many countries in the world today have unreliable legal systems. In such cases, it may turn out that the best use of capital is to invest it abroad, even though it would produce more at home. If fraud or violence is allowed, then my most profitable enterprise may be to hit my neighbors over the head—even though that activity is not particularly productive for the economy as a whole.

If property rights are not well defined, people will often make the wrong decision. For instance, no one owns the ocean. As a result, each fisherman will take as many fish as possible, regardless of the long-term effect on the stock of fish. Anyone who holds back is just letting someone else take more fish. Similarly, if land or capital were the common property of all, they would also be used wastefully. Indeed, much of the land on the medieval manor was common property, and it was overgrazed as a result. One important effect of the enclosure movement, which eliminated this common land, was to make land use more rational.

Again, our picture assumes that people produce, buy and sell, and seek jobs with maximum profits as a goal. In a society of monks, or of primitive tribesmen with ill-developed profit motives, markets may not work very well. Our picture also assumes that the economic goal of any society is the maximization of human satisfaction. One reason why Adam Smith won his argument with the mercantilists was that the objectives of society were changing. The mercantilists had been working for maximum national power, not human welfare. A country seeking national power should perhaps produce its own steel even if importing it is cheaper. And a big population may provide it with a big army even if the individual is left poorer.

By and large, these quibbles aren't very important for us. In the United States we do have a reliable court system. It generally keeps the peace, prevents fraud and violence, and defines most property in a way that makes markets workable. We live in a country where most people undoubtedly do try to maximize their individual satisfactions. We seem to want a society that yields a great deal of individual welfare, even at the expense of some national power. But what works for us may not work for everyone.

ECONOMIC PROBLEMS

There are other underlying assumptions to our picture that may not hold up so well, even in our society. Where they fail, unregulated private enterprise is likely to result in economic problems.

The picture we have drawn assumes, first of all, that there is competition. That is, it assumes an economy made up of many sellers and buyers, none of whom is large enough to control prices. In Adam Smith's day that was not a bad assumption. Most business was small-scale, and monopoly (having only one seller for a product) was possible only if the government granted it. Pure, one-seller monopoly is still rare, but something like a quarter of our GNP comes from industries in which a few producers control most of the output. Another ten to fifteen percent comes from industries in which the government controls business, often preventing competition. In these industries it is not at all clear that just the right amounts of each good will be produced. Instead, output may be restricted and prices raised. We will discuss the problem of monopoly and what is done about it in Chapter 6.

Our picture also assumes that there is competition on markets for the

factors of production. Again, this assumption was not too bad in Adam
Smith's day, when most employers ran tiny shops and trade unions were
virtually illegal. But many modern firms have tens of thousands of
employees; some have hundreds of thousands. If there is only one
employer in town, the wages it pays may be below what the laborers add
to the value of output. Probably more important, about a fifth of the
workers in the United States now belong to trade unions, many of which
are strong enough to set wages above what workers could get in competitive markets. Either way, the market will not work as Adam Smith
thought it would. We will discuss the problems of noncompetitive labor
markets in Chapter 9.

Our picture also assumes that the distribution of land, capital, and
labor among the members of society is acceptable. In that case, a system
that yields incomes according to individuals' productivities and distributes goods to the highest bidders would have much to recommend it.
But what if some people are so poorly endowed with resources that the
most they can produce is worth less than a dollar a day? Would you find
a system acceptable if it let imbeciles and the insane starve? Putting it
another way, if some people are rich and some people are poor, then the
beefsteaks, when sold to the highest bidders, are apt to go to the rich. You
might feel that the poor would get more satisfaction from one more steak
than the rich man will lose if we take one away from him. In that case, we
could increase the satisfaction of wants by redistributing the steaks. The
way income and goods are distributed in a laissez faire private enterprise
system may be wholly unacceptable to you. The result is an economic
problem that will be discussed in Chapters 7 and 8.

The rationale of laissez faire also assumes that all wants and all costs
are adequately expressed on the market. But in fact, many of them are
not. Presumably we get something from defense, for instance. But no one
can make a living running an army and selling its services on the
market—fortunately. If we are going to have defense, then the government will have to intervene and provide it. Actually, Adam Smith
recognized this failure of the market and allowed for it in his book.
Again, the costs of producing such goods as electric power include the
junk that the power plants spew into the air. You and I pay for it in many
ways, from dirty laundry to emphysema. We are becoming more and
more concerned about it. Yet the power company will not take those
costs into account of its own accord. It will produce too much power or
produce it in the wrong ways or both. Only if the government *does*
intervene will this sort of cost of production be taken into account. The
problem of wants and costs that are not expressed on the market will be
discussed in Chapters 10 and 11.

Finally, our picture assumes that the economy will automatically operate in such a way as to utilize its resources fully. In Adam Smith's day it generally did. But at the worst of the Great Depression, we were operating at only two thirds of our capacity. In other words, we could have had half again as much output as we did. Obviously the economy was not maximizing the satisfaction of human wants in that year. The problems of maintaining full employment and the related problem of inflation will be the main concern of Chapters 12 through 17.

It should be obvious by now that pure laissez faire private enterprise is not the best of all possible worlds. No country has ever fully embraced it, and we are far from it today.

MODERN CAPITALISM

The advanced non-Communist countries of the world still have primarily private enterprise economies, but governments intervene in economic decisions in many ways. In this section we will introduce the major actors in such an economy and describe their roles.

OUR BASIC ECONOMIC INSTITUTIONS

Figure 3.1 provides an impressionistic picture of the economy. The basic institutions of the private enterprise part of our economy are households, shown on the left, and firms, on the right.

A **household** is any group of people who live together. Most households are families, but a single individual living by himself is also a "household." Households have two major economic functions. First,

FIGURE 3.1 In the private enterprise part of our economy, firms and households interact on two kinds of markets. Firms sell their products, and consumers buy them, on product markets. Households sell factor services to firms on factor markets.

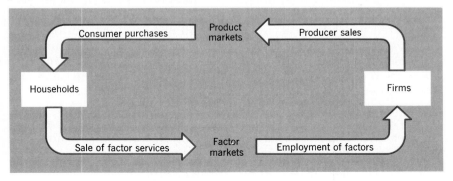

they are our main consuming institutions. In addition, households own the factors of production and supply their services for use in production. This is clearly true of labor. It is also true of land and capital owned by firms, since households own the firms.

A **firm** is any kind of business enterprise. Firms are our main producing institutions. They buy the services of land, labor, and capital and combine them to produce goods and services. The household is familiar to everyone, but many students have only rudimentary notions of modern firms. We will examine them in Chapter 4.

Firms and households meet in two types of markets. The area at the top center of Figure 3.1 represents product markets: where the ships and shoes and sealing wax are bought and sold. There the firms are the suppliers, and households, the buyers. We will examine product markets in Chapters 5 and 6.

Firms and households also meet on factor markets, which are represented by the area at the bottom of Figure 3.1. There the households sell the services of the land, labor, and capital that they own. They receive income payments in return. Firms are the buyers in factor markets. They employ the factor services for use in production. We will study factor markets, particularly labor markets, in Chapters 7, 8, and 9.

The result of these transactions is two sets of flows through each group of markets. They are represented in Figure 3.2. The outer ring is the flow of money. Money passes from households to firms in payment for purchases on product markets. It returns from firms to households in

FIGURE 3.2   Flows through product and factor markets. The outer ring represents the flow of money. The inner ring represents the flow of real goods and services. Product markets are at the top, and factor markets at the bottom.

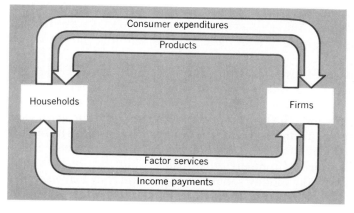

TABLE 3.2   Total federal, state, and local government expenditures (1971)

	DOLLARS (billions)	PERCENTAGE OF THE GNP
Transfer Payments	105	10
Purchases of Goods and Services	109	10
Production of Goods and Services	124	12
Total	338	32

the form of incomes on factor markets. The inner ring represents the flow of real goods and services. This flow goes in the other direction. The products of firms flow to households in the product markets, and the services of labor, land, and capital flow to firms in the factor markets.

The amounts of these flows of expenditures, incomes, output, and employment show the overall level of economic activity. When they fall far below their potential levels we have a depression. When they are near the maximum we have prosperity. Chapter 12 will describe these flows in more detail. Chapters 13 and 14 will try to account for the levels of these flows, and Chapters 15 and 16 will discuss policies to control them.

A MIXED ECONOMY

This picture so far has left out a third major economic institution, the government. It intervenes in many aspects of the economy. We can get some idea of the extent of this intervention from the size and makeup of government budgets. Table 3.2 shows the combined expenditures and receipts of all of the United States' federal, state, and local governments in 1971.

Governments at all levels collect about a third of the GNP in taxes. These funds are used in three different ways. A little under a third of them (about a tenth of the GNP) are transfer payments: payments to households from which the government receives no goods or services in return. Veterans' pensions and social security checks are both transfer payments. These payments redistribute income from the people who pay the taxes to those who receive the benefits, but they leave households to decide how the money should be spent, and they leave firms to produce the goods the households will buy.

Another third of the government budget and about a tenth of the GNP is government purchases of goods and services. The squad cars, school books, ballistic missiles, and sticky tape bought by various levels of government all fall into this category. In such cases the government takes over the consumption decision from the households. However, it still buys the goods and services on product markets. Production decisions are left in the hands of the firms.

Finally, a little more than a third of the government budgets, and about twelve percent of the GNP, is government production. Here the government takes over from both the households and the firms. It produces the necessary goods and services itself. This category includes the operation of the armed forces and the schools, for instance.

Altogether, the government decides what to produce for 22 percent of the GNP. It decides how to produce it for twelve percent of the GNP. The government is clearly a crucial economic institution today. Government budgets and their effects will be discussed in Chapter 10.

Purchases and production are not the only ways the government affects the economy. The 78 percent of the GNP left for the households to allocate among alternative uses, and the 88 percent left for the firms to produce, are still affected by hundreds of regulations, taxes, tariffs, price controls, minimum wage laws, and the like. In some markets these government controls are all-important (public utilities or basic agriculture). In others their effects are mild (most manufacturing and distribution). Government controls will come up in every chapter throughout the rest of this book.

Taxes, transfer payments, production, and regulations—all of these government activities are meant to alter the results of private decisions on markets. Ostensibly they are attempts to solve the problems that would arise on free markets. Most of the transfer payments reflect dissatisfaction with the distribution of income that would otherwise occur. A large proportion of government purchases and production is meant to supply us all with goods and services that would not be supplied in sufficient quantity, or in acceptable form, in a purely private enterprise economy. Defense, police and fire protection, and parks all fall into this category. Another purpose of government spending is to make services such as education and health care available to many who would otherwise have little access to them. Much of the government's regulation of business is undertaken in response to monopoly on product or factor markets. Other intervention is aimed at altering economic decisions to protect the social or physical environment. And a broad purpose of government programs in general is to attain greater economic stability.

The government's attempts to patch up the economy have had mixed success. They often have had unexpected side effects. Many of them have been diverted in ways that advanced the interests of certain groups more than those of the general public. Government purchases and government production have not always been as efficient as possible.

Whether the government's large economic role does an adequate job of patching up the economy is a matter of opinion. Almost everyone is dissatisfied with some aspects of government economic policy. Some economists feel that government intervention has come out badly so often that they advocate something much closer to the laissez faire ideal. Others feel that public intervention is essential, though they almost always can find particular government programs that they want to reform. Still others feel that the problems of a private enterprise economy are so severe, and the attempts to patch it up so unsuccessful, that a completely different economic system should be substituted.

SUMMARY

All economic systems must somehow answer the questions of what to produce, how to produce it, and how to distribute the output. There have been many different ways of answering these questions. In traditional societies the answers are deeply imbedded in custom. In command economies many of these decisions are made by the central authorities.

In a laissez faire economy, individual households and firms, seeking their own best interests, make the basic economic decisions. Under ideal conditions these decisions would result in the production of the goods that consumers valued most, using the most efficient methods. They would be distributed to the people who put the highest dollar values on them. Under ideal conditions, then, a laissez faire economy would result in the maximum satisfaction of human wants possible at a given level of resources and technology, and with a given distribution of resources among persons.

Private enterprise does not work this well in practice for many reasons. There is monopoly in many product and factor markets. Some costs to society do not fall on producers. Some wants are not expressed on markets. Economic instability has often left the economy operating at far below its potential. In addition, most people find at least some aspects of the distribution of income that would occur in unregulated markets unacceptable.

The basic economic institutions in the private sectors of modern capitalist economies are households, which consume goods and services and sell factor services, and firms, which produce goods and services and buy factor services. Households buy, and firms sell, on product markets. Firms buy, and households sell, on factor markets.

Ours is a mixed economy. Government takes over the consumption decision for a fifth of our GNP and the production decisions for an eighth of it. In addition, government controls the private markets in many ways. The various forms of government intervention are attempts to modify the effects of private economic decisions, but they generally work imperfectly.

STUDY QUESTIONS

1   What are the three basic questions that every economy must answer in some way? Try to work out in your mind what each of these questions means.

2   The frontier farm family was a small, almost self-sufficient economy of its own. It was certainly a private enterprise economy, but decisions were not made on markets. How were the three basic decisions made on the farm?

3   The three basic questions described in this chapter are only the most obvious ones. Another is "where to produce?" Who makes this decision in a laissez faire economy? On what basis? What happens to people who produce in the wrong places? What is wrong with the wrong places? Would a commissar do a better job of deciding where to produce?

4   A common criticism of capitalism is that in such a system, production is for profit rather than for use. Is production for profit inconsistent with production for use? Always? Ever?

5   What functions do business losses perform in a laissez faire economy? Does it follow that business losses are a good thing? Always? Ever?

6   Suppose we were to adopt a policy of pure laissez faire in the United States. What functions would be left for the government to perform under such a system? What, if anything, do you think would go wrong under such a system?

FURTHER READING

The amazing variety of ways in which various cultures have organized their economies is laid out in Karl Polanyi, *The Great Transformation* (New York: Octagon, 1973). Of course, the great book expounding and defending laissez faire is Adam Smith's *The Wealth of Nations*, but it is 900 pages long. George Stigler has extracted the more essential parts in *Selections from the Wealth of Nations* (New York: Appleton-Century-

Crofts, 1957), only 115 pages. Robert Heilbroner, *The Worldly Philosophers,* rev. ed. (New York: Simon & Schuster, 1972) provides an entertaining and useful description of Adam Smith's life, thought, and environment, as well as sketches of other great economists, including Malthus, Marx, and Keynes. For a modern advocacy of Smith's principles, see Milton Friedman, *Capitalism and Freedom* (Chicago: U. of Chicago Press, 1962). Friedman also examines the various criticisms of laissez faire capitalism from the point of view of a defender. For a less friendly (some would say radical) criticism, see Richard C. Edwards, Michael Reich, and Thomas Weisskopf, *The Capitalist System* (Englewood Cliffs, N.J.: Prentice-Hall, 1972).

4
BUSINESS
FIRMS

The two basic economic institutions discussed in the last chapter need to be understood before we look at the markets in which they meet. All of us have been members of households all our lives, so they require no explanation. Firms, on the other hand, are quite mysterious to many people. This chapter attempts to dispel some of the mystery.

HOW FIRMS ARE ORGANIZED

ENTREPRENEURS

The principal actor in the tales told in the last two chapters was the businessman, whom economists call the **entrepreneur.** Literally, *entrepreneur* means "undertaker," but that term has been taken over in the English language by the morticians, so we have had to turn to French. The entrepreneur is the man who undertakes business enterprise. He can be thought of roughly as the owner of the business firm. There are some strong qualifications, though, that we will come to later.

The owner of the firm does many things. He commonly puts up capital, and he may provide some of his own labor, but neither of these functions is essential. He could borrow the capital, and he often hires labor. The functions that are inseparable from ownership and entrepreneurship are two: decision making and risk bearing. Of course, the owner can delegate decisions, too, but ultimately his word is final. A hired manager who makes a decision that the owner does not like can be overruled or dismissed. There is no appeal within the firm from the decisions of the owner. Similarly, the owner bears the risks and takes the profits. If things go well and the firm makes profits, they belong to the owner—at least after the Internal Revenue Service has had its cut. If things go badly, he takes the losses.

You can see why the entrepreneur is so important to a private enterprise system. The decisions of what and how to produce are supposed to be made with the objective of maximizing profits. Here is the man who makes the ultimate decisions—and he just happens to take all the profits and losses as well. He has every reason to follow the rules of the game of laissez faire capitalism.

There is more to the entrepreneur than his formal functions, however. Traditionally he has had a mystique about him of self-sufficiency and drive. Many observers believe that the development of a breed of such men played an important role in the economic growth of Western countries and the coming of modern capitalism.

PROPRIETORSHIPS

So who is the entrepreneur in practice? The largest number of firms in The United States are single proprietorships—one-man businesses. There were more than nine million of these generally small enterprises in the United States in 1970. They included most farms and service businesses and a million and a half retailers. Because they are small, however, these proprietorships account for only thirteen percent of all business receipts, despite their large numbers.

The proprietorship is legally very simple. It is just the individual in business. It has all the legal characteristics of the individual in any capacity. You can get a notion of what this status involves by considering the individual in some other role: as an auto owner, for instance. You have complete disposal over your car, so long as you obey the law. And anyone who tries to use the car against your will is engaging in auto theft. Similarly, the proprietor has unlimited decision-making power over his business.

At the same time, the proprietor also has unlimited liability. If your car knocks down a $50,000 pedestrian, it makes no difference that you have invested only $500 in the car. You are responsible for the damages and debts connected with the car to the full extent of everything you own. The same applies to the proprietor. He cannot limit his liabilities to what he puts into his firm. If there isn't enough there to cover its obligations, the creditors can take his house and his insurance policies as well.

Finally, the proprietorship, like the individual, has a limited life. When the proprietor dies or retires, the firm comes to an end. It must be reorganized by inheritance or sale if it is to go on. The proprietor is clearly an entrepreneur of the classic type.

PARTNERSHIPS

The partnership is two or more persons in business. There were about 900,000 partnerships left in the country in 1970. They are especially common in distribution, finance, and services such as the professions. Like proprietorships, they are mostly small. All partnerships together account for only five percent of business receipts.

The law treats the partnership in the same way that it treats any joint undertaking of two or more persons. Barring some side contract, each partner has unlimited decision-making power. If you and I are joint owners of a car, I can drive it to the other end of the country and I will not have stolen it. You have no recourse unless we had an additional contract limiting what I could do with it. Similarly, if we owned a store together, I would be neither stealing nor embezzling if I dipped into the till.

Partners also have unlimited liability.[1] If I knock over the $50,000 pedestrian with our jointly-owned car, you are just as liable for the damages as I am, and you must pay if I cannot. Here no side contract can save you. Similarly, if one partner incurs debts in the name of a jointly-owned store and the store cannot pay, the other partner can lose his house and bank account in meeting the debts.

Finally, the partnership has a particularly limited life. Any time a partner dies or retires, the firm must be reorganized or dissolved. In general, the partnership has pretty much the characteristics of the proprietorship. Its owners are clearly identifiable as entrepreneurs of the old school.

The partnership was important historically. The big businesses of the preindustrial and early industrial period were mostly partnerships. In eighteenth century England you could buy one eighth or one sixteenth or one thirty-second of a ship and bid it goodbye on a trip to the Indies. If and when it "came in," you would be rich. Similarly, the early textile and iron mills were mostly partnerships. But today this form of enterprise is declining, as firms have become larger and longer-lived.

CORPORATIONS

In the last century the corporation has taken over from the partnership as a method for organizing large firms. Today there are one and a half

[1] Some states have a special form of partnership known as a limited partnership. By this arrangement, certain partners put up money and participate in profits, but their liabilities are limited to what they have contributed. There must still be full partners with unlimited liability in such firms, however.

million corporations in the United States, including almost all of the well-known firms. The number of corporations is growing rapidly. They are so common that we tend to think of them as natural, but they are actually rather peculiar legal creatures.

A corporation is a fictitious person, created by the law, that is distinct from its owners. It can own property, incur debt, and sue and be sued, yet its owners neither own the property, owe the debt, nor are involved in the suits. Unlike the proprietorship or partnership, it is characterized by **limited liability**. That is, the owner of the corporation ordinarily risks only what he puts into the firm. If it goes broke, the creditors cannot turn to him to make up any unsettled claims.

The corporation can also have unlimited life. Since it is distinct from the owners, it goes on even if they die or sell out. The present stockholders of United States Steel are practically all different from those who owned it when it was organized in 1901, but U.S. Steel is still U.S. Steel.

The corporation is a recent development as a form of business. Corporations existed in the Middle Ages, but they were largely nonbusiness organizations, such as cities, monasteries, or colleges at Oxford. The corporate form was clearly appropriate in such cases. These entities were intended to go on forever and to be independent of their particular individual members for their existence.

In early modern times, the corporation came to be used for certain special businesses that had particularly public functions, such as the Bank of England and the British East India Company. These corporations were all carefully controlled through their charters, however. Individual charters were drawn up and granted for limited periods by the crown. In return for special privileges, the crown imposed specific obligations on the corporations. By the late eighteenth century, the corporate form became fairly common in banking, insurance, and canal companies, but it still seemed strange in ordinary business. Adam Smith viewed corporations with great suspicion.

When the United States was formed, each state and the federal government had the right to issue corporate charters. At first charters were granted in individual acts of the legislature, but as the nineteenth century proceeded they became more and more automatic. By the start of this century you could form a corporation in certain states (notably Delaware and New Jersey) by doing little more than simply filling out some forms and paying some fees. The rights and obligations of these corporations were as broad as those of an individual. About the only vestige of the old special legal treatment of the corporation today is the fact that it must still pay a special tax, the corporate income tax.

BIG BUSINESS

Only about an eighth of our business firms are corporations, but they account for 82 percent of all business receipts. The bulk of these corporations are partnerships and proprietorships in disguise. A few individuals will form a corporation to attain limited liability and unlimited life, but they will retain all the stock in their own hands. These firms are generally small and behave pretty much as proprietorships and partnerships do.

But the few hundred largest corporations are in a class apart. They have hundreds of millions or even billions of dollars in assets, thousands of employees, and tens of thousands of stockholders. Their stocks and bonds are widely traded on national stock exchanges. The corporate form is absolutely essential for firms of this size. First of all, few individuals could put up all the money needed to finance one of these monsters. The funds must therefore be raised from thousands of investors. These people would be unwilling to contribute if they had to take on all the risks of unlimited liability. Second, large corporations are generally engaged in undertakings that go on for generations. Both limited liability and unlimited life are crucial for these huge firms.

THE EXTENT OF CORPORATE BIGNESS

Many people have expressed alarm at the size of the large modern corporations. The largest, American Telephone and Telegraph, has $55 billion in assets and takes in $19 billion in revenues, more than any state government does. Some 172 of our corporations have more than a billion dollars in receipts each.

The United States is enormous and has room for many huge corporations. But the absolute size of these firms is less important than their role in the national economy. The 200 largest manufacturing corporations account for some 61 percent of all assets (property) in manufacturing. This figure probably exaggerates the role of the big firms somewhat. They have a larger share of assets than of sales or employment because the largest firms use more capital per worker or per dollar of sales than small corporations do. The top 200's share of total manufacturing sales is a bit more than 50 percent.

The role of the top 200 corporations in our economy has been growing. In 1929 they had 48 percent of manufacturing assets. Their share rose moderately during the descent into the Great Depression, declined again during the recovery and World War II, and has been increasing again since then, reaching 61 percent in 1968.

THE EFFECT OF CORPORATE BIGNESS

What difference does it make that the top 200 firms do so much of our business? After all, their share of manufacturing is not, by itself, large enough to seriously threaten competition. And yet this concentration of economic power may have serious effects.

For one thing, the largest corporations do not compete directly on most of the markets in which they participate. On the few where they do compete—for instance, the market for capital—200 firms are easily enough to assure competition. Indeed, the major capital markets such as the stock exchanges are among the most competitive markets that we have. In some individual product markets, a few firms are so huge that opportunities for competition are quite limited. General Motors sells half the cars in the country, and four auto firms account for practically all domestic sales. In steel, the leading four firms do about half the business, and there are many other industries in which the top firms are equally important. But not all lines of business are dominated by a few firms, by any means. The degree of competition on individual product markets will be explored in Chapter 6.

The political impact of the large corporation is a common concern. Certainly the big firms have a great deal of political influence. However, it is not at all certain whether one billion-dollar corporation has more political clout than ten hundred-million-dollar corporations taken together. Indeed, some industries made up of very small firms, such as agriculture, medicine, trucking, and liquor retailing, have been able to get the government to do remarkable favors for them.

There are many powerful pressure groups in society. Not all of them are big business groups, by any means. Individual pressure groups are often able to influence the policies that affect them directly, but they don't always win, even on those issues. They sometimes offset one another. And there is a wide range of policies over which they have little power. For instance, the steel companies have a good chance of affecting government decisions about steel imports, the tax rules that apply to steel, and the environmental controls imposed on the steel industry. But they seldom carry much weight in public decisions about such things as race, social security, the army, international relations, agriculture, oil, or the telephone company. The presence of many powerful pressure groups may lead to a great deal of special-interest legislation, and it may mean that people who don't belong to such groups have less of a voice. Still, we are far from the point where a few firms run everything.

One effect of bigness is unquestioned. The role of an employee or even of an officer is quite different in a large corporation from what it was in a

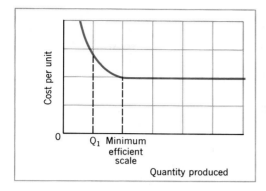

FIGURE 4.1   Costs per unit in a typical industry. At first, costs decline as size increases. But eventually increased bigness produces no further savings in costs. The point at which these gains disappear is known as the minimum efficient scale.

proprietorship. The free-wheeling, self-sufficient entrepreneur is becoming less important on the American scene. He is being replaced by committee members—our well-known "organization men." The character of American society is changing in the process, perhaps for the better or perhaps for the worse. The technicians who inhabit the modern corporation may be more efficient than the old-style entrepreneur, but no one seems to work quite so hard or be willing to take quite as much risk as he did.

THE ECONOMIES OF LARGE SCALE

Bigness has its advantages. Up to a point, larger size means lower cost per unit in most lines of business. Figure 4.1 shows how costs per unit vary with the size of the firm in the typical industry. Costs decline at first as size increases. Opportunities for specialization are increased within a large firm. Also, it is able to make fuller use of large-scale equipment. There are additional savings in such areas as inventories and advertising. These savings don't go on forever, though. In most lines of business there is some **minimum efficient scale** beyond which further gains from large scale disappear. Most American industries contain a number of firms, ranging from minimum efficient scale to many times that size, all of which have roughly comparable costs.

If the firms in some industry were smaller than minimum efficient scale, say at size Q_1, their costs would be higher than they needed to be. Both their owners and the consumers would be likely to be the losers. But such a situation is not likely to last in a competitive market. Any firm that got ahead of the others would have lower costs than its rivals and could undersell them. Ultimately, the inefficiently small firms would have to grow, too, or be forced out of business. Firms at minimum efficient scale or larger don't face such dismal prospects, even when their rivals are much larger than themselves. Most industries contain a number of firms of widely different sizes that have sold on the same markets for decades. This is one of the reasons why economists believe that costs don't vary much with size beyond some point.

Just where that point is depends on the industry. In fields such as apparel, lumber, shoes, and many lines of retailing and services, very small firms can be as efficient as big ones. In many lines of business, however, minimum efficient scale requires huge firms today. It takes at least a half-billion-dollar firm to be efficient in automobiles, steel, or petroleum refining. Even in cement, beer, and tires you need an invest-ment of $50,000,000 to $100,000,000 to reach minimum costs. The American economy is so large that there is room for quite a number of efficient producers in most industries. Still, business firms that are large enough to make their managers into bureaucrats and committeemen are inevitable in large parts of our economy.

STOCKS, BONDS, AND THE STOCK MARKET

THE FINANCIAL STRUCTURE OF THE MODERN CORPORATION

A good way to get a feel for the modern corporation is to examine the securities it issues. They fall into two broad classes, equity and debt.

Equity refers to the owners' claim on the firm. In the corporation, equity is represented by stock. The owner of one share of stock out of a million shares outstanding has a claim on one one-millionth of the firm. If the company earns profits and distributes them as dividends, he has a right to a millionth of the amount paid out. When the firm holds an election to determine the board of directors, he has the right to one vote out of a million. And, in the unlikely event that the corporation should be dissolved, he has the right to one millionth of the remaining assets after the debts have been settled.

Some of the debt of corporations is like everyone else's: short-term bank loans or current bills to be paid. But the long-term debt of a corporation is usually in the form of bonds. A **bond** is a court-enforceable promise to pay a specified amount of interest each year, plus a specified face value at the date of maturity. If the corporation does not pay either the interest or the principal at the promised time, the bondholders can take it to court. If the company is unable to pay, it is bankrupt.

Stocks come in several varieties. A share of **common stock** is a generalized claim on the firm. If common dividends are distributed, the stockholders have a right to participate in them. Under ordinary circum-stances, though, the corporation has no legal obligation to pay any dividends at all. If the firm goes bankrupt, the common stockholder usually loses what he has put up. He can't lose any more than that because of his limited liability.

Preferred stock carries a promise to pay certain specified dividends before any are paid on common stock. In the event of a dissolution, the preferred stockholder has a right to receive the face value of his stock before the common stockholders get anything at all. Yet the corporation has no legal obligation ever to pay dividends or principal to preferred stockholders, either. As a further guarantee, then, much preferred stock today is "cumulative preferred," meaning that any unpaid back dividends on it must be paid before dividends can be paid on common stock. Preferred stock does not usually carry voting rights.

There are several varieties of bonds also. "Debenture bonds" are generalized promises to pay, with no security offered as a guarantee. On the other hand, "mortgage bonds" do offer specific collateral. If the firm goes broke, the mortgage-bond holders can take over the specified assets (for instance a specific building) to the extent necessary to cover their claims. A few corporations even have "income bonds," which carry watertight promises to pay the face value at maturity. But they promise only that interest on the bonds will be paid before any dividends on common or preferred stock. No bonds carry voting rights.

You should not get the notion that corporate dissolutions are common events. They are rare among large corporations. Occasionally one of them may go bankrupt, but even then it usually continues in existence. The Penn Central Railroad went under in 1970, but it was still carrying freight in 1975. What generally happens is that the stockholders' claim on the corporation is erased. The creditors—the bondholders—accept stock or income bonds, or they take bonds of lower value in place of their original claims.

Why are the bondholders willing to make such a settlement when they have a legally enforceable fixed claim on the firm? Because they can expect to receive more money this way. The assets of most large corporations are worth much more as a unit than when sold off in bits and pieces. A railroad is usually worth more than its rails, ties, right-of-way, and rolling stock taken separately. And a soft-drink or cigarette company is surely worth more than its plants, machinery, and inventory. One reason is that loyalties are developed by customers and employees. Another may be just good management that originally put these resources together in a more effective way than you or I could do it. As a result of these settlements, the bankrupt firm usually goes right on operating in about the same business, with about the same personnel

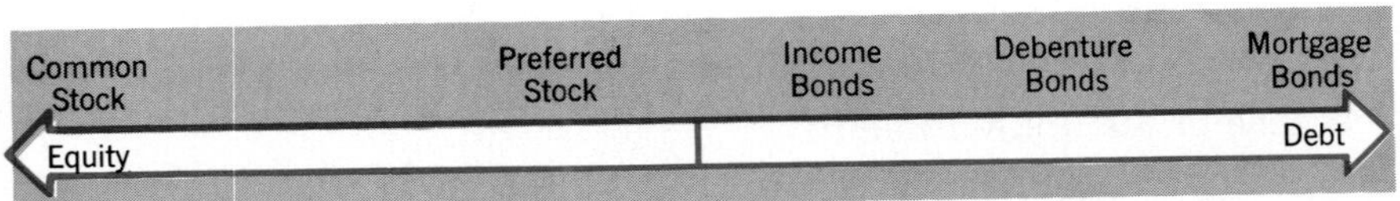

Common Stock		Preferred Stock	Income Bonds	Debenture Bonds	Mortgage Bonds
Equity					Debt

FIGURE 4.2   The securities on the left represent owners' claims on the firm; those on the right are legally enforceable obligations. The distinction between equity and debt is a matter of degree. The various forms of securities actually shade into one another.

except for a few top managers, but with different stockholders. Old corporations seldom die, they merely get reorganized.

By now it should be clear that the distinction between equity and debt is a matter of degree. There is a continuum of securities, as shown in Figure 4.2. It ranges from common stock, with no legally enforceable guarantee at all, to mortgage bonds, with which the guarantee of income and principal is strongest. The various types of securities shade into each other.

STOCK VALUES AND CAPITALIZATION

Why would anyone ever buy stock in a corporation when neither the earnings nor the principal are guaranteed? The answer is that stock prices reflect the anticipated flow of earnings of the corporation. There is always some price at which the stock is a good buy, and when the price gets to that level there will be plenty of demand for it. There will be no further reason for its value to either rise or fall.

To be more specific, suppose that the best guess is that a certain firm will pay five dollars a year in dividends indefinitely into the future. In that case, what is its stock worth? The best way to evaluate the stock is to relate its earning potential to what you could get on your investment elsewhere.

Suppose that you can earn five percent if you invest your money in mortgages or bonds or other stocks. Then you can work out the **present value** of the stock by seeing what is necessary for this stock to yield five percent:

$5 = 5\% \times$ present value.

By dividing both sides of the equation by five percent, we get

$$\text{present value} = \frac{\$5}{0.05} = \$100.$$

In general,

$$\text{present value} = \frac{\text{expected annual income}}{\text{going rate of return}}.$$

If the stock in this example is selling for $75, buy it. You will expect to earn $5/$75, or 6 2/3 percent on your money, while you can earn only five percent elsewhere. If its price is $125, sell. You are getting only $5/$125, or four percent, here. You can make five percent on other investments. At $100 you should be satisfied with what you have and be inclined neither to buy nor to sell, since you are earning the going rate of return.

You have just worked out what is called the **capitalized value** of the expected income from this stock. In the same way, you can work out the capitalized value of any income-earning asset: an acre of land, a machine, a share of preferred stock, or a bond. The capitalized value of an asset will rise if its expected annual income rises. It will *fall* if the going rate of return on *other* investments rises. For instance, suppose that the stock in our example goes right on paying five dollars a year, but that the rate of return on other investments rises from five percent to ten percent. Then the capitalized value of the stock will *fall* from $100 to

$$\frac{\$5}{0.10} = \$50.$$

A promise to pay five dollars a year is worth less if you can get more for your money elsewhere.

The simple formula for capitalized value that we used assumed that the expected income would continue at the same level forever. But if the income from the asset is expected to change in the future (as is likely with a share of stock or an acre of land), or if it will come to an end some day (as do most machines and bonds), the calculations are more complicated. There is no need to go into the details here. But the present value of any future income can always be calculated, whether it will come in one lump, in an irregular stream, or in a smooth, continuous flow. Such calculations are called "discounting," and the rate of return used in making them is called the "discount rate." The formula we used in our example for capitalizing a continuous constant stream of income is a special case of discounting. Actually, the present value of a long-term asset such as a 30-year bond is quite close to the capitalized value of an asset that will go on yielding the same amount of annual income forever. The reason is that income more than 30 years in the future isn't worth much now using present discount rates. For instance, a dollar 30 years from now is worth only 5.7¢ now, based on a ten-percent discount rate.

THE STOCK MARKET

If investors buy and sell sensibly, the price of a stock should approximate the capitalized value of its expected income per share. That bit of information won't make you rich, however. The future income of a stock is hard to predict. Different people will have different ideas about it.

They will base their judgments on the current earnings of the firm, its apparent chances for the future, its assets and liabilities, and assorted rumors, hunches, and "hot tips."[1] As a result, there are usually some people who think the stock's price is too high and want to sell and others who think it is too low and want to buy. When the offers to sell exceed the offers to buy, the stock's price falls. When the offers to buy exceed the offers to sell, it rises. Some shares of a widely held stock are likely to change hands every trading day. Those who go on holding their stock presumably believe that the capitalized value of its future income per share is at least as high as its price.

Some people have been able to do very well speculating on the stock market. Quite a number of them rode the market up in the 1960s, as business prospects in general improved. A few probably did better than average by pure gambler's luck. But the consistently successful speculators are almost always people who have been able to predict changes in the earnings prospects of firms earlier and more accurately than the rest of us. This ability takes a lot of knowledge and skill. The amateur who buys on a "hot tip" usually gets burned by it. Most likely it isn't right. Even if it is, a million other people have probably heard it, too, so its effect has already been reflected in the stock's price.

On the other hand, an only casually informed investor can make about the same return on his money as most others if he buys stock in several firms and just holds it. Stock prices generally reflect the earnings prospects of each firm about as accurately as is possible with the knowledge available to professionals at the time. The well-informed professionals bid up the price of any stock whose market price is low relative to its prospective earnings, and vice versa. Regardless of which stocks the ordinary investor buys, he will earn roughly the same return on his money. That going rate of return reflects the productivity of capital in the economy generally.

CONTROL OF THE CORPORATION

HOLDING COMPANIES AND CONGLOMERATES

Technically, the common stockholders control the corporation through their elected representatives, the board of directors. Actually, there is less there than meets the eye.

---

[1] One thing that has practically nothing to do with the price of a common stock is its face value. Most common stocks have definite values printed plainly on their faces. These numbers are arbitrary and carry no guarantee at all. It is completely possible for a common stock with a face value of $100 to sell for two dollars or for $200, depending on the company's prospects.

For one thing, it takes only 50 percent of the stock plus one share to have complete control of a corporation. But even this figure overstates by a great deal what is really needed for control. A corporation can be partially financed with non-voting bonds and preferred stock. A million-dollar corporation with $500,000 in bonds and preferred stock can be controlled by the holders of only $250,000 in voting stock.

Moreover, modern corporations can hold the stock of other corporations. A corporation whose assets consist of the stock of other firms is known as a **holding company.** Such a company may own controlling interests in a number of subsidiaries. In some instances these subsidiaries may, in turn, own controlling interests in other companies. In the 1920s there were holding companies as many as six steps removed from the operating companies. In such structures it was feasible for a million-dollar interest at the top to control operating companies worth tens of millions.

We still have many holding companies, including such firms as American Telephone and Telegraph, United States Steel, the leading banking and electric power systems in many states, and most of the major **conglomerates**. These last are called conglomerates because they operate in many unrelated lines of business. Some of the biggest of them are International Telephone and Telegraph, LTV, and Litton Industries.

In many cases the holding company device is no longer aimed primarily at pyramiding control. The parent company often owns all the stock of the subsidiaries. The holding company form is retained because of certain tax advantages, because of various government regulations, or because it provides a convenient way to acquire other firms.

Holding companies often do not pay cash for the stock they acquire in their subsidiaries. Instead they commonly offer stocks or bonds in the parent company in exchange for the stocks of the operating companies. Indeed, the stockholders in the firms that are selling out may prefer to receive stock instead of cash. It allows them to avoid paying taxes on the transaction. By taking this route some corporate empires have been constructed with breathtaking speed. A number of the conglomerates were put together in just a few years during the late 1960s. LTV grew from assets of $1.5 million in 1955 to $2.6 *billion* in 1968. Its acquisitions included a bewildering collection of products: from space vehicles and steel to sausages and catchers' mitts.

THE SEPARATION OF OWNERSHIP AND CONTROL

The tale of holding companies *still* overstates what it takes to control a large modern corporation. In many cases the stock is so widely distributed that nobody holds more than a small percentage of the total. As a result, control can be effectively maintained with far less than 50 percent of the stock outstanding.

All widely-held American corporations have stockholders' elections every year. Stockholders need not attend in order to vote. Instead, they receive proxies, which permit them to assign their voting rights to someone else. But ordinarily there is just one list of candidates for the board of directors, most of whom are unknown to the stockholders. And most stockholders who value their time do not do the research needed for an intelligent vote. Ordinarily the proxies are filed in the waste basket. When they *are* used, they are generally assigned to the existing management. As a result, most stockholders' meetings merely endorse the existing board of directors. When one director dies or retires, his replacement is chosen by the remaining members of the board. In practice, the management of a large corporation is usually chosen by itself.

Once in a blue moon there is a "proxy fight" with an opposition slate, so that the stockholders have a choice. However, even these attempts often fail.[2] Only when things in the firm are going very badly compared with other corporations is there any real threat.

A 1963 study showed that in 167 of the 200 largest nonfinancial corporations, no individual or closely associated group held as much as ten percent of the stock. A group with as much as ten percent of the common stock might be able to control. But in most very large corporations, power is apparently in the hands of a management that holds only an insignificant share of the stock.

MANAGEMENT CONTROL AND BUSINESS ETHICS

What difference does it make if most leading firms are controlled by self-appointed managers whom the stockholders cannot remove from office? For one thing, the managers may run the corporation in their own, rather than the stockholders', interests. For instance, they determine their own salaries. These salaries may have little to do with how well they have managed the firm. The management of Lockheed Aircraft, for instance, voted itself a large bonus in 1971 after a year in which the firm almost went bankrupt and was saved only by a large loan guarantee by the government.

---

[2] A much more serious threat to the insiders is that some other firm will try to buy up the stock in their company. The acquiring firm makes a "tender offer" to buy stock from the present stockholders at a specified price, usually above the market price. Stockholders often find these offers difficult to resist. Such "takeovers" were quite common even among firms in the billion-dollar class in the late 1960s.

Management can also use inside information to play the stock market. The employees of a firm can buy stock in anticipation of a good financial report. They can sell in anticipation of a bad one—one that they know about but that outsiders learn of only later. For instance, the officers of Texas Gulf Sulfur once bought stock in their own firm before the rest of the world found out that the company had discovered a valuable deposit of copper. In that case the offenders were punished by the Securities and Exchange Commission (a federal regulatory agency). However, where lesser employees of the firm or their cousins and friends make the purchases, there is little control. As a result of such trading, those in the know can get rich, and their profits are made at the expense of the stockholders who sell to them.

Managers can even manipulate the accounts of a firm to make it look more or less profitable and then sell or buy stock to take advantage of the impression they create. Many of the firms that were taken over by conglomerates in the late 1960s had their accounts revised to show slower depreciation on their plant and equipment, so that their reported profits shot up. The new accounting procedures were usually legitimate, but it took a magician to figure out what was happening.

Managers can simply take advantage of their powerful positions to do themselves favors. They can hire pretty secretaries or erect palatial office buildings on Park Avenue that do the stockholders little good. Most people know someone who can "get it for you wholesale" or someone who received a job because his uncle managed the firm.

The point is not that American businessmen are particularly unethical, but rather that the character of the firm has changed. In the old-fashioned proprietorship, the owner–manager who bought from the company that paid his way to Las Vegas, or who hired his incompetent nephew, wasn't cheating. He was just taking his profits in one form instead of another. But in the large, modern corporation the situation is different. The management is ordinarily in a position of trust. It handles the assets of other people who have no control over them. A public official who accepts favors from suppliers or who hires his relatives is clearly breaking the rules. The management of the large corporation is in essentially the same situation today, but our ideas of business ethics have been slow to change to fit the new conditions. Over the last 40 years, the federal government's Securities and Exchange Commission, the stock exchanges themselves, and the courts have imposed new rules. These rules are designed to prevent such things as deceptive corporate reports or insider trading on the stock market. Nevertheless, the standards of normal managerial behavior are still quite different from those that apply to others in positions of trust.

MANAGEMENT CONTROL AND THE GOALS OF THE FIRM

The separation of ownership and control in the large, modern corporation might have still more basic effects on business behavior. Stockholders can be reasonably expected to want high profits—but stockholders no longer make the decisions. What about self-appointed managers who usually own only tiny portions of the corporation's stock? They might have quite different goals.

Some economists have suggested that such managers might choose a policy of rapid corporate growth, even if they had to sacrifice some profits to attain it. They get higher salaries and more prestige and power as heads of larger firms. Other observers, including occasional businessmen, speak of managers' obligations to their employees, their customers, and society as a whole as well as to stockholders. Presumably such managers would sacrifice some profits, if necessary, for better working conditions, safer products, or a better environment.

If business executives do have weak profit motives for either reason, their firms might perform differently from what is expected in the traditional picture of the private enterprise economy. Profits would no longer necessarily lead firms to produce the right goods in the right amounts at minimum costs.

Many economists believe that the profit motive is still alive and well in the large modern corporation, however. For one thing, the management must make at least reasonable profit rates or the price of their company's stock will fall. Outsiders will find it worthwhile to buy up the stock and take control. Such takeovers will be profitable if the new management can make better use of the company's assets than the old one did. During the late 1960s, many corporations with ho-hum profit records were taken over by outsiders in this way. In some extreme cases, it was even worthwhile for outsiders to buy control of low-profit firms and then put them out of business, transferring the assets of those firms to more profitable uses. Many managements have struggled hard to get their profits up for fear of such takeovers.

In competitive industries, such as textiles, lumber, meat packing, shoes, or retailing, business firms have very little leeway in any case. The profit rates available to the best-managed, most profit-oriented firms are seldom very high in these fields. In such industries, firms that do not take full advantage of their situations are courting bankruptcy or takeover.

Even when the firm has more leeway, management may still have good reason to seek high profits. Since income tax rates on high salaries are high, top executives have taken an increasing share of their incomes in the form of common stock, often purchased at low prices under "stock option" plans. They usually own only a small share of the stock outstanding, but that is not the point. What they do own accounts for a large and increasing part of their personal incomes. As a result, managers often stand to gain a great deal if their firms' profits rise so that the value of their stocks goes up.

A number of economists have attempted to compare the profitability of corporations apparently controlled by management with those controlled by an individual or an identifiable group. Some studies have shown that management-controlled corporations earn moderately lower profit rates than those with identifiable controlling stockholders. But others have found no difference at all between the two groups. In any event, all the studies seem to agree that the effect of management control on profitability is mild if it exists at all.

Many instances of clearly profit-oriented behavior are readily available. Every year hundreds of large firms close unprofitable plants and stores. Hundreds more try to break into new and profitable industries, often at great cost. New techniques or locations are rapidly adopted, sometimes in response to savings that come to only a few percent of total costs. And every year a good number of businessmen are found to be agreeing on prices or are seen descending on Washington in attempts to get better tax treatments, more protection from foreign competition, or less expensive environmental requirements. Some of this behavior may be unseemly, but it is unquestionably aimed at higher profits.

SUMMARY

The crucial functions of the entrepreneur are to make decisions and to take risks. For the owners of proprietorships and partnerships, these functions are combined. Such firms are likely to aim for maximum profits. However, these forms of business are not very suitable for large-scale enterprises because of their limited lives and unlimited liability.

The law treats the corporation as a "person" distinct from its owners. Its owners have limited liability for its obligations, and it can go on for generations though its owners change completely. Stockholders are the owners of the corporation, and bondholders are its creditors. The corporation has a legally enforceable obligation to pay the specified interest and principal on its bonds, but it has virtually no legal obligation to pay dividends on its stock.

The prices of stocks, bonds, and other income-earning assets tend to reflect their capitalized values—their expected annual income divided by the going rate of return on investments. A stock's price will rise if expected future incomes rise or if the going rate of return falls, and vice versa.

Common stockholders have the right to vote for the board of directors of the corporation, but in most large modern corporations stock is too broadly dispersed for effective stockholder control. The top management of these corporations cannot usually be removed by the stockholders. One result is that modern managements, unlike old-line entrepreneurs, are in a position of trust. They control other people's assets. We have developed some legal controls, but our standards of business behavior are still quite different from those that we apply to public officials.

Some observers expect the separation of ownership and control in the large modern corporation to result in a change in business motives. However, the threat of takeover by outsiders, the narrow leeway available for firms on competitive markets, and the increasing importance of stock in the typical management's income all provide good reason for managers to seek high profits.

STUDY QUESTIONS

1   What is a corporation? From a legal point of view, how does it differ from a partnership? How does the large corporation differ from a partnership in practice?

2   Who is the entrepreneur in the large modern corporation? If you have a hard time finding anyone who fits the definition, ask yourself what functions the entrepreneur fulfills. Are these functions fulfilled in a large corporation? Who does them?

3   Are there economies of scale in the college education industry? If so, where do they come from? Try imagining conditions in the economics departments of colleges with varying numbers of students: 500, 1,000, 2,000, 5,000, 10,000, 20,000 and 50,000. About how many professors would there be in the economics department of each school? How many economics courses could each school offer each term? How well prepared would the professors be to teach these courses? How many students would there be in each course? You probably can only make rough guesses about the answers to most of these questions, but you should be able to see some of the possible economies of scale. Do these economies go on indefinitely? For instance does the 50,000-student school have any advantage over the 20,000-student school in teaching economics? Do you think there is a minimum efficient scale in college teaching? If so, about where do you think it falls?

4   How will the prices of old government or corporate bonds change if

interest rates in general go up? You can follow such changes very clearly if you watch the financial pages during a period when interest rates are changing. A rise in interest rates ought to affect the prices of common stocks, also. However, if you try to follow stock prices when interest rates are rising you will find it much harder to see the effect of rising interest rates there. Why should this be?

5   Most stockholders in large corporations such as General Motors or American Telephone and Telegraph pay little or no attention to the annual elections of the boards of directors, because they generally cannot affect the outcome. Many of the same people will take an active part in congressional or presidential elections, and most of them will at least vote in those elections. Why the difference?

FURTHER READING

The antecedents of the corporation and its history in England are developed in an excellent little book by C. A. Cooke, *Corporation, Trust and Company* (Cambridge, Mass.: Harvard U. Press, 1951). It is a scholarly but nontechnical work. Two entertaining, non-scholarly, but generally correct books on the stock market by "Adam Smith" (a pen name) are *The Money Game* (New York: Random House, 1968), and *Supermoney* (New York: Random House, 1972). The classic on the transformation of the entrepreneur in the large modern corporation is Adolph A. Berle, Jr., and Gardiner Means, *The Modern Corporation and Private Property*, rev. ed. (New York: Harcourt Brace Jovanovich, 1969), but it isn't bedtime reading. Two controversial interpretations of the effects of the change are A. A. Berle, Jr., *Power Without Property* (New York: Harcourt Brace Jovanovich, 1959), and John Kenneth Galbraith, *The New Industrial State,* 2nd rev. ed. (New York: Houghton Mifflin, 1971). Both are available in paperback.

APPENDIX TO CHAPTER 4
THE ELEMENTS
OF ACCOUNTING

Accounting is a useful tool in analyzing the modern corporation. The development of accounting practices has helped make it possible to manage huge enterprises efficiently. This appendix offers a once-over-lightly on the main points.

STOCKS AND FLOWS

Two types of statements can be made about almost any economic process. One describes the **stocks** that exist at any point in time, and the other describes the **flows** that occur over a period of time. Figure 4.3 illustrates these concepts. It represents a bathtub with water flowing in and out. The flows can be measured only over time. To describe how much water flowed into the tub, you would have to specify the time period—be it a second or a minute or an hour. If you said that the water was flowing in at twenty gallons a minute, you would mean that twenty gallons would enter the tub if the water continued at its present rate for one minute.

In describing the *amount* of water in the tub you would be giving a statement of stock. Here you could be precise *only* if you measured it at a particular instant. If someone asked how much water was in the tub "today" you could say only that it fluctuated, but as of 10:31 P.M. you could give a specific amount.

There is an obvious relationship between the flows and the stock in this example. The change in the amount of water in the bathtub over a period of time is the difference between the flow in and the flow out. In effect, the *change* in the stock of water is another flow concept, even though the amounts of water in the tub at the start and at the end were stocks.

Most economic measures are stocks or flows. Try it out for yourself. Is our population a stock or a flow? What about the number of births? The GNP? The public debt? You can look the answers up in the footnote.[3]

[3] The population is a stock. The number of births and the GNP are both flows. The public debt is a stock.

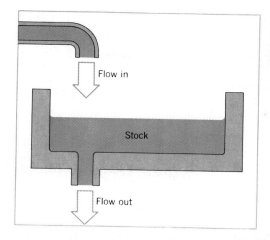

FIGURE 4.3 **The flows in and out of this bathtub can only be measured over time. The stock of water in it can only be measured at an instant.**

THE BALANCE SHEET

Statements of stock about the business firm appear in its balance sheet. Statements of flows into and out of the firm appear in its income statement.

The **balance sheet** lists two types of quantities, the firm's **assets**—what it owns—and its **liabilities** and **equity**—the claims against its assets. Table 4.1 shows a simplified balance sheet. "Cash" is currency and bank accounts. "Accounts Receivable" are bills that the firm has yet to collect from outsiders. "Inventory" is the total stock of materials, goods in process, and finished goods on hand. The allowances for bad debts, shrinkage, and depreciation will be explained presently. "Buildings and Equipment" is self-explanatory. "Good Will" is an estimate of what the firm is worth over and above its tangible assets. It includes such things as patents, trademarks, and the list of loyal customers. They are often a firm's most valuable assets. A company that owned a popular cigarette brand could probably quite easily get the rest of the assets it needed to sell cigarettes. A firm that owned the plant, equipment, and tobacco but had no known brands would have a large investment in advertising ahead of it before it sold many cigarettes.

The **liabilities** of the firm are its debts. "Accounts Payable" are bills the firm has not yet paid. "Notes Payable" are mostly short-term loans, usually from financial institutions such as banks and insurance companies. Bonds are long-term debts.

Equity is the owners' claims on the firm. Common and preferred stockholders have a clear ownership right to the corporation, though it would not go bankrupt if it could not honor their claims. The common and preferred stocks are listed at their face values. The last item, "Surplus," is also part of the stockholders' claims on the firm. It is a residual item. Any excess of assets over liabilities plus the book

TABLE 4.1   A corporate balance sheet

ASSETS			LIABILITIES AND EQUITY		
Cash		$ 50,000	Liabilities		
Accounts Receivable	$100,000		Accounts Payable	$ 75,000	
Allowance for Bad Debts	− 10,000	90,000	Notes Payable	100,000	
			Bonds Outstanding	200,000	$375,000
Inventory	200,000		Equity		
Allowance for Shrinkage	− 25,000	175,000	Common Stock at Face Value	200,000	
Buildings and Equipment	500,000		Preferred Stock at Face Value	100,000	
Allowance for Depreciation	−140,000	360,000	Surplus	50,000	350,000
Good Will		50,000	Total Liabilities and Equity		$725,000
Total Assets		$725,000			

value of stocks outstanding is surplus. It is really just a correction in the arbitrary face values of stock shown on the balance sheet. This explanation will become clearer in a moment.

Total equity (preferred and common stock plus surplus) is just a statement of what the firm is worth to its owners. If a corporation has $1,000,000 in assets and $600,000 in debts, it is worth $400,000 to its stockholders. As a result, the two sides of the balance sheet must always be exactly the same:

Equity = Assets − Liabilities.

DOUBLE-ENTRY BOOKKEEPING

One implication of this equation is that every change in the firm must always be recorded twice. In other words, bookkeepers must make "double entries." We can illustrate the reason with a series of transactions.

Here is the balance sheet for a very simple firm just starting out in business:

ASSETS		LIABILITIES AND EQUITY	
Cash	$1,000,000	Common Stock	$1,000,000
Total	$1,000,000	Total	$1,000,000

The stockholders have just paid $1,000,000 in cash for common stock that just happens to have a face value of $1,000,000. Now the firm sells $500,000 of bonds and uses the proceeds to buy plant and equipment. The balance sheet will look like this:

ASSETS		LIABILITIES AND EQUITY	
Cash	$1,000,000	Bonds	$500,000
Plant and Equipment	500,000	Common Stock	$1,000,000
Total	$1,500,000	Total	$1,500,000

Assets go up by the $500,000 that the plant and equipment cost, and liabilities go up by the $500,000 of the bonds. The totals on the two sides of the balance sheet stay the same. Next, the firm buys $700,000 in inventory for cash. Here is the new balance sheet:

ASSETS		LIABILITIES AND EQUITY	
Cash	$300,000	Bonds	$500,000
Inventory	700,000	Common Stock	$1,000,000
Plant and Equipment	500,000		
Total	$1,500,000	Total	$1,500,000

Cash is reduced and inventory is increased by $700,000. Total assets stay the same, and the balance sheet still balances. Next, let the firm sell $100,000 worth of goods from its inventory on credit for $200,000. The balance sheet now looks like this:

ASSETS		LIABILITIES AND EQUITY	
Cash	$300,000	Bonds	$500,000
Inventory	600,000	Equity	
Accounts Receivable	200,000	Common Stock	$1,000,000
Plant and Equipment	500,000	Surplus	100,000
Total	$1,600,000	Total	$1,600,000

Inventory goes down by $100,000, the amount sold. Accounts receivable of $200,000 are added to assets. These changes aren't enough, however. The total assets have gone up by $100,000 because of the profit made on the sale. In order for the balance sheet to balance, the total on the right has to increase also. The firm doesn't have any more debt than it did before, so the extra $100,000 is listed as surplus. This surplus is part of the owners' equity. The firm is now worth $100,000 more to the owners than it was before the sale.

One thing to note is that the company's cash hasn't changed. A firm can make a profit of $100,000 without having $100,000 more in cash. Its assets did go up, but even this increase would not have been necessary. The firm could have sold the goods for cash and paid off some of the bonds with the proceeds. In that case its total assets would have gone down, not up, in spite of the profit.

Finally, let the accountant embezzle $50,000 in cash. When the theft is discovered, cash will have to be written down by $50,000. The firm is worth less to its stockholders, so the surplus is written down by $50,000 at the same time. Here is the result:

ASSETS		LIABILITIES AND EQUITY	
Cash	$250,000	Bonds	$500,000
Inventory	600,000	Equity	
Accounts Receivable	200,000	Common Stock	$1,000,000
Plant and Equipment	500,000	Surplus	50,000
Total	$1,550,000	Total	$1,550,000

At every point the two sides of the balance sheet must add up to the same amount. If they don't, the company isn't necessarily in trouble. The accountant has just made some sort of a mistake.

ESTIMATES IN THE BALANCE SHEET

The figures in a real balance sheet are seldom nice, round numbers like the ones in these examples. Instead of $50,000 you are apt to find a figure like $54,280.07. Such numbers give the accounts a spurious air of precision. We conventionally assume that round numbers such as $50,000 are approximations, while those spelled out to the last decimal place are the result of exact measurement. Accountants have to use exact-looking numbers to keep control over a firm. Nevertheless, their evaluation of the firm is much less precise than it looks. In fact, practically every asset in the balance sheet is an estimate. Most assets can only be known approximately.

Some typical accountants' estimates show up in our first balance sheet (Table 4.1). They include the allowances for bad debts, for shrinkage, and for depreciation. Take the depreciation item, for instance. The firm knows what it paid for its buildings and equipment. This amount is reported directly in the balance sheet. But it also knows that the buildings and equipment have partially worn out and/or become obsolete since they were acquired. To cover this loss in value the accountants have subtracted an estimated allowance for depreciation from the original values. The result is their estimate of what the buildings and equipment are worth now.

The allowance for depreciation is only an estimate. It could have been made in any number of ways. One simple possibility would be to say that a $10,000 machine that is expected to last for ten years depreciates by $1,000 each year. This scheme is illustrated in Figure 4.4. The machine would be valued at $9,000 at the end of the first year, at $8,000 at the end of the second, and at zero at the end of the tenth. These estimated values would be too low if the machine actually lasted more than ten years and too high if it were scrapped in less than ten years. This system is known as straight-line depreciation.

An alternative would be to allow for faster depreciation at first, and slower later on, as illustrated in Figure 4.5. Such a system would accurately reflect the decline in value for an automobile on the secondhand market. For a growing firm this pattern of depreciation will result in higher reported costs, and lower total

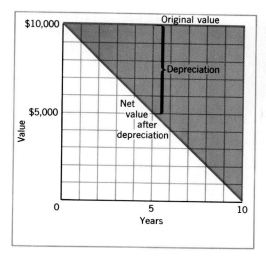

FIGURE 4.4   The net value of a $10,000 asset will vary greatly after a few years, depending on what scheme the accountants use to estimate depreciation. They can assume that the asset depreciates the same amount each year . . .

assets, than straight-line depreciation will. Many firms have adopted some form of accelerated depreciation in recent years. It results in lower reported profits for growing firms, and therefore lower corporate taxes.

Another alternative would be for the accountant to depreciate the machine slowly at first and more rapidly toward the end of its life, as in Figure 4.6. This method results in greater total assets and lower reported costs than straight-line or accelerated depreciation does. Public utilities sometimes follow such an accounting practice because they are allowed a fixed rate of return on the book

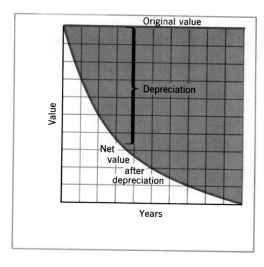

FIGURE 4.5   . . . they can assume that the asset depreciates more rapidly at first and more slowly later . . .

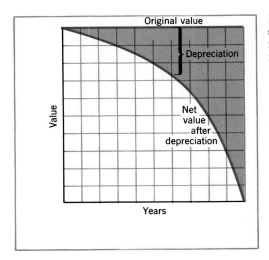

FIGURE 4.6 ... or they can assume that the asset depreciates more slowly at first and more rapidly later.

value of their assets. They will therefore earn more if their books report greater assets.

All of these methods of estimating depreciation are accepted accounting practices. As a result, two identical firms may report quite different assets, costs, and profits without cheating.

The allowances for bad debts and for shrinkage in the balance sheet shown in Table 4.1 are similar estimates. The firm knows from experience that not all of its accounts receivable will be collected. The accountants estimate the actual value of the accounts receivable by subtracting an allowance for bad debts. Similarly, they know that the inventory will decline in value because of pilferage and deterioration. They estimate these losses by subtracting an allowance for shrinkage.

In some balance sheets these allowances are reported as "reserves" for depreciation, bad debts, and shrinkage. This term does not mean that there is a fund of cash around to replace the deteriorated assets. It is just a name for the correction of the original values of the affected items. A firm with large reserves for depreciation isn't rich—it just has old equipment.

Another estimate is involved in inventory valuation. The items in inventory were bought at different times and at different prices. How the inventory is evaluated depends on what assumption the firm makes about the order in which the items in inventory are used. Take, for example, a firm with a 1,000-ton pile of coal. Every week it receives 100 tons and burns 100 tons of coal. Suppose the price of coal is rising. If the firm uses LIFO (last in, first out) accounting, its books will show that it is currently burning the expensive coal that has just been delivered, while it keeps the cheaper old coal in inventory. Its reported costs will be high and the value of its assets, low. If instead it used FIFO (first in, first out) it would put the newest coal in the pile and use the cheaper, old coal. In that case its reported costs would be lower and its reported assets higher than with LIFO.

Of course, this is all just accounting. No one really keeps track of which lumps of coal are actually in the pile. But accountants must follow some rule in valuing inventory. Either method is somewhat arbitrary, and both are considered proper as long as the firm sticks with the one it has chosen. A firm may seem more or less profitable, depending on which practice is followed. If it uses LIFO, its profits and the value of its assets will appear more stable during business fluctuations than if it uses FIFO. Since prices tend generally to rise, LIFO will usually result in lower reported profits and asset values than FIFO.

The wildest estimate of all is "Good Will." Many firms value this item on their books at zero or some nominal figure, though good will is usually quite valuable. Sometimes a firm will report good will at a substantial value. When it does, it usually means that the firm has purchased patents or trademarks or other entire business firms at a price greater than the book value of any tangible property acquired.

The fact that most balance sheet items are estimates should not be taken as a slur on accountants. In fact, it is just the opposite. If the value of each item in the balance sheet were known exactly, there would be little to accounting but bookkeeping. It is the need to make estimates that makes accounting a profession.

THE INCOME STATEMENT

Table 4.2 shows an income statement for our hypothetical firm. It shows the flows of sales, expenses, and profits through the firm. Whereas the balance sheet was reported as of a particular date, the income statement shows receipts and expenditures over a period of time, such as a year.

Many of the items in the income statement are self-explanatory. The allowances for bad debts, inventory shrinkage, and depreciation are estimates of the amount by which the assets involved have declined in value during the year. "Operating Income" shows what is left to cover capital costs of various sorts. The corporation earned $52,000 after taxes, of which $30,000 was paid out to stockholders as dividends. The $22,000 that was left was plowed back into the firm. The balance sheet at the end of the year will show $22,000 more in surplus than at the start.

HOW TO READ CORPORATE ACCOUNTS

A corporation's accounts can give a variety of information about the firm. For instance, in looking at a balance sheet we may be interested in both the firm's solvency and its liquidity. **Solvency** refers to the ability of the firm to meet its

TABLE 4.2   A corporate income statement

Sales		$1,000,000
Expenses		
Materials	$500,000	
Wages, Salaries,		
and Supplements	300,000	
Estimated		
Bad Debts	2,000	
Inventory		
Shrinkage	3,000	
Depreciation	20,000	
Rentals	50,000	− 875,000
Operating Income		125,000
Interest		− 25,000
Net Income		
Before Tax		100,000
Corporate		
Income Taxes		− 48,000
Net Income		
After Tax		52,000
Dividends		− 30,000
Addition to		
Surplus		22,000

debts over the long run. It is shown by the relationship between the firm's assets and its liabilities. A common way of evaluating solvency is the **debt ratio,** the ratio of liabilities to assets. The firm in Table 4.1 had a debt ratio of $375,000/$725,000, or 0.517. A firm with a high debt ratio is likely to be very profitable in good years, when its operating income per dollar of invested capital exceeds the interest rate it pays. On the other hand, it could run a serious risk of bankruptcy in bad years if it is in an unstable industry. Debt ratios over 0.5 are commonly considered to be risky in unstable industries. However, public utilities, which face quite stable demand, often carry that much debt and more.

   Liquidity is the ability of a firm to meet its current commitments as they arise. It is often evaluated by comparing current assets with current liabilities. A **current asset** is cash or something that can be turned into cash in a short period, such as a year. Cash, accounts receivable, and inventory are commonly counted as current assets. A **current liability** is a debt that can come due within a short period. Accounts and notes payable are usually current liabilities. Bonds can also be in this category if their maturity dates fall within the next year. A common index of liquidity is the ratio of current assets to current liabilities, or the **current ratio.** The firm in Table 4.1 has a current ratio of $315,000/$175,000, or 1.80. What is an adequate current ratio depends on the line of business involved. In an unstable business a current ratio of 2.0 or more is often required.

On the other hand, banks often have more current liabilities than current assets.

A firm can go broke because it is illiquid—lacks liquidity—even though it may have plenty of assets to cover its total liabilities. If it cannot cover its payroll and current bills it is still in trouble.

The profitability of a firm is usually evaluated by the way its profits compare to its sales or its equity. The firm in Tables 4.1 and 4.2 had a profit–sales ratio of $52,000/$1,000,000, or 0.052. Its profit–equity ratio was $52,000/$350,000, or 0.149. Is a profit–sales ratio of 0.052 high or low? It is hard to tell without knowing how much capital the firm uses. A profit–sales ratio of 0.052 would be tremendous in food retailing, where annual sales are five times assets. Profit–sales ratios in that field are usually around one percent. But it would be low for electric utilities, where annual sales are a fourth of assets, and profit–sales ratios are more like fifteen percent.

The ratio of profit to equity is more nearly comparable among different industries. This figure shows what a dollar of equity earns in each firm. If management tries to maximize profits, and if markets are competitive, rates of return on equity will tend to move toward equality. If a dollar in one industry earns only five percent while others are earning ten, a profit-seeking management will shift his company's assets into the more profitable lines of business when it can. Similarly, high profits (say fifteen percent) will attract new competition. Profits will tend to fall. As a result of such adjustments, the profit–equity ratio will tend toward equality in all competitive industries. It will never be *exactly* the same in practice, because different firms use different accounting practices and because market conditions and costs for various firms are always changing.

Table 4.3 shows a concrete example: profit ratios for Borden's Milk and Shell Oil in 1971. As you can see, Borden makes a lot less profit than Shell on each dollar of sales. But Borden isn't necessarily any less profitable. Its low profit–sales ratio just reflects the fact that Borden needs only a small investment to produce its output. Most of the production of the milk products it sells is done on the farm. The oil company, on the other hand, operates oil wells, pipelines, refineries, and gas stations. It has to turn oil from reserves in Texas into gasoline in the driver's car. It therefore needs much more capital per dollar of sales than Borden does. The profit—equity ratios show that the two companies were making similar returns. There was little reason for capital to flow from the milk to the oil industry, or vice versa, at that time.

TABLE 4.3   Profit ratios of two firms (1971)

FIRM	PROFIT-SALES RATIO	PROFIT-EQUITY RATIO
Borden	2.9%	8.7%
Shell Oil	6.3	8.7

STUDY QUESTIONS

1 Why must all transactions be entered twice in the books of a business firm?

2 If the income statement of a firm shows a loss, how will the balance sheet change from the beginning to the end of the period covered by the income statement?

3 Try making a balance sheet for yourself. First make a list of all your assets. Then list your total debts. Then subtract the debts from the assets to find your equity (usually called "net worth" in the case of an individual or a proprietorship). If you are like many students, you are apt to find that you have a negative net worth. What does this mean? Why would anyone lend to a person with a negative net worth? (Hint: You have an asset, or at least are acquiring one, which is quite valuable but which you probably didn't include in your list of assets. What is it?)

4 If you were conducting a survey to find the degree of equality in the distribution of personal wealth in your community, which measure would be more appropriate, total assets or total equity (net worth)?

5 A certain corporation has assets of $100 million. Its total equity is $50 million. But the total market value of its outstanding stock is only $10 million. How can this happen? Which figure most accurately reflects the value of the company to its stockholders?

UNIT TWO
COMPETITION
AND
MONOPOLY

5 COMPETITIVE MARKETS

Our picture of modern capitalism in Chapter 3 was painted with a broad brush. Now it is time to analyze more precisely how competitive product markets work.

DEMAND AND SUPPLY

As a first step we must develop an important method of analysis called demand and supply. It can be used to explain factor markets as well as product markets. With some modifications, it can be used to explain the effects of monopoly and to analyze government spending. Economic decisions depend both on what people want and what is possible. Demand and supply analysis give us a way to handle these two fundamental considerations. It is a powerful economic tool that will be used again and again throughout this book.

PURE COMPETITION

Like any theory, demand and supply analysis rests on certain assumptions. First of all, we assume that the buyers and sellers are all seeking their own best interests. We also assume that they know all the options open to them. Finally, we assume that the markets being studied are purely competitive.

The last assumption requires some explanation. **Pure competition** means that buyers and sellers are so many and so small that no one of them can significantly affect the price of any commodity by himself. Each buyer approaches the market as you approach a meat market. The price of sirloin steak will be the same regardless of how much you buy. The same goes for sellers. They are assumed to be in the position of individual farmers. No single farmer can affect the price of beef cattle, whether he produces and sells all he can or stays off the market completely. In the next chapter we will drop this assumption of pure competition. We will then have to modify demand and supply analysis to handle the situation, but the changes will be fairly easy.

DEMAND

Our first concern is with demand. **Demand** consists of the amounts of some commodity—say eggs—that people are ready and willing to buy. What determines the demand for eggs? Why do we buy 27 dozen eggs per person per year instead of more or less? You can make a long list of reasons. It might include a variety of factors:

☐ income per person

☐ the price of eggs

☐ the price of complementary goods, such as bacon

☐ the price of substitutes, such as meat and cheese and perhaps other foods

☐ people's attitudes toward eggs

☐ the quality of eggs

The list could go on. It already presents a problem because our minds are limited. They can juggle only a few variables at a time. Most of us can make a reasonable guess as to what will happen to the amount of eggs bought if incomes rise, or if the price of eggs rises, or if the price of beef rises, or if the Surgeon General issues a warning about the cholesterol in eggs. But what will happen if all four occur at once (a wholly possible event)?

In dealing with this problem, economists take the easy way out. They focus on one variable at a time and assume that everything else is held constant.[1] First we will pay the most attention to price. We will assume that money income, the prices of other goods, consumer tastes, and the quality of eggs do not change. Then, later, we can deal with changes in these other variables.

We know the demand for eggs right now: we can look it up in the newspaper. Say the average American is buying 27 dozen eggs a year at a price of 60¢ a dozen. What would he buy if the price were at 70¢ instead, while everything else was the same? Almost certainly less.

---

[1] Actually it is possible to allow for all the relevant variables at once if you use a computer. Many economists who study the demand for individual commodities in practice do just this. But it seems a little much to expect the reader to buy time on an IBM 360-30 just to be able to follow the text.

TABLE 5.1   One person's demand schedule for eggs

PRICE	QUANTITY (dozens per year)
90¢	18
80¢	21
70¢	24
60¢	27
50¢	30
40¢	33

And at 80¢? Less yet. Table 5.1 contains a plausible, though hypothetical, demand schedule. It shows the quantities that a consumer will buy at various prices. The same relationship is expressed graphically in the demand curve shown in Figure 5.1. It just happens to be a straight line in this example, but that need not have been the case. The one thing we *can* be pretty sure about is that demand curves will slope downward and to the right. That is, the lower the price, the more people will buy. The higher the price, the less they will buy.

Why? There are two basic reasons. The first is called the **substitution effect.** It says that as the price of eggs gets lower, consumers are induced to substitute eggs for other goods. They can now get more satisfaction

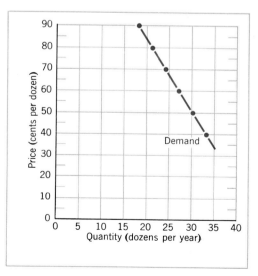

FIGURE 5.1   A demand curve for eggs. It shows the number of eggs per year that a consumer will buy at various prices if nothing else changes.

TABLE 5.2 Several demand schedules for eggs

PRICE	DOZENS BOUGHT PER YEAR BY					TOTAL DOZENS BOUGHT PER YEAR
	PERSON 1	PERSON 2	PERSON 3	PERSON 4	PERSON 5	
90¢	18	0	20	20	5	63
80¢	21	0	20	25	6	72
70¢	24	0	20	30	7	81
60¢	27	0	20	35	8	90
50¢	30	0	20	45	9	104
40¢	33	8	20	50	10	121

from a dollar spent on eggs. Their diets will tend to tilt toward eggs. Conversely, higher egg prices will induce consumers to shift from eggs to meat, cheese, and Cream-of-Wheat.

A second, less obvious reason for the slope of the demand curve is the **income effect.** With a lower price of eggs, while all other prices stay the same, everybody's money incomes will go a bit farther. In effect, we will all be a little bit richer. For most goods, the richer we are, the more we buy. Ordinarily, then, the substitution and income effects both tell us to buy more as the price goes lower. The income effect is a bit less certain than the substitution effect, however. There are goods that we actually buy less of at higher incomes: margarine, flour, tripe. But even the demand curves for these goods will usually slope downward to the right, because the substitution effect is ordinarily much stronger than the income effect.[2]

Table 5.1 and Figure 5.1 referred to a single individual. However, our country has millions of egg eaters. The total demand for eggs in the United States is the sum of all the individual demands of the individual egg eaters. Table 5.2 shows the demand schedules of five different people. They will have to stand for all the millions of people in the real market. The first person is our friend from Table 5.1. The second person doesn't care for eggs, but when the price gets low enough he will feed

---

[2] It may be instructive to work out the case where demand curves slope in the other direction. Suppose that a very poor man spends half his income on potatoes, which he detests. When the price of potatoes falls, the substitution effect says to buy more, but the income effect says to buy less. This time the income effect will win. Potatoes are such a large part of his income that a price drop makes him *much* better off. The result is that he buys more meat and *less* potatoes. Here is a case where people buy less at a lower price. (You might call this example the exception that proves the rule. Exceptions don't ordinarily prove rules, but they *do* show that rules are quite general if the only exception is as far out as this one is.)

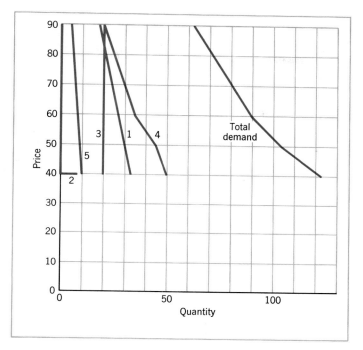

FIGURE 5.2   The total demand for eggs is the sum of all the individual demands at each price.

them to his dog. The third is on a special egg diet prescribed by his doctor. The fourth and fifth are more ordinary consumers. The five schedules are added together in the last column to show the total amount of eggs that all five people will buy at each price.

The same exercise is repeated graphically in Figure 5.2. The five individual demand curves appear at the left of the figure. The total demand curve at the right slopes downward and to the right once more. Each point on the total demand curve represents the sum of the quantities on the individual demand curves at that price.

The particular numbers used in Table 5.2 and Figure 5.2 are not important. Indeed, you have every reason to suspect me when I present you with a specific numerical example; I could be rigging things. Ordinarily we will merely show generalized demand curves that slope downward and to the right like the curve in Figure 5.3. You may supply your own numbers if you like. Any numbers will do, just so long as zero is at the "southwest" corner of the diagram.

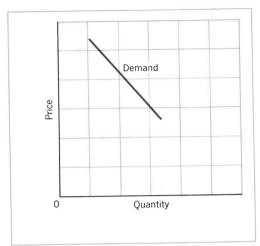

FIGURE 5.3   A generalized demand curve slopes downward to the right. Most of the time we will use simple curves like this one; the specific numbers are not important.

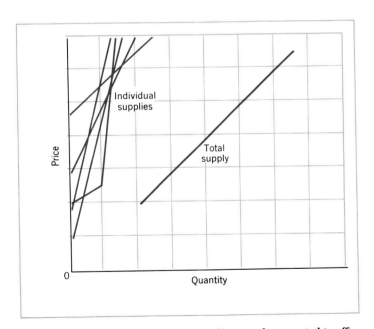

FIGURE 5.4   Supply curves. Most suppliers can be expected to offer more at higher prices, as shown in the individual curves at the left. By adding the amounts each individual will supply at given prices, we get the upward-sloping total supply curve at the right.

SUPPLY

Supply is the quantity of some commodity that sellers are ready and willing to sell. Just as with demand, we can list many factors that affect the supply of eggs. They would include:

□ egg prices

□ the prices of other goods that farmers might produce instead

□ the costs of production

Once again, the list could go on. But, once more, we will focus on price and assume that all the other things are constant. Each individual supplier will be ready and willing to sell a given number of eggs at each price. At a higher price he will probably offer more eggs, because it becomes profitable for him to keep more chickens and to work his farm more intensively. Moreover, farmers who had been raising hogs or cattle will be attracted into the egg business. The result is a series of upward-sloping individual supply curves like those in Figure 5.4. These curves can be summed up horizontally, just as the individual demand curves were, to give us the total supply of eggs. Just as demand almost always slopes downward and to the right, so supply can be usually expected to slope upward and to the right. The higher the price, the more that will be offered.

EQUILIBRIUM PRICE

At last we are able to consider demand and supply at the same time. Table 5.3 couples the demand schedule from Table 5.2 with a plausible supply schedule. These same demand and supply functions are plotted as curves in Figure 5.5.

TABLE 5.3 Supply and demand schedules for eggs

PRICE	QUANTITY OFFERED BY SELLERS (dozens)	QUANTITY SOUGHT BY BUYERS (dozens)
90¢	120	63
80¢	110	72
70¢	100	81
60¢	90	90
50¢	80	104
40¢	70	121

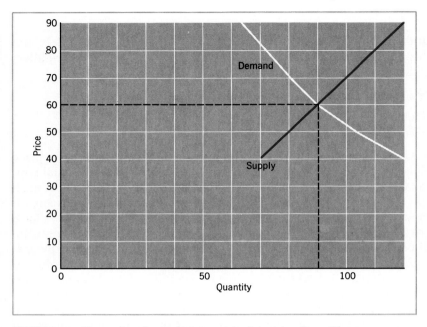

FIGURE 5.5 Demand and supply interact to determine the selling price and the quantity sold. The two curves come from Figures 5.2 and 5.4

Now suppose that at the start of business this year the price is 80c a dozen. What will happen? Sellers will want to sell 110 dozen eggs, but buyers will want only 72. If the situation were to persist for long, there would be lots of disappointed sellers and many rotten eggs. But it won't last. According to Table 5.3 there are many sellers who would be willing to offer eggs at a lower price. Some individuals can be counted on to do so. And as they lower their prices, the general price of eggs will drop. Then two sorts of adjustment will occur. Consumers will buy more eggs, and sellers will offer less. The price will continue to fall until the glut of eggs disappears at 60¢ a dozen. At that price buyers will want to buy just as many eggs as sellers want to sell. There will be just enough eggs to go around and no more reason for the price to fall.

If we start out with a price of 40¢ a dozen instead, just the opposite will happen. Now the buyers will want more than the suppliers are willing to offer. As they bid for the scarce eggs, the price of eggs will rise. As prices go higher, the consumers will cut back and the producers will expand. When the price reaches 60¢ the great egg shortage will have disappeared. No more adjustment will be needed.

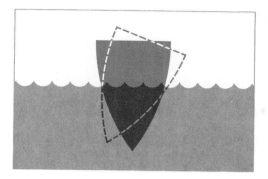

FIGURE 5.6 The ship in color is in equilibrium; the ship outlined in broken lines is not.

Between them, demand and supply determine how many eggs are bought and sold and what the price will be. In economic jargon, we have arrived at an **equilibrium quantity and price.** Equilibrium is a general concept used by physicists, engineers, chemists, anthropologists, and many others. It just means a situation where there is no tendency to change. For example, consider a well-constructed ship, represented schematically in Figure 5.6. Its equilibrium position is straight up in the water (the solid red in Figure 5.6). If the ship is out of equilibrium—as represented by the broken lines—it will tend to return to equilibrium. Once settled in its equilibrium position, it will have no tendency to leave it. The analogy with equilibrium price is complete. Whenever the price is out of equilibrium it will tend to move toward equilibrium. Once it gets there, demand and supply will interact to keep it from rising or falling any further.

CHANGES IN DEMAND AND SUPPLY

So far we have assumed that all variables other than price were constant. Now we can relax that assumption. Let income rise and see what happens. As a result consumers will buy more eggs than before at 60¢ a dozen. The same thing will be true at every other price. Table 5.4 adds a new column to our original table. It shows what happens if income rises. At each price, the quantity sought is higher than it was before. The equilibrium price, therefore, is no longer 60¢. The price will tend to rise until demand and supply are just equal again. This now happens at 70¢. In Figure 5.7 this change shows up as a shift in the entire demand curve from D_1 to D_2. Equilibrium price and quantity change accordingly, from P_1 and Q_1 to P_2 and Q_2.

Similarly, when we drop the assumption that all other things are constant on the supply side, the supply curve can also shift. Suppose

TABLE 5.4   Supply and demand as income changes

PRICE	QUANTITY OFFERED BY SELLERS (dozens per year)	INITIAL QUANTITY SOUGHT BY BUYERS (dozens per year)	QUANTITY SOUGHT BY BUYERS WITH HIGHER INCOMES (dozens per year)
90¢	120	63	80
80¢	110	72	90
70¢	100	81	100
60¢	90	90	110
50¢	80	104	120
40¢	70	121	135

that feed prices fall, so that the cost of producing eggs declines. Then farmers will be willing to supply more eggs at the same price as before, or the same number of eggs at a lower price. In either case the whole supply curve shifts over to the right, as in Figure 5.8. (Notice that an *increase* in supply shows up in a curve that is geometrically *lower* and to the right on the graph.) Equilibrium price falls, and output increases.

It is easy to get confused at this point. What do we mean when we say an "increase in demand"? We might mean the kind of increase that occurs when the price of eggs falls: a movement along the demand curve. But we might also mean the kind of increase that occurs when incomes increase: a shift in the whole demand curve. These two changes are completely different things. They should be kept separate. A *shift* in the demand curve will *cause* the price to rise or fall. Movement *along* the

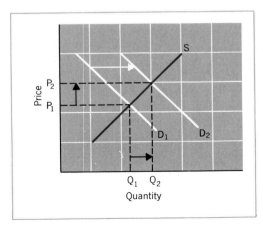

FIGURE 5.7   An increase in incomes leads to an increase in demand. This change is represented by a shift in the demand curve upward and to the right. Equilibrium price and quantity rise as a result.

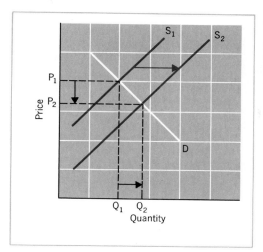

FIGURE 5.8 A fall in the cost of chicken feed results in an increase in the supply of eggs. The supply curve shifts downward and to the right. Price falls and quantity increases as a result.

demand curve is *caused by* a rise or fall in price. (The change in price was caused in turn by an increase in the supply of eggs.) To keep the two concepts straight we will reserve the phrases *increase* or *decrease in demand* or *supply* to mean shifts of the demand or supply curves. These shifts can be caused by changes in incomes, the prices of other goods, costs, or just about anything *except* changes in price. Unfortunately, there isn't any nice crisp term for movements along the curves. We will try to speak of them as increases or decreases in the quantities sought or offered in response to price changes.

It is easy to get the impression that equilibrium means stability, but it need not. In the real world, demand and supply are changing all the time. Adjustments are always being made, and the equilibrium price is moving up and down as a result. Demand and supply analysis is seldom used to estimate the actual equilibrium price. The point of the analysis is usually to find what determines price and quantity and what makes them change. We do not have a complete answer to these questions so long as price and quantity are still changing. When they stop changing we are at equilibrium.

To be sure the principle is clear, it is worth trying other shifts. What effect will a decrease in demand have on price and on quantity? Work it out on a piece of paper and then look the answer up in the footnote.[3] What sort of change will produce a fall in quantity and a rise in price? Try that one too, and then check the footnote.[4]

---

[3] A decrease in both price or quantity.

[4] A decrease in supply.

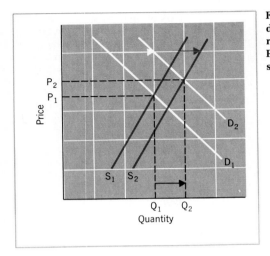

FIGURE 5.9 An increase in both demand and supply will certainly result in an increase in quantity. Price could increase or decrease or stay the same.

What will be the effect of an increase in demand *and* an increase in supply—simultaneously? This situation is the normal one in most industries. Incomes are usually rising, so demand goes up. Productivity is usually increasing, so the supply also goes up. The result is shown in Figure 5.9. Depending on which increases more, the price may rise, fall, or stay the same. (As it is drawn, the price appears to rise. But work out for yourself what would have happened if the supply had risen more, and the demand less, than what is shown.) In any case, output increases for certain.

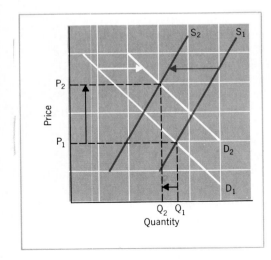

FIGURE 5.10 In a general inflation, the demand for any one product will increase, and the supply will decrease. The price will certainly rise. The quantity could rise or fall or stay the same.

Finally, what is the effect on the price and output of eggs of general inflation—where the prices of most goods are rising? People will be willing to buy more eggs at the same price or the same amount at a higher price, because the prices of substitutes are rising and because their money incomes are increasing. In other words, demand increases. But that is not all. The costs of production are rising too, so the supply decreases. The supply curve shifts to the left, as in Figure 5.10. The result is that output may increase, decrease, or stay the same. But no matter what happens to the output, the price rises with a vengeance. Our discussion doesn't explain inflation, of course. To do that we would have to know why money incomes, costs, and the prices of other goods are rising. But it does explain why prices in any one market rise when there is a general inflation.

IN THE LONG RUN

How much more the sellers will offer when the price rises depends on how much time elapses. Even if the price of eggs doubles today, there won't be any more eggs for sale this afternoon, because it takes time to produce more. But if the price stays up there for a few weeks we will see more eggs appearing, as farmers feed their chickens more. And if prices stay high for several months, the size of flocks will be increased and more farmers will get into the egg business. Many more eggs will appear on the market.

THE SHORT RUN AND THE LONG RUN

Economists often distinguish between the short run and the long run. The **short run** is a period so short that no new facilities can enter production and no old ones can leave. In the steel industry the short run is a period in which the nation's steel capacity is fixed. In eggs it would mean that only the farmers who are now in the business with mature flocks can produce.

The **long run** is a period so long that any new capacity that may be needed can be built, while any old capacity that is not needed will have worn out. In eggs, the long run is long enough for any new farmers who want to enter the business to do so, or for existing flocks to die off so that present producers can leave (perhaps through an increase in the supply of chicken soup).

How long is the long run? The answer differs with the industry. It may take a decade to enter the apple industry, because it takes that long for a new orchard to mature. But it takes only about six months, starting with

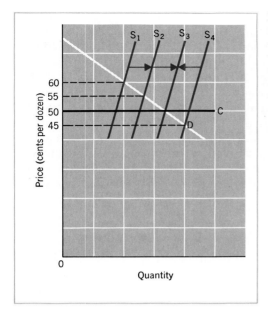

FIGURE 5.11 If equilibrium price in the short run is above cost (as when supply is S_1 or S_2), capacity will expand so that the short-run supply shifts to the right. If price is below cost (as when supply is S_4), resources will leave the industry and supply will shift to the left. When price just equals cost (as when supply is S_3) the industry is in long-run equilibrium.

baby chicks, to have a flock of laying hens. The time needed to leave a business may also be quite different from the time required to enter it. A cement plant can be built in a couple of years, but it takes thirty years for it to wear out.

LONG-RUN ADJUSTMENTS

Now suppose that in the long run, the cost of producing eggs is 50¢ a dozen, regardless of how many chicken farmers there are. This fact shows up in Figure 5.11 as a horizontal line at the 50-cent mark.

In the short run the supply might look like S_1. It is pretty steep because there is a limit to the number of eggs you can get out of a chicken, no matter how you feed it. For the time being the equilibrium price will be at 60¢, well above cost. Farmers will be making a nice profit.

High profits tend to induce new production, however. In this case, the existing farmers will tend to expand their flocks. Other farmers will shift into eggs from different lines of agriculture. As they do so, egg production will go up. The short-run supply curve will shift over to the right, perhaps to S_2 after six months. The price will fall to 55¢. But this price still leaves substantial profits. The process will continue until the price gets down to a level that just covers the 50-cent cost, at short-run supply S_3, perhaps a year after the process began.

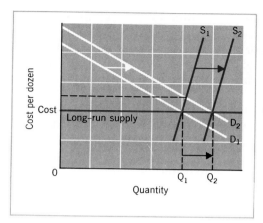

FIGURE 5.12 An increase in demand may lead to a rise in price in the short run. In the long run, however, the higher price induces an increase in capacity, until the price just covers the cost once more.

If farmers make a mistake and too many of them come into the egg business, then the supply might shift all the way to S_4. In that case the price would be 45¢, well below cost. Farmers now would be taking losses. Many of them would get out of eggs as soon as they could. As the flocks were reduced, the short run supply would shift back toward S_3 once more. In this example, 50¢ is the long-run equilibrium price.

Note the role of profits in this story. They are not just raids on the consumers' purses. In a competitive market, profits serve as signals that tell businessmen to expand their productive capacity. The high profits will disappear once that expansion occurs. Similarly, losses tell businessmen to contract production. Losses in business are unpleasant but useful; they are like pain in physiology. Just as pain tells you to take your hand off a hot stove, so losses tell businessmen to stop producing goods on which the public puts little value.

Try one more experiment. Let demand increase, as in Figure 5.12. At first there will be high profits, because the price rises while the cost stays the same. But in the long run, the supply will shift once more until the price reaches 50¢ again. In fact, in the long run, equilibrium price will be 50¢ regardless of where the demand is. The horizontal straight line in Figure 5.12 can be thought of as a long-run supply curve. It shows that—given enough time—any likely amount will be supplied at a price that just covers the cost of production.

OPPORTUNITY COSTS

You may be wondering why anyone would produce eggs at all if he just covered costs and made no profits. The answer lies in the way economists define cost. The **cost of production** is the cost of *all* the inputs employed, *including* those supplied by the owner of the firm. If the owner works in the firm or puts up some of the capital, he must consider the cost of his labor or capital as well as the cost of any labor or capital that he hires from outside. Profits appear only when his receipts exceed all these costs.

But how much does a man's own labor cost him? Certainly more than nothing. If he weren't busy producing eggs he could be driving a truck or managing a supermarket. If he could earn four dollars an hour in his best alternative employment, then he is giving up four dollars for every hour he spends with his chickens. This figure is the cost of his labor to him.

The cost of his capital can be worked out the same way. If he had not put his money into a poultry farm he could have used it to buy stock or real estate or a gas station instead. If his best alternative investment would yield him ten percent, he will not be covering the cost of his own capital unless he makes at least ten percent producing eggs. In other words, when a producer is "just covering costs" in the economic sense, he is making as much on his time and investment as they would yield in any other line of business. When this is true, he has no incentive to leave.

This way of defining costs and profits may look a little arbitrary, but in fact all costs are really determined in this way. The cost of a hired hand is set by what he could get elsewhere. Our egg producer must pay that worker at least as much as he could earn elsewhere or the worker will go to the better job. Similarly, the farmer must pay as much as anyone else for any feed or seed or steel he buys, or he won't get any.

In general, all costs are **opportunity costs.** That is, the cost of any input, whether paid out of the pocket or not, is what it could have earned and produced in its best alternative opportunity for employment. If receipts don't cover all such costs, the firm is taking an economic loss. It would do better in another business.

Opportunity cost is a very important idea. It will appear often in this book. If factors of production yield more than their opportunity cost in one line of business, society must be putting a greater value on what they are producing there than on what they could yield in other possible employments. If they yield less than their opportunity costs, then the public values what they are producing less than what they could produce elsewhere.

COMPETITIVE MARKETS AND ECONOMIC EFFICIENCY

Now back to the egg business. With demand and supply analysis we can see more precisely how competitive markets solve the basic economic

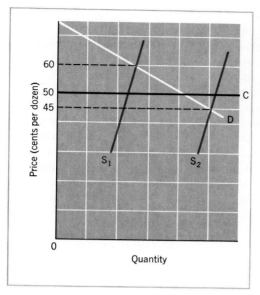

FIGURE 5.13 In the short run, a high price induces producers to use their facilities intensively, and consumers to economize on the scarce product, if supply is short (as when supply is S_1). In the long run the market price induces entry, until the opportunity cost of the last unit produced just equals what consumers will give up to get it.

problems: what and how to produce, and how to distribute the output.

First, consider the short-run equilibrium when supply is like S_1 in Figure 5.13. Not many eggs are produced, so the price is bid up to 60c. This price rise does two things. First, it induces farmers with mature flocks to feed them well, thus helping to alleviate the egg shortage. Second, it squeezes some egg consumption out of the market. Eggs are, in effect, rationed to only those people who are willing to pay at least 60¢ a dozen for them. Eggs are used only for purposes in which they are at least that valuable. In this way we get the greatest dollar value out of the eggs we do have.

Similar reasoning holds if the supply is at S_2. This time the egg business turns out to be rather dreary, but the farmers might as well make the best of a bad situation. They are induced to cut back on egg production. They may be stuck with too many hens, but there is no need to give the hens a high-yielding feed. The price of eggs drops far enough to get consumers to take all the eggs that are produced. Eggs may not be terribly valuable now, but at least they don't rot.

In the first case, rising prices alleviated the egg shortage. But the high price meant that consumers would have been better off if there had been more resources in the egg business to begin with. They were willing to give up 60¢ worth of steak or cabbage or strawberry jam for another dozen eggs. Given enough time to adjust, another dozen eggs could be produced for only 50¢. This 50¢ is the opportunity cost of the eggs in the long run. The resources that could produce 60¢ worth of eggs were producing 50¢ worth of beef or cabbage instead. We would get more out of our resources if some land, labor and capital were shifted out of beef and cabbage production and into eggs. This, of course, is what will happen in the long run in a competitive market like that for eggs.

When egg output was too great, as in curve S_2, the price fell to 45¢. That price meant that consumers were willing to give up only 45¢ worth of other goods for a dozen eggs. But the resources used in egg production would have produced 50¢ in their best alternative employments. Clearly we would have been better off with fewer resources in egg production and more in beef or cabbage. Here again, the farmers will make the correct changes if they pursue their selfish best interests in the long run.

When the egg market reaches long-run equilibrium, consumers will put a value on eggs that is just equal to the opportunity cost. At that point, none of the resources devoted to eggs could produce goods of greater value in any other business. Nor are there any resources employed elsewhere that could produce eggs worth more than what they are presently producing. We can't get any more of value from our scarce resources by shifting them into or out of eggs. Farmers won't have any incentive to make such a shift, either.

The competitive nature of the egg market does something about the *methods* of egg production as well as the quantity. Fifty cents a dozen in the long run is the *minimum* cost attainable. Obviously there are all sorts of ways to produce eggs at a higher cost than that. By feeding the hens champagne and caviar, for instance, we might be able to get the cost up to $100.00 a dozen. In the short run, farmers may make mistakes and use high-cost methods (though surely not as bad as champagne and caviar). But in the long run they have no option. They must get costs down to the 50-cent minimum or take losses. The cost of production reflects what the resources employed could produce elsewhere. The market forces egg producers to use methods of production that minimize the sacrifice of the other goods required in producing eggs.

COMPETITIVE MARKETS IN PRACTICE

Altogether, competitive markets should ration goods so that they are fully utilized in their most valuable uses in the short run. They should also allocate productive resources so that they are used in the most efficient way and in their most valuable employments in the long run. Real-life competitive markets do perform pretty much as this theoretical story suggests, but the picture is too rosy. Problems can arise in reality that the theory ignores.

THE AMERICAN EGG MARKET IN 1973

The experience of American commodity markets in 1973 offered some spectacular examples of how competitive markets work in fact. Bad crops in Russia, India, Africa, and South America resulted in world shortages of wheat and feed grains. Simultaneously, the Peruvian anchovy catch declined disastrously. This decline cut the world's chief source of fish meal and shifted demand to soybeans, the main alternative high-protein feed. In late 1972, the President made an agreement with the Russians to sell them almost a third of the American wheat crop. Finally, in early 1973, the Midwest and the lower Mississippi valley suffered their worst floods in a generation.

The results of all these events was a big increase in the demand for American grains and soybeans, coupled with some drop in supply. The prices of animal feeds took off. In May 1973, foreseeing an accelerating inflation, the Administration froze retail prices though not farm prices. However, rising foreign demand and domestic floods continued to push feed prices up. By June, layer feed cost almost twice as much as it had a year earlier. With feed costs soaring and egg prices fixed, poultry producers cut their output. Egg production fell by nine percent in three months. During June and July, shoppers often found the egg shelves at the store empty.

Figure 5.14 shows what had happened. The high feed prices had shifted the supply of eggs to the left, from S_1 to S_2. Ordinarily, the result would have been a rise in price. However, the price freeze of May prevented that adjustment. With the price frozen at the old level, a shortage developed. One reason for the shortage was that consumers were trying to buy more eggs than they would have at higher prices. Another was that farmers were producing fewer eggs than they would have at higher prices. The drop in output was partly a response by the poultrymen to high feed prices. They reacted by reducing the proportion of protein in their feed. As a result, the number of eggs laid per hen fell from 20 in May to 18.5 in August. This was a typical short-run response to the low prices. But farmers were also making long-run responses. They culled many more older hens from their flocks than usual, and they placed remarkably few new layer-type chicks. The number of layer hens on farms fell from 300 million early in the year to an eight-year low of 281 million in July.

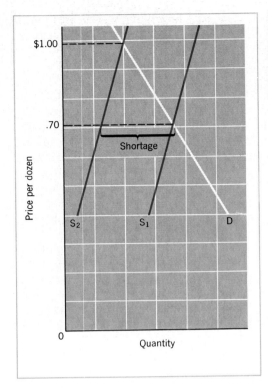

FIGURE 5.14 As a result of a world feed shortage in the spring of 1973, the supply of eggs declined, as from S_1 to S_2. The government's freeze prevented the rise in price that normally would have occurred. The result was a general egg shortage.

Realizing that this trend could mean ever greater shortages later on, the government lifted price controls in July. Egg prices shot up from 71¢ a dozen at retail in June to almost a dollar in August. The egg shortage disappeared, in the sense that anyone willing to pay a dollar a dozen could find eggs on the shelf again. However, no more output was possible at that time.

Egg production picked up in October, and egg prices fell to 87¢ in that month. Feed prices had fallen by then, however, so egg production continued to be very profitable. From August through November the number of layer-type chicks hatched ran about fifteen percent beyond the previous year's levels. The effect of this long-run adjustment wasn't felt immediately, because it takes almost six months for a hen to mature. But the increasing size of flocks led to a large increase in egg production in the first months of 1974. By February the price of a dozen eggs at the farm was down to the price of seven pounds of layer feed, about where it had been for the two years before 1973. The poultry business no longer yielded especially good profits.

Altogether, 1973 saw the creation of an egg shortage by the imposition of price controls while feed prices were rising. It also saw the elimination of the shortage after prices were allowed to rise. The price increase served three functions. In August it merely rationed eggs to those who thought they were worth at least a dollar a dozen. By October the high price of eggs (and the falling price of feed) had induced a short-run output adjustment: a rise in the number of eggs per hen. During the fall it also induced a long-run output adjustment: an increase in flock size. By February 1974, this process had led to enough additional egg production to bring the profits back to normal levels once more.

IMPERFECT FORESIGHT

This tale of 1973 eggs was quite straightforward compared with what can sometimes happen on competitive markets. For one thing, competitive producers are fallible human beings; they foresee the future imperfectly. Mistakes are regular events. In fact, some of the mistakes are almost built into certain competitive markets.

Consider the hog farmer. He must decide how many hogs to raise a year or more before they go to market. He can only guess at what the price will be at marketing time. He is liable to base his guess on prices at the time the baby pigs are born.

The result is illustrated in Figure 5.15. Suppose, to start with, that the price of hogs is above equilibrium for some reason, at P_1. Going by the supply curve, it appears that hog producers will expand their output all the way to Q_2 if they expect the old price to continue. When all those Q_2 hogs actually reach market in year two, however, the price will have to fall all the way to P_2 for all the hogs to be taken. If the farmers in year two assume that the low price will hold in the future, they will produce only Q_3 hogs. Such a small output will force prices up to P_3 in year three. Subsequent steps will yield high output and low prices in year four, low output and high prices in year five, and so forth. The result is a series of price fluctuations, shown in Figure 5.16, that do nobody any good. The price fluctuates because there are thousands of hog farmers, each one producing in his own interest and unable to know what the others are doing at the same time.

Of course, if things were this simple, farmers would soon figure out what was happening to them. In real life, though, both the demand and the supply are constantly shifting around because of changes in income, tastes, the weather, and so forth. Farmers cannot tell for sure what prices will hold when their hogs come to market. That is the whole reason why they tend to assume that last year's prices will continue.

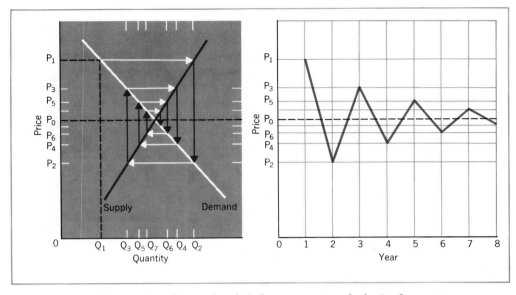

FIGURES 5.15 and 5.16 If producers plan their future output on the basis of current prices, they are likely to make mistakes. A high initial price leads to a large output and low prices. The low price leads to a low output and high prices, and so forth. The result is a series of fluctuations. Output changes appear in white. The price changes that result appear in red.

This bit of analysis has come to be known as the "cobweb theorem" because of the way the diagram looks after a few go-arounds. It seems to be a fair picture of the real-life hog business. Figure 5.17 traces out the actual behavior of hog production in the United States over the last 40 years. It really does follow the fluctuations in the hog–corn price ratio quite closely, but with roughly a two-year lag.[5] This pattern has been going on since the Civil War.

So that you don't think that hog farmers are a case apart, consider the market for college professors. At the end of World War II, when the veterans returned, the colleges were jammed to the rafters and college professors were in great demand. As a result, large numbers of people entered graduate school with a view to joining the prosperous academic

[5] Farmers are less interested in hog prices themselves than in the relation of those prices to costs. The most important cost is feed, mainly corn in the United States, so hog production tends to respond to the ratio of hog prices to corn prices.

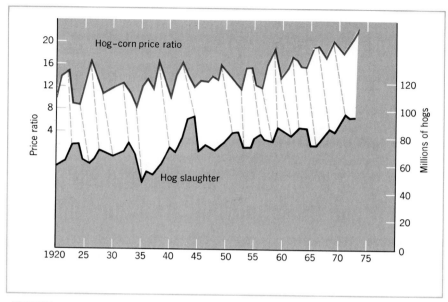

FIGURE 5.17 Hog production has traditionally followed the ratio of hog to corn prices, with a one- to two-year time lag. This diagram traces the fluctuation since 1920, but the pattern has been clear since the Civil War.

life. They finally made it in about 1950, in such numbers that many of them couldn't find jobs. Thereafter, the graduate schools were quiet and empty for a decade. By 1960 there were too few professors again. Salaries started rising at a rate that seemed to make the long, dreary 1950s worthwhile. By the mid-1960s the graduate schools were booming once more. The inevitable has since happened. In the 1970s we have another crop of Ph.D.'s who cannot find work of the sort they planned on when they were graduate students.

In both cases, the hogs and the professors, resources had to be committed far in advance of sale. Neither farmers nor graduate students are given the ability to see the future clearly at that distance. Markets with smaller production lags yield fewer systematic mistakes. Still, situations where resources wind up in the wrong line of business are far from rare in America.

Errors like these are costly to society. They mean that resources are often employed in uses where they produce far less than they might have if their owners had had a clearer picture of the future.

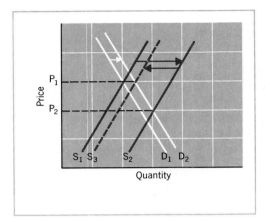

FIGURE 5.18 **Over most of this century, productivity on the farm has grown faster than the GNP, while the demand for farm products has grown more slowly than the GNP. The typical result is shown below. Supply increases by a large amount, demand increases little, and price declines unless a lot of people leave the farm.**

IMMOBILITY

Mistakes also mean a great deal of pain for the owners of the resources involved. They often earn much less than they might have. This is particularly true when the resources, once committed, are immobile —that is, unable to move easily to other employments. The graduate students who trained for jobs that turned out not to exist can't use their heavy investment in human capital to be dentists or airline pilots now. The time and effort they spent in becoming Ph.D.'s is largely wasted.

In some businesses the process of economic growth itself results in regularly recurring surpluses. If the factors employed are immobile, the painful adjustment may be almost continuous.

Take the case of farming: this time all farmers, not just hog producers. Productivity has increased more rapidly in agriculture than in the economy as a whole in most years since the 1930s. As a result, in any typical year, the supply of farm products would increase more rapidly than the GNP unless resources leave agriculture. This change is represented by the shift from S_1 to S_2 in Figure 5.18. But the demand for farm products grows more slowly than the GNP, because we are already well fed; we don't spend much of our added incomes on food as we become richer. In most years, the demand for farm products increases only moderately. This slow growth is shown by the small shift from D_1 to D_2. The result is a surplus at the old price and a tendency for prices to sag. This doesn't happen every year. Sometimes the weather will cut back the growth of the American farm supply, or a crop failure in India or Russia will temporarily boost demand. But Figure 5.18 gives a reasonable picture of events in the typical year.

The sag in farm prices can be prevented if enough people leave the farm. The increase in productivity per person will be offset by the drop in farm population. The supply will be brought back to S_3. But the same story is apt to be repeated the next year.

In fact, a half million or more people do leave the farm each year. That is a tremendous number when you realize that there are fewer than ten million farmers left in this country. Leaving the farm means changing their homes and developing entirely new skills. Conditions severe enough to drive that many people to make such a shift cannot be pleasant. Our economy will produce more of value when these people switch to city jobs. But the people involved must often pay a heavy personal price for what we gain.

PROTECTING PEOPLE FROM COMPETITION

Public policy makers are not very happy with competitive markets that alternately produce too little and then too much, or with markets that leave a residue of people in the wrong jobs, condemned to low incomes until they can find other work. As a result, most advanced countries intervene in one way or another to alleviate the worst of such difficulties.

One old standby in agriculture has been price supports. A case can be made for the government's trying to even out the avoidable fluctuations. If the government had guaranteed a price of P_0 back in Figure 5.15, the hog farmers would have been able to predict the market correctly. The senseless fluctuations would have been avoided.

To some extent, private speculation will serve the same purpose. Speculators try to buy goods when prices are low and sell them when prices are high. If speculators guess correctly, they will add to demand when prices are low and to supply when prices are high. In this way they will even out fluctuations in prices and in the amounts of output that reach consumers. For instance, there is an active market for frozen hog bellies (the raw material for bacon). Purchases and sales by speculators on this market serve to flatten out hog price fluctuations to some extent.

What governments have commonly done, though, has been not so much to even out the peaks and valleys as to bring everything up to the peaks. The result in a typical year can be illustrated in Figure 5.19. The government guarantees a price of P_2, well above equilibrium. This price results in an embarrassing surplus. It is the entire excess of supply over demand at P_2 in Figure 5.19. It occurs for two reasons. First, consumers buy less at the higher price. Second, producers offer more than they would at the equilibrium price, P_1. To make up the difference, the government must buy all the surplus output.

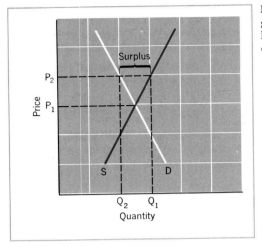

FIGURE 5.19 If the government guarantees a price of P_2 in this market, it will have to buy up the indicated surplus.

A decade and a half ago in the United States, such a policy resulted in government stocks of wheat and cotton that were in excess of a full year's needs. Since then the Department of Agriculture has gotten out of its embarrassing jam by paying farmers to limit their acreage. Their aim was to restrict output all the way back to Q_2 in Figure 5.19. (At any higher output there would still be a surplus, and the price would still fall.) In effect, the government paid farmers to shift the supply curve sharply to the left. These acreage control programs were reasonably successful. But they were also quite expensive, because farmers tended to retire their least productive land and to use lots of labor and fertilizer on the acreage they did plant. And at the same time, a great deal of agricultural land went to waste. An even more fundamental difficulty was that this approach merely perpetuated the underlying problem. Too many resources continued to be used in agriculture, because farming was kept profitable in spite of its excess capacity.

The government has intervened many times to protect industries against the consequences of competition. The agricultural price and output policies are only the best-known case. We have import quotas on textiles, meat, and steel. We have production controls in oil and prohibitions on price competition in such lines of business as airline, rail, and truck transportation. The typical result has been excess capacity, just as in agriculture.

Yet the problems of the people whose farms or factories or skills are in excess supply are very real. We will all be better off if they move into another trade, but the shift is painful for them. A good case can be made that we should help them adjust. Indeed, it may be politically impossible in a modern democracy to do nothing while a large group of people faces severe losses.

An alternative to supporting the market is for the government to help finance the transfer of resources to new employments. In agriculture, government can help by providing training in new, urban skills and by maintaining full employment in the city. In other lines of business government can perform similar functions. It can finance the retraining and moving expenses of people who are in the wrong trades. It can let businesses write off some of their losses for tax purposes, balancing them against profits earned earlier or earned in other businesses of the same firm. Such policies help the losers in the competitive process, but they do not perpetuate surpluses and excess capacity. The public as a whole gains, because resources are transferred more quickly to more useful employments.

SUMMARY

The demand for a product is the amount of it that people are ready and willing to buy. The supply is the amount that producers are ready and willing to sell. In a competitive market, demand and supply interact to determine price and output. At equilibrium price, the quantity demanded just equals the quantity supplied. There is no further reason for price to change.

In competitive markets, high profits will induce suppliers to increase their capacity, while losses will induce them to cut back. In either case, the adjustment will continue until the price just equals the cost of production. Profits and losses disappear in the long run. In long-run equilibrium, all producers are forced to use minimum-cost methods. Moreover, the last factors of production employed in each industry add just as much to the value of output there as they would in their best alternative employments. Society could not gain anything by shifting them to other industries.

In practice, competitive markets work imperfectly, because producers may make systematic errors in predicting prices. They may alternate between too much and too little output. Such errors can result in many painful years for those whose skills and equipment are committed to the wrong industries.

Governments often try to reduce the pain by supporting prices or by restricting output. Such policies make life pleasanter for those in the industry, but they often result in large surpluses or excess capacity. They also impede long-run adjustments. If, instead, governments were to pursue policies that increased the mobility of labor and capital, they would still help the unlucky. At the same time, they would make the economy more efficient by getting resources into their most productive employments.

STUDY QUESTIONS

1   The table below shows the demand and supply for "gimlets" in 1980.

PRICE	QUANTITY SUPPLIED PER YEAR	QUANTITY DEMANDED PER YEAR IN 1980
$13	200	650
12	300	600
11	400	550
10	500	500
9	600	450
8	700	400

The gimlet industry is purely competitive. The minimum attainable cost of producing gimlets is $10. This cost per unit will be the same in the long run regardless of the size of the gimlet industry. In 1981 the discovery of an important new use for gimlets leads to a doubling in the demand for them. That is, in 1981, consumers are ready and willing to buy twice as many gimlets at each price as they were in 1980. Work out the new demand schedule on a piece of paper. You might want to plot the two demand functions and the supply function on a piece of graph paper as well. Now answer the following questions:

a. What is the short-run equilibrium price in 1981?

b. How did it get there?

c. What, if anything, is good about that price? In particular, do you feel that consumers are better off at that price than at a price of $10 *in 1981*? (Be careful. A low price is nice if you get gimlets, but it's just a source of frustration if you don't.)

d. What is the long-run equilibrium price?

e. How does it get there after the doubling of demand that occurred in 1981?

f. How many gimlets will be produced in long-run equilibrium?

g. What, if anything, is good about the long-run equilibrium price? In particular, do you feel that consumers would be better off if the government kept the price at $8 instead? (Be careful, again. Consider two cases: One is where the government just sets a price of $8 and enforces it. The other is where the government pays enough of a subsidy that businessmen find it profitable to produce gimlets even with a price of $8. In the second case, remember that consumers pay taxes also.)

2   What will be the effect of each of the following on the equilibrium price and quantity of beef? In each case work out in your own mind whether and how demand and/or supply will be affected. Then see how the change in demand and/or supply affects price and quantity.

☐ A rise in the price of feed

☐ A rise in the price of pork

☐ A rise in both prices

☐ A rise in the price of feed and a fall in the price of pork

☐ A fall in the price of feed and a rise in the price of pork

3   The government decides the price of bread is too high and rolls it back from 50¢ to 40¢. Use a diagram to work out what will happen in the short run. How is the result likely to change in the long run?

4   What is the opportunity cost of your time spent in studying? Is it the same at 3:30 P.M. as at 10:30 P.M?

5   I own my own house. Part of my standard of living is the shelter I receive from my house. I don't report that as part of my income for income tax purposes, but the services my house give to me are included in the Gross National Product. How should those services be valued for inclusion in the GNP?

6   A technological change reduces some good's cost of production per unit. What is the effect of this change on price, quantity, and profits in the short run? In the long run?

FURTHER READING

Supply and demand is developed with many ramifications in a readable classic by Hubert Henderson with the straightforward title, *Supply and Demand* (New York and London: Cambridge U. Press, 1958). A good place to get a more thorough and advanced understanding of how competitive markets work is Robert Haveman and Kenyon Knopf, *The Market System*, 2nd ed. (New York: John Wiley, 1970). For a more complete analysis of the problems and policies associated with agriculture see Leonard Weiss, *Case Studies in American Industry*, 2nd ed. (New York: John Wiley, 1971), Chapter 2.

APPENDIX TO CHAPTER 5 ■
THE ELASTICITY ■
OF DEMAND AND SUPPLY ■

In Chapter 5 the analysis of demand and supply was deliberately kept as simple as possible. Here it will be explained further. The concepts introduced in this appendix will not be needed in reading the rest of the book, nor in most of the readings cited at the ends of the chapters. They do turn up in a great deal of economic literature, though. Readers planning to go further into economics may want to work through this appendix.

The concepts discussed here are more than just theoretical tricks. They can be used to analyze problems for which the bare-bones concepts presented in the chapter are insufficient.

THE ELASTICITY OF DEMAND

CHANGES IN QUANTITY AND PRICE

As we have seen, different products have different types of demand curves. Some things are staples that we cannot do without. Others are things that we will readily dispense with if the price is too high. An important aspect of the demand for any commodity, therefore, is how responsive it will be to price changes.

The responsiveness of demand to changes in price is known as the **elasticity of demand.** Economists define it as the percentage change in the quantity purchased, divided by the percentage change in price. This relationship can be symbolized as:

$$\frac{\dfrac{\Delta Q}{Q}}{\dfrac{\Delta P}{P}}$$

Q and P stand for quantity and price, respectively. The Greek letter delta (Δ) is the symbol for "change in . . . ." Therefore, $\Delta Q/Q$ is the percentage change in Q: the amount of the change in Q divided by the whole amount of Q.

TABLE 5.5   A demand schedule

PRICE	QUANTITY SOUGHT BY BUYERS
10	100
9	110

In the demand schedule in Table 5.5, for instance, we see that as the price drops one unit (from 10 to 9), the demand goes up by ten units (from 100 to 110). The elasticity of demand, therefore, is about

$$\frac{\frac{\Delta Q}{Q}}{\frac{\Delta P}{P}} = \frac{\frac{10}{100}}{\frac{1}{10}} = \frac{0.1}{0.1} = 1.0$$

However, this arithmetic is a little ambiguous. You might have noticed that if we had considered the effect of an *increase* in price instead of a *decrease,* the elasticity estimate would have been

$$\frac{\frac{10}{110}}{\frac{1}{9}} = 0.818$$

To be unambiguous, we must measure elasticity using the change in quantity that occurs with an infinitesimal change in price. But infinitesimal changes are hard to show in numerical examples. One way around this difficulty is to use the average price and quantity over a range of prices. We can express it mathematically as

$$\frac{\frac{Q_2 - Q_1}{Q_1 + Q_2}}{\frac{P_2 - P_1}{P_1 + P_2}}$$

In our example, then, elasticity of demand would be

$$\frac{\frac{10}{210}}{\frac{1}{19}} = \frac{.0476}{.0526} = .905$$

This measure is known as **arc elasticity.** It is a useful approximation in numeri-

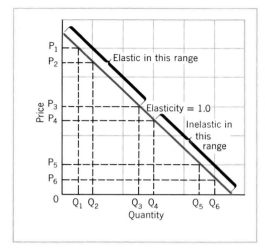

FIGURE 5.20   Elasticity of demand is not constant throughout a straight-line demand curve. The drops in price from P_1 to P_2, P_3 to P_4, and P_5 to P_6 are all equal in absolute terms. But they might represent price cuts of 10%, 20%, and 50%, respectively. The resulting percentage increases in quantity are distinctly not proportional.

cal examples. The actual estimates made by economists in real markets are almost always expressed in terms of percentage rates of change in quantity divided by percentage rates of change in price at a given point. The ambiguity involved in numerical examples is thereby avoided.

When the elasticity of demand for a commodity is greater than 1.0, economists describe the demand as **elastic.** In that case, a small decrease in price will cause a large rise in the quantity sought. When the elasticity is less than 1.0, the demand is described as **inelastic.** In that case, even large changes in price have little effect on the quantity sought.

Evaluating elasticity of demand from a curve is a little tricky. The demand curve in Figure 5.20 does *not* have an elasticity of 1.0 throughout, as you might have expected at first glance. It is true that a given change in price results in the same change in quantity anywhere on the curve. But elasticity deals with *percentages* of change, not with absolute quantities. Thus, at high prices, a drop from P_1 to P_2 might be only a ten-percent drop in prices. However, it results in a doubling in quantity, from Q_1 to Q_2. The elasticity there is well over 1.0. When the price is low, a halving of price from P_5 to P_6 brings only a ten-percent increase in quantity, from Q_5 to Q_6. There the elasticity is much less than 1.0. Right in the middle of the demand curve a twenty-percent fall in price, from P_3 to P_4, results in a twenty-percent increase in quantity, from Q_3 to Q_4. The elasticity of demand is 1.0 at the midpoint of a straight-line demand curve.

Figure 5.21 shows demand curves that are elastic and inelastic throughout. The vertical demand curve has an elasticity of zero, because the quantity bought is the same regardless of the price. The horizontal demand curve has an elasticity

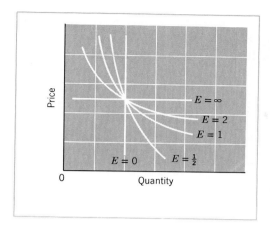

FIGURE 5.21 Five demand curves of constant elasticity. The flatter of any two intersecting curves is always the more elastic.

of infinity, because a tiny drop in price would lead to an infinite increase in the quantity bought. In between are other demand curves, with elasticities ranging from ½ to 2.0. The steeper of any two intersecting demand curves will always be the less elastic of the two at the point of intersection. On the steeper curve, a small change in price has less effect on the quantity sought.

THE ELASTICITY OF DEMAND IN PRACTICE

Economists have estimated the elasticity of demand for many commodities. Table 5.6 shows some of these estimates. They can be used to tell us the effect of a price change on the quantity of any commodity sold. Our original elasticity formula amounted to

$$\text{Elasticity } (E) = \frac{\%\Delta Q}{\%\Delta P} \,.$$

It follows that

$$\%\Delta Q = E \times \%\Delta P.$$

Apples have an elasticity of demand of 1.3. Therefore, a ten-percent fall in the price of apples will lead to a

$$1.3 \times 10\% = 13\%$$

increase in the quantity of apples sold. A similar drop in the price of wheat, however, would result in only a two-percent increase in the amount of wheat sold.

Why is the demand for wheat inelastic while the demand for apples is elastic?

TABLE 5.6   Elasticity of demand for various goods

COMMODITY	ESTIMATED ELASTICITY OF DEMAND
Automobiles	0.8–1.5
Electric power for residential use	1.0
Steel	0.2–0.4
Cotton	0.1
Wheat	0.2
Corn	0.3–0.5
Apples	1.3
Peaches	1.5
Beef	0.8–1.1
Pork	0.7–1.0
Lamb	1.8–2.3
All meats	0.4–0.6
All food	0.2–0.5

Why is the demand for beef more elastic than the demand for meat in general, or for food in general? The best answer has to do with the availability of substitutes. If there are good substitutes for a commodity, buyers will readily switch to other goods when the price goes up. Demand will thus be relatively elastic. If there are no substitutes, buyers will go on consuming almost as much at a high price as at a low price. Demand will be inelastic.

This is the reason for the perplexing difference between the elasticities of demand for beef, for all meat, and for food. Pork and lamb are good substitutes for beef in most consumers' eyes. But the substitutes for all meat, such as eggs and cheese, are much more distant. And there are hardly any substitutes at all for food in general. When the price of beef goes up, therefore, buyers shift readily to pork. When the price of meat goes up they shift more reluctantly to eggs. But when the price of food in general rises, they shift only slightly to gasoline and cigarettes.

It is fairly common to hear goods with elastic demands described as "luxuries" and those with inelastic demands described as "necessities." There may be an element of truth to that rule, but there are many exceptions. Are cigarettes and liquor necessities? They certainly have inelastic demands. People go right on buying those commodities even though they bear heavy taxes resulting in prices far above production costs.

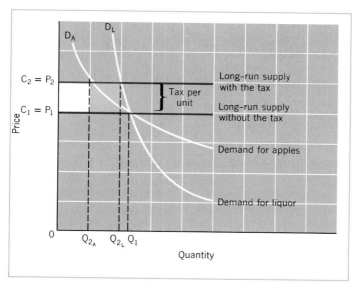

FIGURE 5.22   A tax on liquor will reduce the quantity sold proportionately less than a tax on apples will. The government can collect a lot of taxes on liquor, and the distillers will not object as much to a tax as the apple growers would.

ELASTICITY AND TAXES

It is no coincidence that cigarettes and liquor, which have inelastic demands, are heavily taxed. The government can raise a good deal of revenue from such taxes precisely because consumption is little affected by high prices. If a tax were imposed on a commodity such as apples, for which the demand is elastic, consumption would fall off sharply at the higher price.

This relationship is illustrated in Figure 5.22. To make the comparison easier, apples and liquor are assumed to have the same production cost. We also assume that their demand curves intersect at the long-run equilibrium price. Then we impose the same tax per unit on both products (maybe with apples measured in bushels and liquor in quarts). Cost per unit in both industries rises by the amount of the tax. So will price when they reach long-run equilibrium again.

The government's tax receipts consist of the tax per unit times the quantity sold. The tax per unit is the height of a side of one of the rectangles. The quantities sold at the new price are the lengths of their bases. Since the altitude times the base of a rectangle is its area, the areas of these rectangles represent the total tax receipts. The white rectangle represents the government revenue from the apple tax. The government's receipts from the liquor tax are represented by the red and white rectangles added together. Clearly the liquor tax is a much more effective revenue-raiser.

There is another reason why governments don't impose taxes on apples: If they did there would be a very loud howl from the apple growers. Such a tax would cut deeply into apple sales. A large proportion of the growers would have to go out of business before they reached long-run equilibrium again, and they all would be miserable until price got up to C_2. Distillers would resist a tax less, because it would cut liquor sales only mildly.

ELASTICITY AND PRICE FLUCTUATIONS

The elasticity of demand also affects the stability of prices. Figure 5.23 compares the effect of a given increase in supply on the price of two commodities with elastic and inelastic demands, say apples and wheat. When the supply of apples increases, the price needs to fall only slightly to get consumers to take up the additional output. When the supply of wheat increases by the same amount, the price must fall a long way to clear the market. In general, the more elastic the demand, the more stable prices will be as output fluctuates.

ELASTICITY AND TOTAL RECEIPTS OF SELLERS

An important aspect of the elasticity of demand is the effect of a change in price on the sellers' total receipts. (The sellers' receipts are the same as the total expenditures of the buyers of that commodity.) A drop in price has two effects. First, the goods that would have been sold anyway, even at the higher price, now are going at a lower price. There is a loss of receipts on them. The amount of this

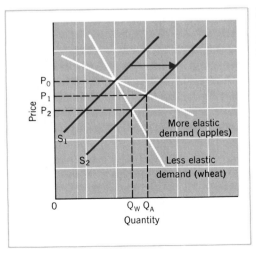

FIGURE 5.23   The more elastic the demand is, the greater is the fall in price caused by an increase in supply.

loss is the quantity formerly sold times the change in price, or $Q \times \Delta P$. At the same time, however, the drop in price results in the sale of more goods that could not have been sold at the higher price. There is an increase in receipts here. This gain is the price times the additional quantity sold, or $P \times \Delta Q$. Our formula for elasticity is

$$\frac{\dfrac{\Delta Q}{Q}}{\dfrac{\Delta P}{P}} \ .$$

which can be rearranged to read $P \times \Delta Q/Q \times \Delta P$. The elasticity of demand, therefore, is equal to

$$\frac{\text{the gain in receipts from new sales (due to a price decrease)}}{\text{the loss in receipts (from a lower price) on goods already being sold}} \ .$$

If demand is elastic, this ratio will be greater than 1.0. The gain from a price decrease is greater than the loss. A drop in price for a product with elastic demand will increase the total receipts of its sellers. If demand is inelastic, on the other hand, a fall in price will induce so few additional purchases that the total receipts of sellers will decline. And if the elasticity of demand is just 1.0, the total receipts of sellers will be the same regardless of the price.

This relationship is pictured in Figure 5.24. In both graphs, the total receipts at

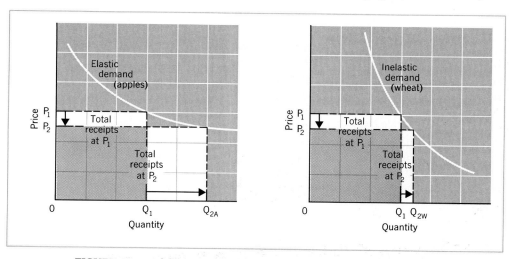

FIGURE 5.24   A fall in price will increase the total receipts of sellers if demand is elastic, but will decrease them if demand is inelastic.

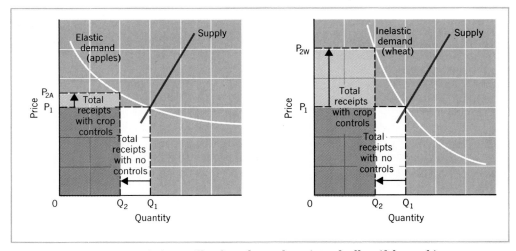

FIGURE 5.25   Output restrictions will reduce the total receipts of sellers if demand is elastic, but will raise them if demand is inelastic.

a given price are the price times the quantity sold, or the area of the rectangle formed with the axes. At a price of P_1, for instance, the total receipts are the area of the rectangle with sides OP_1 and OQ_1. At P_1, both the commodity with the elastic demand and the one with inelastic demand produce the same total receipts. But when price drops to P_2, the rectangle becomes larger where demand is elastic and smaller where it is inelastic.

Fluctuations in supply on unregulated markets will have quite different effects on the receipts of suppliers of different products. Whether they gain or lose depends on the elasticity of demand. In apples, where demand is elastic, a good crop will not reduce prices by much, so total receipts will increase. On the other hand, in the wheat market, where demand is inelastic, a bumper crop means a big drop in price. Farmers will receive less in total receipts for their products in a good crop year than in a bad one. A crop failure actually makes wheat farmers as a whole better off. (But, of course, an individual farmer who cut production would only lose, because acting alone he would have no effect on the market price. Looking at it another way, the demand for *his* wheat is infinitely elastic because there are such good substitutes—other people's wheat.) If the elasticity of demand is about 1.0, as with beef, the receipts of sellers will be about the same whether prices are high or low.

ELASTICITY OF DEMAND AND CROP RESTRICTIONS

Crop restrictions will always raise prices. Whether they raise farmers' incomes,

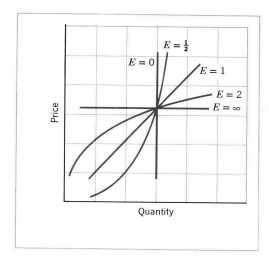

FIGURE 5.26 In general, the flatter of two intersecting supply curves will be the more elastic.

however, depends on the elasticity of demand again. This problem is illustrated in Figure 5.25. If the Department of Agriculture were to restrict the output of apples from Q_1 to Q_2, the price of apples would rise only to P_{2A}, and the apple growers' total receipts would actually decline. But when wheat output is reduced from Q_1 to Q_2, the price rises sharply to P_{2W}. Wheat farmers' receipts are increased.

The "basic commodities," for which the Department of Agriculture actually does maintain crop restriction programs, are corn, wheat, cotton, tobacco, and rice. All of them have inelastic demands. Actually, as crop restrictions work these days, the farmer receives money for the land he doesn't plant as well as for the crops he sells.

THE ELASTICITY OF SUPPLY

The way the quantity of a product offered responds to price changes can also be described in terms of elasticity.

MEASURING THE ELASTICITY OF SUPPLY

As you might expect, the more responsive output is to price, the more elastic supply is. The formula for elasticity of supply is the same as for demand: $\%\Delta Q/\%\Delta P$. Figure 5.26 shows several supply curves with constant elasticities. Once again, the steeper of any two intersecting curves is the less elastic.

ELASTICITY OF SUPPLY AND ADJUSTMENT TIME

The elasticity of supply depends on how much time the sellers have in which to adjust to a price change. The quantity of eggs coming to market today will probably be the same whether the price doubles or halves or stays the same. In other words, the supply of eggs on one day's notice has an elasticity of zero.

In the short run, producers already in the business have enough time to adjust the outputs from their existing factories or farms. The short-run supply curves of most goods, therefore, have elasticities of more than zero but less than one. How elastic the supply is in the short run depends on how easy it is to adjust production. The short-run supply of most individual farm products is fairly elastic, because many farmers can shift from one crop to another fairly easily. If the price of soybeans goes down compared with the prices of corn and oats, we can expect quite a lot less soybeans next year.

The same is not true of the supply of *all* farm products together, however. If the price of all such products falls sharply, the amounts coming to market won't change a great deal in the short run. Farmers may cut back on their use of fertilizer and purchased feed, but they have nothing else to do with their time or land in the short run. They'll go on producing just to eat and pay their taxes.

ELASTICITY OF LONG-RUN SUPPLY

In the long run, when producers have enough time to enter or leave the industry, supply is much more elastic. In fact, the elasticity of supply is infinite in "constant cost" industries—industries in which costs are the same regardless of how much is produced. This is the situation we assumed in Chapter 5. It is a convenient assumption, because it makes analysis easy. It is also close to the truth over a wide range of outputs in many industries. Given enough time to build more plants, the cost of producing shirts or shoes is probably about the same whether the industry has twenty plants or 200.

This is not true in all industries, however. In primary industries, such as coal mining or agriculture, the quality of natural resources varies from place to place. When output is low it can be concentrated in the lowest-cost areas. But to get higher levels of output we have to mine narrower seams of coal. We have to plant crops on land that is poorer or farther from the main markets. Prices must be higher in order for production to be profitable in these higher-cost operations.

A long-run adjustment in such an industry is illustrated in Figure 5.27. Initially, demand is D_1 and short-run supply is S_1. The equilibrium price is P_1. Then demand shifts to D_2. In the short run, the price rises to P_2. But this higher price leads to an expansion of industry capacity and higher costs. When the short-run supply has shifted to S_2 the industry is in long-run equilibrium again. Now the price will be P_3, somewhat higher than P_1 because of the higher costs.

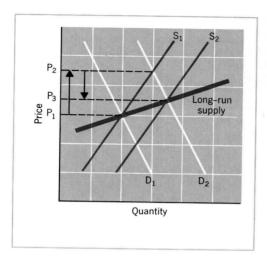

FIGURE 5.27 In an increasing-cost industry, an increase in demand will result in an increase in output and, therefore, in cost and price. The long-run supply is the thick upward-sloping curve.

Some industries may have decreasing costs—that is, their long-run supply curves slope downward to the right. When the industry is small, producers must provide many services for themselves. But when it is larger, other firms step in. Foundries, machinery makers, and technical schools specialize in the supplies, equipment, and skills that the industry needs. The costs of production will fall as the industry grows. Figure 5.28 illustrates how this type of growth would affect the market price. Start with demand and short-run supply at D_1 and S_1 again. Then let demand rise to D_2. Prices may rise at first to P_2. But as the industry expands (as short-run supply shifts to the right), costs will fall. By the time the

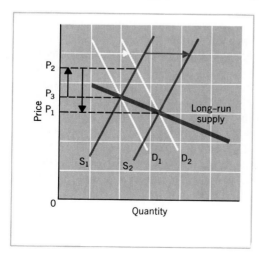

FIGURE 5.28 In a decreasing-cost industry, an increase in demand may result in an increase in price at first. Ultimately, however, increasing capacity will lead to a decrease in price.

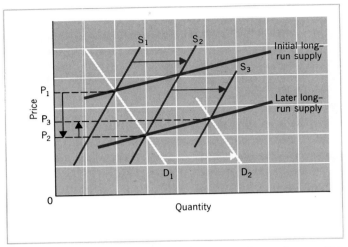

FIGURE 5.29   **In this industry, costs increase as demand grows. Yet technological changes may still result in a fall in costs and a lower long-run supply.**

industry reaches long-run equilibrium once more, the price will have fallen to P_3, a level lower than where we started.

Not all changes in costs are caused by changes in the size of the industry, by any means. Most industries make technical improvements whether they are expanding, contracting, or standing still. These improvements reduce cost if the prices of the resources stay the same. Such cost reductions apply at any industry size. They represent a downward shift in the whole long-run supply curve.

Agriculture, for instance, has experienced very rapid improvements in productivity over the last 40 years. At the same time, its output has increased. Yet agriculture's long-run supply curve certainly slopes upward and to the right because of the varying productivity of farm land. Figure 5.29 shows how these facts can be reconciled. Technical improvements such as better seed result in a fall in cost. Therefore, the long-run supply would shift downward and to the right. As a result, the long-run equilibrium price would fall, and quantity would increase, even if the demand stayed at D_1. In fact, the demand for agricultural goods does increase, as incomes and population grow. But even allowing for a shift in demand from D_1 to D_2, prices still fall overall, from P_1 to P_3. This drop in price and increase in quantity occurs in spite of the rising long-run supply curve.

Now take an industry with constant or decreasing costs (a horizontal or downward-sloping long-run supply curve). It can have *rising* costs and *rising* long-run equilibrium prices even while its output increases. This is the case if its costs of production are rising because of inflation. This happened in many manufacturing industries during the late 1960s and early 1970s. You may want to work this case out yourself on a piece of paper.

STUDY QUESTIONS

1   The following table shows portions of three demand schedules:

PRICE	Q_1	Q_2	Q_3	INITIAL SUPPLY	SUPPLY AFTER AN INCREASE
$5	22	20	16		
$4	25	25	25		
$3	30	33	40		
$2	38	50	70		

a. For each demand schedule say whether demand is elastic, inelastic, or what.

b. In the column market "Initial Supply" pencil in a supply schedule such that equilibrium price is $4.

c. In the last column pencil in another supply schedule such that supply increases at each price.

d. Assuming that the same supply schedule applies for each of the three goods, what is the new equilibrium price for each good?

e. In which case does the increase in supply cause the largest decrease in price? The smallest? Why?

f. What happens to the total receipts of sellers in the three cases as a result of the increase in supply? Why?

2   What effect do you think the development of the trucking industry and the construction of the Interstate Highway System has had on the elasticity of demand for railroad services? Why?

3   You are in charge of the produce section of a supermarket. It's noon on Saturday. The store closes at 6 P.M. and is closed all of Sunday. You have a lot of bananas that you are pretty sure won't make it to Monday. You are considering cutting their price to get rid of them. Should you? Does it make any difference that the bananas cost you five cents a pound when you bought them? How will the elasticity of demand get into your decision?

4   Which is more elastic, short-run or long-run supply?

6
THE
MONOPOLY
PROBLEM

Much of the American economy today is characterized by big business. The press, Congress, and many of the public seem to be continuously suspicious that the huge oil or auto or electrical equipment companies are engaged in monopolistic conspiracies against the public. The Communist governments picture our economy as one characterized by "monopoly capitalism." This chapter will look at what monopoly is, what is wrong with it, how serious the problem is, and what is done about it.

THE EFFECT AND EXTENT OF MONOPOLY

PURE MONOPOLY

The most extreme case of monopoly is **pure monopoly.** In that instance there is only one seller of a commodity—say, light bulbs—and no possibility of any new sellers. The pure monopolist can be analyzed using the diagram in Figure 6.1. Assume, as we did in Chapter 5, that in the long run his costs per unit stay the same, regardless of how many light bulbs he chooses to produce. If he wants more bulbs, all he has to do is build another plant just like those he already has. This is probably a reasonably accurate picture of most manufacturing, once a firm reaches the level of output where it is realizing all the economies of scale. At any rate, the assumption makes the analysis easier.

In a competitive market, price is automatically determined by supply and demand. This is not so in monopoly. An individual light bulb monopolist makes a conscious decision about what price

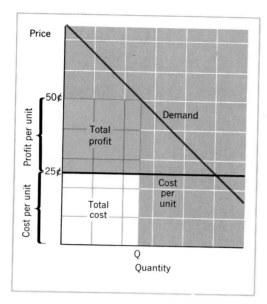

FIGURE 6.1 The most profitable price for a monopolist is where the light red rectangle is as large as possible. This means a price well above the cost per unit.

should be. And in setting his price he will also be determining the output, because consumers will be willing to buy only so much at each price.

Now let us assume that the monopolist tries to maximize his profits. His total profits show up in Figure 6.1 as the profit (price minus cost) per unit times the quantity sold. These numbers form sides of the pink rectangle in Figure 6.1. Since the product of two sides of a rectangle is its area, the monopolist's total profit can be represented by the area of that rectangle. The monopolist will try to pick a price at which this area is at a maximum. That price will clearly be well above the cost per unit. It will just as clearly be well below the level where he sells nothing at all. Having set the price, our monopolist has also set the output. If he is sensible, he will build enough capacity to satisfy consumer demand at that price. He doesn't need much more than that. There are no rivals or new entrants to force his price down to the minimum cost per unit as there are in the long run in competitive markets.

THE EFFECT OF MONOPOLY PROFITS

Setting the price above cost has two basic effects. First, it makes the monopolist rich. Second, it misallocates resources. Remember that cost per unit reflects what the resources used could produce in their best alternative employment. In this case suppose that light bulbs cost only 25¢ each to produce but that the monopolist's most profitable price is 50¢. The consumers who do buy light bulbs are willing to give up 50¢ worth of eggs or socks to get another light bulb. Yet the land, labor, and capital that would produce another bulb are out producing only 25¢ worth of eggs and socks in competitive markets. If we could shift these inputs into the light bulb industry we would get more value for our scarce resources. But the monopolist will not do it. He is out to maximize profits, as any entrepreneur is supposed to do in a market economy. But in this case he winds up producing too little and charging too much for it.

This picture may seem a little abstract for real-life firms, but it is correct in its essentials. Real monopolists may be more than willing to increase sales. Indeed, they may use ads and salesmen to try to push the demand curve over to the right. The one thing they will not do to increase sales is to cut price to the point at which it just covers costs.

In real life, monopolists often face the threat of potential competition if their prices get too high, and this threat may limit them. They may face demand curves like ED in Figure 6.2. There are some buyers for light bulbs even at very high prices. But a monopolist who charges those prices is apt to see the light bulb market taken over by new producers or by imports. In that case he is likely to set his price at a level near E, so that new competition is not attracted too fast. As long as he is setting his price at all above cost, though, he still is restricting output and misallocating resources.

There is another, more obvious effect of monopoly. Monopoly commonly yields high profits. The monopolist earns high profits not

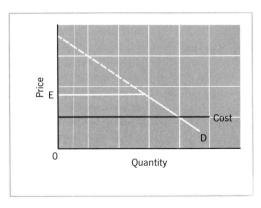

FIGURE 6.2 The monopolist in this example will face the entry of new competitors if he sets his price above E. His customers will gradually disappear.

as a temporary reward for producing the right goods at low cost, but as a permanent result of his powerful position. He is richer—and we, his customers, are poorer—merely because he occupies a strategic position in the market.[1] Many people object to such a seemingly arbitrary redistribution of income from us to him. But whether it is good or bad is up to you to decide. It is strictly a value judgement.

OLIGOPOLY

Pure monopoly is fairly rare in the United States. The electric utility and the telephone company fall into this category, but they are regulated by the government. In the unregulated industries a few firms such as IBM, Xerox, Kodak (in film), and the local newspapers in many towns have near-monopolies. Still, taken all together, even these nearly pure monopolies account for only a small percentage of the GNP. A much more common situation is **oligopoly,** in which two or three or four or a half-dozen firms account for the largest part of an industry's output.

Consider a hypothetical light bulb industry with two hypothetical oligopolists, General Electric and Westinghouse, as shown in Figure 6.3. The price right now from both firms just happens to be 50¢. (We will see how it got there in a minute.) Now say GE considers reducing its price. If Westinghouse could be counted on to keep the old price, GE would soon pick up the entire market. It could make a killing by making just a small price reduction—perhaps to 40¢. All of Westinghouse's customers would quickly shift to GE. But, of course, Westinghouse won't hold still. The first rule of American business is to "meet your competition." So Westinghouse will meet the reduction to 40¢ as shown in Figure 6.3, and both companies will wind up with about the same market shares as before. Both companies will now be less profitable. Actually, the people at GE will probably be able to figure this out in advance. It is highly unlikely that they'd try cutting prices to pick up more sales. They would cut their price only if they expected to gain even when Westinghouse followed. That

---

[1] You can buy the stock of some monopolistic corporations, but probably you cannot get rich in the process. The stock market will capitalize the monopoly profits, and the stock will sell at a higher price as a result. When you buy at that price you will not be earning any more on your money than if you bought any other stock. The monopolist who sold out to you still has his boodle even if he has now put it into municipal bonds. On the other hand, if you are smart enough to buy stock in a firm today that becomes a monopolist next year, then you *will* participate in the monopoly profits. They will show up as a rise in the value of your stock when the firm gets its monopoly.

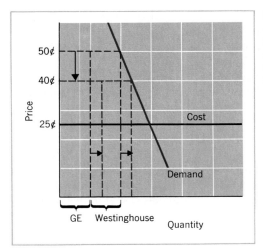

FIGURE 6.3 The result of a price cut by an oligopolist, if his rival meets the new price, will be an increase in the quantity sold by both firms but not much change in their relative market shares.

would be the case if they expected increased profits at the lower price even though Westinghouse followed. But, of course, a monopolist would also cut his price if he thought it would increase profits.

GE might even consider a price increase. The circumstances are shown in Figure 6.4. In this case, both firms would be better off at a higher price, so Westinghouse would be apt to follow. If it didn't, GE could always back down. In an oligopoly, then, price is likely to go up whenever the industry as a whole will gain from the move. Of course, a monopolist would raise his price in the same circumstances: he *is* the whole industry. On the other hand, Westinghouse would not be likely to follow the price increase if it did not increase profits. But a monopolist wouldn't raise his price, then, either.

Altogether, our two oligopolists are likely to wind up in a position very close to that of a single monopolist. It really makes no difference which of the two firms leads the way. The other will generally follow if the move is profitable. Of course, GE and Westinghouse could have gotten to the same point by sitting down and agreeing on price, but that method happens to be illegal in the United States. Oligopolists have been known to collude anyway, but deliberate price fixing is not usually required. They can reach a monopolistic result even if they act independently, as long as they keep each other clearly in view.

A light bulb industry with 200 sellers instead of two would also be better off if its members would keep the price at 50¢. But they

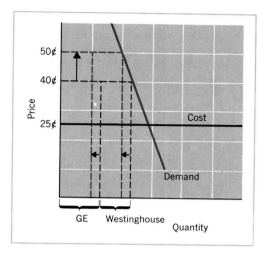

FIGURE 6.4 An oligopolist would find a price increase profitable if his rival could be expected to follow suit, and if industry profits are higher at the greater price.

couldn't do it. Any one member of the industry could probably get away with a price cut because he would be so small a part of the total that his move would go unnoticed by the others. And once some firms started picking up customers by price competition the others would have to follow. The process would continue until the price got down to cost per unit, where further price cutting is unprofitable. For oligopoly pricing to work, there must be so few firms that each one automatically takes the others' likely behavior into account.

This picture of oligopoly is a little too simple. In the real world all sorts of quibbles are necessary. For instance, suppose that one firm had lower costs than the other. Then the low-cost firm would probably prefer a lower price than the high-cost firm. The low-cost firm is likely to win the argument. Or suppose that GE thinks that demand is much more responsive to price reductions than Westinghouse does. Demand curves like the one in Figure 6.3 aren't easy to measure in real life. An executive at GE can't just look in the morning paper for an accurate curve. All he can do is make educated guesses and hope that he's right. If GE expects a relatively large response to a price reduction, it will tend to opt for lower prices. Westinghouse will have to go along even if it is against its management's better judgment. Or maybe one of the two hasn't figured out how the oligopoly game works or has a public-spirited management that keeps price low out of the goodness of its heart. The other has no choice but to go along. And even if the two do not compete in prices, they are likely to spend a lot of

money on product and packaging design or on advertising and salesmen. This sort of competition may be of value to consumers if it results in
improved products. On the other hand, it may just increase the cost
while giving consumers no more than annual style changes and uninformative commercials.

   In general, oligopoly is not the same as monopoly. It is a big box
into which we have dropped a great variety of industries, ranging all
the way from light bulbs to gasoline. What holds for the light bulb
producers probably does not hold for gas stations. Oligopoly can result in situations close to monopoly. But it can also produce results
close to those of pure competition. Economists are generally agreed,
however, that the fewer sellers there are, the closer an industry is
likely to come to the monopoly result.

CONCENTRATION

The extent to which a few firms dominate an industry varies from
market to market. Table 6.1 shows the shares of the top four firms in
each of a number of important manufacturing industries in 1967.
Technically, these percentages are known as **concentration ratios.** In
some cases the industry as a whole embraces more than one market.
That is the case when the products are sold regionally, as petroleum
products are. Gasoline produced on the east or west coast is virtually never sold in the Midwest, and midwestern gasoline is seldom,
if ever, sold on the two coasts. It is also the case when the products
of an industry do not compete with one another. For instance, tran-
quilizers and antibiotics don't compete, even though both are products
of the drug industry. In these cases the table shows concentration ratios
for the most appropriate major submarkets for which information is
available.

   As you can see, American manufacturing ranges all the way from
tight oligopoly (automobiles, aluminum, tires, cigarettes, and light
bulbs) to intense competition (lumber, furniture, apparel, and textiles). Where we draw the line between oligopoly and competition is
to some extent arbitrary. Most economists would probably count as
oligopolistic those industries in which the top four firms do half or
more of the business. They would consider industries in which the
top four do no more than 25 percent to be competitive. Some of the
industries in the in-between category belong in one class and some
in the other. Many have features of both. Altogether, roughly half of
our manufacturing is oligopolistic and the other half is competitive.

TABLE 6.1   Concentration ratios in selected product markets (1967)

COMMODITY	SHARE OF MARKET HELD BY TOP FOUR FIRMS
Automobiles (passenger cars, knocked down and assembled)	99%
Primary aluminum	91
Light bulbs	88
Cigarettes	81
Household soap and detergents	77
Complete military aircraft	77
Tires and tubes	71
Miscellaneous acyclic (organic) chemicals	47
Steel	
Hot rolled bars, shapes, plates, and structural shapes	62
Hot rolled sheets and strip	56
Steel pipe	37
Steel wire	33
Drugs (1958)	
Antibiotics	59
Tranquilizers	55
Veterinary	45
Vitamins	27
Refined petroleum products (1963)	
Pacific	65
East North Central (Great Lakes)	46
West South Central (mainly Texas and Louisiana)	42
Wheat flour	37
Paper	
Sanitary paper products (facial tissue, toilet paper, etc.)	61
Coarse (for bags, etc.)	39
Container board (for cardboard boxes)	35
Book paper	27
Cotton broad woven fabrics	30
Fresh meat	27
Footwear	27
Paints and varnishes	23
Canned fruits and vegetables	23
Men's and boys' suits and coats	17
Wood household furniture	11
Lumber (1963)	
Pacific	16
South Atlantic	5
Dresses	7

TABLE 6.2   The major sectors of the economy (1971)

SECTOR	BILLIONS OF DOLLARS	PERCENTAGE OF GNP
Agriculture, forestry, and fishing	$ 33.5	3.1%
Mining	17.1	1.6
Construction	50.7	4.8
Manufacturing	259.9	24.7
Transport, communications and public utilities	91.9	8.7
Wholesale and retail trade	180.8	17.2
Finance, insurance, and real estate	150.7	11.6
Services	122.7	11.6
Government	140.9	13.4
Net income earned abroad	6.9	0.6
Total GNP	$1,050.4	100.0%

Manufacturing accounts for only about a quarter of all economic activity today. Table 6.2 shows the breakdown of the American GNP into its major components. Some of these sectors are very competitive. They include the unregulated parts of agriculture, forestry, and fishing, coal mining, residential construction, most retail and wholesale trade, real estate, and many services. On the other hand, metal mining, local banking, and about half of manufacturing are quite concentrated. In some other industries, such as construction and medicine, competition is limited by unions or professional associations. This leaves oil production (oil wells), the regulated parts of agriculture, and transportation, the public utilities, and communication where the government controls entry or output or price, or all three. Finally, in one eighth of the economy, the government does the production itself. Adding up all the percentages in Table 6.2, approximately a quarter of the economy is characterized by unregulated monopoly or oligopoly, another quarter is operated by or regulated by the government, and about half can be counted as effectively competitive.

This statement gives us only a rough picture of the nature of our economy. There are competitive aspects of many oligopolistic industries, and some limits on competition exist in some of the unconcentrated industries. Moreover, other economists would classify some industries differently. Still, anyone who does his job conscientiously will wind up with a large concentrated sector *and* a large competitive one. The Communists speak of the American economy as typified by "monopoly capitalism." Some other people speak as if it were generally competitive. Neither group is correct. We have large elements of both.

THE COST OF MONOPOLY

What do we lose as a result of monopoly and oligopoly? Rates of return on stockholders' investments are seldom more than twenty percent in even the most monopolistic of industries. Many firms in concentrated industries earn much less than that. Moreover, even competitive industries earn something like eight percent.

Actually, the difference between the profit rates in competitive and concentrated industries is probably understated, because accounting practices tend to understate high profits and overstate low ones. Even allowing for some distortion in corporate reports, though, the difference between monopoly and competition is less than catastrophic. All corporate profits together come to only ten percent of the GNP. Adding in the noncorporate sector of the economy and allowing for some understatement of profits would increase this figure only moderately. Perhaps as much as half of actual profits—and certainly less than half of those that are actually reported—are earned in the unregulated monopolistic quarter of the economy. Roughly half of *these* profits would be earned even if the sector were competitive. This process of elimination leaves us with pure monopoly profits of only two or three percent of the GNP—or around $30 billion. These monopoly profits represent what the owners of firms with monopoly power earn at the expense of the rest of us as a result of their powerful positions. They are richer—and nonmonopolistic consumers are poorer—by that amount.

This statement does not tell the whole story, however. High monopoly prices result in the use of some of our land, labor, and capital in industries where they produce less valuable goods than they could elsewhere. In addition, some concentrated industries have higher costs than necessary. For instance, high prices make it worthwhile for steel and cement companies to serve customers far from their plants. These customers could be more cheaply served by closer mills. Drug, soap, and cereal companies spend about ten percent of their receipts on advertising, much of it uninformative and mutually offsetting. In some industries (steel and cement are good examples again) high prices have induced producers to build more

capacity than is needed. All the economic wastes resulting from
monopoly have been estimated at as much as six percent of the GNP,
or maybe $60 billion. These wastes are in addition to excess
monopoly profits. Their cost comes out of the consumers' pockets,
too. In this case, however, the producers are no richer for it.

On the other hand, we couldn't attain a perfectly working competitive economy no matter how hard we tried. As a result, these estimates of monopoly and oligopoly profits and economic waste exaggerate what consumers could gain from policies designed to reduce
monopoly. Probably we could gain as much from one or two years of
economic growth as we could conceivably gain by an all-out effort to
make the economy more competitive. The losses from monopoly
aren't insignificant, but they aren't our most important problem,
either.

ECONOMIES OF SCALE AND TECHNOLOGICAL PROGRESS

A common defense of monopolies is that the losses they cause are
made up for by the economies of large scale. Furthermore, it is argued that more concentrated industries can make greater contributions to technological progress. Economists have examined both
claims carefully during the last decade.

On the economies of scale, the general finding is that the American economy is so huge that it can support many firms of efficient
size in most industries. There are a few exceptions. We do not have
room for more than a very few diesel engine plants of efficient size.
In the less densely populated parts of the country, cement production is bound to be concentrated in one or a few plants, largely because the product is so bulky that it cannot be shipped very far. But
the much more common situation is like that in steel or petroleum
refining. There, plants of the most efficient scale account for less
than two or three percent of total output each. These plants may
produce hundreds of millions of dollars worth of output, but our
economy is so big that it can easily accommodate them. The United
States is large enough to have both the economies of scale *and*
competition in most industries.

The problem of technological progress is harder. It is true that big
business accounts for a disproportionate part of our total expenditures on research and development. But more than half of that research is government-financed. Smaller firms, in fact, get more patents per dollar of private research expenditure than big ones.
Perhaps more important, a disproportionate share of the big break-

throughs have been made by one or a few individuals working either alone or in companies that were small when the inventions were made. For instance, the Polaroid process, Xerography, and the computer were all the work of one or a few individuals. Large labs sometimes do produce important inventions, such as the atom bomb or the transistor, but their advantage lies more in making improvements in engineering than in original breakthroughs.

When it comes to adopting the new techniques once they are discovered, some large firms clearly have an advantage. Many new techniques require large scale. Yet, many times, the relatively small firms of an industry—or even complete outsiders—have been the innovators. In some cases new techniques or products have been ignored by leading firms until someone else introduced them. For instance, IBM stuck to its old tabulating machines until Univac showed that computers were commercially valuable. IBM also refused to buy the Xerography process when it received an early offer from the inventor. Only after the huge success of Xerox Corporation did IBM enter the copying machine field. Moreover, competitive industries are capable of adopting new processes quickly. Witness the rapid spread of hybrid corn in agriculture, or of the supermarket in retailing. Once a new technique becomes known it is adopted among small firms about as fast as among large ones.

If rivals could copy successes *instantaneously,* of course, there would be little incentive for competitive firms to adopt something new. There would be no payoff from successes to offset the inevitable failures. But that is not the way the world works. In even our most competitive industries the successful pioneers stand to gain, at least for a few years. The first firms to adopt the supermarket made a bundle before everyone else had copied them.

Altogether, bigness probably helps in some aspects of progressiveness, especially in the development of new techniques, once invented. Bigness probably also aids in their adoption where the new developments require large scale. But, as we have seen, we have room for both bigness and competition in most industries. We would probably have a no less progressive economy if American industry were less concentrated.

MONOPOLY POLICY

Monopoly is a substantial though not a catastrophic problem. What can be done about it? We have two major approaches. In the largest part of the economy we try to preserve or restore competition through enforcement of the antitrust laws. In another part of the economy we let monopoly exist but try to regulate it.

ANTITRUST

The main antitrust laws are the Sherman and Clayton Antitrust Acts. The Sherman Act prohibits agreements that restrain competition and acts that are meant to create or maintain monopoly. The Clayton Act bars specific practices such as mergers, tying sales (where if you want my product x you must buy my product y), exclusive dealing (where if you want to carry my products you cannot carry my competitors'), and price discrimination (charging one buyer less than others for the same goods). All the Clayton Act prohibitions apply only "where the effect may be substantially to lessen competition." The Sherman Act was passed in 1890 and the Clayton Act in 1914. However, the most active period of antitrust enforcement has been in the years since the 1930s.

The most important parts of the antitrust laws today are the prohibitions of anticompetitive agreements and mergers. It is as illegal to agree on price or on market shares as it is to drive down the wrong side of the street. Collusion still goes on, of course, but it must be secret, and the agreements cannot be enforced at law. The Justice Department succeeds in turning up a few dozen cases of collusion every year, though they are often small. The law can do little about the members of a tight oligopoly who merely march in step without actually making formal agreements.

The merger law is even more important today. For years the antitrust laws had little effect on mergers. Many of the huge corporations that make up American business, such as United States Steel and American Can, were formed in enormous mergers at the turn of the century, well after the Sherman Act was passed. These mergers often combined entire industries and created nearly pure monopolies. Another wave of mergers occurred in the 1920s, creating such firms as Bethlehem Steel and General Foods. The second wave of mergers seldom created pure monopolies, but they made many oligopolistic industries much more concentrated. Since 1950, when the Clayton Act was tightened up, however, we have had much stricter enforcement. Today we virtually prohibit any acquisition by major firms of significant competititors, or of important suppliers or outlets, in even moderately concentrated industries.

Nevertheless, we underwent yet another merger wave in the 1960s. This time the acquisitions were conglomerate in character. That is, they combined firms in different industries or different regional markets. The Justice Department brought suit against several of the biggest of these mergers and succeeded in taking the steam out of the movement, but none of the cases ever reached the Supreme Court. As a result, we still don't know if the law applies to such combinations. There is a great deal of disagreement among economists as to whether conglomerate mergers are anticompetitive at all.

Some conglomerate mergers may actually enhance competition. This can happen if a powerful firm acquires a small firm from another industry and turns it into a strong competitor. For instance, National Steel, an important steel company, acquired a small aluminum fabricator and used that foothold to become one of only nine major aluminum producers in the country. Other conglomerate mergers have served to eliminate weak management. Still, some economists believe that mergers of very large firms with other firms that are leaders in concentrated industries will lessen competition. If they were prevented from acquiring leading firms, the large firms might enter these industries by acquiring small firms and building them up. Whatever else, conglomerate mergers certainly can create big firms.

One thing that the antitrust laws have seldom accomplished is the dissolution of powerful firms. In 1911 the government won cases against the oil and tobacco monopolies. Today we have eighteen major oil companies and six cigarette companies, instead of one of each. Right after World War II, following another successful case, Alcoa was required to give up its control of Aluminium, Ltd., the Canadian aluminum company. Moreover, the government sold the aluminum plants it had built during the war to firms other than Alcoa. Today we have nine aluminum producers instead of the one we had before the case. There have been half a dozen smaller dissolution cases since, and a current case against IBM could turn out to be more important than any of its predecessors. Such actions have been rare, however. They occur only where a single firm accounts for the bulk of an industry's output, and even in these cases the government sometimes loses. The law has hardly ever been used to break up the leading firms in industries controlled by two or three firms, such as automobiles, glass, or heavy electrical equipment.

The courts have generally been reluctant to break up big firms. For one thing, there is a fear that going companies will be made less efficient if they are dissolved. Moreover, it generally is not possible to recoup the exceptional profits earned by the people who established the monopoly. Those people have most likely sold their stock to you and me. The prices of the stock already reflect the expected monopoly returns. Therefore, you and I are only getting the same return on our investments that we could receive anywhere else. The dissolution of a well-established firm would harm the present stockholders, most of whom are "innocent bystanders." As a result, many people see little to be gained from such dissolutions.

Altogether, we have antitrust laws that do a reasonable job of discouraging collusion and that do an excellent job of preventing the creation of new monopoly by merger. But they do little about eliminating monopoly where it already exists. This may be enough. Very few firms have been able to attain dominance in their industries by internal growth alone. Generally, concentration tends to decline slowly where mergers are prevented. If we can just continue to enforce the law as we have in the last two decades, we may gradually be able to attain a more competitive economy.

Some people advocate much stricter antitrust laws, laws that would make little firms out of big ones in many industries. Others feel that the law as it is now enforced is too severe. To a large extent the difference between the two views reflects value judgments. The argument is basically about the fairness of a system that "protects innocent bystanders" or one that permits some people to get rich at the expense of the rest of us because of strategic positions they have acquired. As with all value judgments, you, the reader, will have to decide for yourself.

REGULATION

In some lines of enterprise, such as the public utilities, the government has permitted or even created monopoly and then tried to regulate it. The general principle has been to set prices that cover costs and then to require the regulated firms to serve all comers.

Actually, this task is much harder than it looks. For one thing, it makes government responsible for deciding what reasonable costs are. When a firm is guaranteed that prices will always be set high enough to cover costs plus a reasonable return, it has little incentive to keep costs down. This is especially true if the decision-maker actually has something to *gain* from the higher costs. For instance, an increase in managers' salaries shows up as an increase in costs for the firm. It will ordinarily be covered by the rates that the regulators allow. There is little reason to economize on such salaries. Moreover, accountants can define costs in wondrous ways if you don't watch them. And finally, what *is* a reasonable rate of return? The regulators have been all over the map on that question. Altogether, regulation, even at its best, is an imperfect substitute for competition.

Regulation is often not at its best. The Interstate Commerce Commission (ICC), which regulates the railroads and trucking, has acted mainly to prevent price competition in these industries in recent years, and it has kept new trucking companies from entering the business. Economists who have examined the case have concluded that the main effect of the ICC today is to keep the cost of freight transportation several billion dollars a year higher than it needs to be. Similarly, the Civil Aeronautics Board (CAB) has seen its main business as that of keeping the airlines profitable. It has prevented the creation of *any* new trunk (main-line) airlines over four decades of enormous growth. It has kept eager potential entrants out of new routes. It has regularly prevented domestic fare competition. The airlines, prevented from picking up new customers by cutting price, have done so by adding more flights. As a result, we have had lots of half-empty planes flying across the country. In the early 1970s the CAB approved agreements to limit the numbers of flights on specific routes. Now about the only ways left for the affected airlines to compete is in advertising and pretty stewardesses.

The Federal Power Commission (FPC) has set the price of natural gas so low that it has discouraged exploration for new reserves. At the same time the low price has encouraged widespread industrial use. Both of these effects have contributed to a general gas shortage. The Federal Communications Commission (FCC) has prevented cable television companies from bringing more than two or three channels from other cities into the hundred largest cities. Largely as a result of FCC regulation, most American cities have only three or four TV channels while most cities in Japan, a much poorer country, have six. The list could go on. Time and again the regulators have seen their job as not only to prevent monopoly profits, but also to keep their wards profitable, even if it requires higher costs or poorer service than might be possible.

Probably a majority of economists feel that regulation is the best option available in cases like local electric and telephone companies, where the economies of scale make monopoly inevitable. But most economists also feel that we should think twice before extending regulation to industries where even oligopoly is a reasonable alternative. The regulated industries just have not performed that well, even when compared with quite concentrated industries in the unregulated sector.

CARTELS

The government sometimes intervenes in the market to *prevent* competition instead of promoting it. An agreement to prevent competition is known as a **cartel.** Our government has created and enforced quite a number of cartels over the years. The agricultural price policies discussed in Chapter 5 have this effect. So does the "prorationing" of oil, a policy carried on by the major oil-producing states. State agencies specify output quotas for individual oil wells. They thereby control the total oil supply. This system of output controls, along with import quotas on foreign oil, helped keep the domestic price of oil far above world levels during the 1950s and 1960s. It was estimated that Americans were paying about seven billion dollars a year more for petroleum products in the early 1970s than they need have. The high prices led to the drilling of thousands of superfluous oilwells. Only a small minority of these wells represented new exploration. Many were drilled in the middle of well-established oil fields, merely because another well meant another quota. The United States has 90 percent of the world's oil wells while producing less than a third of the world's oil.[2]

In the fall and winter of 1973 the countries of OPEC (the Organization of Petroleum Exporting Countries) made this whole structure obsolete by quadrupling the royalties they demanded of the oil companies. They became the most powerful cartel in history, charging prices many times the cost of production and leaving the prices that had been maintained by state prorationing in the United States far behind. One result was an all-out, worldwide search for non-OPEC oil. Another was an unexpectedly intense effort by consumers to economize on petroleum products.

Another case of government intervention to prevent competition is the system of resale price maintenance, or "fair trade," laws of a majority of states. Under these laws, manufacturers can specify a minimum price below which retailers cannot sell. In this way they prevent price competition at the retail level. Fortunately, most manufacturers have abandoned attempts to enforce "fair trade" prices. But in fields where such policies are still pursued, such as

[2] For two decades we had excess capacity in oil. Flush wells (where the oil comes up because of natural pressure) were required to produce at far less than capacity —sometimes as low as 30 percent in the early 1960s. By the early 1970s, however, this excess capacity had disappeared. Wells are now permitted to operate at their maximum allowable rates. But we still have far more oil wells than are needed to exploit our known resources fully. As a result, American oil costs much more to produce than foreign oil does. Quotas on imports of foreign oil were finally suspended in 1973.

drugs, toiletries, liquor, and small appliances, retail prices are kept up artificially. High-cost distributors are protected.

Not only do cartels impose monopoly prices, but they result in high costs of production as well. When the government guarantees a high price in an industry, it induces new producers to enter. It also takes the pressure off of unneeded or high-cost producers who would otherwise leave. The result, ordinarily, is excess capacity. Entry into the cartelized industry will continue until it is no more profitable than any other industry. In this case, however, the profits disappear because of higher costs rather than lower prices. Because of cartels we find ourselves with too many farmers, too many oil wells, and too many drug stores. Cartelized industries usually run at far below capacity and, therefore, waste many resources. The protected producers may earn exceptional profits when the cartel is first established. But after the high prices have induced unnecessary expansion, the producers are no better off than they would be in another industry.

In spite of the predictable bad results of cartels, Congress and the state legislatures have displayed a strong inclination to establish them. There is almost always someone around petitioning the legislature for protection against "ruinous competition." Even though the cartel may seem temporary when set up, it generally turns out to be permanent. After a cartel has induced a great deal of excess or high-cost capacity, its members become dependent on the high prices just to break even. The removal of the cartel then would mean disaster for them.

SUMMARY
Monopoly and tight oligopoly restrict output and increase price. They thereby make the economy less efficient and make insiders rich at the expense of the rest of the country. About a quarter of our economy is unregulated monopoly or oligopoly, mostly the latter. Another quarter is government operated or controlled, and about half is competitive. Monopoly profits account for a few percent of the GNP, but the economic waste due to monopolistic restriction of output and oligopolistic practices that increase costs may account for several percent. In most industries the United States is so large that it can have both competition *and* firms that are large enough to reap economies of scale and gains from new technology.

Our policy approaches to monopoly are all imperfect. Antitrust is reasonably effective in preventing the creation of new monopoly by collusion or merger, but it has done little to eliminate existing monopoly. Regulation works imperfectly at best, and in some lines, such as transportation, it has worked to raise prices and induce inefficiency. Publicly created cartels, such as those in agriculture and oil, almost automatically result in excess capacity and high costs. Altogether, antitrust may be imperfect, but the unregulated sector, where it holds sway, has performed quite well compared with the sector controlled by the regulators or the cartels.

STUDY QUESTIONS

1   You drive into Noplace, Ohio, and find only one motel. Is the Noplace Motor Lodge a pure monopolist? Try drawing the demand curve that it faces tonight. Then try drawing a second demand curve showing how many customers it would have over the next decade if it set various prices and left them there for the decade.

2   "I'm not a monopolist, I have a competitor," said the president of United States Widgets, Inc. He's right, too. There is another important producer of Widgets. What difference does that make? Does the presence of another producer make the Widget industry "competitive"? Does the fact that there are only two sellers make the industry monopolistic?

3   The antitrust laws prohibit all collusive agreements among competitors. They also prohibit most mergers among competing firms, at least if both firms are large enough to attain the economies of scale. But by and large they do not require the breakup of large firms, even if there are only a handful of sellers in the market. Are these three policies consistent? Should one or another of them be changed?

4   Most large cities control taxis. They almost all set taxi fares. In addition, in such cities as New York and Chicago the number of taxis is set by law. The only way to get into the taxi business is to buy a "medallion" from someone who is already in the business. What would be the effect of a large increase in taxi fares on the price of a medallion? If you chose to go into the business by buying someone else out, would you make monopoly profits? Do you think that taxi fares are likely to be at competitive levels?

5   In Washington, D.C., taxi fares are also controlled, but in that case anyone with a valid license can go into the taxi business. What would be the effect of a large increase in fares in Washington? Would taxi drivers there make monopoly profits?

6   The major banana-producing countries of Central America are considering a large tax on the exportation of bananas (of about five cents a

pound). Would this banana tax be monopolistic? What would be the tax's effect on the price of bananas to consumers? There are several dozen countries in the world with conditions that would permit them to grow bananas. What do you think will happen to those other countries' banana crops if the Central American countries impose their tax?

FURTHER READING

The effects of monopoly, competition, antitrust, and regulation in electric power, steel, and retailing are analyzed in Leonard Weiss, *Case Studies in American Industry*, 2nd ed. (New York: John Wiley, 1971). Another good set of industry studies appears in Walter Adams, ed., *The Structure of American Industry*, 4th ed. (New York: Macmillan, 1971). Willard Mueller, *A Primer on Monopoly and Competition* (New York: Random House, 1970) offers a good run-down on the monopoly problem and antitrust. Louis M. Kohlmeier, Jr., *The Regulators* (New York: Harper and Row, 1969) is a striking, interesting, and accurate picture of the Federal regulatory agencies, written by a leading journalist.

APPENDIX TO CHAPTER 6 ◼
THE THEORY OF MONOPOLY

The analysis of monopoly in Chapter 6 was intentionally simplified. Economists have developed a method to describe the monopoly price precisely. That analysis is briefly outlined in this appendix, though the concepts developed here are not necessary for an understanding of the rest of the book.

MARGINAL REVENUE

The monopolist faces a demand schedule like the one shown in Table 6.3. The more he tries to sell, the lower the price he must charge. The third column of the table shows total receipts. They are just price times quantity. They increase less than proportionately with output because of the as-

TABLE 6.3   **A monopolist's demand and revenue schedules**

SELLING PRICE	QUANTITY SOLD PER DAY	TOTAL RECEIPTS PER DAY	MARGINAL REVENUE PER DAY
$10	0	$0	
			$9
$9	1	$9	
			$7
$8	2	$16	
			$5
$7	3	$21	
			$3
$6	4	$24	
			$1
$5	5	$25	
			–$1
$4	6	$24	
			–$3
$3	7	$21	

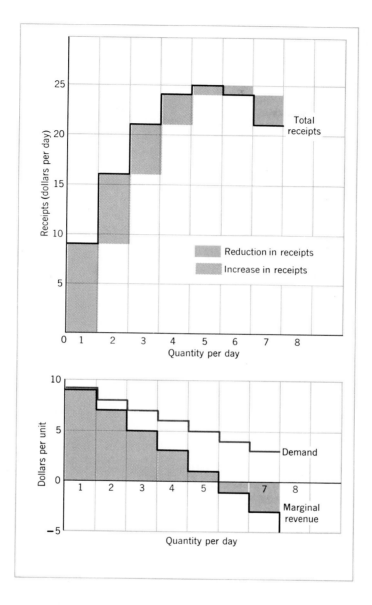

FIGURE 6.5 *(top)* If the monopolist cuts his price, he sells more. His total receipts (price times the quantity sold) will increase at first. At some higher level they would fall off again because of the low price.

FIGURE 6.6 *(below)* The changes in receipts as output increases are the monopolist's marginal revenue. The bars on this marginal revenue chart come from Figure 6.5. The monopolist's demand curve is also shown.

sociated price reductions. The last column in Table 6.3 shows the firm's **marginal revenue**—that is, the addition to receipts that arises from one more unit of output.

This schedule is reproduced as a bar chart in Figure 6.5. The dark line is total receipts. Marginal revenue shows up as the shaded areas—the pink additions to receipts and the grey reductions in receipts as compared with each previous step. The demand schedule appears as the red steps in Figure 6.6. Marginal revenue is shown there, too, as a series of pink or grey bars.

After the first unit sold, the marginal revenue is always less than the price, because the firm is selling some goods it would be able to sell anyway at a higher price. For instance, to go from an output of three units a day to four, it must reduce the price from seven dollars to six. It receives six dollars on the additional unit sold, but it loses three dollars on the three units it could have sold anyway without reducing the price. The addition to receipts from the additional unit sold is, therefore, $6 − $3 = $3.

The extent to which marginal revenue falls below price depends on the elasticity of demand. If the demand is very elastic, a drop in price will bring many more sales, so marginal revenue will be high. On the other hand, if the elasticity is as low as 1.0, the total receipts of the firm will be the same regardless of its output. The marginal revenue from one more unit of output will be zero. If elasticity is less than 1.0, a reduction in price will result in a fall in total receipts, so marginal revenue will be negative. A profit-maximizing monopolist would always raise his price as long as the elasticity of demand is less than 1.0.

MAXIMIZING PROFITS

To make the largest possible profit, the monopolist must compare his marginal revenue with his costs. Figure 6.7 shows such a comparison. It is drawn to a larger scale than Figure 6.6, to make the comparison easier. The story will be simpler if we continue to assume that cost per unit is the same in the long run, regardless of the quantity produced.

Let's assume that cost per unit is $3.00. It will clearly pay the monopolist to produce the *first* unit, since that will add $9.00 to his receipts and only $3.00 to his costs. His profit goes from zero to $6.00 in the process. Now try a second unit. The marginal revenue in going from one to two units per day is $7.00, compared with only $3.00 of additional production cost, so his profit per day increases. Profits continue to increase so long as the marginal revenue is greater than the cost of producing the additional unit. But the step from three to four units adds just as much to receipts as it does to costs. Going beyond that point would mean net *reductions* in profits.

Demand curves are more commonly thought of as continuous curves like

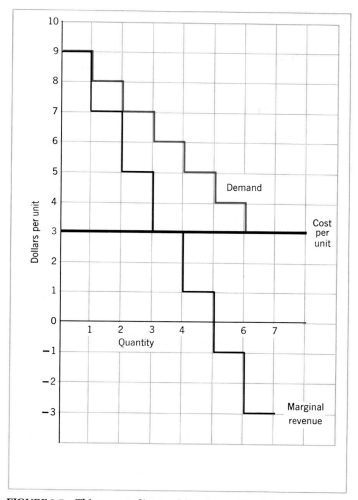

FIGURE 6.7 **This monopolist would find it profitable to produce the first three units, because each one adds more to his receipts than to his costs and therefore increases his profits. The fourth unit neither increases nor decreases his profits. After that, increased output adds more to cost than to receipts. Profits are greatest where marginal revenue equals cost.**

the one in Figure 6.8, rather than as sets of steps. When we use such a demand curve, marginal revenue becomes a continuous curve as well. The most profitable policy for the monopolist is to expand until marginal revenue just equals the cost of an additional unit, and no further. Expansion

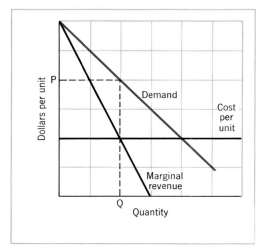

FIGURE 6.8 Here the monopolist faces a continuously downward-sloping demand curve. The marginal revenue curve is always below the demand curve. The most profitable price and output is where marginal revenue equals cost per unit.

adds to his profits for a while, but it won't ever be carried far enough to bring the price into equality with the cost per unit. As long as there is a downward-sloping demand curve, the most profitable price will always exceed the cost of an additional unit.

The less elastic the demand is, the greater the excess of price over cost will be. This is natural. Remember that the elasticity of demand for a product depends on the availability of substitutes. Goods with close substitutes have elastic demand. Monopolists facing less elastic demands have only relatively distant substitutes to compete with; they can raise prices to higher levels as a result. Firms with good substitutes for their products are hardly monopolists at all. In the extreme case of the competitive firm, the price is the same regardless of how much the firm produces. In that case the price *is* the same as marginal revenue, and the firm has no reason to restrict its output at all.

THE EFFECT OF MONOPOLY

The effect of monopoly pricing is analyzed in Figure 6.9. The most profitable price in this example is P. The associated output is Q_1. From a social point of view we would prefer the firm to produce at Q_2, where the price would just equal the cost of the last unit produced. At that point the last resources employed by the monopolist would produce just as much as they would in their best alternative employment. But a profit-maximizing monopolist would not willingly expand his output that far.

The white rectangle at the lower left corner of Figure 6.9 represents the

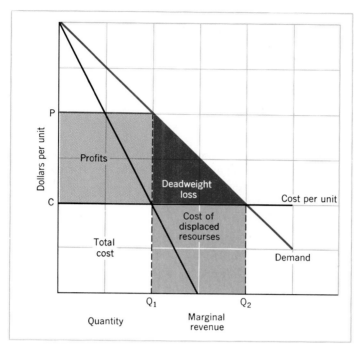

FIGURE 6.9   The monopolist charges a price of P and restricts output to Q_1 in the process. His profits are equal to the area of the pink rectangle. Society loses output equal to the area of the red triangle.

monopolist's total costs—just his cost per unit times his output. The pink rectangle is his monopoly profit in excess of the opportunity cost of his capital (profit per unit minus cost times the quantity sold). The less elastic the demand is, the more he will raise price over cost per unit. His total profit will be greater as a result.

The grey rectangle represents the additional costs he would incur if he expanded until price equaled cost per unit. The grey area does not reflect a net loss to society, because the resources he doesn't use are not left unemployed. They are in other industries, producing as much as their opportunity costs.

This leaves us with the red triangle. It *does* represent an economic loss. Consumers are willing to pay the amounts shown by the demand curve for additional units of the product in question. But the resources that might have produced these goods are actually producing things worth only as much as the grey area. The red area between the demand and the cost curve, therefore, shows the additional value that these misplaced resources could produce if the industry were not a monopoly.

Economists have attempted to estimate the value of this loss. For the economy as a whole it comes to less than one percent of the GNP. The sum of monopoly profits (the pink area) is considerably larger. As shown in the chapter, it is something on the order of three percent of the GNP. It is not a net loss, however. The monopolist gains and the rest of us lose, but the economy as a whole which includes all of us is poorer only by the extent of the dead weight triangle.

STUDY QUESTIONS

1   A certain monopolist faces the demand schedule shown below. Work out his marginal revenue between each level of output and the next. In the long run he can produce any amount of his product at five dollars a unit. Find the most profitable level of output, using marginal revenue. Check your answer by working out his total profit at each level of output.

PRICE	QUANTITY
13	0
12	1
11	2
10	3
9	4
8	5
7	6
6	7
5	8
4	9

2   In the example given above, what would be the best level of output from the point of view of society as a whole? What does society as a whole lose due to his charging too much and selling too little as a result?

UNIT THREE
THE
DISTRIBUTION
OF
INCOME

7
FACTOR
MARKETS
AND
INEQUALITY

So far, our main emphasis has been on product markets. Now we will turn to the markets on which the services of the factors of production are bought and sold. These markets are equally important. They determine wage rates and the rates of return to capital. In the process they also determine how the factors of production are employed. Factor markets affect not only the allocation of resources but also the distribution of incomes. As a result, discussions of the way they work often produce strong emotions.

FACTOR MARKETS
HOW PRODUCT AND FACTOR MARKETS ARE RELATED

The roles of product and factor markets are illustrated in Figure 7.1. It is a mildly more complicated version of the circular flow diagram from Figure 3.1. The two basic economic institutions, households and firms, have the same functions that they had there. This time, however, the individual product and factor markets on which they meet are represented by supply and demand diagrams.

The two diagrams at the top represent product markets like those discussed in Chapters 5 and 6. Of course, in the real economy there are thousands of individual product markets. We have reduced them to two simply to fit them on the page. The demand on these product markets arises from households. Supply comes from the firms. Prices and consumer tastes determine how the households' consumption is distributed among the various products. The same prices (or, in monopolistic mar-

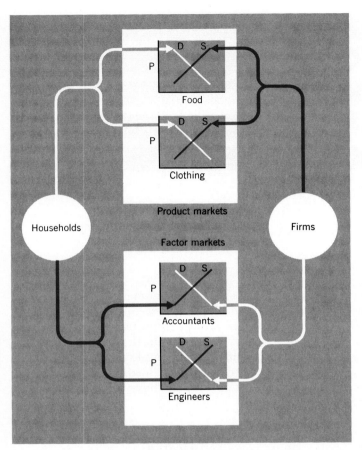

FIGURE 7.1 **Households and firms meet on two kinds of markets: product markets, where households buy and firms sell, and factor markets, where firms buy and households sell.**

kets, the demand curves themselves) interact with production costs to determine how much of each good the firms produce. Product markets may result in more or less desirable production and consumption decisions. Their results depend on how competitive the markets are, how accurately the firms foresee the future, and how well informed consumers are. In any case, some decisions, good or bad, will certainly be made there.

In this chapter we shift our attention to the factor markets, represented at the bottom of Figure 7.1. Again we show only two of them, though there are thousands in the real world. They include the markets for the services of stenographers and lumberjacks, for downtown real estate and Texas oil pools, and for all other sorts of labor, land, and capital. The households own these factors of production either directly or indirectly. Households account for supply in the factor markets. Firms are the buyers here; they determine the demand. The prices of the factors of production—the wage rates of various sorts of labor, the rents on various sorts of land, and the rates of return on various sorts of capital—are all determined in factor markets. These factor prices influence the households in choosing among alternative employments for the factors they own. They also guide the firms in deciding which combinations of factors to use in production. Factor markets may work well or poorly, depending on the degree of competition and the amount of foresight of households and firms. We will start out with a picture of factor markets under the best of conditions. We will take up some of the realistic imperfections later.

THE DEMAND FOR LABOR

By far the most important factor markets are those for labor. Wages and salaries account for 76 percent of all factor payments. But this figure actually understates the importance of labor, because it leaves out the earnings of the self-employed, such as the doctors, farmers, and unincorporated shopkeepers. Assigning two thirds of their incomes to labor, it turns out that somewhere around 81 percent of all factor payments are labor incomes. We will therefore focus on the markets for labor. Much of what is said, though, can be applied to other factors as well.

To understand the firm's demand for labor it is necessary to introduce a new concept, the **marginal product.** The word "marginal" refers to the effect of a small change. Marginal product, therefore, is the change in output that results from small change in an input. For instance, consider the employer of a particular type of labor, say electrical engineers. Let the technology used and the other factors employed by the firm remain fixed. Then as the number of electrical engineers is increased, we should see diminishing returns. After some point, each additional engineer should add less to the total output than the previous one did. The principle is the same one we know from our potato patch in Chapter 2.

Marginal product can be illustrated with a hypothetical electric clock firm. Its outputs are given in Table 7.1. You can see from the table that if the firm were to employ no electrical engineers at all, it could produce

TABLE 7.1   Output of a clock manufacturer

NUMBER OF ENGINEERS	TOTAL OUTPUT (clocks)	MARGINAL PRODUCT (clocks)	VALUE OF MARGINAL PRODUCT (at $10 per clock)
0	10,000		
		4,000	$40,000
1	14,000		
		3,000	$30,000
2	17,000		
		2,000	$20,000
3	19,000		
		1,500	$15,000
4	20,500		
		1,000	$10,000
5	21,500		
		500	$5,000
6	22,000		

10,000 clocks a year. With one engineer it could produce 14,000 clocks. In other words, the first electrical engineer employed can add 4,000 clocks to the firm's output. These 4,000 clocks are his marginal product.

A second engineer adds less to output than the first. Perhaps his jobs are less essential, or maybe he must share equipment and the help of the other staff with the first engineer. The 3,000-clock difference between the outputs with one and with two electrical engineers is the marginal product of the second man. A third electrical engineer adds even less to total output than the second one did. His marginal product is still lower, and so forth. If the firm were to employ six electrical engineers it would have to use the last one to sweep the floors. His marginal product would be very low.

Notice that the differences among the marginal products of the various electrical engineers are *not* due to differences in their abilities. You can hire the engineers in a quite different order and get the same result. The decrease in marginal product is strictly a matter of diminishing returns. As long as other factors are held constant, there is a limit to how much the firm can produce, regardless of how many engineers it hires. As it approaches that limit, additional electrical engineers add less and less to its output.

The value of the marginal product is crucial in determining the firm's demand for a factor of production. In a competitive industry, the value of the marginal product can be computed by just multiplying the marginal

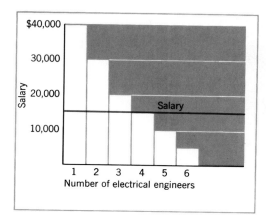

FIGURE 7.2 Each bar on this chart represents the value of the marginal product of another electrical engineer at a clock factory. The most profitable level of employment is where the value of the last engineer's marginal product just equals his salary.

product by the price of the product. The value of the marginal product is derived in the last column of Table 7.1. (We have assumed that electric clocks sell for ten dollars apiece, so 4,000 additional clocks mean $40,000 additional receipts, and so forth.) The value of the marginal product from the schedule in Table 7.1 is reproduced as a bar chart in Figure 7.2.

Now suppose that the going salary for electrical engineers is $15,000. The firm would certainly employ at least three electrical engineers, because each of the first three would add more to the value of output than he costs. Substantial amounts would be left over to pay other factors of production and to add to profits. If the firm added a fourth engineer, it would increase receipts by just as much as it had to pay him. It would not matter to the firm whether or not it added this man. But if the value of his marginal product were just a bit greater than $15,000 it would clearly pay the firm to hire him. A profit-maximizing firm would certainly *not* hire a fifth or a sixth electrical engineer, however. These workers would add less to receipts than they did to costs. They would therefore reduce profits.

This result is quite general. It holds for any profit-maximizing competitive firm. As long as another unit of any factor of production adds more to receipts than it does to costs, the firm will employ more of that factor. The firm will stop when the value of the factor's marginal product just equals its price. When the last unit of each factor employed adds just as much to the value of output as it costs, then the firm will be maximizing profits. It has no further reason to expand.

The value of the marginal product schedule in Table 7.1 actually

TABLE 7.2 Demand schedule for electrical engineers

SALARY	NUMBER OF ENGINEERS
$50,000	0
$40,000	1
$30,000	2
$20,000	3
$15,000	4
$10,000	5
$5,000	6

traces out the firm's demand for electrical engineers. For instance, if the going salary for engineers were $20,000, the firm would hire only three of them. At $30,000 it would hire two, and so forth. Table 7.2 gives us a complete demand schedule for electrical engineers at this firm. The bar chart in Figure 7.2 shows exactly the same relationship. It is the firm's demand curve for electrical engineers.

We can arrive at the overall demand for electrical engineers by adding up the firms' demands for them. This is exactly what we did with the demand for eggs in Chapter 5. In Figure 7.3, the individual firms' demand curves appear at the left. We can read off the numbers of electrical engineers who would be hired by each firm at $15,000 and add

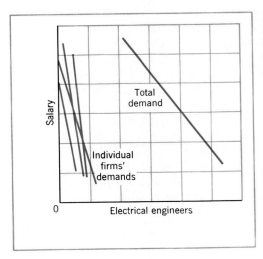

FIGURE 7.3 By adding up the individual firms' demand curves, like those on the left, we get the total demand for the factor of production: in this case electrical engineers.

them up to get the overall demand at that salary. A similar addition of individual demands at $30,000 yields another point on the overall demand curve. Since most firms will employ fewer engineers at higher salaries, the overall demand will slope downward and to the right.[1]

THE SUPPLY OF LABOR

The supply of labor also depends on the wage rate, but in a peculiar way. Try it out for yourself. How much would you work if the wage rate were a dollar an hour? Or two dollars? Five? Ten? A hundred dollars an hour? The answer differs with the individual, but if you are like most of us, there comes a wage rate above which you would not work any more hours. In fact, at even higher wages you would probably work less, not more. The reason is that at higher wage rates you would be richer. No doubt you'd want to use some of your added income for more goods. But you would want more leisure time too, unless you just can't think of anything to do with more spare time. Certainly the workers of the country as a whole have behaved this way. As wage rates have risen, we have worked shorter hours, taken longer vacations and coffee breaks, started work at a later age, and retired sooner. Of course, these changes were often the result of bargaining by unions, but the goals of the unions probably reflect the values of their members in this respect. They could have earned more pay if their working time had not been shortened, but generally they took part of their higher standards of living in more leisure as they became richer. The implication is a supply curve for labor like that shown in Figure 7.4. After some point, higher wages will induce individuals or the population as a whole to work less, not more.

The supply of labor on any one labor market has a more orthodox shape, however. In the short run there are only so many trained electrical engineers. The short-run supply curve, therefore, is close to a vertical straight line like the one in Figure 7.5. Notice that it tails off at the bottom. The reason is that if engineering wages were terribly low—say a dollar an hour—many engineers would choose to drive trucks or sell ice cream instead of doing the job they were trained for.

In the long run, the supply of electrical engineers depends on alterna-

---

[1] Actually, the total demand curve for electrical engineers will be steeper than the sum of the individual firms' demand curves. As you add to the total number of electrical engineers employed you add to the output of the types of goods they produce. This increased output will result in a fall in the price of those goods. However, we can ignore that complication for now. At any given price for electrical goods, each firm will still employ electrical engineers out to the point where the value of their marginal product still just equals their going salary.

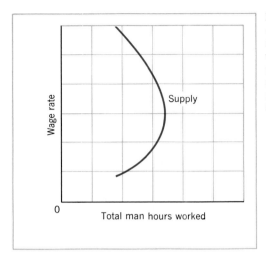

FIGURE 7.4 The amount of labor offered by the population as a whole may not respond much to higher wage rates. In fact, it is possible that people will work less as their wage rates rise. They would be taking part of their higher incomes as leisure time.

tive employment opportunities. Young people starting out could be dentists or accountants or lawyers instead. They will choose electrical engineering only if it is expected to give salaries and other benefits that are as high as, or higher than, what they could earn in their best alternative occupations. There are some people who would be electrical engineers at almost any wage, but their number is limited. To get more people into the profession we have to pay more. The higher the salary, the more young people there will be who will find electrical engineering

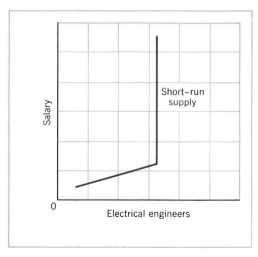

FIGURE 7.5 In the short run the stock of trained workers in a given field is very nearly fixed. At very low wages, though, many would go off into low-skilled jobs.

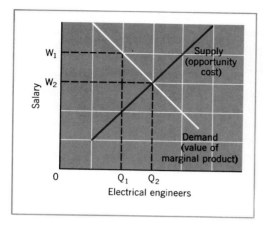

FIGURE 7.6 The long-run supply of labor of any one type slopes upward and to the right because of the differing opportunity costs of different workers. The long-run equilibrium salary equals both the value of the marginal product and the opportunity cost of the last worker hired.

their best bet. In other words, the supply of electrical engineers depends on the potential workers' *opportunity costs*, the highest amount they can earn in any alternative employment. The result is an upward-sloping long-run supply curve like that in Figure 7.6. Any other occupation would have the same sort of curve.

EQUILIBRIUM WAGE RATES

Both the demand and the supply curves for electrical engineers appear in Figure 7.6. The demand curve reflects the values of their marginal products. The long-run supply curve reflects their opportunity costs. Say that in the short run there are too few electrical engineers, perhaps Q_1. Then the going wage will be well above opportunity cost, at W_1. This high pay will attract more people into the field, and the salary will tend to fall. When it reaches W_2, where it just equals the opportunity cost of the last person attracted in, there will be no more tendency to change. We will then be at long-run equilibrium. The same type of analysis could have been applied to office space or Iowa land or waitresses or machinists. In the long run, in competitive factor markets, the wage will equal *both* the value of the marginal product *and* the opportunity cost of the factor involved.

A strong case can be made that competitive factor markets allocate resources in the most efficient possible manner among employments. For one thing, each employer expands his business to the point where the value of the marginal product of each factor he uses just equals its price. As a result, we can't add anything to the value of output by shifting factors from one firm to another. The last electrical engineer hired by

General Electric adds just as much to the value of output there as he would at Westinghouse or at the Little Corner Electric Clock Company. This principle applies in both the short and the long run. A commissar trying to direct labor to different employments couldn't do any better.

In addition, in long-run equilibrium, each worker is in his most productive employment, and we have the right level of employment in each occupation. Each factor is earning a wage at least as high as its opportunity cost. The last man employed in each occupation is earning just what he would earn, and therefore what he would add to the value of output, in his best alternative employment. Our commissar could not add anything to the value of output by shifting workers from one occupation to another. Shifting the last engineer into dentistry would reduce the value of electric clock output *at least* as much as it would increase the value of false tooth production. If all factor markets are competitive and in long-run equilibrium, we get the maximum possible output from our scarce factors of production.

IMPERFECTIONS IN PRACTICE

As usual, competitive factor markets work less perfectly in practice than in theory. Few firms consciously line up marginal products with wage rates. In fact, many managers don't even know what "marginal product" means. Their ignorance of terminology by itself doesn't hurt. Any competitive firm that succeeds in maximizing its profits is equating the values of marginal products with wages in spite of itself.

In practice, however, employers have only a rough idea of what the profit-maximizing combination of inputs would be. They simply make what seem to be "workable" production and employment decisions. They aim at "satisfactory," but not necessarily maximum, profits. For instance, a survey asked southern businessmen how they would respond if local wages were raised to the level of wages in the North. The most common response was that they would increase efficiency. This answer implied that they were not operating in the most efficient way to start with. Faced with a tougher competitive situation they would move closer to the point where marginal products equal factor prices.

Similarly, young people entering the labor market have only a rough idea of what salary levels are like. They are bound to be even vaguer about what the prospects for their chosen occupations will be several years hence, when they will be looking for jobs. Most likely you are preparing for a career. You can check for yourself. Who earns the most and who earns the least in the following list: lawyers, accountants, engineers, and college professors? If you are like half the students in my own classes, you lined them up wrong. You can check the answer in the footnote.[2] If workers regularly guess wrong, they will tend to wind up in jobs where they earn less than they might have received in other employments.

Though these quibbles are important ones, the standard analysis of competitive factor markets still yields a reasonably accurate picture. Even if firms don't precisely equate marginal products and factor prices, they have to come close to doing so. Otherwise they will take losses. For the average manufacturer, profits plus taxes is only about seven percent of sales. The difference between maximizing profits and making "satisfactory" profits in such a case is not very great. This is especially true of firms selling on competitive product markets.

Similarly, even though a majority of workers don't have any clear idea of what their alternatives are, some do. And it takes only a minority of people to make the market work. As long as more people leave poor jobs than leave good ones, labor markets will tend to adjust in the right direction. There is plenty of evidence that they do. For instance, net migration is quite consistently out of low-wage states and into high-wage states. Nevertheless, workers, like everyone else, sometimes make mistakes. Also, most people are not very mobile after they get past their twenties. While average wages probably do tend to reflect marginal products and opportunity costs, there are many people in this country who are in the wrong employments.

INEQUALITY

The behavior of factor markets is the subject of much concern. Factor markets determine the distribution of income, an issue about which people have strong opinions. How equitably incomes will be distributed depends on how well different individuals are endowed, and on what those endowments can earn on factor markets.

[2] Lawyers earn the most and accountants earn the least. According to the 1970 census, median earnings were $19,466 for lawyers, $13,520 for engineers, $12,215 for college professors, and $11,639 for accountants. However, the rates of pay in these professions will undoubtedly have changed by the time the people now in school have finished their training. For instance, professors' salaries were relatively high at the time of the census because of the shortage in the 1960s. They will probably rise less during the 1970s than those in some other professions.

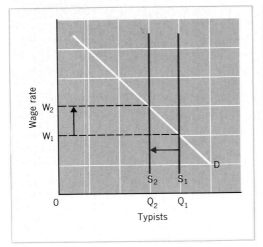
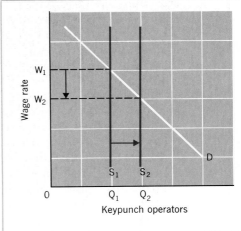

FIGURES 7.7 AND 7.8 In the long run, differences in pay for jobs requiring equal ability will tend to disappear on competitive labor markets. Workers will tend to leave low-paying jobs (typists) and move into better-paying jobs (keypunch operators).

WAGE DIFFERENCES

To some extent, competitive markets tend to move us toward greater equality. Consider the markets for typists and keypunch operators, represented in Figures 7.7 and 7.8. At first, the short-run supplies (S_1) interact with the demands to yield a higher wage for keypunch operators. But this situation can't last. The two jobs require about the same degrees of skill, so the greater wage for keypunching will tend to attract labor away from typing. And as the shift occurs, wages will tend to fall for keypunch operators and rise for typists. Eventually they will be about equal, at W_2. That point should approximate long-run equilibrium.

The same results hold if Figure 7.8 represents conditions in a low-wage state such as Arkansas, while Figure 7.7 refers to a high-wage state such as California. Again, the flow of labor between factor markets will tend to equalize wages of persons with equal abilities. Such adjustments don't occur instantaneously. They may take generations, and before they are complete new changes in demand will occur. Interstate income levels have been moving toward equality for the last four decades, but they still have a way to go.

This story will carry us only so far. Consider the markets for structural steel workers who must work on girders many stories above the street and those of the rest of us who work on the ground. The structural steel

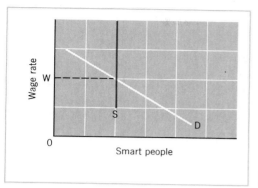
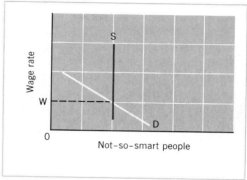

FIGURES 7.9 AND 7.10 Wages of smart people tend to be higher than wages of not-so-smart people, but in this case there is no way for workers in the low-paid category to shift into the high-paid one.

workers earn more per hour, but most of the rest of us crane our necks and say "they can have it." Even in the long run, wage rates will not equalize if there are differences in the attractiveness of jobs over and above the wages. Wage rates for indoor work tend to be lower than wages for comparable work at ten below zero or 100° above out of doors. Similarly, jobs that are very unstable because of the weather or business fluctuations tend to pay more per hour than steady jobs.

An important element in the character of a job is the amount of training it requires. If an employer insists on hiring people with four years of college he will have to pay more than for workers taken right out of high school. Economists have examined salary differences among the professions. They compared the training costs for different professions, including the potential income given up while the trainee is in school. These costs turn out to be quite close to the differences in the capitalized values of the worker's lifetime income in most cases. In other words, investments in medical or legal or engineering educations yield about the same rates of return as investments in stocks and bonds.

Some wage differences reflect differences in the natural endowments of the persons involved. Consider the markets for smart people and for not-so-smart people, in Figures 7.9 and 7.10. In this case the wage rate differs greatly. The reason is that their marginal products differ. If this difference were something you could adjust for by going to school or to a beauty salon this wage difference would tend to fall to a level reflecting the cost of adjustment. But it cannot possibly do so. We were made with these differences, and they won't go away. Even in competitive markets, we can expect inequality in wage rates that comes from more than just the differences in the attractiveness or training requirements of different jobs.

Finally, in the real world there are barriers between jobs that arise because of human institutions. Some of the best jobs in society have fences built around them by trade unions or state occupational licensing laws. The wage rates in plumbing or medicine are high enough to attract lots of us in. However, most of us can't get there, because the United Brotherhood of Plumbers and Pipefitters and the state board of medical examiners have set difficult requirements for entry. At the same time, some of the worst jobs are filled by women and blacks because widespread discrimination in employment has kept them out of better-paying jobs.

THE EXTENT OF INEQUALITY

A good deal of information is available on the degree of inequality in modern society. Figure 7.11 shows the distribution of income among American families in 1970. Technically it is a **Lorenz curve.** It shows the cumulative percentages of total income earned by cumulative percentages of all families, starting with the poorest. For instance, the poorest 20 percent of the families earn only 5.5 percent of all family income after taxes. The poorest 40 percent earn 17.5 percent of family income. The poorest 60 percent earn 34.9 percent, and the poorest 95 percent (that is, all but the richest five percent) earn 85.6 percent of all family income. If there were perfect equality, the Lorenz curve would be a straight

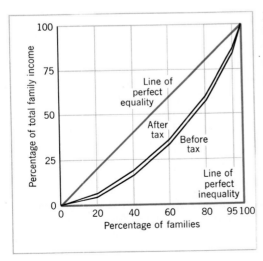

FIGURE 7.11 Lorenz curves show the percentage of total personal income received by successively richer percentages of all families. The more bowed such a curve is, the less equally distributed income is.

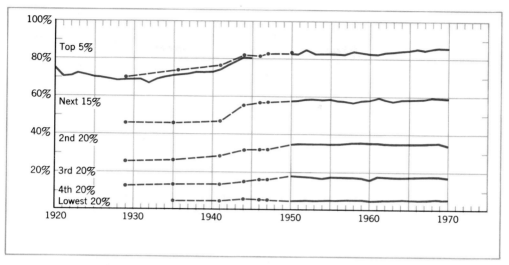

FIGURE 7.12   There has been one significant change in American income distribution since 1920, a shift to greater equality during the World War II period. Otherwise the shares of the various income classes have remained remarkably stable.

diagonal line from the "southwest" to the "northeast" corners. If there were complete inequality, the curve would trace out the "southeast" boundary of the chart. No one would receive any income except the richest family. In general, the more bowed the curve, the greater the inequality.

The outer of the two black lines in Figure 7.11 shows the distribution of incomes before the personal income tax; the inner line shows after-tax incomes. The American income tax has little effect on the distribution of incomes. American after-tax incomes are somewhat less equally distributed than those in Scandinavia. But they are more equally distributed than incomes in most other non-Communist countries.

American incomes have become more equally distributed over the years. Figure 7.12 traces out the shares of the various income groups since the 1920s. Most of the change occurred during World War II. Since then, income shares have remained remarkably stable.

REASONS FOR INEQUALITY

Competitive factor markets do allocate resources efficiently, but you don't have to like the income distribution that results. If everyone earned just his marginal product, then the insane and the infirm—who can produce very little—would starve. Practically everyone would find such a distribution of income unacceptable.

Why does inequality exist? Some of it is only temporary. In any one year some people will do very well, and others will report low incomes because of illness, unemployment, retirement, student status, or plain bad luck. Lifetime incomes will be more equally distributed. Even on a lifetime basis, however, a great deal of inequality still exists.

Part of the reason for this inequality in incomes is the difference in the attractiveness of jobs. But this argument doesn't get us very far. By and large, the nicest jobs are also the best-paying ones. It is the well-to-do who generally have the air conditioned offices.

Much of the inequality is due to differences in ability and training. Table 7.3 shows annual earnings by race, sex, and education in 1970. Read down any column and you will find income rising with education. But Table 7.3 also shows the effect of some of the barriers between jobs. Read across any row and you will find that women earn less than men, and that black men earn less than white men of the same educational class. Black women do as well as white women partly because a much larger proportion of white women workers are wives who do not have jobs at all or who work only part-time.

Monopoly on product and factor markets also contributes to inequal-

TABLE 7.3   Median incomes* of persons 25 and older (1970)

YEARS OF SCHOOL COMPLETED	WHITES		BLACKS	
	MALES	FEMALES	MALES	FEMALES
1–7 years	$3,786	$1,440	$3,168	$1,290
8 years	$5,536	$1,815	$4,340	$1,605
9–11 years	$7,591	$2,388	$5,617	$2,395
12 years	$8,960	$3,380	$6,380	$3,491
1–3 years of college	$10,048	$3,616	$8,083	$4,558
4 or more years of college	$12,840	$5,995	$9,290	$7,744

*The median income is the income earned by that person who is at the midpoint of the income distribution in each grouping. Half the people in each of the groups earn more than the median, and half earn less. The median income should be distinguished from the mean, or average, income. The mean income is the total income of each group divided by the number of persons in the group. The median income of a group is usually lower than the mean, because there are ordinarily some individuals in the group with very high incomes. They pull the mean up but do not affect the median.

ity. Most of the great fortunes were created by the formation of monopolies. Whether or not the rich still own stock in the monopolistic firms, they originally got their wealth from them. The mere existence of monopoly acts to keep the rest of us poor. As we saw in Chapter 6, we pay more for the goods produced by monopolistic industries. At the same time, by restricting output, monopoly reduces the employment opportunities in the high-paying industries. It thereby keeps too many people in the low-paying trades. Output is restricted in automobiles and steel, for instance. As a result, too many people are competing for jobs in competitive fields such as agriculture and textiles.

There is good evidence, too, that monopolistic industries discriminate more than others. Competitive firms must take every employment advantage they can, just to stay profitable. Monopolists generally pay high wages and pick and choose to get "desirable" employees. Race seems to be one element of "desirability" for many employers. At least, the percentage of minority employees in good jobs in concentrated industries is much lower than that in unconcentrated industries. Monopolists are not necessarily more racist or sexist than the rest of us. They are just under less competitive pressure to minimize costs.

Powerful trade unions have similar effects on factor markets. By raising wages in the industries they control, they keep too many workers in nonunion industries. Wage rates in those industries are lower as a result. Moreover, some unions have long-standing policies of excluding minority groups. This is particularly true of the unions in highly skilled trades. This is part of the reason why poverty is heavily concentrated in the nonunion, unconcentrated fields, such as agriculture and the services. Workers in these lines would do better in other industries, but they cannot get in.

THE DISTRIBUTION OF WEALTH

A large part of the very high incomes in this country comes from property, such as stocks, bonds, and real estate. Figure 7.13 shows Lorenz curves for before-tax income and for personal wealth in 1970. Personal **wealth** is defined as individually-owned assets minus debt.

The wealth curve in Figure 7.13 refers to nonhuman wealth, such as stocks and bonds. But the most important asset for most people is themselves—their inherited talents and acquired skills. Nature did not distribute talent nearly so unevenly as nonhuman wealth is distributed. An occasional person may be two or even three times as smart or pretty or strong as the average one, but very rich people have hundreds of times as much property as the average person owns. You can add to your

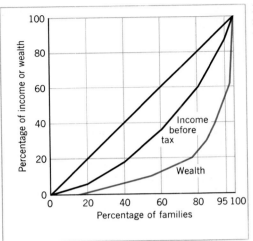

FIGURE 7.13   Wealth in the United
States is much less equally distributed than income is.

human capital a bit by investing in health care and education, but these
investments have severely diminishing returns. Your mind and body are
strictly fixed factors. After a point, more trips to the doctor or another
year of school won't add much to your productivity. On the other hand,
you can go on piling up stocks and bonds indefinitely with no decline in
their rate of return. As a result, human capital could not possibly be so
unevenly distributed as nonhuman wealth is.

In the case of nonhuman capital, by contrast, parents can transfer

Nonhuman capital can also be passed from generation to generation.
Human capital is "fully depreciated" by the end of a person's life; one
can't pass it on to his children. The children will inherit some more or
less valuable talents, and one can certainly make *new* investments in
their health and education. But few parents can, by their own efforts,
provide their children with human capital that will yield as much as
$20,000 or $30,000 a year in this way. Most parents, even among the rich,
cannot provide their children with even that much human capital.

In the case of nonhuman capital, by contrast, parents can transfer
everything they own to their children except for the tax collectors' cut.
Their stocks and bonds and real estate do not die with them the way their
talents and training do. The next generation can start with the total that
was accumulated in their parents' lifetimes and build from there. As a
result, nonhuman capital *can* accumulate from generation to generation.
It may grow very large in some families. A large proportion of the people
who now have great wealth owe their fortunes mainly to the head start
they received through inheritance.

Wealth is even less equally distributed in England than it is in the

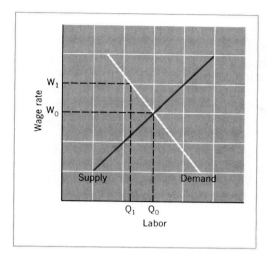

FIGURE 7.14 A minimum wage law, setting the wage at W_1, would reduce employment opportunities in any occupation in which the law affected the wages actually paid.

United States. However, over time, the distribution of wealth there is becoming somewhat more equal. It also became more equal in the United States between 1929 and 1949, but since then we seem to have been moving in the opposite direction again. Inequality in wealth is increasing while income distribution remains about constant. This development is at least partly due to the fact that the rich are taking a large part of their income in capital gains, which contribute to wealth but are not included in reported income.[3]

INCOME DISTRIBUTION POLICIES

What is the right distribution of income? This is almost entirely a matter of value judgment. There seems to be fairly widespread agreement, though, that greater equality would be a good thing if nothing else were to change. I have taken votes on this subject in my classes regularly, and invariably the vast majority has voted in favor of greater equality.

But how to get there? We have tried various routes. All of them are imperfect, and some of them are positively counterproductive.

MINIMUM WAGE LAWS

One possibility is the minimum wage law, which prohibits employers from paying less than a specified wage rate. The effect of this law is analyzed in Figure 7.14. If the minimum wage is set below W_0 it won't

[3] A capital gain is an increase in the value of an asset during the period it is owned. Capital gains are taxed at a lower rate than other income.

make any difference. The market-determined wage will prevail. At a higher level, such as W_1, the minimum wage law will have an effect. However, it is not at all certain that it will make for greater equality. The people who still have jobs may be better off, but employment opportunities covered by the law will fall from Q_0 to Q_1. This drop could mean greater unemployment, or it could merely mean that more people will be in uncovered occupations such as baby-sitting or self-employment. Either way, the people squeezed out by the minimum wage will be poorer.

In practice, the United States minimum wage is so low that it does not affect most factory workers. The occupations that it does affect are those of blacks, teen-agers, women, and some low-paid workers in the South. Some of these people's jobs may evaporate if the minimum wage rate rises. Minimum wage laws make industries less inclined to move to low-wage regions, because they can no longer benefit from the plentiful labor there. As a result, too many people are left hoeing corn on the hillside. Again, there is evidence that black teen-age unemployment rates go up when the minimum wage is raised. In general, a minimum wage law may well make inequality more severe, rather than less so.

If a minimum wage does limit the employment possibilities of many of the poor, it makes the economy less efficient in the process. If the poor are forced into unemployment or into jobs where they are less productive than they might be, their contribution to our total output is reduced accordingly. A major source of our economic growth through history has been the shift of excess labor out of agriculture and other low-productivity employment. If minimum wage laws affect mobility at all, they act to impede this shift.

THE GOVERNMENT BUDGET AND INEQUALITY

A second approach to changing the distribution of income is through the government budget. The federal, state, and local governments together collect about a third of the GNP in taxes and pay it out in expenditures. Incomes will be more or less equally distributed depending on who pays those taxes and who benefits from those expenditures.

On the tax side, incomes would be more equally distributed after tax than before if the rich paid a higher percentage of their incomes in taxes than the poor. This is true of the income tax, the most important federal tax. Even there, however, the change in income distribution due to the tax is small, as we saw in Figure 7.11. The personal income tax accounts for only a little over a third of all tax revenues, however. Many of the other taxes fall as heavily on the poor as on the rich. And some taxes collect a larger percentage of poor people's incomes than of rich people's incomes. This is especially true of state and local taxes. Altogether, the degree of income inequality is little affected by taxes.

Taxes certainly do affect the distribution of income among individuals, however. Some pay much more than a third of their incomes in taxes. Others pay far less. How much each person pays depends on how he earns his income, whether he owns his home or rents, what sorts of goods and services he consumes, how much he saves, what state and city he lives in, and many other things. But there just isn't any systematic tendency for taxes to fall more heavily on the rich as a group than on the poor, or vice versa. Some rich people pay lots of taxes, but so do some poor people. And there are others in both groups who pay low taxes. Each of the major taxes and whom it hits hardest will be discussed in Chapter 10.

The government also affects the degree of inequality through its transfer payments and the services it provides to different people. The overall effect of these expenditure programs is to make living standards more nearly equal. One reason is that some (though not all) of the transfer payment programs go mainly to the poor. Another reason is that many public services are available on an almost equal basis to everyone, regardless of income. For instance, everyone has access to primary and secondary education with no tuition charges. This service represents only a small percentage increase in standards of living for the rich, but free grade school and high school is a very large percentage increase in the standards of living of the poor. The effect of government expenditure programs will also be discussed in Chapter 10.

REDUCING BARRIERS TO MOBILITY

A third approach to reducing income inequality is to eliminate the barriers that prevent movement between occupations. If we all had equal chances to be plumbers or doctors, their wages would be less out of line with those of other workers. If women and blacks had equal chances at good jobs with the rest of our population, there would be fewer poor people.

In many cases, the barriers to entry into the good jobs are more than just discrimination in employment. To get a good job you must have access to a suitable education. An important reason why the poor stay poor from generation to generation is that they do not have those educational opportunities. The special training needed for a good job often requires an investment of money that the poor do not have. A strong case can be made for having public grants and loans to cover such investments.

But even if people have a free choice of employments when they start out, many will still wind up in the wrong jobs. In some cases they just make mistakes. In other cases the jobs that looked good at age twenty turn out to be poor jobs later on because of such things as technical change, shifts in consumer tastes, or new competition from abroad. Ideally, these people should switch to new jobs, and perhaps to a new part of the country. But such changes are often difficult, especially for people over 40. One way to reduce the inequality that results from these changes would be for the government to help finance retraining and moving. The federal government has had a manpower training program since 1962. Economists have found that, on the average, people who took part in the program improved their economic positions as compared with similar persons who did not.

There would be a similar case for a relocation program. The government could help pay moving expenses for those seeking to leave depressed areas. Some countries, notably Sweden, have gone a long way in this direction. We do have a demonstration program, but it is tiny: only five million dollars a year. Congressmen are generally unenthusiastic about programs that help their constituents move away.

The removal of barriers to mobility would help reduce inequality. It would also improve the allocation of resources. With fewer barriers we will make better use of our peoples' abilities; we will get more output out of our total resources. Even the most ardent advocate of laissez faire capitalism should find this approach to greater equality attractive.

INCOME SUPPORT AND EMPLOYMENT

Even in a fully competitive labor market, with no barriers to mobility, there would still be a great deal of inequality. Some people have such low marginal products that they are bound to be poor so long as what they earn depends on what they can add to output. This is true of the aged, the severely disabled, the insane, and many mothers who have young children and no husbands. Our main way of dealing with this source of inequality is through direct government payments. These measures will be discussed in the next chapter.

Another important reason for low incomes and inequality is unemployment. Equality increased in this country in the early 1940s. One major reason was the reduction in unemployment that occurred with World War II. Since the war, we have always had higher levels of employment than we did in the 1930s. Policies to maintain high levels of employment will be discussed in Chapters 12 through 17.

SUMMARY

The demand for factor services depends on their marginal productivities. The supply depends on their opportunity costs. In competitive factor markets the price tends to settle where it equals both the value of the marginal product and opportunity cost. The result is a system that allocates factors to their most efficient employments. The system works imperfectly because of poor information. Still, wages tend to reflect marginal products and opportunity costs even if only some of the participants in the market are well informed and only some workers are mobile.

The distribution of income that would result from well-working factor markets would be quite unequal. The reason is partly that people differ in their factor endowments and partly that there are barriers to movement between jobs. Many of the barriers are man-made. They include union rules and state licensing laws that keep most people out of good jobs. They also include discrimination that keeps women and blacks in poor jobs. The differing factor endowment is partially due to nature, but much of it is man-made also. Much of the difference between the poor and the middle class comes from differing investments in human capital, such as health care and education. The high incomes of the very rich are largely due to their ownership of large amounts of property.

The distribution of income in the United States has become somewhat more equal over the last half century, primarily because of a large change during World War II. It has remained remarkably stable since the war. Property is far less equally distributed than income, partly because individuals can accumulate more of it than of human capital, and partly because it can be passed from generation to generation.

Various efforts have been made to reduce inequality. Minimum wage laws do little to make incomes more equal. They may actually make them less so, because they reduce the employment opportunities of the poor. Taxes do not affect the degree of income inequality much, because they fall about as heavily on the poor as on the rich. But government transfer programs and services do make for greater equality. The removal of barriers to entry into good jobs and the provision of better education to the poor would work both to increase equality and to improve the allocation of resources. But even with more equal opportunities and greater mobility, there would still be a good deal of inequality. Income assistance for the disadvantaged and policies to keep unemployment low are important means of increasing equality further.

STUDY QUESTIONS

1   Go back to Table 2.2 on page 37. Work out the marginal product of labor at the various levels of employment shown there. Now work out the value of the marginal product assuming that potatoes sell for four dollars a bushel. What would be the most profitable level of employment if the wage were $80 a year? Does that wage sound a little low? I told you I didn't know much about growing potatoes. The example clearly assumed South Asian or eighteenth-century technology.

2   Would you mow my lawn for 20¢ per hour? For 50¢ per hour? For $1.00 per hour? For $2.00 per hour? For $5.00 per hour? Or what? What considerations determined the wage at which you were willing to take the job? Would the wage at which you would take the job have been different if you were a peasant in India? Why?

3   Check the footnote on page 183. Median incomes ranged from $11,639 for accountants to $19,466 for lawyers in 1970. In spite of the wide range in expected incomes, there were lots of students starting out in all four of those professions in 1970. In two or three cases it turns out that more students were entering professional training than would be able to find jobs a few years later. Why did anyone train to be an accountant, engineer, or college professor when the average lawyer could earn so much more?

4   Over most of the 1940s, 1950s, and 1960s, the lower ranks of the army were filled by the draft. Today we have a volunteer army. Buck privates earn more than twice as much as they did in the late 1960s. This big raise seems to have been necessary to get adequate numbers of enlistees when the draft was abandoned. Compare the draft with a volunteer army in terms of equity. Who pays for the army now? Did the same people pay for it during the draft? (Hint: What did it cost the draftees to be in the army?) Now compare the two systems in terms of efficiency. How much civilian output was lost by using the draft to select workers to be put in the army? Is more or less civilian output sacrificed when we fill the army using voluntary enlistments? (Hint: What is the opportunity cost of enlistees? Was that also the opportunity cost of draftees?) One concern that has been expressed recently is that a disproportionate number of the volunteers turn out to be black. Why should this be?

5   What effect do you think the following had or would have on the extent of income inequality in the United States:

☐ the draft

☐ social security

☐ large-scale unemployment

☐ laws prohibiting discrimination by sex or race in employment

FURTHER READING

Good places to read further on the workings of the labor market are Richard Freeman, *Labor Economics* (Englewood Cliffs, N.J.: Prentice-Hall, 1972) and Allan Cartter and F. Ray Marshall, *Labor Economics*, rev. ed. (Homewood, Ill.: Irwin, 1972). Both are good texts on the subject. Edward Budd, *Inequality and Poverty* (New York: Norton, 1968) contains a good set of readings on the degree of inequality and what might be done about it.

8
POVERTY
AND
RACE

Regardless of how they feel about the degree of inequality in the country, most people are offended by the persistence of poverty in a nation as rich as ours. In this chapter we will discuss that problem, giving special emphasis to the position of minority groups.

THE EXTENT OF POVERTY

THE MEANING OF POVERTY

What constitutes poverty is a matter of definition. For the last fifteen years our government has had one. For an urban family of four, poverty was defined as an income below $4,275 in 1973, or the amount that would buy the same standard of living in other years. The government statisticians adjust this income level for larger or smaller families and for people living on the farm, where living costs are lower.

The official poverty level is essentially arbitrary. By this standard, half of our population would have been poor in 1929. At the turn of the century a family with a standard of living comparable to what $4,250 will buy now would have been considered well-off. We have obviously changed our idea of what constitutes poverty as we have become richer.

Yet a $4,250 income means a very low standard of living. It would provide a family of four with a diet long on starches and including only occasional cheap cuts of meat. They would probably live in slum dwellings. Such an income does provide a black-and-white television set, but probably not a car. Families with incomes of $4,275 spend, on the

average, a third of their incomes on food, compared with eighteen percent for the rest of us. They still do not eat very well. Of course, many of
the poor receive less than $4,275.

THE INCIDENCE OF POVERTY

In 1970, 12.5 percent of the American population was "poor" by official
standards. Some of these people were only temporarily poor. They
included businessmen who had had a very bad year and workers who
were temporarily unemployed. Students and retired people often have
incomes below the poverty line, though their incomes are higher over
most of their lifetimes. Nevertheless, surveys have shown that the majority of the American poor are poor for most of their lives. By and large,
Americans don't *become* poor except for short periods. Most of our poor
were born into poor families and stayed that way.

Poverty is not evenly distributed over the population. Most of the poor
are that way for very real reasons. In 1970, about 21 percent of the aged
were poor, 38 percent of those in households headed by women were
poor, and 32 percent of the non-whites were poor. These figures compare with only seven percent of those in households headed by white
males of working age. In short, very few of the poor are that way by
choice.

In two thirds of the poor families in 1970, at least one person had a job.
Some 32 percent of the farmers were poor, as were 33 percent of those in
personal service work, such as housecleaning or baby-sitting. Only four
percent of factory workers were poor by the government's standards.
Only a minority of the poor—less than a third of them—were on welfare.

Forty percent of the poor were children. Going by past experience, a
large proportion of these children will remain poor when they grow up.
The nutritional, medical, and educational environment of poverty keeps
them that way. Poverty is a long-term trap.

Measured by an absolute standard, poverty in this country is decreasing. In 1959, 22.4 percent of all Americans were poor (using the official
standard adjusted for changes in the cost of living). By 1970 this number
was down to 12.6 percent. At these rates of change, poverty would
disappear completely by the mid-1980s. But it is doubtful that it actually
will. Poverty is falling much more slowly in some groups than in the
country as a whole. Though the overall percentage of our population in
poverty was nearly cut in half between 1959 and 1970, the percentage of
persons who were poor in families headed by women fell only from 50.2
percent to 38.4 percent. Most of the reduction in poverty has been due to

the general growth of the country; the degree of inequality has remained practically constant.

WHAT TO DO ABOUT POVERTY

For the able-bodied poor of working age, the best solution to poverty is to make them eligible for better jobs. One way to do this is to reduce the barriers restricting their chances for the good jobs. But more is needed. The poor have low marginal products because of inadequate health and education. For migrant farm laborers, poor southern farmers, and ghetto dwellers to make it onto the American gravy train, they have to have better nutrition and education than are currently available.

TRANSFER PAYMENTS

Many of the poor could not earn good incomes even if they had adequate opportunities and educations. This is clearly true of the aged, the disabled, and women with young children. Yet hardly anyone would let these people starve simply because of their low marginal products. Even where there is an able-bodied male present, if his productivity is very low his poverty is imposed on his family as well as himself.

Such poverty calls for **transfer payments,** payments for which no services or goods are received. We have a maze of transfer payment programs in this country, but they work imperfectly. In 1970 all government transfers to individuals cost $78 billion at the federal, state, or local level. But much of this money did not reach the poor. The largest program is social security. It is estimated that 63 percent of the social security beneficiaries would be poor without these payments. But many of them would have property, particularly houses, to supplement their low incomes. The next largest transfer payment program is veterans' pensions. Some 54 percent of the recipients would *not* be poor if the program did not exist.

Since a large proportion of the American poor are on the farm, one might think that the agricultural programs would serve as means of reducing poverty, but they do very little. Price supports and farm subsidies are distributed roughly in proportion to the amounts that farmers sell or the amounts of land that they can retire. Poor farmers have little land. They produce very little and consume a large part of what they do produce, so much of their output never reaches the market. Most of the Department of Agriculture's help, therefore, goes to the larger farms. The top twenty percent of the farmers are estimated to receive 67 percent of the boodle. These people are seldom rich by urban standards, but most of them would qualify as middle-class. The farm poor receive little agricultural assistance. Hired farm laborers receive none at all.

IN-KIND TRANSFERS

Many of our transfer programs provide help **in kind.** That is, the government gives goods or services instead of money. The largest such program is Medicare, a federal health insurance program covering persons eligible for social security. It has been estimated that only about a third of the people helped by this program would be poor without it (though 63 percent of them would be poor if they lacked both social security and Medicare). A related program is Medicaid, which finances medical services for welfare recipients in many states. One probable effect of Medicare and Medicaid has been to increase the incomes of doctors. In many cases they served the poor anyway before Medicare and Medicaid came along, often on a low- or no-fee basis. Now they can charge full fees for their services.

A second in-kind program distributes food to the poor. There are several such programs, but by far the most important is food stamps. These coupons are distributed free to families with no income. They are sold to other families with incomes under $4,000, at prices that depend on income. The percentage of income charged for the stamps rises with income itself, until it reaches 27 percent in the $2,000 to $4,000 income class. In all cases the stamps are worth more in groceries than the recipients pay for them. Food stamps are available on the same basis throughout the country to anyone with a low enough income, whether he has a job or children or not. The food stamp program has grown very rapidly in recent years. Congress seems more willing to give food than money to the poor. A major purpose of the food stamp program, at least when it began, was to keep up the demand for farm products.

A third in-kind transfer program is public housing. We spend a half a billion dollars a year on low-cost housing projects, mostly in our big cities. The results have been mixed. Those who get into the projects benefit from low rents, but the poorest people are seldom eligible, because participants must pay a portion of the costs. In general, public housing projects have involved the destruction of more housing units than they replace. Rents for nonparticipants have therefore been forced up. The housing projects have provided employment for builders, and they have sometimes improved the looks of the central cities. But their help to the poor has been less clear. In the late 1960s the government began leasing existing housing for the poor and paying them rent subsidies. Both of these programs have as yet been quite small.

In general, transfers in kind have often missed the mark. They have frequently been expensive for what they did achieve. A major reason is that these programs have often been meant to benefit other groups, such as the builders and the farmers, at least as much as they did the poor.

Another reason why in-kind transfers are an expensive way to aid the poor is that they limit consumer choice. Say the apartments in a government housing project rent for $100 less than they cost. This $100-dollar discount gives the occupant something, but probably not as much as $100 in cash would.[1] With the cash itself he could live elsewhere. He could put some of the money into more food or bus fares if he preferred. The money is worth more to the recipient because it can be spent on the things that seem most valuable. Putting it another way, the cost of providing a given standard of living for a poor family is lower if the government gives them money than if it gives them things. Give the gift that means the most: cash.

WELFARE

An increasing portion of our transfer programs is in the form of direct money payments to poor people. These programs include aid to families with dependent children and various programs to aid the blind, the disabled, and the aged not eligible for social security. Altogether, these programs came to $14.5 billion in 1970. That figure is less than a quarter of the total of social security, Medicare, and veterans' benefits. We will refer to this group of programs as **welfare.** Welfare payments grew rapidly throughout the 1960s, because benefits rose while eligibility standards were made easier. And still, only 29.5 percent of the poor families in 1970 received welfare payments.

Welfare is the subject of great controversy. In most states, families with an able-bodied man present are not eligible for payments. One result is that welfare provides an incentive for the breakup of families. A man can improve his wife's income by abandoning her. Also, about fifteen percent of the total cost of welfare comes from administration of the programs. A large part of this expense is for checking on recipients' eligibility. Eligibility and the level of benefits vary from state to state. Some of the poorer states have benefits so low that even those who receive them are still in deep poverty. One result of the differences

---

[1] In a few extreme cases, in-kind transfers turn out to be worth nothing at all to the recipients. A few public housing projects have had such low occupancy rates that they have had to be torn down. The poor preferred to live elsewhere in spite of the subsidy.

between state programs is that they create an incentive for the poor to move to the more generous states.

As welfare is usually administered it leaves recipients little incentive to work. Until 1967, welfare brought the incomes of eligible persons up to some specified level. Any time they earned anything, their welfare checks were reduced by the same amount. Under rules adopted in 1967, the welfare check falls by only two thirds of such earnings. In other words, someone on welfare can now keep 33¢ out of every dollar he earns. Since working costs something in bus fares, baby-sitting, and the like, people who couldn't earn more than the amount of their welfare checks anyway still have little reason to work. As a result of such perverse incentives, welfare can create permanent paupers.

THE NEGATIVE INCOME TAX

An alternative to welfare that has been proposed by both liberals and conservatives is the **negative income tax.** The personal income tax falls on income above certain levels that are determined by the number of personal and dependent exemptions. Because of those exemptions it seldom affects people with incomes in the poverty range. The negative income tax plan proposes that the government make transfer payments *to* people whose incomes fall below some specified level. In other words, the government would make up some of the difference between poverty incomes and the specified levels.

Figures 8.1 and 8.2 may make the proposal clearer. Figure 8.1 illustrates the present situation for families that are not on welfare. Earned income is the diagonal straight line. (In effect, the graph just says that at any given income level, you receive that many dollars.) But now the income tax steps in; the red line shows the income after tax. Low incomes are entirely covered by exemptions, so there is no tax on them. At these levels, earned income and income after tax are the same thing. But at some point the exemptions run out. From there on up, after-tax income rises more slowly than earned income.

Figure 8.2 adds the negative income tax. (For simplicity, the negative tax is shown as ending at precisely the income level where the regular, positive tax begins. This coincidence isn't necessary, however.) With the negative income tax, families below the cutoff point receive transfer payments to bring them up to the dark line. Families with no earned income at all receive a basic grant to live on. As they earn more money, the transfer payments they receive fall. For instance, say the basic grant is $3,000 a family, and the tax rate is 50 percent. Then a family with no earnings would receive $3,000. One that earned $1,000 would receive a

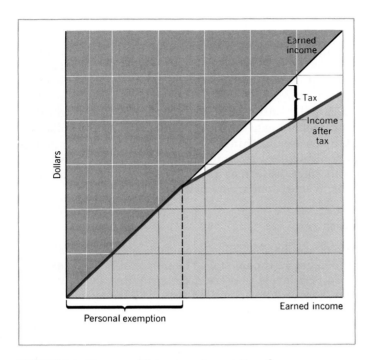

**FIGURE 8.1   Because of the personal exemption, the very poor pay
little or no income tax. For incomes above the level of the personal
exemption, after-tax income rises more slowly than earned income.**

transfer payment of $2,500, bringing its total receipts to $3,500. Total
receipts would continue to rise by 50¢ for every additional dollar earned,
up to the cutoff point of $6,000.

One of the arguments for the negative income tax is that it gives the
recipient incentive to work. It certainly does, compared with welfare.
However, many of the people who would be eligible for transfer payments under the negative income tax are not now receiving welfare. The
additional payments to them would reduce their incentives to work, if
anything. Their incomes would be higher than before, so they might
decide to take more leisure. A tax rate of 50 percent on anything they did
earn would further reduce their incentive. We could increase the incentive to work by lowering the tax rate—for instance, by having the transfer
fall by only 33¢ for every extra dollar earned. But the cost to the government rises rapidly as the tax rate falls. With the same basic grant of
$3,000 but a tax rate of 33 percent, every family earning less than $9,000
would receive some kind of transfer.

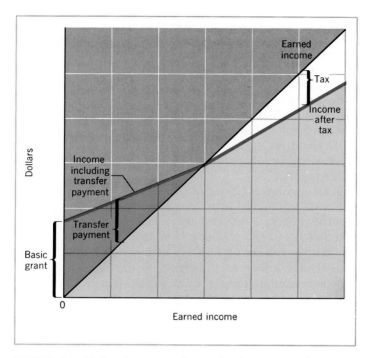

Earned income

Tax

Income after tax

Dollars

Income including transfer payment

Transfer payment

Basic grant

0

Earned income

FIGURE 8.2 Under the proposed negative income tax, the poor would receive government payments if their income falls below a specified level.

Incentives to work should be particularly weak if we were to retain in-kind transfers at the same time we adopted a negative income tax. Food stamps, public housing, and many aids to education are all available only to persons with incomes below specified levels. Taking all of these benefits into account, a poor family might be better off staying poor than earning an income only slightly above these levels. This could be the case even if the negative income tax rate were quite low.

The negative income tax *would* help to keep families intact, because all families would be eligible, including families with male heads. It should also reduce administrative costs, since everyone with low incomes would be eligible. And it would not exclude people who were too proud to apply for welfare or people in states that have very restrictive welfare laws.

The negative income tax would almost certainly help reduce poverty and distribute incomes more equally. But it would cost the government more than welfare does, because it would apply to many people who are not now covered. It would also make transfers to many more people with low, but not poverty, incomes. Some people in high-income states are concerned because the basic grant is likely to be smaller than the welfare payments that they are already providing. Furthermore, the overall effect of the program would be to transfer large amounts of money from the rich states to the poorer ones. (Most people in the rich states would be paying tax, while many in the poor states would be receiving payments.) Others worry that the negative income tax would serve to encourage the birth of additional children, because the basic grant would rise with family size. However, at present the same criticism is true of both welfare and the regular income tax.

A limited negative income tax program was proposed by the Nixon administration in 1970 and again in 1971, but neither bill was passed. However, some of the programs that already exist have taken on features of the negative income tax in recent years. Though a majority of the poor don't participate in the welfare program, welfare recipients can now keep a third of any income they earn. In 1973 Congress established a Supplemental Security Income program that replaced a variety of programs for the disabled, the blind, and the aged with a negative income tax. The large and controversial group containing able-bodied persons of working age was not affected by the program. All of the poor *are* eligible for food stamps. And the net transfers involved in food stamps decrease as the recipients' incomes rise. We seem to be gradually introducing the negative income tax by the back door.

An alternative to welfare or the negative income tax is the family allowance. Most of the Western European countries and such other countries as Canada have had these payments for years. They give fixed sums per child to *every* family. A family allowance program is even more costly than a negative income tax that transfers the same amount of money only to the poor. Moreover, family allowances provide all families with an incentive to have more children.

MINORITY GROUPS AND POVERTY

Perhaps the most serious domestic problem facing the United States today is the position of minority groups. Minorities have a disproportionate share of poverty. Half the American Indians, a third of the blacks, and a quarter of the persons with Spanish surnames are poor by the official definitions. These groups together account for 30 percent of the poor. We will focus on the blacks here simply because blacks account for 70 percent of all these minorities. Much of what is said applies to other groups as well.

The poverty of minority groups is long-standing, but it has become more noticeable as they have crowded into the centers of our large cities in the years since World War II. The problems of deteriorating urban life are closely associated with that of minority poverty.

THE ORIGINS OF BLACK POVERTY

The most important fact of black history is that blacks have always been second-class citizens or worse in America. Unlike other groups who came as hopeful immigrants and were able to battle their way into the middle class within a few generations, the blacks came as slaves and were kept that way. Only eleven percent were free on the eve of the Civil War, in 1860. Most of the slaves seem to have been adequately fed and cared for, and some were trained in valuable skills. By and large they were treated as the valuable assets that they were, but hardly as prospective free men. It was a felony in most southern states to teach slaves to read. Just four generations ago, in 1870, 80 percent of the black population was illiterate, compared with twelve percent of the whites.

After the Civil War the black condition was converted into what was effectively serfdom. Most blacks were landless sharecroppers, tied to their particular landlords by debt. They did go to school, but under conditions that were hardly designed to produce much education. Some 89 percent of the black population was in the South just before World War I, and 77 percent as late as the start of World War II. Most of these people were still on the farm.

During the industrial booms of the two world wars, substantial numbers of blacks moved to the northern and western cities. Even more blacks moved after World War II, when the mechanization of cotton farming resulted in the extinction of most sharecropping farms. By 1970, 47 percent of the black population was in northern and western cities, 34 percent was in southern cities, and only nineteen percent was left in the rural South.

In the old South, blacks were segregated from the white population by law. There was and is no such legislation in the North, but segregation persists. Black movement into white neighborhoods is strongly resisted, and if it does occur, the whites move out. The postwar construction of freeways has helped whites escape to the suburbs. The desegregation of schools by the courts in the 1960s probably increased the incentive for whites to move. Families who might have been willing to live in mixed neighborhoods were often unwilling to send their children to the inferior schools that the blacks attended.

THE GHETTO

Blacks left in the all-black ghetto face worsening conditions. Police protection, education, and even such simple services as garbage collection are typically poor. Food chains tend to build their new stores in the suburbs, where the high demand is, and to abandon the ghettos to obsolete, high-cost stores. The result is that blacks pay more for the same goods. The poverty and hopelessness of lives in the ghetto generate disease and crime.

The market for urban real estate worsens the situation. More blacks are constantly moving into the ghettos from the rural South. And meanwhile, the local black population is growing. As a result, the demand for housing in the ghetto increases. The result is shown in Figure 8.3 by the shift from D_1 to D_2. If the boundaries of the ghetto were not to change at all, the housing supply would be a vertical line like the one shown. The piling in of more black families while black incomes were rising would result in high and rising rents in the ghetto when compared with rents for similar dwellings in white areas. In practice, the wall around the ghetto is not a rigid one today. As ghetto conditions deteriorate, better-paid blacks try to buy housing outside the ghetto. The result is powerful racial tension in the new neighborhood, followed by a new escape by fearful whites. Eventually the ghetto expands. Ghettos have spread quite rapidly in recent years, and as a result, rents are only moderately higher in the ghetto than in white areas today.

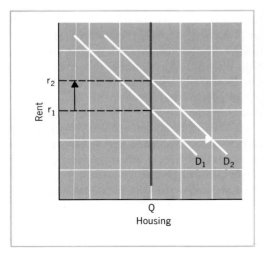

FIGURE 8.3 If the boundaries of the ghetto were rigid, black immigration to the cities and rising black incomes would mean higher rents in the ghetto than outside. In fact, the boundaries have expanded fast enough that the rent differential is quite small.

Job opportunities tend to disappear in the ghetto. In earlier times, the white immigrant population was located right next to the mills where the jobs were. Since then, highways have improved, security in the central cities has deteriorated, and city land prices and taxes have risen. For all these reasons, the factories have moved to the suburbs along with the white population. The transit systems of most cities were built to bring people to the heart of the city from its fringes. They are ill-designed to take blacks out to where the new jobs are. The result is that black workers, often without cars, must either travel for hours to reach work or else take poorer jobs.

A large proportion of the blacks are marginal workers. They can get jobs at prevailing wages only when labor is in short supply. Figure 8.4 shows unemployment rates among white men, black men, and black teen-agers. The 1971 recession meant unemployment rates of four per-

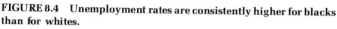

FIGURE 8.4   Unemployment rates are consistently higher for blacks than for whites.

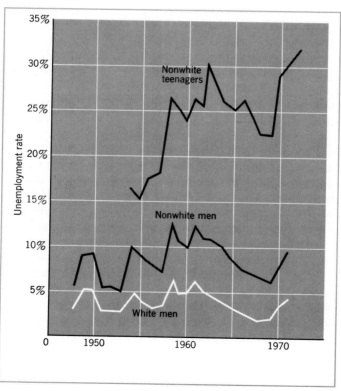

cent for white adult men. But it meant seven percent for the black adult men, and 30 percent for black male teen-agers. Unemployed youths are left to become social problems in the city streets. Studies have shown that urban black earnings rose relative to whites' during the prosperous 1940s and early 1950s. They did so again during the boom of the 1960s. But in the recession years in between, blacks lost ground.

The marginal position of the black worker is only partly due to lower skills. Many employers have systematically discriminated against blacks in hiring. The restrictive rules of trade unions have closed many jobs to them. These obstacles break down most easily when labor is in short supply.

But many blacks *are* short on skills, too. Under slavery, some blacks were trained at urban skills and were rented out by their masters. After the Civil War, these skilled black workers entered the urban labor markets. Over the next generation, however, pressure from the new unions succeeded in excluding black workers from most skilled jobs.

The problem of low black incomes has been intensified by the low quality of black schools. In the South, the segregated school system almost invariably offered blacks an education that was far inferior to the one provided by neighboring white schools. But in the North today, conditions turn out to be not a great deal better. Located in the older parts of town, black schools tend to be dilapidated and overcrowded. Faced with difficult teaching conditions in the ghetto, many of the teachers who can do so find jobs elsewhere. What are left are the inexperienced or less effective teachers plus a few highly motivated heroes. Perhaps exceptionally high salaries would attract better teachers into the ghettos, but it is the suburbs that pay the better salaries.

The result of this situation is inferior training. Blacks score several grades behind whites of the same grade levels in achievement tests. A twelfth-grade education for a black yields a test score comparable to that of a white ninth-grader. Northern school systems are no better than southern ones in turning out black workers who can earn high incomes. A survey taken in 1967 showed that the earnings of blacks who had been educated in the rural South were actually higher, if anything, than those of blacks who received the same number of years of education in the big cities.

By moving north the black worker did improve himself. Black income levels for any given combination of age, education, and region of origin are a good deal higher in the North than they are in the South. Moreover, blacks who grow up in the North tend to complete more years of school than blacks in the South, and they earn more as a result.

POLICIES TO RELIEVE MINORITY POVERTY

ANTI-DISCRIMINATION LAWS

During the 1960s, Congress and the states enacted a great deal of legislation intended to deal with these problems. Open housing laws prohibited discrimination in the sale or rental of housing. Fair employment practices acts prohibited job discrimination by the employer or the union. The effectiveness of these laws has been questioned. It is difficult to tell whether a black house buyer or job applicant is turned down because he is black or for other reasons. But in any case, these changes were associated with improved conditions for blacks. Provisions on property sale contracts that prevented resale to minority groups became unenforceable. As a result, the ghetto was able to expand more readily in response to increased population. This expansion had two effects. It kept rents down, and it gave blacks access to the better housing being abandoned by whites.

A study was made of states with and without fair employment practices acts in 1959 (before the federal law was passed). It showed that the differential between average black and white wages was smaller wherever the laws were on the books. This had not been the case before the laws were passed. In other words, black wages rose faster relative to white in states that had such laws. By now a fair employment practice law is federal legislation. It applies everywhere.

In 1959, the effect of an additional year of education on black incomes was very slight compared with that of whites. Discrimination in employment was apparently so severe at that time that blacks had little incentive to stay in school. In 1967 black incomes for each age–education class were still far below those of whites with similar educations. However, the *additional* effect of another year of education for a black was as great as for a white person. Blacks at least have the incentive to train for better jobs today.

INCREASING BLACK PRODUCTIVITY

The artificial barriers to mobility by blacks have been reduced, though by no means eliminated. The number of blacks able to benefit from the new opportunities was disappointing, however. It now seems clear that the mere removal of discriminatory barriers is not enough to eliminate the problem. Something must be done to increase the blacks' marginal productivities as well.

The basic problem is to make black workers more employable. Many people have stressed the importance of improving educational opportunities. Merely equalizing expenditures per student between the suburb and the central city is not enough. More money must be spent per student in the ghetto than elsewhere if the student there is to have the same educational opportunity as one in the suburbs. This money is becoming harder to find as the tax resources of the central cities decline. It takes state and federal funds raised in the richer parts of the country to finance such a program.

If we can't overhaul ghetto schools, an alternative is to get the black student into the suburbs. The removal of legal segregation has not done so to any great extent because of remaining, hidden restrictions. Even well-to-do blacks find it hard to move into the suburbs. Of course, the poorest blacks cannot afford high-cost suburban housing at all. In a few cases, attempts have been made to integrate schools by busing students outside their neighborhoods. These programs have met with massive resistance, especially when whites are supposed to be bused into the ghettos. Most of the busing programs are now stalled. In any case, many observers are skeptical about the value of taking young children to schools far from their homes.

Another approach is to scatter public housing for the poor throughout the suburbs. This approach could result in permanently mixed neighborhoods with no threat of overwhelmingly black schools, since the black share of the population would be largely determined by the amount of public housing available. Such a program would probably require state or federal funds and administration. Not only would it be costly but it would also have to cross city boundaries. The location of public housing in middle-class, white neighborhoods has met strong resistance.

FINDING EMPLOYMENT OPPORTUNITIES FOR BLACKS

Some observers doubt that improving the quality of black education will accomplish much by itself. They often turn to programs that affect black jobs directly.

One possibility is to require that some specified percentage of a firm's employees be taken from minority groups. The government has put pressure on firms and institutions that receive government contracts or grants to hire minorities. Such programs do improve job opportunities for some blacks, but the employer can still pick and choose. The less productive blacks are apt to remain poor.

Some people go further and propose that the government become an "employer of last resort," hiring the unemployed itself, regardless of its needs. The low quality of public services in the ghettos suggests that quite a few more people could be usefully employed there. The government already has a variety of programs to employ the poor in general, and minorities in particular. More than a million people were enrolled in these programs in 1971. And more than half of them were blacks, especially teen-agers. Yet the unemployment rate among young blacks is still enormous.

Probably the most important thing the government can do to raise the opportunities of blacks is to keep the level of employment high. This policy could mean inflation, as we will see in Chapter 14. Preventing inflation may well seem worth a three- or four-percent adult —white—male unemployment rate. But it is more questionable whether it is worth a 30-percent unemployment rate among minority young people. These are the rates that have gone together in the past.

More has been done to eliminate the disabilities of the black over the last two decades than over the entire period from the end of the Civil War until the late 1950s. Perhaps the most important change was the vote. Half of the black American population gained the right to vote by moving to the North, where there were no legal voting restrictions. For the remaining half, the Voting Rights Act of 1964 eliminated the old restrictions. Able to participate at last in the election of government officials, blacks can perhaps hope to influence government in their own favor just as other groups do.

Something has been accomplished economically. The percentage of blacks in poverty fell from 56 percent in 1959 to 32 percent in 1970. Median black family income rose from 41 to 62 percent of median white family income in the same years. But the huge problems that remain are disappointing to many. A heritage of centuries of slavery and serfdom is not easily overcome in a few years.

SUMMARY

Poverty is heavily concentrated among the aged, women, and minority groups. It is declining rapidly because of the growth in the economy as a whole, but it remains serious among people with low marginal productivities. To eliminate it we must break down the barriers that prevent access to good jobs and we must provide better nutrition and education for the poor. But many of the poor will still be unable to earn good incomes because of disabilities such as age, illness, or dependent children. Many of the in-kind transfer programs are meant to help other groups as well as the poor. Welfare does help the poor, but less than a third of them participate in that program. It is criticized because it weakens incentives to work, encourages the breakup of families, and is costly to administer. A negative income tax would avoid many of these faults, but it would be expensive.

Minority groups are especially likely to be poor, because of inadequate training and high barriers to better housing and jobs. Moreover, minority groups are badly prepared to take advantage of new opportunities when they do appear. Programs to eliminate such disabilities will require state or federal money, because central city tax resources are severely limited. Perhaps the best bet for future progress is a policy of maintaining high employment levels.

STUDY QUESTIONS

1   "The poor are that way because they want to be" — do you agree?

2   Do you expect poverty to disappear by 1990? Why or why not? Suppose that by then no family has an income below the equivalent of $4,250 in 1973 dollars. Do you think that most people would feel that poverty was gone?

3   If we could eliminate all racial and sexual discrimination, would we, in the process, eliminate all poverty among disadvantaged groups?

4   Under a full negative income tax some self-supporting students, some businessmen who had bad years, some persons who have taken religious vows of poverty, and even some hippies and residents of skid row would be eligible for transfers from the government. Do you think they should be? How large a proportion of the poor fall into these groups? Is it worth cutting them out if you also cut out the working poor (more than half the total)?

5   There is a good deal of evidence that some employers discriminate in hiring. Yet many people believe that efficiency in production requires free choice in hiring and firing. Can we prevent discrimination in employment without interfering with that freedom of choice? Do you think the attempts to prevent discrimination that have been made result in inefficiency?

FURTHER READING

Good places to read further about the poverty problem and the programs designed to deal with it are in Alan Batchelder, *The Economics of Poverty,* 2nd ed. (New York: John Wiley, 1971), Joseph Kershaw, *Government Against Poverty* (Chicago: Markham, 1970), and Theodore Marmor, *Poverty Policy* (Chicago: Aldine, 1971). The negative income tax proposal is well explained and analyzed in James Tobin, "The Case for an Income Guarantee," in the Summer 1966 issue of *The Public Interest*. For an absolutely fascinating history of American black slavery, which shatters a myth on every page, see R. W. Fogel and S. L. Engerman, *Time on the Cross* (Boston: Little, Brown, 1974). An excellent analysis of economic policies oriented toward black poverty is James Tobin, "On Improving the Economic Status of the Negro," in *Dædalus* (Fall 1965).

9
LABOR
UNIONS

Our earlier discussion of factor markets assumed that they were competitive. But in many labor markets, either a large employer or a trade union—or both—is in a dominant position. In those cases the market behaves quite differently.

THE EXTENT AND CHARACTER OF UNIONISM
THE COMING OF THE UNIONS

Labor unions are fairly new developments on the American scene. They hardly existed before the Civil War. In the succeeding decades they managed to organize many of the skilled trades, but they left most unskilled and semiskilled workers unorganized. This situation persisted until the 1930s. It meant that most of the low-income workers and most of big business were untouched by unionism. Figure 9.1 traces union membership as a percentage of nonagricultural employment over this century. Unions accounted for ten percent of the labor force or less until the mid-1930s.

Then a revolution occurred that extended unionism to most northern and western industrial workers. The government played a major role in the revolution. Before the 1930s, when the government intervened in labor disputes, it was usually on the side of the employer. The courts upheld contracts in which employees had to agree as a condition of work not to join a union. They often issued injunctions preventing strikes. In the 1930s such "yellow dog contracts" and anti-strike injunctions were outlawed. A National Labor Relations Board was established in 1936. Its job included holding shop elections to determine what union, if any, was to represent the employees in a plant and certifying the winning union as bargaining agent. The employer was prohibited from firing people for union activity or from discriminating against them in any

FIGURE 9.1 Until the 1930s unions played a minor role in the economy. Their successful organization in the late 1930s and 1940s changed the character of industrial labor markets in a basic way.

way. About all he could do to keep the union out was to argue. In this new setting the unions were able to win election after election. By the end of World War II the revolution was complete.

The extent of the unions since then has been limited mainly by the availability of workers who can be easily organized. Unions are still weak in most white-collar trades and in industries where employers are many and small. The share of unions in the labor force has actually been declining slightly in recent years because of the growth in white-collar jobs (clerical, sales, managerial, and professional) relative to blue-collar.

THE STRUCTURE OF AMERICAN UNIONS

Most unions have both local and national organizations. The locals represent the workers in particular plants or particular localities. The locals are parts of national unions (or "internationals" if they have Canadian locals) that represent the trade as a whole. In industries that sell on a local market, such as construction, the locals tend to do most of the negotiating. But in industries that sell nationally, such as automobiles and steel, the nationals commonly bargain for major contract provisions on a company-wide or industry-wide basis. The locals in such industries deal mainly with local work rules and grievances.

The skilled trades unions such as the Airline Pilots Association or the United Brotherhood of Carpenters and Joiners represent all members of a particular skill, regardless of where they work. These groups are often described as **craft unions.** Many of the unions organized in the 1930s represent all workers in a particular industry such as automobiles or steel. These unions are called **industrial unions.**

Unions accounting for 77 percent of all union members belong to the AFL–CIO (American Federation of Labor–Congress of Industrial Organizations). Some important unions such as the Teamsters and the United Auto Workers do not belong. The AFL–CIO is not a union; it does no bargaining. It represents the union movement in political matters and attempts to settle jurisdictional disputes among its members. It sometimes sponsors organizing campaigns in new areas. For instance, the AFL–CIO contributed to an effort to organize agricultural workers during the late 1960s.

WHAT THE UNIONS ACCOMPLISHED

Wages and working conditions improved in the industries organized by the new unions of the 1930s, but they improved in most other industries as well. The largest part of the gain was simply the result of growth in the per-capita GNP. Similarly, most of the unionized trades pay more than average nonunion jobs, but the same trades generally had high wage rates before the union came.

Yet the unions do seem to have raised wages for their members somewhat. Economists have made dozens of studies of the impact of the unions on wage rates. Some have compared wages before and after the coming of a union with wages in lines that were organized or unorganized throughout the period. Others compared wages between union and nonunion cities in localized industries, such as local transit. Still others compared the earnings of individuals with given age, sex, education, type of residence, and type of industry to see the effects of differing degrees of unionism.

The results of these studies are fairly consistent. A few unions seem to have raised wages very little compared with nonunion wages. They include ones that cannot strike, such as some of the government workers' unions, and ones that organize only part of their jurisdictions, such as the textile workers. But most of the semiskilled industrial unions, such as those in autos, steel, and rubber, add something like five to ten percent to their members' wages. Unions in the skilled trades, such as machinists and printers, are generally able to raise wages ten to twenty percent. In a few cases, such as those of airline pilots and skilled con-

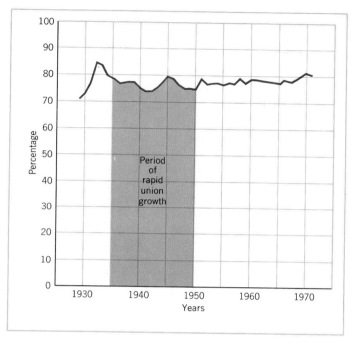

FIGURE 9.2 **The share of labor in national income. This share has remained remarkably stable despite the spectacular growth of unionism between 1935 and 1950.**

struction workers, the wage advantage from unions may reach 25 percent.

These results probably understate what the unions have accomplished, for one and possibly two reasons. First, these calculations generally ignore fringe benefits. These benefits have probably improved more in the highly unionized industries than in unorganized ones. Second, a recent census survey which asked individuals about union membership (in 1967) seemed to show that unions have greater effects on wages of unskilled and semiskilled workers than earlier studies had suggested. The correct figure for semiskilled industrial unions may be more like fifteen to twenty percent than five to ten percent.

Whatever they have achieved for their own members, the unions have done much less for labor generally. Figure 9.2 shows the share of labor in the total factor payments over the years.[1] The coming of the union in the late 1930s and early 1940s is hardly noticeable.

[1] Technically it is wages and salaries plus two thirds of self-employment income as a percentage of the national income. National income is the sum of all factor payments.

UNIONS PRO AND CON

Labor unions are monopolistic combinations of workers. Yet many people who oppose monopoly on product markets are willing to accept monopoly here because they believe that unions help low-income people and make for greater equality.

UNIONS AND INCOME DISTRIBUTION

Many unions, especially in the skilled trades, raise wages by restricting the number of workers in their trades. Through the apprenticeship system, they control the number of workers trained, and they prevent employers from hiring nonunion workers. The result is illustrated in Figure 9.3. Unions limit the number of eligible workers to Q_1 and force the wage up to W_1 in the process. People kept out of the good jobs must look for work elsewhere. The supply of labor in nonunion employments is greater, and nonunion wages are lower, as a result.

The semiskilled industrial unions do not generally have such restrictions on entry, but the effect of their wage policies isn't much different. As long as they can bargain for above-market wages they will accomplish the same thing. If they win a wage of W_1, employment will be restricted to Q_1 automatically. Employers who must pay high union wages take on fewer workers as a result. High wages for auto and steel workers mean poorer job opportunities for the rest of us.

By and large, trade unions do not represent the poor. Only four percent of workers employed in manufacturing and mining and three percent in

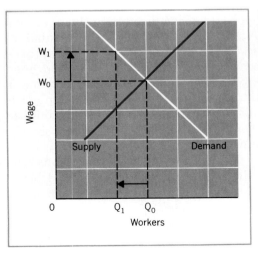

FIGURE 9.3 Whether the union restricts the number of workers in an industry to Q_1 or demands a wage of W_1 and lets the employer decide how many workers to hire, the effect will be fewer jobs in the unionized industry.

transportation are poor by the official definition. These are the sectors where unions are strong. By contrast, 32 percent of those employed in agriculture, 33 percent of those in personal services, and ten percent of those in the retail trade are poor. Unions are weak or nonexistent in these sectors. By raising their own wages and restricting employment in highly-paid trades, the unions very likely make the poor poorer.

Monopoly on factor markets, like monopoly on product markets, results in the misallocation of resources. When unions raise wages, they leave some workers in nonunion trades, where they produce less than they might if employment could be expanded in the unionized trades. As a result, our economy's total output is lower than it might be.

The effects of unionism must be put in perspective. On the average, unions raise wages by ten to twenty percent. Union members are about 25 percent of the labor force. As a result, the difference between union wages and union members' opportunity costs would come to two or three percent of the GNP. This difference is of the same order of magnitude as the sum of monopoly profits on product markets. Neither is insignificant, but they don't shake the earth, either.

MONOPSONY

The effect of the union might be quite different if the employer is in a dominant position in the local labor market. The big employer is then a **monopsonist,** the only buyer. He can use his monopsony power to keep wages low, at W_1 Figure 9.4, by restricting employment. At this low wage he will get only those workers who have low opportunity costs.

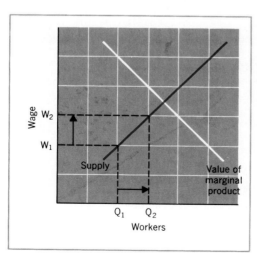

FIGURE 9.4   **A monopsonist could pay workers less than the value of their marginal products and hire only Q_1 workers. If a union came along and forced him to pay a wage of W_2, he would have no reason to restrict employment. Both the wage and employment opportunities could increase.**

Now suppose a union comes along, and that it can bargain for a higher wage, say W_2. Thereafter the monopsonist will be unable to push wage rates down by restricting employment. In this case, therefore, the union serves to raise both wages and employment opportunities.

Economists have examined social security records for various labor markets to find the extent of monopsony. Their general conclusion is that monopsony is rare. In only 2.6 percent of the cities studied did the leading firm employ as many as twenty percent of the workers in their local markets. A major reason is that the majority of workers in most communities are in the distribution and service trades.

If any firm does have monopsony power in labor markets, it is the employer of specialized labor in small towns. One case might be a firm that employs married women in the smaller mill or mine towns. These women often do not have the option of moving elsewhere, because their husbands work there. One reason why women's wages are low may be that they often have monopsonistic employers. In general, the unions have done little for such workers. Certainly the large firms in big cities, where the unions are strong, seldom have much monopsony power.

TABLE 9.1 **Wage increases in various trades during inflations**

| | (1)
INDUSTRY | WAGE INCREASES (PERCENT) IN THE YEARS | | | |
		(2) 1939– 1948	(3) 1953– 1958	(4) 1966– 1969	(5) 1969– 1971
Industries with strong unions	Tires	76%	23%	14%	9%
	Steel	99%	33%	14%	12%
	Motor vehicles	76%	19%	19%	17%
	Trucking	*	*	16%	21%
	Railroads	78%	30%	17%	21%
Industries with weak unions	Crude oil and gas	96%	17%	14%	16%
	Drugs	105%	26%	19%	8%
	Cotton textiles	189%	12%	18%	9%
	General merchandise retailing	103%	21%	23%	11%

*Not available.

WORKING CONDITIONS AND GRIEVANCES

Many observers feel that the overall effect of unions is good in spite of their monopolistic restraints because they improve working conditions. Before the unions, the employer was in a position to make arbitrary employment decisions. Hiring, firing, and discipline were often left to the shop foreman. He could be quite capricious, and the worker seldom had any recourse. In periods of unemployment it was common to find a foreman receiving kickbacks—a share of the workers' wages—in return for full-time work at a good job. Even when he was honest, the foreman could be a tyrant.

One of the major effects of the union was the development of systematic grievance procedures. Arbitrary layoffs or disciplinary actions can now be appealed to a neutral **arbitrator.** He hears both sides, and the union and the employer agree in advance to accept his decision. This procedure eliminated many strikes over minor issues. It has also dealt with many issues that were simply ignored before the unions came.

UNIONS AND INFLATION

To the man in the street, a serious problem with unions is that they seem to contribute to inflation. But once more, the economists aren't so sure. Union demands certainly do contribute to high wages and prices. But the wage rate the union would ask for would be higher than its members' costs *whether or not* there is inflation.

In practice, union wages rates rise no faster in periods of rapid inflation than do nonunion wages. Table 9.1 compares wage increases in a group of highly unionized industries with those in industries where unions are weak. Percentage wage increases are shown in four periods of inflation. Column 2 covers the World War II period, and column 4 shows wage increases during the period of accelerating inflation during the war in Vietnam. In both periods the industries with weak unions showed wage increases as great as, or greater than, those in the highly unionized industries. One reason was that union wages were often set by long-term contracts. They could respond to inflation only after a lag. Another reason was that employers in unionized industries knew that they would have to live indefinitely with any increases they granted. In nonunion industries, wages rise merely because of labor shortages over which the employer has no control.

The situation is different, however, when inflation is accompanied by unemployment. This is illustrated in columns 3 and 5, which show wage increases in the 1950s and the early 1970s. In those years there was a good deal of unemployment, and most labor markets were not a bit tight. Unions could still raise wages. But in the nonunion industries, where market forces played a more important role, wages rose more slowly.

Altogether, unions probably contribute to the sort of creeping inflation that sometimes occurs in spite of some unemployment. If anything, though, they slow down the all-out inflations that occur when labor markets are tight. Taking the two effects together, unions probably act to postpone inflation but also to make it last longer.

UNIONS AND DEMOCRACY

Some people favor unions because of their effect on political democracy. It takes more than the vote to participate fully in government decisions. The well-organized groups in society, such as large corporations and farmers, are able to get a disproportionate number of government decisions made in their favor. Politically, the urban working class was largely unorganized before the coming of the unions. Today it is a strong power bloc, able to work as a group in dealing with the administration and Congress. In large part, the unions are the reason.

At the same time, many unions, especially the newer ones created in the 1930s, have often been leaders in advocating greater equality. Their goals have included full-employment policies, taxes that fall heavily on the rich, legislation against discrimination, and improved welfare laws (though labor's support for the last two goals has cooled noticeably in recent years). The adoption of such policies may well have done more to reduce inequality and poverty than high union wages did to increase it.

As might be expected, the union's political power is often used to promote special union interests. Unions are the main proponents of laws that set high minimum wages. These laws help to protect union members from low-wage competition. In recent years, as competition from imports has increased, unions have become leading advocates of import quotas. In regulated trades they have often been able to get rules favorable to themselves. In many communities, for instance, the building trades have succeeded in preserving building codes that prevent the use of labor-saving materials and techniques. The Teamsters, who organize the truck drivers, are among the main supporters of the ICC rules against rate competition between railroads and trucking.

UNION PRACTICES

Labor unions are widely accepted today, but many of their practices are still matters of wide debate.

STRIKES

One controversial feature of the union is the strike. In competitive labor markets, anyone willing to pay the going wage can hire help. Even when there is a monopolist or a monopsonist there is still a going price. Anyone willing to pay the monopolist's price or accept the monopsonist's wage can do business. But in unionized labor markets we have both powerful buyers *and* monopolistic sellers. If they disagree on the terms of employment there will be a work stoppage. No output will occur at all.

Many people find such events undesirable because they hurt others besides the disputing parties. Yet that is the stuff of which collective bargaining is made. Unions would have little power on labor markets if they did not have the right to withhold labor when the terms of employment were unacceptable. Labor unions that couldn't strike would be little more than pressure groups.

Some people who accept the right to strike in the abstract still try to find the party that is to blame whenever a strike occurs. But, in a sense both sides are to blame, since either one could end the strike by meeting the other side's demands. Perhaps we should say that the side that makes the unreasonable demand is to blame. But this responsibility is hard to determine in practice. An outsider can seldom tell which demands are unreasonable. In an economy in which most wage rates rise in most years, for instance, an employer who offers no more than last year's terms is really proposing to drop behind. At any rate, the announced demands of employers and unions are seldom what either of them realistically expects to get. Both of them ask for more than they actually expect as a matter of effective bargaining. The outsider usually cannot tell what the realistic demands are, or whether they are reasonable or not. Informed observers usually don't even try.

The man in the street often exaggerates the cost of strikes. Figure 9.5 shows the man-hours lost because of strikes as a percentage of total man-hours worked over the last 45 years. Only in 1946, right after World War II, did the time lost through strikes exceed one percent of the total man-hours employed. In the typical year this figure is only a few tenths of a percent. Even so, these low percentages exaggerate the effect of strikes, because it is often possible to make up for strikes by building up inventories in advance or by filling accumulated orders after the strike is over. As a result, the loss in output is even less than the reported loss in man-hours.

Most strikes are small, local affairs. Consumers are little affected if one of the meat-packing companies is on strike or even if all of the talcum

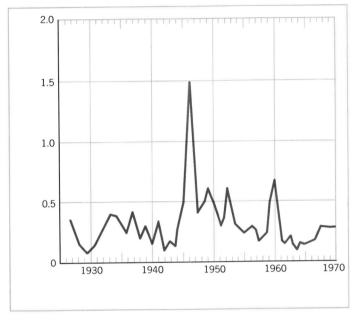

FIGURE 9.5   The percentage of total man-hours lost in strikes since 1925. Only in 1946 did we lose as much as one percent of our labor time.

powder plants in the country go out. The public can simply let the disputants take whatever punishment they choose to absorb.

NATIONAL EMERGENCY STRIKES

The situation is quite different, however, when strikes tie up the whole steel industry or all the ports on the East and Gulf coasts for long periods. Then thousands of steel users or the whole range of export industries may be set back. One of the most difficult problems of labor policy is what to do about such **national emergency strikes.**

One approach is the temporary injunction. Under the Taft–Hartley Act the government can get an injunction prohibiting a strike for 80 days if the courts find that it creates a national emergency. When this law was passed in 1947, the unions, remembering the injunctions used to break strikes in the 1920s, opposed it as a "union-busting" measure. But as it has worked out, Taft–Hartley injunctions have been rare. Only 28 were issued in the first 22 years of the act, from 1947 through 1968. Most of these injunctions were in the defense industries, on the docks, or, occasionally, in a basic industry such as steel. The injunctions may merely postpone the strike, but more often than not a settlement is reached during the 80-day period. The union retains much of its bargaining power while the injunction is in force, because it has the right to go back on strike when the injunction expires. Such injunctions have never come close to "busting" any union.

Although the Taft–Hartley injunction itself has been used sparingly, the government has become involved in the settlement of many big strikes. Government tries to bring public pressure to bear on the unions and employers to settle. Sometimes it even proposes terms. Outside observers conclude that these terms have often been more generous than what the union would have won if the government had kept hands off.

COMPULSORY ARBITRATION

A common proposal at the time of big strikes is **compulsory arbitration.** Under that procedure the strike is ended immediately. The parties to the dispute then have to present their cases before an independent public arbitrator, and they are bound by his decision. Employers and unions both generally oppose compulsory arbitration. They are willing to leave disputes over work rules or grievances to mutually agreed-upon arbitrators. A few unions, such as the steel workers, have even negotiated contracts under which they agree to the arbitration of any contract changes over a specified period. But unions usually want to keep the crucial contract terms in their own hands.

Most students of labor economics are skeptical about the value of compulsory arbitration, anyway. They feel that the costs of strikes are too small to warrant such a drastic solution. Under compulsory arbitration the union and the employer would both become pressure groups attempting to affect contract terms by political means. The resulting contracts might be less desirable than those reached through free collective bargaining under the threat of strike.

Compulsory arbitration may not work, anyway. If a union were dissatisfied with the result and went out on strike in spite of the prohibition, it is doubtful whether the public would stand for wholesale imprisonment of strikers to make the arbitrated settlement stick.

A variation on compulsory arbitration was proposed by the Nixon administration. It would have required disputants who could not settle an issue between themselves to present their "final offers" to an independent arbitrator. The arbitrator would then choose one of the two offers. He would not be allowed to split the difference between them. Presumably this system would lead both union and management to propose reasonable terms. It might make disputes easier to settle, but like compulsory arbitration, it would probably not solve the problem of a really determined union. (The Nixon proposal was not passed by Congress, but a similar plan was adopted voluntarily by major league baseball for settling individual player salary disputes.)

THE CLOSED SHOP AND THE UNION SHOP

Many people who accept the idea of unions and strikes still find some union practices undesirable. A common target of criticism is the **closed shop,** in which the employer is forbidden to hire nonunion workers. The closed shop permits the union itself to determine who is eligible for covered jobs. Many unions have had policies that keep out minority groups or limit the number of workers in their trade. Under the closed shop, the unions govern access to jobs as well as to union membership.

The main argument for the closed shop is that it protects the union against **free riders,** employees who do not join the union but still participate in any benefits that the union wins in their shop. Since joining the union costs money, in the form of dues, the workers would have little incentive to join unless there were a closed shop.

The closed shop is prohibited under the Taft–Hartley Act, but the **union shop** is permitted. This arrangement leaves the hiring decision to the employer, but requires that after a certain period, anyone hired must join the union. The union is protected from free riders but does not determine who gets the jobs.

Some people object to the union shop also. They feel that any rule that requires union membership is an invasion of personal rights. Some nineteen states, mainly in the South and West, have **right-to-work laws,** which prohibit both the closed and the union shop. These laws have limited effects, however, because only a small proportion of union members are in the states where they exist. None of the major industrial states has a right-to-work law.

The ban on the closed shop has done little to weaken the hold of the craft unions over the makeup of their work forces. These unions still control access to most skilled jobs through their apprenticeship rules. Moreover, in such fields as construction and seafaring, the employers must go to union hiring halls to get workers. This arrangement assures that only union men will be hired.

The closed shop or related provisions that had the same effect have been common in the older skilled craft unions, such as the construction trades. The more broadly based industrial unions, such as the automobile, rubber, and steel workers, have never had closed shops. Many of them do have union shops.

FEATHERBEDDING AND ADJUSTMENT ASSISTANCE

Another union practice that is widely criticized is **featherbedding.** That is the term for union rules that prevent the introduction of labor-saving techniques or that require the hiring of unneeded workers where new techniques have made their jobs obsolete. For instance, the railroad unions for years required the employment of firemen on diesel engines, where they were not needed. Similarly, the painters have opposed the use of spray guns and rollers; they have also limited the size of paint brushes. Such rules clearly make the country as a whole poorer. They often increase the demand for workers in the trade involved, though.

The problem of displaced workers is real enough. We all gain at their expense when technological improvements occur. A strong case can be made for having programs that retrain obsolete workers, help them to find new jobs, and pay their moving expenses. In that way we can help displaced workers and still benefit from technological advance. The government set up a program that offers such retraining under the Manpower Development and Training Act of 1962. Studies show that the program improved the job opportunities of the participants. A large proportion of these workers were not persons displaced by technical change. Instead they were persons who had never been trained in a skill at all. The program turned out to be one of the more effective means of eliminating poverty in general.

Some unions, such as the meat packers, have contract provisions that require employers to help any workers they displace. Employers must either find the workers other jobs within the firm or pay them large settlements if they prefer to look elsewhere. Some steel companies have contracts that provide for the workers' participation in the financial gains from any specific improvements. Provisions such as these deal with the displacement problem, and they still let us gain from technological advances, rather than suppressing them.

Like the closed shop, featherbedding is most common among the skilled craft unions, such as the printers and carpenters. Their members have specific skills to protect. The general, semiskilled worker in an industrial union has less to lose from any given technical change, because he can be shifted fairly easily to another job in the same firm.

VIOLENCE, CORRUPTION, AND UNION DEMOCRACY

Occasional reports of violence in connection with strikes receive a great deal of publicity. Violence is seldom involved in ordinary disputes over wages and working conditions, however. It is much more common when a union is trying to win recognition or to prevent the elimination of the union in a plant. It was a frequent occurrence in the 1930s, when unions were fighting for their lives; both sides engaged in it. "Scabs," people who took jobs in struck plants, were sometimes beaten up or even killed. At the same time, the strikers were sometimes attacked by company guards. In the famous "Memorial Day Massacre" of 1937, some eighteen strikers were killed during an attempt to organize the steel mills. Such occurrences are rare now that the unions are generally accepted and employers no longer attempt to operate struck plants.

Some unions have been marked by corruption. When union leaders are subject to little control by their members, they sometimes use their power to extort personal favors from the employers at the expense of the workers they are supposed to represent. The union officials involved have often been associated with the underworld, and they maintain their power by threats of violence. Corruption of this sort is especially common where the bargaining power lies with small locals that receive little public attention, such as those of the Teamsters and the construction unions.

A major reason for such corruption is undemocratic organization. Most unions hold regular elections of officers, but until the 1960s it was about as rare for the leadership of a large union as for the management of a large corporation to be voted out of office. Some union presidents even passed their jobs on to their sons! The existing union leadership had control of the election machinery. It also could dictate the content of the union newspaper. With those weapons at its disposal, it could seldom be successfully challenged.

The Landrum–Griffin Act, passed by Congress in 1959, attempted to assure fair union elections. It required secret ballots, equal access to membership lists by all candidates, and elections at least every five years. Since then, successful challenges to existing leadership have become much more common. Presidents have been voted out of office in such important national unions as the United Steelworkers, the International Union of Electrical Workers, the American Federation of Government Employees, and the United Mine Workers. One effect of increased union democracy has been more militancy on the part of the unions. The claims and promises of contenders for union office have raised the expectations of the workers. There are still cases of far-from-democratic procedures in some unions, however. The 1969 United Mine Workers' election was marked by charges of vote buying, dishonest vote counts, and violence. Shortly after the election, the losing challenger and his family were murdered. Union officials were convicted of planning the killing. The leadership at that time has since been voted out of office.

SUMMARY

Unionism became general in American industrial employment only in the 1930s. Its effect has been to raise wages somewhat over opportunity costs in industries in which the union organizes the entire jurisdiction. But to the extent that the union does raise wages, it restricts employment opportunities of nonunion workers, resulting in a misallocation of resources. Unions have also served to make working conditions less arbitrary and have made possible the fuller participation of the working class in the democratic process.

The strike is an essential feature of the union as we know it. Usually the cost of strikes is minor, but a few national emergency strikes have been met by the government with injunctions or intervention in the collective bargaining process. Both approaches have had mixed success. The alternative of compulsory arbitration is opposed by most managements, unions, and students of labor markets. It would transform the union into a pressure group.

Both the closed shop and the union shop protect the union against free riders, but the closed shop gives the union the power to determine who will get jobs. Featherbedding rules prevent technological improvement to protect workers' jobs. As an alternative, assistance in retraining and moving could both help the displaced workers and give us the advantages of technical progress. Corruption and undemocratic practices have marred the records of some unions. Widely criticized union practices, such as the closed shop, featherbedding, and corruption, are characteristic of a minority of unions. The broad-based industrial unions have generally been free of such faults.

STUDY QUESTIONS

1 Compare labor unions with producers of a particular good who make collusive agreements. What are their goals with respect to prices and wage rates, respectively? Which of the two are more powerful? Are they treated similarly by the government? Should they be?

In 1949 Britain was by far the largest importer of beef in the world. At that time it purchased all its beef through its Ministry of Food. At the same time Argentina was by far the most important exporter of beef, and all of its sales were made through its Agriculture Department. The Ministry of Food and the Argentine Agriculture Department had a long-term contract specifying the price of beef. Then, in 1949, Britain devalued the pound. The Ministry of Food wanted to buy at the old price in terms of pounds. The Argentines wanted the old price in terms of American dollars, and therefore almost half again as many British pounds for its beef. The disagreement lasted for more than half a year. Argentina was filling up with aging cows while British housewives made do with small amounts of canned corned beef. Do you see any parallel between this story and a labor dispute? Why did things come out as they did in this case? Why don't we see such stoppages more often on commodity markets?

Why do some unions oppose labor-saving devices? Where would you expect the opposition to be, in slowly- or in rapidly-growing industries? In trades that require highly specialized skills or in those that involve general semiskilled workers?

What is the difference between the closed shop and the union shop? Do the two lend themselves equally well to racial discrimination on the job? Does the union have less power over the number of workers employed under the union shop than under the closed shop? What if the union just insists on a very high wage? Won't that limit the number of workers by itself?

One argument against compulsory arbitration is that it gives the disputants an incentive to make extreme demands, because the arbitrator is likely to split the difference between their demands. How would the proposal that the arbitrator be required to choose either management's last offer or the union's last demand solve this problem?

A problem in analyzing union behavior is to decide on what the goals of the union are. Compare the wage that would prevail on a competitive labor market if there were no union with the following two possibilities: (a) the wage that would prevail if the goal of the union was the maximum possible membership drawn exclusively from that industry, (b) the wage that would prevail if the goal of the union was the highest wage consistent with full employment for union members. (Hint: If the union followed this goal strictly, would it ever want to see any new workers hired to replace those who died or retired?) In fact, most unions seem to operate somewhere between these two extremes.

FURTHER READING

A good paperback on trade unions is Derek Bok and John Dunlop, *Labor and the American Community* (New York: Simon & Schuster, 1970). Good texts on the subject are Lloyd Reynolds, *Labor Economics,* 5th ed. (Englewood Cliffs, N.J.: Prentice-Hall, 1970) and Neil Chamberlain, *The Labor Sector* (New York: McGraw-Hill, 1971). On the coming of the union see Henry Pelling, *American Labor* (Chicago: U. of Chicago Press, 1960). An interesting set of readings on unions appears in William G. Bowen, *Labor and the National Economy,* rev. ed. (New York: Norton, 1973).

UNIT FOUR
THE
PUBLIC
SECTOR

10 GOVERNMENT EXPENDITURES AND TAXATION

No discussion of the economy would be complete without a careful look at the government. Government expenditures at the federal, state, and local levels are a third of our GNP. Taxes and transfer programs are our most important means of affecting the distribution of income.

BIG GOVERNMENT

In 1902 all the governments in the United States combined spent $1.7 billion. Only 29 percent of this money came from the federal government. By 1971, governments in the United States were spending the astronomical sum of $338 billion. Some 65 percent of these expenditures were federal. How did the government get so big?

THE GROWTH OF THE PUBLIC SECTOR

Part of the growth of our government was merely growth in the economy as a whole. It costs more to provide the same services to more people. And as we have gotten richer we have bought more of most things, including the services rendered by the government. Indeed, the demand for such traditionally government services as education and highways has increased faster than the GNP.

The government sector has grown *much* faster than the GNP, however. Figure 10.1 shows government expenditures as a percentage of the GNP

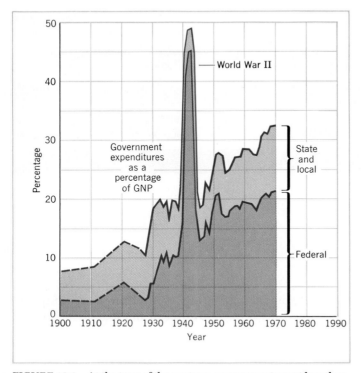

FIGURE 10.1 At the turn of the century, government spent less than a tenth of the GNP, and under a third of that amount was federal spending. Today, government spending equals a third of the GNP, and two thirds of that amount is federal.

and splits them up between the federal, state, and local sectors.[1] The public sector has clearly become a larger and larger part of the economy over the years. This trend shows little sign of slowing down. The federal government has grown relative to state and local governments since 1900, but the state and local shares of the GNP are increasing, too.

WHY GOVERNMENTS GROW

One reason that government has grown so much has been the shift of functions to it from other institutions in society. Intercity transportation is one such case. In Grandpa's day it meant railroads. Private companies

[1] About $30 billion, or roughly twelve percent of all federal expenditures in 1971, took the form of federal grants-in-aid to state and local governments, which they then spent. These sums are assigned to the federal government in Figure 10.1.

provided the roadbed as well as the rolling stock. But today, autos, trucks, and buses move on highways built by the government. The airlines use airways maintained by Washington and airports built by the city fathers.

In addition, the minimum standards that we are willing to accept for the poor have gone up. At the turn of the century we could largely ignore the sharecropper, but today his descendants are much too visible in the central cities to be ignored. In total, our various transfer programs account for 31 percent of all public spending, and they are rising rapidly. They represent one of our most important efforts to attain greater equality.

CENTRALIZATION

The long-term shift in emphasis from state and local to the federal government reflects, in part, the growth of a more interdependent national economy. When we traveled by train or buggy we didn't much care whether a poor state had bad roads or not. When poor blacks stayed in the South, the rest of the nation could ignore their bad educations and low incomes. But as our economy has become more interdependent, we have felt a need for more nearly uniform standards of highways, welfare, and education. As a result, we have channeled federal money to the states and let the federal government take over some state and local functions in order to assure more uniformity.

The federal government has taken over other programs simply because of its greater taxing power. A city or a state that raises its taxes far out of line with other areas of the country is apt to see its industries moving away. A high tax rate is no use to it if there is nothing left to tax. To maintain local prosperity, the city or state may have to forego expensive programs even if the need is great. But the federal government has no such deterrent.

Though the federal government has grown much more than state and local governments since the turn of the century, the state and local governments have also increased in importance. In fact, in the 1960s, state and local government expenditures grew faster than federal spending. This growth was made possible, in part, by large grants from the federal government.

DEFENSE

One of the most important reasons for the growth of government in general, and of the federal government in particular, has been the change in our position in the world. At the turn of the century the United States was a second-rate power in a peaceful world. Our defense expenditures were small. Today we are the leading power in a much less peaceful world.

Table 10.1 gives some idea of what our world position costs us. Defense and international affairs are clearly part of this cost. The space program is more arguable, but one suspects that it would be much less costly if we were not in a race with the Russians. The veterans' benefits are the costs of wars we have fought in the past. So is most of the federal debt. Most of the debt was incurred during World War II. It rose from $47 billion at the start of the war in 1941 (and half of that amount dated from World War I) to $227 billion in 1945. The debt in the hands of the public has hardly risen since. It was $230 billion in 1970. Altogether, our international position accounts for a third of all public spending and more than half of the federal budget.

Defense expenditures are particularly hard to control. The public is in a poor position to evaluate them, because many of the projects are secret and require a great deal of technical knowledge to be understood. Even members of the administration and Congress who have access to the necessary information make many decisions in the dark. The reason is that other countries' projects are secret, too, and the development of a new weapon takes many years. The safe thing to do often seems to be to go ahead with a project. If it turns out badly or is unnecessary, we lose a few billion dollars. But if we don't build it, and a potential enemy does, we may face disaster. The defense contractors and the armed forces tend to promote this point of view.

Our methods of procuring weapons also tend to push costs up. When

TABLE 10.1 Cost of American International Obligations (1970)

ITEM	COST (billions)
Defense	$80.2
International affairs and finance	3.6
Space	3.7
Veterans' benefits	8.7
Interest on the public debt	14.0
Total	$110.2

the Defense Department hires personnel or buys gasoline or underwear it does business on about the same basis as other agencies. However, about a third of its spending is for advanced weapons systems such as aircraft and missiles. These weapons are usually at the leading edge of new technology. The government cannot set exact specifications in advance. The costs of development and production are very difficult to estimate. There is a good chance that a project will be cancelled in midstream because it isn't working out well or because changes in technology or in other countries' weapons make it obsolete.

The risks in this sort of enterprise would be vastly greater than those in most of private business if the government bought in the usual way. Enormous commercial failures like Ford Motors' Edsel or RCA's computer business involved losses of a half billion dollars or so. Some defense contracts have had cost overruns of as much as eight billion dollars. Some projects are probably unnecessary. Also, the military does have a tendency to "gold plate" the weapons they do acquire. But even wih angelic generals we'd still have the problems of high risk and uncertainty, nonetheless.

A system of sealed bids with fixed-price contracts seems unworkable in advanced weapons procurement. What the government does instead is to negotiate contracts under which the contractor receives a fixed fee, while the government pays all or most of the costs. This arrangement leaves the contractor with little incentive to keep costs down. What counts for him is the quality and timeliness of his product. He may be willing to incur high costs in order to improve its performance and get it out fast. The government tries to keep costs down by close supervision. But this scrutiny costs something, too, because it takes lots of paper work, and confusion naturally arises whenever there are two bosses.

The result of this contracting system has typically, though not always, been high-quality weapons delivered about on time, but at costs wildly higher than those estimated in advance. Costs have often been two or three times the original estimates.

There have been several attempts to revise this system, but their success has been limited. Weapons procurement will probably continue to be astronomically expensive as long as we feel a need to keep as far ahead as possible in the defense race.

THE BUDGET PROCESS AND BUREAUCRACY

Some of the growth of government budgets probably is the result of the very way that government spends its money. Many government programs are open-ended commitments. When the government promises to cover a certain percentage of the medical bills of the poor, or to support the price of wheat at a given level, it commits itself to expenditures that it cannot really control. Many of these programs are small in their early years. Congress may adopt them without a great deal of concern. But by the time millions of people come to be dependent on them it is very difficult to cut them back.

Second, the government often provides a large part of the costs of specific state and local programs. This support may lead those governments to carry the programs too far. The federal government pays 55 percent of the cost of sewage treatment plants and 90 percent of the cost of freeways, for instance. As a result, such projects look very cheap to state and local governments. They are apt to buy more, and fancier, sewage plants and freeways than they would if they had to pay the whole bill.

Again, bureaucracies seem to have a built-in tendency to grow. Once an agency is set up, its staff has a stake in its continued existence and growth. Putting an agency out of business is almost impossible. At budget time it will put in an exaggerated list of needs. The central budget authorities may cut some back, but they are in a poorer position than the agency itself to judge where cuts will be least harmful.

There is no reason to believe that bureaucracies are more difficult to handle today than they were in 1900, of course. The federal budget process is certainly more rational now than then. But government spends a third of the GNP now against a tenth of it then. Consequently, the errors that do arise are apt to cost more as a percentage of GNP than they used to.

ECONOMY IN GOVERNMENT

Table 10.2 shows the major expenditures of the government in 1970. They are huge. As a result, there is a constant cry for economy in government.

"Economy" has two possible meanings here. One is for the government to provide the same services at less cost. Everyone is for this; to oppose it would be like coming out in favor of sin. The problem is how to accomplish it. A general cut in every agency's budget might perhaps induce some improvements in efficiency. The main effect, however, would be to provide fewer services.

The best way to improve efficiency in government, as in business, is to improve our methods of accounting, management, and personnel assignment. There is plenty of room for such improvements, but they are not the sort of thing that Congress is well designed to achieve. Merely

TABLE 10.2   Federal, state, and local government expenditures (1970)

ITEM	EXPENDITURES (BILLIONS OF DOLLARS)			
	FEDERAL	STATE	LOCAL	TOTAL[1]
Defense and international relations	84	—	—	84
Veterans' Administration	9	—	—	9
Space	4	—	—	4
Interest on the public debt	14	1	3	18
Post Office	8	—	—	8
Social security and retirement funds	42	3	1	46
Public welfare	10	13	7	18
Education	9	30	39	56
Highways	5	13	5	17
Health and hospitals	5	5	5	14
Agriculture and natural resources	9	2	1	11
Unemployment insurance	3	3	—	3
Housing and urban development	3	*	2	3
Air transportation	1	*	1	2
Police	*	*	5	5
Fire protection	*	*	2	2
Sanitation	*	*	3	3
Parks and recreation	*	*	2	2
Other	5	10	6	15
Total	211	80	82	320

[1]Totals do not add up, because intergovernmental grants-in-aid are included at the federal and state levels, while expenditures financed by those grants are included in state and local columns. The grants are excluded from the totals column to avoid double counting.

*Less than 0.5 billion.

cutting a budget does little to bring about such improvements.

The other meaning of "economy in government" is "cut government programs." Go through the expenditures in Table 10.2 yourself and see if there aren't programs you would propose cutting. Doubtless you can find some. But don't be too confident that your proposals could be adopted. Every big expenditure in the list has a large constituency that supports it—otherwise it wouldn't be there. At the state and local levels, in particular, you can be sure that the pressures for these services are strong. Most state and local governments have had to raise taxes again and again in recent years to cover their expenses. Raising taxes is not a good way for governors, mayors, and legislators to get reelected. You can be sure that they will incur such burdens only if the pressure for them is very great.

THE ECONOMIC ANALYSIS OF GOVERNMENT EXPENDITURES

PUBLIC GOODS

But why can't private enterprise provide these services instead of the government? In a few cases private enterprise would be feasible. The post office might be run by a profitmaking corporation. Intercity highways might be built—and the tolls collected—by private enterprise. But even these examples would fall into the public utility class if they were privately operated. Most items in the budget are public for a good reason. They are expenditures for goods that the market would not supply in large enough quantity if the government did not intervene. And transfer payments, of course, are meant to redistribute income directly, something private enterprise would not do at all.

A **public good** is one that everybody can enjoy without diminishing the enjoyment of others, and from which it is impossible to exclude people from participating. Defense is a good example. Everyone benefits from defense, whether he pays for it or not. The quibble about excluding people is important. A movie fits the first half of the definition. One person's enjoyment of it does not hinder another person from seeing it. But one *can* exclude people from movies, so it pays private enterprise to provide them to paying customers. Defense is different. If it is provided for one person it is provided for all.

If we were to leave defense to private enterprise, we wouldn't get much defense. One submarine on patrol might be worth five dollars a year to me, two dollars to you, 50¢ to one of your friends, and so forth. If we added up the values put on it by everyone in the country, the total might well come to more than the cost of the sub. Yet a private firm probably still wouldn't find it profitable to operate the submarine. The reason is that most of us wouldn't be willing to pay the firm what we thought the sub was worth. Each individual would be inclined to let the others pay, knowing that the sub would be there whether he paid or not.

In fact, the only way to get the subs out there is to make a joint decision and force everyone to contribute toward its cost.

This characteristic of public goods is known as the "free rider problem." The unions face the same problem, because each worker knows he will benefit from the union whether he pays dues or not. The union's services are public goods for the workers affected. To solve the problem, unions try to get union shop provisions in their contracts, which force everyone in the affected shop to pay dues. In the same way, public expenditure decisions force everyone to pay. The government does this by using taxing power.

Figure 10.2 illustrates the demand for a public good—say submarines again. The curves toward the bottom of the diagram are individuals' demand curves for submarines. Each curve shows the value an individual puts on having one, two, three, or more submarines on patrol. As

FIGURE 10.2   The demand for a public good is the vertical sum of individual demands for it. In other words, it is the sum of the values that the individuals in society put on it. It is correct to add these values together, because one person's benefits from the public good do not diminish other people's enjoyment of it.

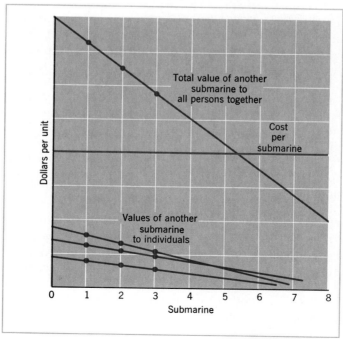

the diagram is drawn, no one puts a high enough value on submarines to pay for even one of them by himself. Without government spending, therefore, we would have none at all. Yet the total value of submarines to all the individuals taken together is quite large. This value is shown by the total demand curve in the upper part of Figure 10.2. The first point on that curve shows the total of the values put on one submarine by the individuals of society. The second point is the total value of a second submarine to all people in society, and so forth. The upper curve is just the sum of the individual demand curves added vertically.

This total demand curve can be compared with the cost curve for submarines, also shown in Figure 10.2. Taking everyone's values into account, it appears that society as a whole would find five submarines worth their cost, but not a sixth. Yet private enterprise, responding to private demand, would not find even one submarine profitable. Only by government action would we actually get the five submarines.

Many of the things bought by the government are not pure public goods. For instance, assume that the government did not provide schools or fire departments. Many of us would still be willing to pay for those services. It would probably be worthwhile for private enterprises to provide us with them. But the education and fire protection we would get would probably not be sufficient. The reason is that education and fire protection both yield **external benefits.** That is, consumption of them benefits other people besides those who use them directly. The rest of us would benefit from your education as well as you, for example. It is generally believed that a community of educated people is much more productive and stable than one in which many are illiterate. Yet, left to their own devices, many parents might be unwilling or unable to pay the $1,000 per student per year needed to educate their children. The rest of us put some value on the education of those children, too. But, for those parents who don't value education so highly, no mechanism exists to collect payments from the rest of us, short of government. Similarly, if you buy no fire protection, my house is endangered as well as yours. I would be willing to pay a little to have *everyone's* house protected, but again there is no mechanism for me to do so, short of government. Because of the public element of education and fire protection, the government provides these services and collects taxes to pay for them. This is the case in all the developed countries in the world today.

Conversely, one can think of a "public bad." It would involve **external costs**—that is, costs that fall on others besides the people who make the decisions. For instance, everyone in the neighborhood participates in the smell from a pulp mill, whether he wants to or not. These people might join together and pay the pulp mill to suppress the smell or tax it until it does so. But these remedies would require government again.

COST–BENEFIT ANALYSIS

It is not easy to decide what the correct level of output of each public good should be. The government must estimate the value to all citizens, taken together, of a bit more of each program. Then it must compare that value with the costs. Presumably this is what governments have been doing all along. In recent years, though, public officials have formalized such evaluations in a process known as **cost–benefit analysis.** Government officials try to estimate the dollar value of the benefits received and compare them with the costs incurred for each project undertaken.

This task isn't easy. Consider a proposed freeway between towns A and B. The benefits would consist of the gasoline, tires, and time saved in driving between the two towns. It would also include the costs of accidents avoided on the freeway that would have occurred on the existing roads. The value of the saving in gas and tires can be determined by finding the amount of traffic between the two cities and multiplying that by the estimated saving per car and truck. The time saved can also be evaluated in money terms, using the average wage of the drivers. Even the saving from improved safety can be approximated if you calculate the capitalized values of the earnings of people who would have been killed or disabled on the old roads. (One thing that should not be included, however, is a reduction caused by the freeway in the price of truck-delivered goods. Potatoes may become cheaper, but they do so *because* of these savings in gasoline, driver time, and accidents. To include both the price reductions and the cost reductions that caused them would be double counting.)

These benefits, whatever we figure they are, will be distributed over the future. Yet the costs of the freeway come now. To make the two figures comparable we need to find the capitalized value of the benefits. That calculation raises another issue: what cost of capital to use. It won't do to use the low interest rate paid by the government, because most public projects are not paid for by borrowing. The money usually comes from you and me as taxes. The appropriate cost of capital to use in capitalizing the benefits from a public project, therefore, is the average return that taxpayers would have gotten on their money. That's what we give up when the government takes our money to pay for freeways.

When all this is done, the benefits from the freeway must be compared with the cost of building it. Many of the costs are straightforward, but there are problems here also. Some costs are nonmonetary. You have to put a dollar value on any harm that the freeway will do to the landscape and on damage from the smog that its extra traffic will add to the atmosphere. There is obviously a very large element of judgment in assigning values to such costs. Cost–benefit analysis can't usually be precise.

If the estimated value of all of the benefits from a government project turns out to be at least as much as the estimated costs, then the project is worthwhile. Cost–benefit analysis, if properly applied, will enable the government to supply goods and services at levels where the last unit supplied is worth just as much as it costs. This is just the sort of result that is achieved by a competitive market in the long run for private goods.

As it is actually applied, cost–benefit analysis often does not work this well. The people who do the analysis are agencies like the Bureau of Public Roads and the Army Corps of Engineers. These organizations have a vested interest in building more roads and dams. As a result, if they are not watched carefully, they tend to overestimate the benefits and understate the costs. Such miscalculations are particularly likely because the people who really do watch them most closely are usually the congressmen in whose districts the roads and dams are to be built. They have a vested interest in the projects, too.

Cost–benefit analysis is most commonly applied to projects that come in lumps, such as particular stretches of freeway or particular dams. In principle, however, it should be applied to government services of a continuing nature as well, such as schools and the police department. Often a government service that would pass the cost–benefit test if taken as a whole includes elements that do not. For instance, public education is generally accepted as worth the price. However, that fact does not mean that every gymnasium and every course is worth its cost. Theoretically, cost–benefit analysis should be applied to each element of each program. Often it is not. The result may be that generally useful programs are expanded too far.

On the other hand, governments are limited in the amount that they can collect in taxes. They may not have the funds to carry out all of the projects that pass the cost–benefit test. In that case they must ration funds to these projects whose benefits exceed costs by the greatest amount. The ultimate decisions must be made by elected officials who can ride herd on the bureaucrats.

GRANTS-IN-AID AND REVENUE SHARING

The sources of public funds affect decisions about government spending. When the people who benefit from a program also pay for it, the resulting government services are apt to be worth what they cost. But not all public programs are financed that way. About $30 billion of federal expenditures are in the form of **grants-in-aid** to state and local governments—that is, transfer payments to state and local governments, usually for specific purposes. States also make grants-in-aid to local governments. To the governments that receive these grants the programs involved seem cheap. On such terms, the local officials will spend almost any amount that the granting government will let them get away with. For instance, the federal government pays about 90 percent of the cost of freeways built as part of the interstate system. As a result, many freeways have been built that probably did not pass the cost–benefit test.

One way around this problem that has been advocated by some liberals and conservatives alike is **revenue sharing.** Under revenue sharing the federal government would make general grants to state and local governments with no strings attached. There would be no requirement that the funds be spent on any particular types of programs. The recipient governments would then have no incentive to use the funds wastefully because anything saved would mean lower state and local taxes. The federal government, with its greater taxing power, would be able to raise whatever funds are required.

The revenue sharing proposal is controversial. Many people fear that the funds would be misused, because state and local governments are sometimes poorly run. In addition, there is widespread concern about how the funds would be distributed among the recipient governments. People in rich states fear that too much money would be siphoned off by the low-income states. People concerned about the problems of the cities fear that the states will get too large a part of the total. Blacks are concerned about the effects of putting more money and decision-making power in the hands of the southern states. Revenue sharing will certainly *not* solve the problem of waste at the local level if it is simply added to the tied grants rather than substituted for them.

A limited general revenue sharing bill was passed in 1972. The Nixon administration also proposed a series of special revenue sharing bills that would give state and local governments grants for use in broad areas such as education or transportation. These grants would substitute for specific grants in the same areas. The recipient governments had mixed emotions about these proposals. They generally welcomed the money, but they objected to the loss of the somewhat larger specific grants that it would have replaced. The special revenue sharing proposals were not adopted. Congress was apparently unwilling to give up its control over the state and local programs it supports. One reason may be that Congressmen can win points with voters by getting "free" highways, sewage systems, college buildings, and the like for their districts.

PAYING FOR THE GOVERNMENT

WHY TAXES?

Once government expenditures are decided upon, some way must be found to pay for them. The government could simply print more money to pay its bills, or it could borrow the money it needs. But most government expenditures are not financed in either of these ways. State and local governments have very little choice; they can't print money, and they have very limited borrowing power. The federal government could use either approach. Yet it also pays for most of its expenditures with taxes, even though taxes are much more painful. Why?

The basic reason why we have taxes is that there would be a great deal of inflation if the government printed or borrowed money to cover all of its needs. It would buy a large part of the economy's output, but consumers would have little reason to cut back their expenditures. Total public and private demand for goods and services would greatly exceed our ability to produce them. Prices would be bid up as a result.

Taxes *do* give consumers plenty of reason to reduce their spending. Their take-home pay is less, and they spend less as a result. The right amount of taxes to collect to avoid inflation may be more than or less than the amount of government expenditures, depending on the situation. What the right amount of taxes is will be discussed in Chapter 15.

STANDARDS OF EQUITY

But what sort of taxes should we impose? The most debated issue here is the **equity,** or fairness, of taxation. What tax system will allocate the burden of government fairly among the members of society?

"Equity" and "fairness" are vague terms that have different meanings to different people. What is fair is another value judgment. Nevertheless, certain standards of equity have wide acceptance. One is the **benefit principle:** Let each person pay according to the amount that he benefits from government services.

The gasoline tax is one that meets the benefit standard quite well. People pay the tax in proportion to the amount that they use the roads. And even people who do not own cars pay their share of it. It is included in the cost of any goods they consume that are delivered by truck. Those people are using the roads indirectly to that extent. Local assessments for sewers and street improvements and the social security tax also meet the benefit principle in a rough way. This sort of taxation corresponds closely to the way goods are paid for on private markets.

The benefit principle won't get us very far, however. How do you allocate the benefits from national defense, for instance? Similarly, it cannot be used to pay for transfer or subsidy programs. It would be self-defeating to collect taxes from veterans and farmers and then pay the money back to them as benefits. The same problem applies to public education. One of the purposes of public education is to attain greater equality. That goal would be poorly served if parents had to pay the full cost of their children's educations.

To pay for public services where the benefit principle cannot be applied, many people feel that the **ability-to-pay principle** is fair: Let each person pay for government according to his ability. Many people interpret the ability-to-pay principle to mean that taxes should be set so that all persons make equal sacrifices. But this simple statement leaves many questions unanswered. How do you measure ability to pay? What taxes would allocate costs by that principle?

The most commonly used standard of people's ability to pay is their income. Table 10.3 compares the effects of three different types of tax on a person who earns $5,000 and on another who earns $10,000. The first is **regressive.** That is the term for a tax that collects a higher percentage of low incomes than of high incomes. The general sales tax in most states is a regressive tax. A poor person has to spend most of his income on goods and services to live; he therefore pays sales tax on most of his income. A richer person can save a good deal of his income. Since he pays no sales tax on what he saves, his sales tax payments are a smaller percentage of his income than they are for the poorer person. Incomes are less equally distributed after a regressive tax than before it. In this example, the poor person's income was 50 percent of that of the richer person. But his after-tax income was only 48 percent of that of the other.

The second example shows the effect of a **proportional** tax. It collects the same percentage of income from all taxpayers. In this example it collects ten percent of the income of both persons. The general sales tax is close to a proportional tax in those states where food is exempt. The tendency for richer people to save more of their incomes is just about offset by the tendency of poorer people to spend a higher percentage of their incomes on food. After-tax incomes are just as equally distributed as before tax incomes in this case.

The last example in Table 10.3 is a **progressive** tax. It collects a larger percentage of higher incomes than of lower incomes. Our leading progressive tax is the federal income tax. Incomes are more equally distributed after tax than before tax when the tax involved is progressive.

Now back to ability to pay. Which tax imposes as much sacrifice on the rich man as on the poor? It is up to you to decide. If you are like the vast majority of students I have questioned, you will vote for the progressive tax. But no one else can answer the question for you. There's no way to hook up brains to see how much another dollar means to different taxpayers. In making decisions between regressive and progressive taxes you are deciding what constitutes **vertical equity**—that is, equity among different income groups.

Regardless of how you answered the question about vertical equity, you are likely to feel that **horizontal equity** is fair. In other words, most people feel that persons with the same income should pay the same tax. "Loopholes" that let some people pay lower taxes than others in the

TABLE 10.3   Three forms of taxation

		LOW INCOME	HIGH INCOME
	Income before tax	$5,000	$10,000
	Ratio of low income to high income	50%	
REGRESSIVE TAX	Tax rate	10%	6%
	Tax	$500	$600
	Income after tax	$4,500	$9,400
	Ratio of low income to high income after tax	48%	
PROPORTIONAL TAX	Tax rate	10%	10%
	Tax	$500	$1,000
	Income after tax	$4,500	$9,000
	Ratio of low income to high income after tax	50%	
PROGRESSIVE TAX	Tax rate	10%	15%
	Tax	$500	$1,500
	Income after tax	$4,500	$8,500
	Ratio of low income to high income after tax	53%	

same economic situation strike many people as inequitable. This judgment applies the ability-to-pay principle once more.

EFFICIENCY

Equity is not the only criterion we employ in choosing among taxes. Taxes have varying effects on the efficiency of the economy as well. For instance, excise taxes are generally inefficient compared with the income or general sales tax, because they distort consumer decisions. (An excise tax is one that is collected as part of the price of a particular type of good. Examples are our cigarette and liquor taxes.) Consider the tax that used to be levied on windows in colonial New England. Its chief result was that houses were built all over New England with a minimum of windows. The total money collected in taxes was no lower as a result. That amount depended on the town's need for schools and roads. But New England houses were gloomier than they had to be.

An important aspect of efficiency is the way that taxes affect incentives. Their influence may be either positive or negative. The possibilities are illustrated by the labor supply curve shown in Figure 10.3. It is the same overall labor supply curve we saw in Figure 7.4. Suppose you are earning a wage of W_1. A tax would reduce your effective wage to W_2. You would be less inclined to work with it than without it. You earn less per hour of work, but you get just as much out of an hour of leisure as you would if there were no tax. On the other hand, if your pre-tax wage rate were W_3, you would be set back to W_4. You would be

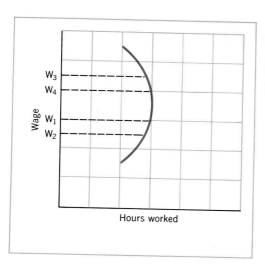

FIGURE 10.3   An income tax might produce either an increase or a decrease in incentive to work, depending on the worker's income level. The curve is the labor supply curve from Figure 7.4, page 00.

inclined to work more, not less. You would put in more time in order to keep an acceptable level of after-tax income. Which situation applies depends on the individual. Every person has his own labor supply curve. But most of the evidence suggests that the average American is in the range where he will work less, the higher his wage. At least, historically, we have put in shorter hours as our wage rates have risen. If this is so, taxes will make people work more, not less.

If any tax does have a negative effect on incentives, however, it is a progressive one such as the income tax. A progressive tax takes a larger percentage of any *additional* income earned than it takes of income generally. It is doubtful, however, whether even the income tax, our most progressive tax, has a negative incentive effect. Studies of the work habits of highly paid persons, such as doctors, lawyers, accountants, and business managers, in both Britain and America, have shown no tendency for them to work less in response to the highly progressive taxes imposed during World War II. A probable reason is that they like their work or the power or prestige that their jobs convey. They apparently are little affected by the heavy taxes they must pay on the last bit of income earned.

Some people have argued that the income tax discourages risk-bearing. They point out that the government takes a large part of incomes when they are high, but it does not participate in losses. Actually, under our present tax laws, government does participate in losses to some extent. The taxpayer can average his income over a period of four years. Moreover, if the taxpayer has a diversified set of investments, he can offset his losses on any one investment against gains made on others. As a result, the government does participate in many losses as well as profits. In any event, the American income tax falls especially lightly on capital gains, which is the form in which a large part of profits comes to individuals.[2] There is little evidence that Americans became less willing to bear risks in the years beginning with World War II, when the income tax became much heavier.

ALTERNATIVE TAXES

Table 10.4 shows the amount of different taxes collected by government at various levels today. We will discuss the advantages and flaws of each of these taxes in turn.

---

[2] Capital gains are increases in the value of property held. If you buy a share of stock at $50 and sell it at $75 you realize a capital gain of $25.

TABLE 10.4   **Taxes by level of government* (1970)**

TAX	AMOUNT (BILLIONS OF DOLLARS)			
	FEDERAL	STATE	LOCAL	TOTAL
Personal income tax	90	9	2	101
Corporate income tax	33	4	—	37
Social security tax and retirement funds	42	10	1	53
Excise taxes and motor vehicle registration fees	16	16	1	33
Sales tax	—	14	2	16
Property tax	—	1	33	34
Other taxes	10	3	—	13
Total	191	57	39	287

*Note: This table does not include incomes of government enterprises such as the post office, government-owned utilities, liquor stores, hospitals, universities, public housing, sewerage, and water. Including all of these revenues, total government receipts were $334 billion, and total government disbursements were $333 billion in 1970.

THE PERSONAL INCOME TAX

The personal income tax is the most important federal tax. It is a progressive tax and meets the vertical equity standard well, in most people's opinion. It also has a particular advantage from the tax collector's point of view. Its progressive character means that the amount of money it collects rises *faster* than income. As a result, the federal government automatically finds itself with larger revenues as the GNP rises.

The income tax meets the horizontal equity standard much less well, however. Over the years, many special provisions have been introduced that help some people more than others. They are often regarded as "loopholes" in the tax law. For instance, the interest on state and local bonds is completely exempt from the federal income tax. As a result, these bonds have been bid up to prices where they yield very low rates of return *before* taxes. They are seldom good investments for ordinary citizens. But they are excellent for people in high tax brackets, who would have to give up a large portion of any other type of interest in taxes.

Incomes in the form of long-term capital gains also get a tax break. A long-term capital gain is an increase in the value of property that has been held for more than six months. If you sell such property you pay only half as much tax on the difference between your purchase and your selling price as you would pay on ordinary income of the same amount. In fact, if you are rich enough, you might pay even less than half. The maximum tax rate on long-term capital gains is 32½ percent, regardless of your tax bracket. Even that tax can be avoided. If you hold the property until you die you avoid the tax on capital gains completely. Your heirs will have to pay inheritance taxes (though there are ways around them, too), but any capital gains that occur during your life will be completely exempt. If your heirs ever sell the property they will calculate their capital gains only from the date on which they inherited it.

A third "loophole" consists of depletion allowances. People who invest in mineral properties—oil, iron ore, coal, and so forth—are allowed to deduct a percentage of their receipts from the output of those properties when they calculate their taxable incomes. For instance, the owner of an oil well can deduct 22 percent of the value of the oil extracted. There is a case for having some sort of depletion allowance on minerals. After all, the businessman who invests in a machine can deduct a part of his initial investment each year as depreciation, up to a total equal to what he paid for the machine. The depletion allowance is supposed to give the same sort of adjustment to investors in oil. Yet in practice, depletion allowances greatly exceed the amount that is needed to recoup the initial investments. The Treasury Department has estimated that for the average oil well the appropriate depletion rate is only about three percent of annual receipts instead of the official 22 percent. The oil companies have several other tax advantages as well. One result of all these benefits is that oil companies pay practically no income tax. Another result is that they have been led to drill far more oil wells than are needed. We produce a third of the world's oil, but we have 90 percent of the world's oil wells.

Not all the "loopholes" are for the rich. Homeowners receive non-money income in the form of housing on which they pay no income tax. The person who rents an apartment, on the other hand, must pay for his housing out of his taxable cash income. One result is that many people have been induced to build homes who would otherwise rent. This situation makes the builders happy.

These four "loopholes" are just a few out of many. The income tax law is riddled with special provisions that benefit particular groups. In most cases, some sort of public purpose is used as justification. For instance, the tax exemption on state and local bond interest permits those governments to borrow money cheaply from the public. When Congress considered dropping this provision in 1969, a horde of state and local officials descended on Washington to argue against the move. No change was made. Similarly, the special treatment of capital gains is defended as a way to reduce any tendency for the income tax to discourage risk-bearing. Depletion allowances are supposed to encourage oil exploration and thus reduce our dependence on foreign producers (though the provision applies to oil produced by American firms abroad as well as at home). These arguments for special tax treatment make varying amounts of sense—but watch them closely. They are usually made by people who pay less tax because of the loopholes.

Loopholes make for horizontal inequity, and they cost the government billions of dollars each year in lost tax revenue. They also distort many economic decisions. Taxpayers spend days and weeks finding ways around the income tax. More important, many observers feel that we invest too much in state and local bonds, houses, and oil, and too little in other things. Our economy is less efficient as a result.

A major reason for the many loopholes is that the tax rates on large incomes are so high. Many people advocate that most deductions and exemptions simply be eliminated. This change would bring in so much additional revenue that general tax rates could be reduced substantially. The result would be a more equitable and efficient tax system—and much less effort devoted to filling out tax forms.

THE CORPORATE INCOME TAX

The corporate income tax brings in an amazing amount of revenue, because the tax rates are very high: 48 percent in the mid-1970s. The corporate income tax meets the vertical equity standard reasonably well if the tax really falls on the stockholders, because the owners of corporate stock are mostly relatively rich. But some economists feel this tax is, at least partially, shifted to consumers and workers. If the portion shifted is as great as 50 percent, then the tax would probably be regressive. At any rate, the tax has all the defects of the personal income tax as far as horizontal equity goes. The same sort of loopholes apply here also.

Some economists feel that the corporate income tax puts an unwarranted burden on that particular form of business. People who invest in corporations pay 48 percent of their firms' profits in taxes, and they also pay personal income taxes on any dividends they receive. People who invest in proprietorships and partnerships merely pay the personal income tax on their profits. One result might be that too much of the country's capital is invested in proprietorships and partnerships and too little in corporations.

An alternative to the corporate income tax would be for the corporation to report to the stockholders their share of its profits. They would then have to pay personal income taxes on that amount. It wouldn't matter whether the profits were paid out as dividends or reinvested in the firm. This system would also eliminate the present incentive for a corporation to retain and reinvest profits whether or not that is the best way to use those funds.

THE SOCIAL SECURITY TAX

The social security tax is a proportional tax on earnings from work up to a cutoff level provided by law ($13,200 a year in the mid-1970s). The tax does not fall on income that is unrelated to work, such as welfare checks. It is therefore a progressive tax for persons with incomes under $8,000. In 1970, people in the $7,000 to $8,000 income class paid seven percent of their incomes in social security taxes. Those in the $0 to $2,000 class paid only 3.8 percent. The main reason was that a large part of the poor people's income was in the form of welfare and other transfers.

Social security taxes are regressive at higher incomes, however. People with incomes over $25,000 paid only 4.4 percent of their incomes in social security tax. One reason was that they paid no tax on earnings from work above the legal cutoff level. Another was that any interest and dividend income that they had was also exempt from the tax.

The social security tax is usually defended as a benefit-principle tax. However, it doesn't meet the benefit principle very well in the case of a second income earned in one family. A working wife pays the tax but gets little in return for it. The retirement benefits for a couple are not very much higher if the wife has been paying the tax during her working years than if she had stayed home.

EXCISE TAXES

Excise taxes are taxes imposed on particular commodities, such as telephone calls, liquor, or gasoline. The government imposes them on the producers of these goods. However, they don't stay there for long. Figure 10.4 shows why. Say a tax of ten cents a dozen is imposed on eggs. The tax, therefore, increases the cost of producing a dozen eggs by ten cents. The producers would supply the same number of eggs only if the price were ten cents higher than it was before the tax. The public, however, will not want as many eggs at the higher price. The result in the short run is a new supply curve: S_2 in Figure 10.4. The equilibrium price increases from 40¢ to 45¢ as a result of the excise tax.

This price rise isn't the end of the story, however. Production costs, including the new tax, are not entirely covered by 45¢. Producers, therefore, will tend to leave the egg business. This exodus continues until the supply curve finally reaches S_3. At that point the price has risen by the full amount of the tax, to 50¢. In the long run the entire tax is shifted to the consumer, the egg business is just as profitable as any other one once again, but fewer eggs are produced and sold than before.

Businessmen generally resist excise taxes on their products. They fear both low profits in the short run and the discouragement of sales in the long run. The more that the rising price discourages consumption, the greater is their resistance.

Economists tend to agree with the businessmen here. Excise taxes have the same effect as when a monopolist sets his price above cost. The consumer is induced to cut back his consumption of the taxed good and switch to other things that offer less satisfaction per dollar of actual production cost.

Not all excise taxes lead to inefficiency, however. Benefit-principle taxes such as the gasoline tax impose the cost of public services on the beneficiaries. They force those people to take public costs into account.

FIGURE 10.4 **The effects of an excise tax. If a ten-cent tax is imposed, the cost of production is increased by ten cents, from 40¢ to 50¢ a dozen. The producers would continue to supply S_1 eggs only at a price of 50¢. But the public will not want as many eggs at the higher price. The result is a short-run equilibrium at S_2 and 45¢. At this price egg producers are taking a loss. They drop out until the supply reaches S_3. At that point the price has risen by the full amount of the tax, ten cents.**

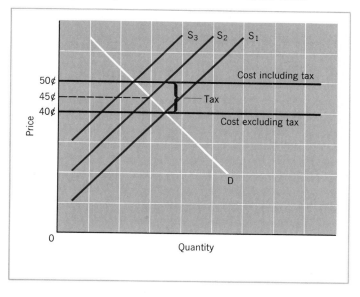

Again, a tax on some product whose use the government wants to discourage would alter consumer decisions; it would push them in the direction that society wanted them to go. Presumably this is the point of our tobacco and liquor taxes. (One suspects, however, that the real reason for these excises is that government can get away with them. Consumers will go on buying tobacco and liquor even when the price is high.) A tax on socially costly activities, such as the discharge of pollutants into the air and water, imposes social costs on the businessman, who would ignore them otherwise. Such taxes would make the economy work more efficiently.

SALES TAXES

The sales tax is the most important single source of revenues for state governments across the country. Sales taxes fall on most goods. Therefore, they do not distort consumption decisions as much as excise taxes do. They meet the horizontal equity standard reasonably well, too, because all consumers pay them on all the goods they buy. Many economists feel, however, that sales taxes do not meet the vertical equity standard. They are regressive in effect, because the rich save a larger proportion of their income than the poor do. And they are particularly regressive if they exempt such services as lawyers' and doctors' fees, as they do in most states. The reason is that the rich spend a much larger proportion of their incomes on such services. A sales tax can be made approximately proportional if food is exempt, because the poor spend more of their incomes on food than the rich.

One proposal that has received a good deal of attention recently is a federal **value-added tax.** Under this tax, manufacturers would pay the tax in proportion to their sales minus the value of what they bought from other firms. Production costs would be increased by the amount of the tax. They would therefore be passed on to the consumer in the long run. As a result, the value-added tax would amount to a federal sales tax. It would have all the advantages and defects of a sales tax.

PROPERTY TAXES

The main revenue source for local governments is the property tax. When we were a rural country and most of our property was in the form of land, property holdings were a reasonably accurate index of an ability to pay tax. Today, however, when most property is in other forms, the tax falls on only one sort of wealth.

The property tax is not easy to administer, either. The amount paid depends on how the property is assessed. These evaluations can be quite arbitrary. Local assessors have been known to give breaks to their friends, to put high assessments on properties owned by out-of-towners, and to negotiate low assessments for factories they want to keep in town. Even in the best of circumstances, assessors' estimates of property values are bound to be wrong fairly often. The result is that some property owners pay more tax per dollar of actual property value than others. Also, rates vary widely from one locality to another. Communities containing large industrial properties have large tax bases, and they are thus able to set relatively low tax rates.

The main argument for the property tax is that we have it—so removing it now would yield windfalls to property owners. After all, the value of a piece of property reflects the capitalized value of the after-tax income that it yields. The property tax reduces that income; therefore it lowers the capitalized value of the property. The price of any piece of property reflects the tax on it, and the person who buys it can expect to receive the going rate of return on his investment. To remove or reduce the tax would be to make him a gift.

Since property taxes depend on assessed valuations that are often fixed for years, they do not rise proportionately with the GNP. Consequently, local governments are generally strapped for funds. They have become increasingly dependent on grants from state and federal governments to meet their needs. We are in an ironic situation in which the cities, which contain the bulk of our wealth, are unable to meet their expenses.

ALL TAXES TOGETHER

All taxes have their faults, so we must choose among alternative evils in finding a way to pay for government. Perhaps the ideal tax in most people's eyes would be a moderately progressive income tax with all the loopholes plugged. But you shouldn't hold your breath until it is enacted. The persons who benefit from the loopholes are many, and they have lots of political clout.

In general, federal taxes are relatively progressive, while state and local taxes are regressive. Taking all levels of taxes together, the American system is mildly regressive at the low-income end. The poor pay little or no income tax, but they do pay the regressive sales and excise taxes. The overall tax structure does finally become progressive at very high income levels—over $25,000. All taxes together fall least heavily on the middle class.

One effect of the greater progression of federal taxes, as compared with state and local taxes, is that federal revenues rise faster than the GNP. At the same time, state and local governments are constantly searching for new sources of revenue. This problem is one of the incentives behind the revenue-sharing proposal. Shifting more of the taxes to the federal level would relieve the pressure on state and local governments. It would also make the overall effect of taxes more progressive.

But the government does other things besides collecting taxes. Its transfer payments, especially social security and welfare, increase poor people's incomes by a large percentage, while raising the incomes of the well-off very little. In addition, public services that are available to everyone free, such as primary and secondary education, are worth a large percentage of poor people's incomes. Services that are worth the same dollar amount per student are a much smaller percentage of middle-class incomes. Any attempt to decide how the benefits are distributed among the various income classes involves arbitrary decisions. It is a matter of judgment how we assign the benefits from public goods such as defense. Still, with any plausible allocation, the poor get much more from government than the taxes they pay. One study based on 1970 data compared transfer payments and services minus taxes for different income classes. The study showed that the net effect of all government action was, roughly, a doubling of the incomes of the poor (those with incomes of under $4,000). There was some net gain for each income class up to $10,000. There was a significant net reduction in income plus government services minus taxes for the group over $25,000. The overall effect of government budgets, then, is distinctly on the side of greater equality. Of course, within each income class there are people who get a lot from government activities relative to what they pay in taxes, while others get little. The overall effect of government budgets probably does fit commonly held ideas of vertical equity, but it leaves a lot to be desired with respect to horizontal equity.

SUMMARY

The government is big. It has grown because of increasing GNP, the shift of responsibility for the poor to the government, and especially because of our increased international commitments. The federal government has grown more than state and local governments because of international obligations, increased regional interdependence, and the greater taxing power of the federal government.

The main economic functions of the government are to redistribute income and to provide public goods (things from which we all benefit and from which individuals who do not pay cannot be excluded).

Cost–benefit analysis provides a means of determining whether government programs are worthwhile, but in practice it is often used to justify projects that the bureaucrats want.

The amount of taxes to be collected depends on government spending and on what is needed to prevent inflation. The most widely accepted criteria for assigning the tax burden of the government equitably are the benefit principle and the ability-to-pay principle. In addition, taxes should distort private decisions as little as possible.

Personal, and probably corporate, income taxes meet the vertical equity criterion well, but many people feel that loopholes keep them from being very equitable among persons with the same incomes. The social security tax meets the benefit principle passably, though a working wife usually gets much less for her taxes paid than her husband does for his. Excise taxes lead to economic inefficiency unless we seriously want to discourage the products taxed. Sales taxes are regressive but reasonably efficient. The property tax falls on only one form of wealth, assessments are arbitrary, and it doesn't respond much to changes in GNP. Still, it is about all that local governments have. Overall, our tax system is mildly regressive in the income ranges where most of our population is located. However, the net effect of all the government activities moves us toward greater equality. Many people argue for revenue-sharing as a means of making state and local spending more rational, of enabling state and local revenues to rise with the GNP, and of making our general tax system more nearly progressive.

STUDY QUESTIONS

1   The growth of government spending as a percentage of the GNP has often been described as "creeping socialism." Look through the expenditure items in Table 10.2 and try to make a judgment of what groups in society are the main supporters of each item. Now look through your list of groups and see if you would classify some of them as socialists, or at least as being clearly on the political left. How much of total government expenditure do you think would continue if the political left were not there? Look through the list again and try to decide what parts of the budget would be supported by the political right.

2   What is a public good? Are the following public goods?

☐   a light house

☐   a freeway from New York to Boston

☐   the city streets in Boston

☐   a television program broadcast by a network station

☐   a beautiful hill covered with oaks and maples with a clear stream at its base about fifteen minutes from town

Does it make any difference in the last case whether the property is owned by a farmer or by the city?

3   Local service airlines receive a subsidy from the federal government which comes to about $100,000 a year per small city served. (That is not the formula for awarding the subsidy, but it is how the numbers come out.) There is a constant tug of war between certain of the smaller cities and the local service airlines over whether they should be served or not. Why the tug of war? Suppose the federal subsidy were abolished but the cities were permitted to negotiate subsidies of their own with the airlines. The subsidy necessary to induce local air service would probably be greater for small cities than for large ones, because the small stops would generate less traffic. If you lived in a city of 100,000 would you be willing to pay a subsidy (maybe one dollar per person per year) in addition to what you pay for any air tickets you buy? If so, why? If not, why not? If you lived in a city of 10,000 would you be willing to pay the subsidy needed to induce local air service (maybe $25 per person per year)? Which do you think is the more equitable way of handling local air service, a federal subsidy or optional local subsidies? Which would lead to more efficient decisions about which small cities should be served?

4   Suppose that a family with a $5,000 income pays $500 a year in taxes. How much do you feel a family with an income of $10,000 should pay if the tax is to be equitable? One way of thinking of it is to try to judge what tax on the $10,000 family would impose the same sacrifice on that family as $500 imposes on the $5,000 family. Here are some possible taxes for the $10,000 family: 0, $250, $500, $750, $1,000, $1,250, $1,500, $1,750, $2,000, $2,500, $3,000, $3,500, $4,000, $4,500, $5,000, $5,500, $6,000. Pick the one that you think allocates the burden of government most equitably. There is no way any one can call your answer wrong. It's strictly a value judgment. However, you may want to know how your value judgment stacks up with others. I have been taking votes on the subject in my classes for years and I have almost always gotten the same result. You can look it up in the footnote.[5] Have you chosen a regressive, a proportional, or a progressive tax?

---

[5]   In my classes, the most popular tax for the $10,000 family has almost always been $1,250. In most classes, the clear majority has voted for that tax.

5   Among those opposed to revenue sharing are several organizations that represent blacks and quite a few congressmen, including some whose constituents seem to favor the program. Why should these people oppose federal revenue sharing?

FURTHER READING

A good place to read more on federal expenditures and taxation, including the various proposals for reform, is Charles Schultze, Edward Fried, Alice Rivlin, and Nancy Teeters, *Setting National Priorities: The 1974 Budget* (Washington, D.C.: Brookings Inst., 1973); a new edition is published each year. Robert Haveman, *The Economics of the Public Sector* (New York: John Wiley, 1973) is a good paperback on government finance in general. The concept of public goods and their ramifications is well explained in Chapter 2 of Robert Bish, *The Public Economy of Metropolitan Areas* (Chicago: Markham, 1971). The alternative taxes in use, and proposals for their reform, are skillfully analyzed in Joseph Pechman, *Federal Tax Policy*, rev. ed. (Washington, D.C.: Brookings Inst., 1972).

11 THE ENVIRONMENT AND THE CITY

Everyone seems to be concerned about the environment today. Brown, poisonous air, evil-smelling lakes and rivers, cluttered landscapes, and congested streets have become normal for many of us. While we were growing richer in things we were becoming poorer in the quality of our environment.

As we shall see, our environmental problems have much in common with the public goods we discussed in the previous chapter. The environment is one area where the government must intervene if life is to stay tolerable. In deciding how it should intervene, and how much, we will be dealing with many of the issues raised in Chapter 10.

THE ENVIRONMENTAL PROBLEM

POLLUTION IN THE PAST

We are not the first people who have had environmental problems. From the time people first gathered in cities until the late 1880s, man was regularly visited by fire and pestilence. The last great city fires (other than those caused by earthquake or war) occurred in the late 1880s. Until this century, disease kept city death rates above those on the farm. We finally solved these ancient problems with sewers, vaccines, public water supplies, and fire departments.

From the Industrial Revolution through World War II, many of the cities of the world were shrouded in coal smoke that closed off the sky and blackened buildings and laundry. Coal made the London fog into an inpenetrable brown wall. With different fuels and new technology we have eliminated much of the soot. You can see the sky in Pittsburgh again, and London fogs are almost white once more. The cities of northern Europe are now washing centuries of grime off their public buildings. The Louvre and Notre Dame appear again as they were meant to be seen.

POLLUTION AND CITIES

Although we have conquered some serious and even deadly environmental problems in the past, new ones seem to arise at an accelerating rate. There are good reasons why.

One is that we have gathered into larger and larger cities. When our country began, only five percent of the population lived in towns of 2,500 people or more. Now 74 percent do. Philadelphia, our largest city then, had 40,000 inhabitants. Today 40 percent of our population lives in 33 metropolitan areas of more than a million people each. An almost continuous chain of metropolitan areas, containing 35 million people all told, stretches from Boston to Washington. Another, of eleven million, extends from Santa Barbara through Los Angeles to San Diego. A third, of nine million, runs from Milwaukee through Chicago to Benton Harbor, Michigan.

This concentration of people has caused many of our environmental problems. When Americans lived on isolated farms, what they did had little effect on their neighbors. But in the nineteenth century, when they crowded into wooden cities that still used wells and privies, one person's disease or fire easily spread to others. Today, if our people, cars, and power plants were spread evenly over the country, they would be no more densely distributed than they are in Iowa. We would have few immediate problems of congestion, smog, or solid waste.

Our cities will continue to grow, but from now on they won't expand much faster than our population as a whole. There simply isn't much rural population left for them to absorb. Even with slower urban growth, however, our environmental problems will continue to mount if nothing is done about them.

THE ENVIRONMENT AND ECONOMIC ACTIVITY

The laws of physics assure us that matter can be neither created nor destroyed (except for small amounts turned into energy in nuclear reactions). When we "consume" beef or gasoline or pulpwood, therefore, the elements they are made of don't disappear. They become body tissue, sewage, garbage, carbon dioxide, paper, junk dissolved or suspended in our rivers, and so forth. As the amounts of materials we use in production and consumption increase, so must the tonnage of goods or waste. They must go somewhere. Some materials become durable goods, postponing the problem of their disposal. Some scrap is recycled. But so far, the bulk of our waste material has simply been emitted into our atmosphere or waters or dumped onto the land.

The environment absorbs a great deal of this waste. Carbon dioxide is converted to oxygen and fixed carbon by plants. Organic materials in the water or on the land are turned into plant foods by bacteria. There are limits, however, to how much of our junk our environment can handle for us. In the case of some inorganic materials, such as mercury or DDT, those limits are quite tight.

Physics also tells us that energy can't be created or destroyed (except for nuclear fission or fusion, once more). Therefore, all the energy we release when we burn fuel must either be put to useful work or go elsewhere. Most of it becomes heat. Some goes up the smokestack, and some is dissipated in the cooling water of power plants. A lot is lost by the heating up of engines and electric power lines themselves. Ultimately, most of it is radiated into space. Yet along the way, we have succeeded in heating up our cities and some of our rivers and lakes quite noticeably.

So far our use of energy has increased quite consistently with our GNP. One reason is that we've taken much of our rising standard of living in the form of warmer houses in winter, air conditioning in summer, and more travel. A more basic reason is that increased energy consumption has been one of the main *means* by which we have increased our productivity.

It is clear that we cannot go on inserting more heat and junk into our environment forever. GNP can still grow, however, if we can increase the efficiency with which we use energy (better insulated houses and more efficient motors), if we can recycle more materials, or if we can shift our consumption toward goods and services that use less energy and materials.

WORLD DISASTERS

Alarms about environmental damage have become commonplace in recent years. Still, a catalogue of the main ones is probably worthwhile.

Some environmentalists predict disaster. They have warned us we will run out of oxygen. Carbon dioxide may accumulate in our atmosphere, raising air temperatures worldwide. If that happens, the polar ice caps will melt and our coastal cities will be swamped. The heat we release in increased energy use may work in the same direction. DDT or oil spills may kill the ocean plankton, thus cutting off much of the cycle that converts carbon dioxide into oxygen. A sky full of supersonic jet exhaust may lead to a permanent cloud cover and to the destruction of the ozone layer that protects us from ultraviolet rays.

Some of these theories have not held up very well on close examination. Calculations show that if we burned all of our known combustibles we would reduce the oxygen supply only slightly. Carbon dioxide is accumulating much more slowly than once was expected. Air temperatures have actually been falling mildly, rather than increasing, over the last two decades. (However, the changes are well within the ranges observed in the past, and they might be reversed in the future.)

The global disaster theory that has received the most support so far is that we will choke off life with certain toxic inorganic elements or compounds that nature does not break down very readily, such as mercury and DDT. The effect of supersonic transport planes is also worth very close study. And the other theories should surely be tested further. But it does not seem as yet that the day of disaster is at hand.

Our main emphasis in environmental policy has so far been on the less spectacular, local effects of pollution. Here the effects are often well known.

AIR AND WATER POLLUTION

The major air pollutants are carbon monoxide and various hydrocarbons coming mainly from motor vehicles, sulfur oxides from the burning of coal and oil by industrial and power plants, and nitrogen oxides and particulate matter from both sources. Carbon monoxide in sufficient concentrations will kill you. Its level sometimes becomes dangerous at busy intersections in large cities. Sulfur oxides are serious irritants themselves, and some of them turn into sulfuric acid—not a nice thing to breathe into your lungs. Hydrocarbons plus nitrogen oxides plus sunlight plus stagnant air produce smog. Smog looks awful, irritates eyes, damages trees and shrubs, and intensifies asthma. Particulates include such poisonous stuff as lead.

Once in a great while, a combination of adverse local air quality conditions has sent hospital admissions soaring and killed significant numbers of people on the spot. Statisticians can relate day-to-day changes in disease and death rates to changes in air quality in a few of the largest cities. Similarly, death rates from lung diseases are seriously worse in cities with bad air pollution. Many scientists worry about the long-term effects of frequent exposure to carbon monoxide, sulfur oxides, or smog, even if those substances never reach levels that will kill on contact. At the very least, most big-city dwellers agree that air pollution is unpleasant.

The largest part of water pollution is organic waste. A little less than a quarter of this matter is household sewage. Most of the rest is industrial waste, especially from the chemical and paper industries. These substances may be unpleasant to us, but they serve as nutrients for bacteria and algae in the water. (Algae are the microscopic plants familiar to us as the scum on stagnant pond water.) As they grow and break down the waste matter, they also use up much of the oxygen dissolved in the water. Carried far enough, this process will produce murky water that smells bad and suffocates fish.

Waste heat from power plants can also damage restricted bodies of water. High water temperatures reduce the oxygen in the water, slowing the breakdown of organic matter and sometimes killing fish.

Some inorganic materials cause special concern. Accumulations of mercury have caused a number of horrible deaths in Japan. The accumulation of DDT is supposed to threaten a number of bird species and has been found in alarming amounts in mothers' milk. There is quite a number of other potential poisons in the water in some places. Few people take in enough of them at any one time to notice the effect, but the combined results of years of exposure are uncertain and worrisome.

Water treatment can eliminate dangerous bacteria. Still, water derived from a polluted stream may not taste very good. The main problem of water pollution in most communities is not its direct effect on health but what it does to the color, smell, and fish life of our lakes and rivers. Water pollution has destroyed much beauty and many recreational opportunities.

SOLID WASTE

Materials that don't go into the air or water must go somewhere. Durable items may be stored in your garage or laundry room for a while, but ultimately they will be disposed of. Nondurable goods wind up as sewage or garbage soon after use. Altogether we generate about a ton of solid waste per person per year—three fourths of it from households.

Disposing of garbage and trash can be a problem. It is especially troublesome in the big cities, where garbage can amount to millions of tons a year. We can burn some of it, but burning adds to air pollution.

Some trash is hauled out to sea. A little is recycled, but even that approach is not always helpful. Recycling paper, for instance, requires washing out a great deal of ink and filler. Those wastes further pollute the rivers. Most solid waste is buried. By now, suitable sites where garbage won't pollute the ground water are becoming scarce in many localities. Some cities have to ship their garbage long distances to get rid of it.

THE LANDSCAPE, CONGESTION, AND JUNK

The environment also includes the landscape. The person who covers my favorite hillside with a housing tract makes my life a little less worth living. Repeat that development a thousand times and you get Los Angeles. As we have become richer and more mobile we have chopped more and more land into large lots and built houses on them.

The loss of agricultural land is probably *not* a problem. The farmer who has to decide between raising hogs or housing chooses on the basis of which activity offers him more money. If he sells out to a developer, it must mean that the capitalized value of what he thinks he could net raising hogs is less than what prospective homeowners are willing to pay for the land. The land will go into the use that consumers value most highly. If we ever do run short of hogs, their price will go up. At that point farmers will be less inclined to sell out to developers.

The farmer and the developer are not likely to pay much attention to what effect their transaction has on natural beauty, however. They *don't* get paid for that. If the decision is left purely to private enterprise we will get miles and miles of uninterrupted city, which can be depressing.

We also get miles and miles of automobiles as our spread-out urban population tries to go to work or to the beach. The result is bumper-to-bumper traffic at 5:30, a downtown decorated with acres of parking lots, and baffling congestion on downtown streets.

That is not the end of our troubles, either. There are the ever-present beer cans in the streets and parks, the roar of jets near the airports, and the jam of people at Yosemite, Yellowstone, and Jones Beach. These things can't kill the way carbon monoxide and mercury can, but they all lessen the quality of life.

THE ECONOMICS OF POLLUTION

What has gone wrong? Why do individual decisions made by rational persons seeking the good life lead to such deplorable results?

EXTERNALITIES

All of these breakdowns in the environment arise from **externalities.**
They are side effects of individual actions that fall on persons other than
the one who makes the decisions. The farmer who keeps my favorite
hillside in fields and oak trees is providing me with an **external benefit**
from his farming business. I have to pay him for his pork, but I get the
beauty for free. He'll ignore my feelings about the landscape in deciding
what to do with his land.

Similarly, when I drive to work, I contribute to smog, and I slow
everyone else on the freeway down a bit. I am imposing **external costs** on
everybody else. I have to take gasoline and tires and my own time at the
wheel into account; if they cost me more than riding the bus, I'll take the
bus. But I don't bear the cost of the extra smog and congestion that I
impose on you. Even if these considerations say I should take the bus, I'll
still be inclined to drive if the costs that fall on me are less than the cost of
the bus.

PUBLIC GOODS AGAIN

Another way of saying the same thing is that our air, water, landscape,
streets, and highways are peculiar kinds of property. They are just as
important a part of our resource base as our farms and factories. Unlike
the farms and factories, however, they are owned by everyone jointly.
With only a few (mostly recent) exceptions, anyone is free to use them in
any way he likes, and at no charge. When an individual has clear title to a
resource and to the goods and services it produces, he has a strong
incentive to use it in the most efficient way. But when resources are
jointly owned, no individual has any such incentive.

What all this means is that clean air and water and beautiful landscapes
are similar to public goods: We all benefit from them, and no one can be
excluded. As with public goods, government must intervene if we are to
have the quality and type of environment we want. Private decisions on
markets won't give them to us.

THE BENEFITS AND COSTS OF A BETTER ENVIRONMENT

The losses due to pollution vary greatly with its intensity. Let's suppose
there is only one pollutant, say sulfur dioxide. At the levels that exist in
most places it is hard to detect any effect at all. At the levels that exist in
some middle-sized cities and quite a few big ones it will turn the tips of
pine needles brown. In other big cities, long-term exposure to it causes

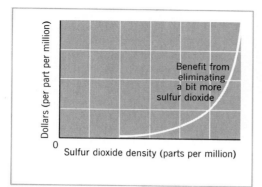

FIGURE 11.1 The benefits from pollution control. Starting at the far right of the diagram, where pollution is intense, a moderate cutback in pollutants will yield large benefits to society. But further cutbacks yield smaller and smaller benefits.

respiratory diseases. (Though, so far, cigarettes have done a better job on that count.) At very high levels that have occurred only on rare occasions so far, it kills some people outright.

For most people, brown tips on pine needles are not nearly as serious as widespread lung disease. It seems pretty clear, then, that the benefits gained by reducing sulfur dioxide pollution follow a pattern like that in Figure 11.1. Take a large industrial city. Cutting the sulfur dioxide in half, say, will save lives. Cutting it in half again will improve the shrubbery. Eliminating the sulfur dioxide that is left after that won't yield much, if any, further benefit.

Now consider the costs of controlling air pollution. They also vary greatly. Much of the pollutant can be eliminated fairly cheaply by just burning low-sulfur coal. Cutting back further requires the installation of scrubbers that may be able to wash half the remaining sulfur oxides out of smoke before it is emitted. This equipment will add more to costs. (They are in operation only in experimental plants at present.) Eliminating the rest of the sulfur dioxide would be terribly expensive, if not impossible. The result is a cost curve like that in Figure 11.2. Sulfur dioxide density is highest at the right-hand part of this diagram. Burning low-sulfur coal brings us back to the middle of the diagram. Scrubbers bring us further to the left. Costs become very great when low densities are attempted.

Similar curves could be drawn for most pollutants. A lot of the pollutants in sewage can be removed cheaply by just holding the sewage in tanks and letting the solid matter settle. More pollutants can be taken out by more thorough treatment, but at a higher cost. We could have perfectly pure water coming out of the sewage treatment plant if we distilled our sewage, but that process would be very expensive. At the same

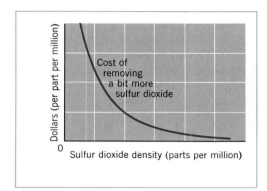

FIGURE 11.2 The cost of pollution control. The first cutbacks in pollution are easy to accomplish and hence not very costly. But the cost per unit removed rises as we try to cut back further and further. The complete removal of all pollutants would involve very high costs, if we could do it at all.

time, some organic discharge into the river may actually improve fish life by providing more nutrients. More than that amount will seriously reduce dissolved oxygen and kill some fish. More yet will make the river into a very unpleasant neighbor.

Similarly, the cost of controlling automobile emissions rises rapidly as you take more and more of the carbon monoxide and hydrocarbons out of the exhaust. Auto owners have become acutely aware of this fact, as the cost of the pollution devices on their new cars has risen and their gas mileage has declined. At the same time, moderate emissions do little harm, while heavy emissions yield Los Angeles smog.

OPTIMAL POLLUTION LEVELS

Now put Figures 11.1 and 11.2 together, as in Figure 11.3. The rising curve shows the benefits from a cleaner environment; the declining curve represents the costs of attaining it. Say we are at point P_1, where

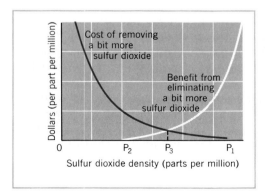

FIGURE 11.3 There is an optimal level of pollution, where the cost of removing one more unit of pollution just equals the benefits to be gained by removing it. The two curves come from Figures 11.1 and 11.2. The optimal level will often be greater than none.

we have made no attempt to control pollution at all. There, the benefits to our population from making some improvement will clearly outweigh the cost. As we cut pollution back, the additional benefits from a further cleanup become smaller, while the further costs rise. If we get over to point P_2, we will be paying very high costs for the last one-percent reduction in sulfur dioxide intensity and getting very little in return. The place to stop is P_3, where the last bit of sulfur dioxide we eliminate costs just as much to remove as it would cost us in damage to plants and people if it were left in the air. Taking any more sulfur dioxide out of the air would benefit us less than it cost to remove.

Just where the optimal level of pollution falls is a matter of debate. It is difficult to measure the benefits of pollution control. Moreover, the situation differs from city to city. Some cities have sulfur dioxide levels so low that with no controls at all there would be little or no damage to the environment from that source. The cost and benefit curves for such a city are shown by the white curves in Figure 11.4. The fact that they do not meet at all means that it would be more costly to remove sulfur dioxide than to leave it in the air. As the city develops, the volume of sulfur dioxide emitted by its industries is likely to rise. The damage from pollution will increase, so the cost curve will shift to the right, perhaps to C_2. Now there are significant costs from pollution. Some controls are called for. Yet again, it would not pay to impose controls that would reduce environmental damage to zero. Controls cost money themselves.

The Supreme Court recently interpreted the Environmental Protection Act to mean that an environmental plan that involved a significant deterioration in the environment would not be acceptable. This rule may be

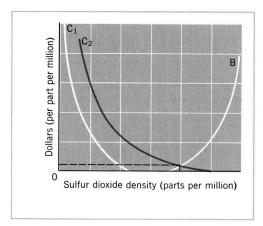

FIGURE 11.4 In a city where sulfur dioxide is no problem, the cost and benefit curves look like the white curves below. Its optimal pollution control policy would be none at all. Economic development might gradually shift the cost curve far enough to the right to make active pollution controls worthwhile, but at a higher level of pollution than before.

a good one in areas where pollution is already a problem. Since few controls have been in effect in the past, the benefits from cutting back pollution in those areas will almost certainly exceed the costs over quite a wide range. But in areas where pollution has not been a problem the rule means either that economic development is to be prevented, or else that controls must always be tight enough to keep pollution at the zero level. That is almost certain to mean that pollution will be cut back to levels where the cost of removing the last pollutants exceeds the benefits from removing them.

Since this argument may sound a little heartless, perhaps it would pay to look at another pollutant for which the man in the street bears the costs of control directly. Most people would probably be willing to pay a good deal more for their cars and get much poorer gas mileage if it would save thousands of lives a year. But fewer people would be happy about the arrangement if all they were doing was keeping some pine needle tips from turning brown. And many people would probably object if pollution had no noticeable effects in their part of the country at all. In fact, we have adopted automobile emission rules on a nationwide basis, although total emissions are at safe levels in many parts of the country. Perhaps this is the only practicable way to control cars, since they are sold on a national market. Furthermore, auto owners often move during the lifetimes of their cars. Yet the automobile rules do have the effect of moving us to the left of points like P_3 in Figure 11.3 in many communities.

WHOSE COSTS AND WHOSE BENEFITS?

It is likely to be much more expensive to cut pollution at some sources than at others. For instance, it is cheaper to build pollution controls into new plants or cars than to install them in old ones. The cheapest way to reduce smog or sulfur dioxide by a specified amount would be to cut emissions drastically at sources where it is easy to do so, and cut them mildly or little at all at sources where it is very costly. A rule that says that all emitters of a certain pollutant must cut emissions by x percent will often not be the best one.

Benefits also differ from person to person. For people who spend most of their lives in the centers of the largest cities, cleaner air may be a matter of life and death. Cleaner water and beautiful landscapes may be worth a lot to people who spend their free time at the beach or in the hills, but they are of little value to the slum-dweller. Even the benefits from cleaner air are mainly a matter of more attractive surroundings in many smaller cities.

The costs of pollution controls ultimately fall on the consumer. He may pay for them directly, as in the case of auto emission controls. Or he may pay indirectly, as the prices of consumer goods go up in response to higher production costs. The slum dweller may be willing to pay higher prices to prevent his early death, but if all he gets for them is cleaner water at a beach that he never visits, he might prefer a better diet.

The bulk of the pressure for a better environment has come from the middle class; the poor have not seen it as a major goal. An all-out effort to improve the environment may well mean, in effect, a better life for the middle class that is paid for, in part, by the poor. Whether a better environment is worth such a result is another value judgment. You must decide for yourself. One way out of the dilemma would be to accompany our efforts to improve the environment with a greater effort to reduce poverty.

ENVIRONMENTAL POLICIES

The next question is how to get power companies and auto drivers to take their external costs into account. This problem certainly takes government intervention. But just how should the government proceed? There are three major alternatives.

REGULATION

First, the government can attempt to control pollution by direct regulation. We have done this at the federal level through the Environmental Protection Agency (the EPA). Many states have created similar agencies. These government regulators issue orders to specific polluters to cut back their emissions. The companies involved aren't happy about having their costs raised, so they often seek less demanding rules or try to delay the effective dates of the orders. The EPA is unlikely to insist on the impossible. Still, what is possible depends on the techniques of the industry. An industry has little incentive to put large amounts of its own resources into this sort of research and development.

The EPA has direct control over emissions from any new stationary sources of pollution. These sources include new power plants, pulp mills, steel mills, and so forth. The EPA also directly regulates standards for new cars. It supervises state regulation of other plants and old cars. Its new-car standards have been tough. In 1973, Congress extended the deadline for the accomplishment of those standards, partly because of the energy crisis and partly because of the auto companies' claims that with a little more time the requirements could be met at a much lower cost. Detroit may well have been right, but it is always hard for the EPA and the public to tell. The auto producers have an obvious advantage in postponing the deadline. This sort of situation is typical. The environmental authorities have often been told that strict enforcement of their requirements would result in the closing of a plant. In some cases it probably would. But the plant owners are apt to say so even when closing isn't imminent. As always, the life of the regulator is not easy.

The EPA's rules do increase costs in the affected industries, and therefore they increase prices. And price increases in turn shift consumer choices. As the emission controls on cars have become more stringent, car buyers have shifted to smaller cars. The main adjustment of the power plants to emission controls so far has been to shift to low-sulfur fuels. This change has raised the price of those fuels, and utility rates have gone up accordingly. It is too soon to know for sure whether consumers will change their power consumption as a result of higher prices. But previous studies have shown that, given enough time to buy different types of equipment and to insulate their houses, consumers are quite responsive to differences in electric rates. Similar changes in consumption should be expected when other external costs are imposed on the consumers. Indeed, such adjustments are a major purpose of the program.

In general, the regulatory approach has all the problems it has in other settings: delay, vague standards, and direct orders that are sometimes too costly for the pollution they avoid and sometimes too mild. At the very least, this system gives the firms being regulated strong incentives to try to influence the regulators and Congress. At the same time, their incentives to look for solutions to our environmental problems may not be so strong. In evaluating the EPA it should be remembered that the agency is new. Most regulatory agencies are at their best when they are first established, while the issues they are to deal with are still hot. As time passes, they tend to become more protective of the industries they were meant to regulate. It would not be astounding if the EPA went the way of the Interstate Commerce Commission and the Civil Aeronautics Board later on, when its fervor cools.

SUBSIDIES

A second possible approach is to pay people not to pollute. The federal government and some state governments have permitted very rapid depreciation of pollution control equipment for tax purposes. This policy reduces the taxes of firms that install the equipment. Our largest environmental subsidy program, however, has been aimed at reducing water pollution. Since 1956, the federal government has paid up to 55 percent of the cost of municipal sewage treatment systems that meet its standards.

Such subsidies provide incentives for firms and municipalities to cut back on their pollution. There is a serious problem with such programs, however. Subsidies for pollution equipment shift much of their cost from the polluters. As a result, the prices of the polluters need not rise. Consumers have little reason to shift away from goods that involve serious pollution. At least, as the subsidies have been set up so far, they have gone to all firms or cities that have installed the specified equipment. Those bodies are paid strictly according to the cost of the equipment, rather than on the basis of the effects they have on the environment. Many of the plants have not been urgently needed, and in any case, many people object to the idea of paying the very people who are causing the problem.

The federal water program has been widely criticized. Between 1956 and 1969, Washington paid out $5.4 billion toward the installation of sewage treatment plants. Most of the money went to suburbs and small towns, many of which produced little sewage or were located in places such that little treatment was needed. The subsidies were paid for plant construction, but the operating costs had to be borne by the towns. As a result, many towns wound up not using their new plants effectively. In 1969, the General Accounting Office concluded that the quality of the nation's water was getting worse, not better, in spite of all the money that had been spent.

A major reason for the persistence of water pollution is that most of it is industrial. About half of all industrial discharges are treated by municipal sewage plants at fees that are kept below total cost by federal subsidies. These industrial polluters have little incentive to change their production methods or product designs to reduce pollution, because pollution doesn't cost them much.

Because of the poor results of this program, Congress set out to revise it in 1971. A tax on industrial pollutants was proposed, but it never got out of committee. Instead, Congress extended the subsidy program. It authorized expenditures of up to $20 billion for the period 1971 to 1975, and set as a national goal the *elimination* of serious discharges from *all* sources by 1985. The job of eliminating all water pollution would be so expensive that it simply would not be worth the cost. More likely the goal just will not be met.

POLLUTION TAXES

A third possibility is to set a tax on pollution—so much per ton. President Nixon proposed a tax on sulfur oxide emissions of power plants in 1970. There is a good case for also taxing the heat that power plants discharge into our waters. In addition, automobile owners might be required to take their cars in for emission tests at regular intervals. Their license fees could depend on the results of those tests. Or they might be issued embossed plastic cards, indicating a tax rate based on the tests. Gas stations would use these rates in determining the taxes on the gasoline they sell. Producers of bottles, tin cans, paper containers, and plastic containers might be required to pay a tax, so much per ton again, based on the costs of disposing of their individual products.

Though many economists have advocated them for years, such taxes are still few and far between. Since they are unfamiliar, we will look at them in greater detail than at regulation and subsidies. Taxes have several advantages. First of all, they would induce polluters to search for ways to cut pollution just as they try to cut other costs. One strategy would probably be to turn the pollutants into saleable commodities. Sulfur is valuable now, but it still doesn't usually pay to extract it from power plant exhausts. If the power company were forced to pay for the external costs of any sulfur emissions, it might be profitable to recapture and package the sulfur in its smoke. And you would certainly think good engineers could find uses for the waste heat that power plants throw away. With high enough taxes on its discharge into the rivers, they might start using it to heat and air condition houses instead. (Perhaps surprisingly, hot water can be used to operate air conditioners.)

A pollution tax would let the polluters themselves decide the difficult question of who should cut back on emissions. The issue would be decided automatically on an individual basis. When pollution controls cost the company less than the pollution tax, they will be adopted. When they cost more than the tax, the firm will just pay the tax and go on polluting. As a result, we will cut back pollution in the places where it is easiest to do so.

Whether the polluter installs controls or just pays the tax, his costs of production will rise. As a result, the prices of goods with a high pollution content will rise. Consumers will tend to shift to more pollution-free goods.

In the case of automobiles, the tax would fall on the auto owners rather than the manufacturers. It would encourage owners of old cars to install anti-smog devices. And it would discourage individuals from disconnecting their cars' emission controls, something they have an incentive to do now. As a gasoline tax, the auto pollution tax would encourage people to keep their gas consumption (and air pollution) down by buying smaller cars and, perhaps, by using public transport more often. An automobile company that developed a better pollution device could save its customers money. Therefore, auto producers would compete in developing efficient emission control systems.

In the case of containers, the tax should make returnables more popular. Products in nonreturnable containers would cost more by the amount of the tax. Products in returnable bottles would be no more expensive than now, but there would be a larger deposit on the bottle, and therefore a greater incentive to return it. If container taxes represented the estimated cost of disposing of each type of material, producers and consumers would be induced to shift to ones that are easy to dispose of. If consumers stuck to nonreturnable containers, it would mean that they valued their own time and storage space more than the full production cost *plus* disposal cost of the containers.

To be effective, of course, pollution taxes would require periodic checks to be sure that the correct taxes were being paid. However, effective regulation requires periodic checks also. Auto emission inspections are easy. They take less than a minute per car. It would not take much more trouble to monitor the emissions of power plants and big industrial polluters. Small ones could be spot-checked, and their tax returns could be compared with their outputs to uncover any gross misreporting. The container tax need not be any more difficult to collect than the cigarette and liquor taxes. And, of course, we already do collect taxes on gasoline at the retail level. In general, American tax collectors have been remarkably effective. That is more than can be said for American regulators.

If correct pollution taxes were imposed, the difficult regulatory questions about where discharges should be cut back, and by how much, would be avoided. So would the delay and the inevitable pettifogging arguments about what controls *might* cost if imposed on a particular plant.

There is still the problem, though, of what tax rates to set. This decision is not hard in the case of containers, whose costs of disposal are easy to determine. But it is difficult to be precise about the external costs of power plant and auto emissions. It is easy to imagine the power companies or the automobile and gasoline producers pulling strings to get low tax rates. Yet tax rates aren't fixed forever. If we do not get the environmental effects we want, we can just raise them. There would undoubtedly be a fight, but the issue would still be clearer than a controversy in a little-noticed regulatory proceeding. It would be, quite openly, the people who wanted a better environment versus the people who didn't want to pay the extra tax.

Some environmentalists fear that companies subject to these taxes would simply raise their prices and go right on polluting. Even if they did, the tax would still work to shift consumers to non-polluting goods and services because of the higher price. Moreover, if we then raised taxes when our environmental objectives were not attained, the industry would ultimately pay an especially heavy tax. Sooner or later the tax would surely be heavy enough to affect production as well as consumption decisions.

Though taxes of this sort have been proposed again and again, they have seldom been put into effect. This seemingly strange behavior on the part of governments that have been continuously strapped for funds can be partly explained by the pressures on them. The affected companies have generally been actively and ardently opposed to pollution taxes. Yet they have often been willing to go along with regulatory schemes that have, ostensibly, the same objectives.

MANY APPROACHES

We do not have to depend on one policy tool exclusively. We wouldn't have to dismantle the regulatory machinery if we passed a set of pollution taxes. In fact, the taxes would make the regulators' jobs easier by giving companies an extra incentive to comply.

At the same time, regulation can deal with some problems that don't lend themselves to the tax solution. We probably *do* want absolute prohibitions on very dangerous pollutants, such as mercury and DDT. It is hard to imagine a tax that would solve the problem of our deteriorating landscape. Rules that require abandoned strip mines to be graded and landscaped seem the only realistic alternative to an absolute prohibition on strip mining, something that would cost us quite a lot.

The value of subsidies is less clear. The strongest case for them may be simply that they are popular. Perhaps they could be used to help firms that face terribly expensive transitions now that external costs suddenly count. As a long-run policy, however, subsidies tend to keep business in polluting industry rather than inducing them to leave.

THE SPECIAL PROBLEMS OF THE CITIES

Air and water pollution can occur anywhere, but they are especially acute in the cities. The cities have many other problems as well. A complete account would include crime, corruption, racial tensions, congestion, and the drabness of miles upon miles of buildings. There is not enough room to cover them all, so this chapter will confine itself to the last two.

CONGESTION

One of the most irritating features of city life is the snail's pace of commutation into town and the massive jam on the city streets when you get there. Cities have been battling this congestion for years.

A common approach is to build bigger and better freeways. Yet the number of cars always seems to expand to fill them as fast as they are built. Meanwhile, the traffic snarl in midtown gets worse with every new lane of freeway opened.

Another approach is to try to induce people to ride buses, subways, and trains to work. That is not easy to do. As more people drive, public transit systems all over the country have run into financial trouble. They have had to raise their rates and cut the number of runs to cut costs. But that remedy just induces more people to drive. Most cities have wound up subsidizing their public transport systems. A few cities, such as Toronto and those of the San Francisco Bay area have even built shiny new subway systems in an effort to woo commuters back to mass transit. But the main effect of the Toronto system was to get the people who were already riding public transit downtown faster and more comfortably. Most of the drivers still drove. We have not had enough experience with Bay Area Rapid Transit to know if it has persuaded commuters to switch. Anyway, there is something peculiar about having to subsidize the richest people in the world so that they won't drive in from the San Francisco peninsula or from the outer suburbs of New York!

The problem is basically one of externalities again. When I drive to work, I produce smog. I also slow up everybody else on the freeway and on the downtown streets. We could estimate the effect of adding one more car to a major artery that carries 10,000 an hour at commuting time. If it slowed all 10,000 cars down by, say, a half a second each, the total cost would come to about 1.4 man-hours of time lost (assuming one commuter per car)! These costs fall on you, not me, when I drive. I ignore them. Once again, government must step in to solve the problem.

Regulatory solutions are not very likely here. The city of Rome has barred private cars from parts of the downtown area, but few other cities are likely to copy that policy. We might prohibit truck deliveries at rush periods—but that move would push costs up and drive firms out of the city. And, as we have seen, subsidies for mass transit have not helped much, either. Sometimes they leave the poor subsidizing the rich.

A CONGESTION TAX

What about a tax here? Again, a number of economists have proposed one. Why not tax people for using the freeways or the downtown streets at rush hours? One possibility would be to require a special license plate for vehicles that are used on congested routes at rush periods. Another would be to put meters on all vehicles, install electronic devices on congested routes that would activate the meters when they went by, and bill the drivers on the basis of the number of rush-hour trips recorded. If that scheme sounds far-fetched, how about a special tax per stall on parking lots? (It should include parking space provided by employers —their staffs commute, too.) A few cities, such as San Francisco and New York, are so located that they could literally charge admission to vehicles coming into the city. Yet what most cities tend to do, instead, is to set their bridge and tunnel tolls on the basis of construction costs. In fact, some cities perversely remove the tolls altogether when a bridge is paid for.

The right tax on rush-hour traffic might be pretty high. If one more car at rush-hour really did cost 1.4 man-hours one way, the external costs of driving to work could be ten or twenty dollars per car *per day*.

A congestion tax would not solve all congestion problems. If a lot more people are going to ride the bus, there had better be a lot more buses. Frequency of service is an important element of the quality of mass transit. Therefore, even more people will switch to public transit as the number of buses increases.

One of the problems with public transit is that it is jammed at rush hour and almost empty at midday and at night. The transit company has to hire enough drivers and have enough buses for the two peak periods of the day anyway, so the extra cost of providing services at 11:00 A.M. and 9:00 P.M. is not much more than the extra fuel consumed. There is a good case for reducing fares at non-commuting hours. That reduction would probably induce some people going downtown at those off-peak times to leave their cars at home. The downtown jam would be reduced further. Only a few cities, such as Boston, have tried this scheme. It is much more common for them to issue low-priced monthly tickets to commuters, the very people who are imposing high costs on the system.

There might still be traffic jams at rush hour, even with a congestion tax. If these jams are bad enough, the city will have to put in more freeways. An extra lane is worth building if its cost, including added congestion costs downtown, is still less than what commuters are ready to pay to get downtown. If we had congestion taxes, we probably would not build freeways as fast as we have, but we would still build them.

An important effect of congestion taxes, higher rush-hour commuting fares, and a slowdown in freeway construction is that it would be more expensive to get into town. The result might be a shift of more business to the suburbs. This development would relieve congestion, but the city fathers and downtown merchants would not be very pleased. This may be one reason, in fact, why few cities have tried congestion taxes. Instead, most of them are subsidizing buses and trains and building lots of freeways.

THE CITYSCAPE AND URBAN SPRAWL

An important part of the environment for city dwellers is the miles of buildings without a break within which they must live. Deteriorating slums spread for miles around the downtown district. Farther out, the buildings are in better shape. Yet open spaces are often fewer in the suburbs than in the central city. One might think that the richest people in the world, a people whose most spectacular contribution to the arts has been in architecture, could have worked out a more rewarding way to live.

The major reasons for urban sprawl are the huge populations of our big cities and the rapid means of transportation available to us. Most people are unwilling to live much more than an hour from work. Until the mid-nineteenth century the main way of getting to work was walking. As a result, most city dwellers lived within three miles of downtown. Cities were very compact. Then came public transit: first horse cars, then streetcars, and finally subways. By the turn of the century the big cities extended as much as eight miles from their centers, and some rail commuter lines extended tentacles of the city even further out. Today, with automobiles and superhighways, it is possible to commute twenty miles or more in an hour. The biggest cities have spread out accordingly. Since commuters are no longer dependent on rail lines, the open spaces between these lines have filled in with houses. The result can mean up to twenty uninterrupted miles of buildings.

They are uninterrupted because of externalities again. Open space in the city is worth a lot to most of us, but an entrepreneur cannot make money by providing it. We can enjoy it without paying the owner anything. By and large, he will not continue to provide this free service for long. As the value of his property rises he is almost bound to sell out to the developer.

When people moved to the suburbs they were under the impression that they were surrounded by miles of open space and that no special provision had to be made to preserve it. Back when suburbs were strung out along railroad tracks this may have been true, but in the automobile age it generally is not.

ZONING AND PARKS

What can be done about urban sprawl? One solution is regulation again. The city fathers usually pass zoning ordinances governing how land can be used. Zoning laws are much less effective in controlling land use than most people think, however. They are sometimes able to keep commercial establishments or apartment houses out of single-family residential neighborhoods, though even these achievements are difficult. But the owner of residential land that would be much more valuable in commercial use has a strong incentive to try to get a "variance," or exception, allowed. Time after time, the zoning authority or city council has given in. It is even harder to force a landowner to leave his property as open space by means of zoning. A rule that tries to keep urban land in orchards and fields is almost certain to break down. It would often keep land in uses worth $1,000 an acre when it could be worth $30,000 an acre in urban use.

   Probably the sprawl can't be stopped, but it is still possible to save some open space. The way is for the city to buy it. Traditionally, open space has meant parks. They have a pretty low priority in most cities' budgets. They have often been sacrificed to freeways and parking. Yet they can make a huge difference in the quality of urban life. Central Park in New York occupies some of the most valuable land in the world. Yet most people seem to feel that it is a good use of the real estate. An effort to sell it off for apartments would be almost a sacrilege. Cities that did not allow for their own Central Parks as they grew have usually regretted it. The suburbs that do not make provisions for parks now are apt to regret it, too, in the future.

SLUMS

The problem of the slums is harder. These ugly areas of rundown and sometimes substandard housing have been blamed for crime, drugs, disease, and practically every other problem that occurs there. Actually these problems, and the slums themselves, are the result of poverty rather than faulty architecture. As we have seen, the incomes of the poor have gone up quite rapidly in recent years. Though it is hard for some people to believe, so has the quality of slum housing. A census of housing is taken along with each national census of population. In 1950,

35 percent of all occupied housing units lacked either hot water, a private flush toilet, or a private bath. In 1970 this figure was down to seven percent.

Slums are still no fun to visit and worse to live in. They are usually in the older sections of town, and they are almost never kept up. There is a good reason for their condition: poor people can't pay much rent. A family earning $4,000 a year (just under the poverty line) can't afford much more than $20 a week, or $90 a month, in rent. You don't get much housing for that kind of money. In new, well-maintained buildings you won't even get a one-room apartment in most cities. The best bets for most poor families are the older areas abandoned by the better-off. But old buildings cost more to maintain than new ones. You can't provide much maintenance for three- or four-room apartments that rent at $90 a month and make any money. The result is that this kind of housing quickly runs down.

The poor condition of slum housing is often blamed on greedy slum-lords and racial discrimination. The "slumlord" theory is very doubtful. The owners of slum housing may have to be obnoxious if they are to collect rent from their poor tenants, but they are not monopolists. Slum housing in most cities consists of many small parcels with great numbers of owners, none of them (except the government) owning more than a tiny proportion of the total. Slum rents settle at whatever level is needed to keep the units occupied, so long as the rent covers the taxes, heat, and unavoidable maintenance. If it won't even earn that much, the properties will just be abandoned.

The racial discrimination hypothesis is more plausible. As we saw in Chapter 8, when blacks are restricted to a well-defined ghetto area, rents in that area will tend to be bid up as black populations and incomes rise. Offsetting this pressure, though, is the tendency for the ghetto to expand because of the difference between property values inside and outside. The net result today is that ghetto rents are only moderately higher than rents for comparable housing in white neighborhoods. The main reason why so much black housing is substandard is that so many blacks are poor.

WHAT TO DO ABOUT SLUMS

Nobody likes slums. The cities have been trying to eliminate them for generations. Along the regulatory route, most cities have passed laws that set minimum housing standards. These laws are widely violated in the slums. And if they were strictly enforced, many slum landlords would find it more profitable to abandon their buildings than to meet the standards. The improving quality of poor people's housing is due not so much to these laws as to rising incomes of the poor.

Another regulatory approach is rent control. It was maintained in New York City from the end of World War II until recently, and it is periodically proposed elsewhere. By keeping rents down, rent control gives slum landlords even less reason to maintain their properties than they would have without it. New York has lagged far behind other cities in the improvement in housing quality for the poor. Rent control does mean lower rents for the poor who already have housing, but young people or new arrivals must often "buy the furniture" or make some other form of surreptitious payment to landlords or existing tenants to get a place to live. Altogether, some slum dwellers have gained and others have lost because of rent control. On balance, it is doubtful whether the poor of New York as a group benefited from it.

In the postwar years we have made massive efforts to tear down slums and replace them with decent buildings. One program is public housing. As we saw in Chapter 8, it usually helps the poor people who get inside, though they would often be helped even more if the government just gave them the money directly. Poor people on the outside gain nothing from public housing, since the developments usually provide no more housing units than are torn down to make room for them. When public housing began in the early postwar years, it at least seemed more presentable than the slums it replaced. But today, many people have come to question the beauty of rows and rows of identical buildings.

"Urban Renewal" is a much bigger undertaking. Under this federal program, cities with approved plans buy up property in decayed areas and demolish the slums on it. They then either resell it to private developers or use it for such public purposes as schools, hospitals, and parks. The federal government covers two thirds of the losses on these transactions; state and local governments absorb the other third. These costs came to a billion dollars a year in 1970, against half a billion a year for public housing.

Until the mid-1960s, most urban renewal land went into housing for the middle class. It also supported businesses to serve them and public facilities to make the areas attractive to them. The poor lost their low-cost slums and were pushed into more expensive housing. Since that time, however, an increased part of the urban renewal land has gone into public housing. The program now helps at least some of the poor as well as the middle class.

The main purpose of the urban renewal program is to make the central parts of the cities more "usable." To planners, that means attracting middle-class people and businesses back downtown. Obvious gainers have been some "slumlords" who sold their property to the city for more than the city got for it from developers. Other gainers were the downtown merchants and property owners, who benefited from the return of some well-heeled customers to the central parts of the city. It is not at all clear that the increase in the productivity of this central land was worth the public resources put into it.

Urban renewal did not eliminate the slums, either. It just moved them elsewhere. In their new areas the poor were no more able to pay rents necessary for proper maintenance than they were in the old slums. The result was that their new neighborhoods quickly deteriorated.

There have been some efforts to improve conditions in the slums by increasing the rents that the poor can pay. The government now subsidizes rent paid by poor people in excess of 25 percent of their incomes, or their payments on purchased houses in excess of twenty percent of their incomes, up to a limit. But most of the funds are for *new* low-cost housing. Since new housing for the poor is limited, only a minority of the poor receive these payments.

The amount of housing built for the middle class under the government's Federal Housing Authority and Veterans' Administration loan guarantees is far greater than that provided by housing programs for the poor. These middle-class programs may have done as much as all the others in improving slum housing. When the middle-class owners and tenants moved into their new homes, their old ones were added to the housing supply available to the poor. This process is one of the main reasons for the rapid improvement in the quality of slum housing since World War II.

A further step that governments can take to improve life in the slums is to provide them with better public services, such as garbage collection and police protection. Both are notoriously worse in the slums than elsewhere.

All in all, however, our best bet for permanently eliminating slums and the evil conditions found in them is to raise the incomes of the poor. The full-employment, antidiscrimination, and welfare policies that have done so much to reduce poverty have done more to eliminate slums than all these other programs put together.

PAYING FOR IT ALL

Pollution controls, mass transit, parks, and slum programs cost money. Yet all over the country, central city tax bases are being eroded by the exodus of the middle class and businesses to the suburbs. Some of the smaller cities and even a few of the newer large ones are still able to annex new land as they spread out. But most of our big cities are hemmed in by independent suburbs. These suburbs enjoy most of the increase in local tax base. Tax rates in the central city have had to go up. Yet a tax increase pushes more people and businesses to the suburbs and raises the rents needed to prevent abandonments in the slums.

Clearly some way of making the suburbs pay for central city services is needed if the quality of city life is to be improved. Our main way of arranging it has been grants-in-aid from federal and state governments. They can tax the suburbs, even though the cities cannot. Federal and state payments are mostly matching grants, whereby the donor pays a share of local expenditures for specified purposes. This sytem has induced cities to spend large amounts of money for freeways and urban renewal, where the federal government picks up much of the tab. Revenue sharing gives the cities money for the purposes they value most, but so far, cities have been lukewarm about such plans. The reason is that the revenue sharing so far proposed comes to less than the matching grants that it replaces.

Some people have advocated **metropolitan government** as a possible solution to many urban problems, including city finance. A single authority would govern the whole metropolitan area, not just the central city. Such a body would be better able to deal with area-wide services such as freeways, public transit, airports, parks, and sewers. It would also have access to the suburban tax base, so it could pay its own bills more readily. Metropolitan government has been adopted by such cities as Miami, Nashville, Indianapolis, Minneapolis–St. Paul, and Toronto. Usually the old cities and towns that it embraces retain some power over some policies, such as zoning or schools, and some taxing power to go with it. Metropolitan government has been resisted in most metropolitan areas, however, because the suburbs are reluctant to share their rich tax bases. Also, their citizens fear that the poor, and especially the blacks, will move into their neighborhoods. Another reason is that suburban officials don't want to lose their power and their jobs.

SUMMARY

Externalities—costs and benefits that fall on others rather than the decision makers—abound in our urban society. They arise because anyone can use our common property, the environment, in any way he likes, and there is no incentive to conserve it. The result is a great variety of serious problems. Many of them, such as smog, polluted water, ugly land- and cityscapes, and congestion are getting worse. In sufficient densities, pollution can threaten the health of plants, fish, animals, and humans.

Nevertheless, the optimal amount of pollution is not zero, but the level where the benefits from the last reduction in pollution are equal to its costs.

Regulation of pollution can improve the environment, but it involves hard questions about who is to cut back how much. It is also subject to delay, vague standards, and pressure groups. Subsidies for pollution controls are a popular proposal, but they do nothing to discourage the production of pollution-generating goods. Taxes on emissions would give business an incentive to search for efficient control methods. They would also discourage the consumption of pollution-producing goods. But taxes have been little used to date, perhaps because of the polluters' own preference for regulation.

Congestion and the deteriorating cityscape are also due to externalities. Congestion has not been solved by traffic regulation and subsidies for mass transit. Congestion taxes would shift some of the rush-hour load to public transit, but they have not been used much. One reason is that they keep people and business away from downtown. Efforts to improve the cityscape by zoning are undermined by pressure from landowners whose property is worth more in other uses than those prescribed by the zoning rules. The only effective way to preserve open land, in the city and suburbs alike, is for the government to buy it and reserve it as parks.

The basic problem of slums is that poor people can't pay enough rent to cover full maintenance. Rent controls keep rents down for those who get in early, but they discourage the maintenance and improvement of slum dwellings. Public housing helps some of the poor; cash would help more. Urban renewal eliminates old slums but often leads to new ones. It may hurt the poor, and it certainly helps the landowners and middle-class residents of the inner city. The most effective way of eliminating slums is to raise the incomes of the poor.

The escape of the middle class and business into politically independent suburbs has removed much of the cities' tax base, which is needed to cope with urban problems. Grants-in-aid from federal and state governments tend to distort city expenditures. An alternative that might better deal with many urban problems is metropolitan government, but it is usually opposed by the suburbs.

STUDY QUESTIONS

1 In each of the following cases, check to see if there are externalities. Are they external benefits or external costs? On whom do they fall?

☐ My car loses its muffler and makes a terrible racket wherever it goes.

☐ The availability of my car in the University parking lot every day makes it possible for several of my colleagues to walk to work, because they can count on a ride home if it rains.

☐ My car is out of tune and burns a lot more gasoline per mile than it would if it were in tune.

☐ I park my car on a busy street at rush hour, thus blocking one of the four lanes on that street.

☐ I finally give up on my car and sell it to a junk dealer, who uses it and others to adorn a local hillside.

2   Studded snow tires were introduced in the late 1960s. Many drivers in northern states bought them, because they make it much easier to drive on slippery streets and roads. Unfortunately, they also caused a good deal more wear on highways than ordinary tires did. Here is a clear-cut externality. The driver with studded tires imposes costs on the general public. Because of these external costs, many northern states have intervened. Some have completely prohibited studded tires. Almost all have prohibited them from April through October. Another possibility is to impose a studded-tire tax. It would be illegal to drive a car with studded tires without a tax sticker on your windshield, which must be renewed every year. Which approach do you prefer? With respect to the tax, how would you go about deciding how much to charge per car per year? Would it make any difference in your views about the tax if you knew that everyone with studded tires would go on using them anyhow, tax or no tax?

3   "There is an optimal level of pollution, and it is almost certainly more than zero." Do you agree? How would you find the optimal level of pollution?

4   Zoning ordinances and urban renewal programs have both been associated with graft and political scandals in many cities. Why do you think this happens?

5   Compare the following as methods of improving conditions in the slums:

☐ urban renewal

☐ building codes

☐ FHA- and VA-insured loans that finance the purchase or construction of new housing

☐ public housing

FURTHER READING

There are many books on the environment today. A famous statement of possible disasters appears in Barry Commoner, *Science and Survival* (New York: Viking, 1966). One of the most balanced and complete statements of current economists' views on the environment is A. Myrick Freeman, R. H. Haveman, and A. V. Kneese, *The Economics of Environmental Policy* (New York: John Wiley, 1973). Some others in paperback include Paul W. Barkley and David Steckler, *Economic Growth and Environmental Decay* (New York: Harcourt Brace Jovanovich, 1972) and E. G. Dolan, *TANSTAAFL* (New York: Holt, Rinehart and Winston, 1971). The title of the last is an abbreviation of "There ain't no such thing as a free lunch." Christopher Tunnard's and H. H. Reed's *American Skyline* (New York: Mentor, 1955), is an excellent history of the American City. The problems of urban transit and slums and many other urban issues are well covered in an excellent collection of articles by Matthew Edel and J. Rothenberg entitled *Readings in Urban Economics* (New York: Macmillan, 1972). Most of the articles are easily within the reach of an interested non-specialist.

UNIT FIVE
AGGREGATE
DEMAND
AND
SUPPLY

12 FLUCTUATIONS IN OUTPUT AND PRICES

Until now we have focused on the behavior of markets for particular goods or factor services. Those topics are collectively referred to as **microeconomics.** Now we will turn to broader questions: general levels of output and employment and prices in the economy as a whole. These topics constitute the field of **macroeconomics.** First we will look at the fluctuations in economic activity that have occurred during this century. Then, in Chapters 13 through 16, we will examine the reasons such fluctuations occurred and what can be done about them.

OUTPUT, INCOME, AND WELL-BEING

THE GNP

Our main measure of the level of economic activity is the gross national product, the total output of final goods and services in the whole country. We have already used this concept many times, but it is worthwhile now to stop and spell out how it relates to other measures of economic activity.

The economy as a whole can be illustrated using the familiar schematic picture reproduced in Figure 12.1. There is a continuous flow of output from firms to households and a counter-flow of expenditures from households to firms through the product markets at the top. The dollar values of these two flows are exactly the same. The value of goods

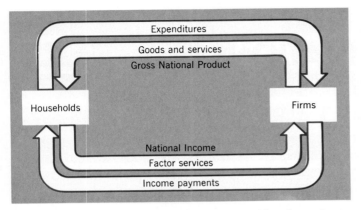

FIGURE 12.1   Gross national product measures either the total output or the total expenditures in a country's economy; they are two sides of the same picture. Similarly, national income measures either the total employment of all factor services or total incomes. And GNP and national income rise and fall together, because output and employment are two sides of the same transactions.

purchased is the other side of the value of goods sold. Both expenditures and output are measured by the GNP.

It is convenient to break the GNP down into its major components. The most important one is **consumption,** with which we are all familiar. A second is **investment,** which in this context means the purchase of goods and services to add to the capital stock. It does not include purchases of stocks or bonds or other securities, because there is no output connected with those transactions. A third element of the GNP is **government purchases.** This category includes not only all government purchases, but also government production of goods and services. Government transfer payments are not included, however, since the government receives no goods or services in return for them. Finally, there are **exports,** which are also part of the total output of our firms. On the other hand, some of our consumption, investment, and government purchases are in the form of imports. Imports are not part of domestic output and must be subtracted from total expenditures to get GNP. Altogether, in 1971, the American GNP was broken down as follows:

Consumption	$ 662 billion
Investment	+ 151 billion
Government purchases	+ 233 billion
Exports minus imports	+ 1 billion
Gross national product	$1,047 billion

NATIONAL INCOME AND DISPOSABLE INCOME

There is a second pair of flows through the factor markets. These flows consist of income payments from firms to households and sales of factor services by households to firms. Here again, the total income payments equal the total value of factors employed. The two flows can thus be measured by a single concept, the **national income.** This statistic is commonly broken down according to the factors employed. In 1971 it broke down as follows:

Wages, salaries, and supplements	$642 billion
Net interest	+ 36 billion
Rental incomes earned by persons	+ 24 billion
Corporate profits	+ 81 billion
Incomes of unincorporated businesses	+ 68 billion
National income	$851 billion

The national income and the gross national product are themselves two sides of the same picture. The costs incurred by firms are mostly income payments. They consist of wages, interest, rents, and purchased materials. Wages, interest, and rents are incomes directly; purchased materials represent income payments made by other firms. The difference between the value of outputs and costs is profit, which is also income.

The GNP does not equal the national income because of certain accounting complications. (They will be discussed in the appendix to this chapter.) Nevertheless, GNP and national income almost always move up and down together. This point is very important. It underlies the whole discussion in the next two chapters. Any increase or decrease in output automatically carries with it an increase or decrease in incomes.

It is important to realize that the national income is not the sum of all the incomes of all the households in the country. To arrive at the amount of income available to households we must add in the transfer payments they receive. We must also subtract the taxes they pay and any profits that are retained by corporations. The result is yet another economic measure, **disposable income.** It corresponds roughly to "take-home pay." It is the amount of money that individuals have to spend or save as they like. Disposable income generally moves with GNP and national income, but the fluctuations are less severe.

The relationships among the various national income and GNP concepts is spelled out in greater detail in the appendix to this chapter.

GNP AS A MEASURE OF YEAR-TO-YEAR OUTPUT CHANGE

GNP is our most widely used measure of economic activity. We look at its year-to-year changes to measure the intensity of booms or depressions. We take its long-term changes as an index of our overall economic progress. Yet there are problems with using the GNP in these ways. Some, but not all of them, are corrected for by the Commerce Department, which computes these figures in the United States.

For one thing, the GNP is measured in dollars, which change in value from year to year. During an inflation the GNP may rise much faster than our actual output. The same amount of goods as last year would simply have a higher dollar value because of rising prices. Similarly, a depression can look worse than it really is when measured by the GNP, if prices are falling. Using the GNP to measure economic activity is like measuring the height of a child with a yardstick that changes in length from year to year.

To deal with this problem the Commerce Department also computes the GNP in dollars of constant purchasing power. That is, it works out what the GNP would be if prices were always the same as they were in some base year. This adjustment is referred to as "deflating" the GNP. The measure of GNP that results is called the **real GNP,** the **deflated GNP,** or the **GNP in constant dollars.** Real GNP *does* reflect year-to-year changes in physical output reasonably well.

GNP AS A MEASURE OF ECONOMIC WELFARE

Real GNP can give us some idea of our overall well-being. But even the GNP is only an imperfect measure of long-term changes in standards of living. For instance, real GNP tripled between 1929 and 1970. Yet American standards of living did not triple in those years. One important reason is that our population grew. The real GNP *per person* just about doubled in the same years.

Even real GNP per person leaves out a lot of things that affect the quality of life, however. Our actual standards of living could conceivably have grown faster or more slowly than that measure would indicate. For one thing, some of our output merely goes to replace plant and equipment that is wearing out or becoming obsolete. Logically, therefore, depreciation should be subtracted from our GNP figures for both 1929 and 1970.[1] Just as logically, we should also subtract any depletion of our natural resources or any deterioration in our environment that

---

[1] This subtraction is done in the formal accounting system used by the Department of Commerce. The result is the **net national product,** described in the appendix. NNP grew just about as fast as GNP from 1929 to 1970.

has taken place in the interval. At the same time, we should add to the GNP the value of any new mineral deposits we have found and any improvements in our environment.

A second problem is that the GNP contains quite a lot of things that do not contribute directly to our standards of living. Instead, they are the costs of attaining it. To illustrate, the time and gasoline you use in getting to work show up in the GNP as consumption. They are really part of the cost of your work, just like the time you put in on the job. The resources we devote to police, defense, and controlling pollution are similar. These so-called "regretables" may be necessary, but they are not services that contribute to our satisfaction. The increases in congestion, crime, international tensions, and pollution that have occurred over the past generation have led to much higher costs of commuting, police, defense, and pollution control. Yet we are no better off as a result.

A third problem is that the GNP leaves out all the housekeeping and maintenance services that households do for themselves. As a result, the GNP goes up when I take my car to a car-wash but not when I wash it myself. It is increased when I buy bread instead of baking it myself. In each case, the same services are involved, but the GNP is higher when I pay others to perform them. To some extent our increasing GNP merely reflects the fact that an increasing part of our output is being sold on the market.

A fourth, and related, problem is that the GNP doesn't include any value for leisure time. Yet leisure is certainly an important part of our standard of living. Between 1929 and 1970, the average work week fell from 48 hours to 38 hours. Housewives' leisure time probably increased by an even greater amount because of the increased use of appliances and the services of commercial laundries and bakeries. A much larger proportion of wives have jobs today than did a generation ago. Yet most of them still have more leisure time than "nonworking" wives did then.

Where do all these considerations leave us? Two well-known economists tried to estimate a measure of economic welfare for the years 1929 to 1965 by adjusting the real GNP for all of these errors and omissions. They added in estimates of the value of leisure, household production, and new resource discoveries in each year. They subtracted estimates of depreciation, resource depletion, environmental deterioration, the time and other costs of commuting, and the "regretables." They concluded, when all this was done, that their measure of economic welfare had increased about as fast as the real GNP per person between 1929 and 1965. In other words, our great increase in leisure was just about offset by our large increase in expenditures on "regretables," mainly defense.

If you ask Grandpa (or someone else who remembers 1929) whether he is twice as well off now as he was then, he is likely to deny it. Many people feel no richer at all. Yet by an objective standard we most certainly are better off. Death rates have fallen for every age–sex group. Life expectancy has increased from 60 to 71 years. Our work week has fallen by a fifth, and most of us now have paid vacations, a rare privilege in 1929. We live in less crowded and much better-equipped houses. In 1929, half of our households lacked either hot water, a private bath, a private flush toilet, or all three. Only seven percent of them are so deprived now. Almost all of us have telephones, refrigerators, and television, and 44 percent of us have air conditioning. In 1929, fewer than half of the households had phones, fewer than ten percent had refrigerators, and, of course, none had television or air conditioning. Even traditional prerogatives of the very rich, such as private swimming pools, trips to Europe, and two or more cars have become available to much of the middle class.

The reason that Grandpa may not feel any richer now than he did then is that his aspirations have increased along with his income. He did not feel deprived without air conditioning back when no one else had it. But today, if he lives in a hot part of the country, he probably considers it essential. The same applies to most of the other improvements in his life style, even the better health and increased leisure. How well-off you feel depends on how close you come to attaining the standard of living you consider adequate or normal. Since these standards rise at the same time that GNP per person does, we may be no happier today than Grandpa was in 1929.

EMPLOYMENT AND PRICES

Our main concern for now will be with year-to-year fluctuations, rather than with long-term changes in standards of living. For this purpose, real GNP seems the best single measure to use, though it doesn't catch all the important aspects of economic instability. Some other measures are discussed here.

EMPLOYMENT

Economists studying economic fluctuations are concerned about levels of employment and unemployment. The Bureau of the Census regularly surveys the American population to determine how many persons are working or actively seeking work. The sum of such persons is known as the **labor force.** The percentage of the labor force without jobs is the **unemployment rate.**

We can never attain a zero unemployment rate. There are always some people who have just quit their jobs and are looking for new ones. Inevitably there are some young people and women who have just entered the labor force and are looking for work. Even during World War II, when the economy was running full-blast, the unemployment rate never fell below one percent. In more normal times, the minimum unemployment rate is more like four percent. When economists and politicians speak of **full employment,** therefore, they mean unemployment rates near this minimum.

Many European countries regularly attain lower unemployment rates than we do. For instance, in the most prosperous years of the 1960s, the unemployment rate reached 1.9 percent in Britain, 1.6 percent in France, and 0.3 percent in Germany, using the American method of calculating it. In the United States the lowest level reached in these years was 3.5 percent. Our high unemployment rates are concentrated among young people, women, and blacks. Adult white male unemployment rates in the United States are similar to those in Europe.

PRICE INDEXES

A third important aspect of economic activity, in addition to total output and employment, is the amount of inflation or deflation that is underway. At any given instant there are always some prices that are rising because of rising demand or costs of production. At the same time others are falling because of falling demand or costs. It takes a rise in the *average* level of prices to be called an inflation.

Price levels are measured by price indexes. The most familiar of these indexes in the United States is the **Consumer Price Index,** compiled by the Department of Labor's Bureau of Labor Statistics. It measures the cost of a fixed market basket of goods, consisting of items bought by an average, urban, working-class family. The makeup of the market basket is determined in surveys taken about every ten years.

The construction of a price index is illustrated in Table 12.1. Suppose that the average family bought the goods shown in the table in the indicated amounts. It won't do to simply average the prices of the individual items, because we consume much more of some goods than of others. Instead, we find the total value of the whole market basket. The totals turned out to be $1,000 in 1967, and $1,300 in 1973.

No one is interested in the absolute value of this market basket. Price indexes are always expressed as percentages of the values at some given base year. The year currently being used as the base for the Consumer Price Index is 1967. In other words, the value of the market basket in each

TABLE 12.1   Construction of a price index

ITEM	QUANTITY	AVERAGE PRICE IN 1967	TOTAL VALUE IN 1967	AVERAGE PRICE IN 1973	TOTAL VALUE IN 1973
Beef	500 lbs.	$0.80	$400	$1.25	$625
Bread	200 loaves	$0.25	$50	$0.30	$60
Shoes	5 pair	$20.00	$100	$25.00	$125
Gasoline	1,000 gals.	$0.30	$300	$0.34	$340
Electricity	5,000 kwh	$0.03	$150	$0.03	$150
Totals			$1,000		$1,300
Percentage of base year total			100%		130%

subsequent year is reported as a percentage of the 1967 value. In the example in Table 12.1, the 1973 price index is $1,300/$1,000 = 1.30 = 130 percent. These calculations are just an example, but in fact, the actual consumer price index *did* stand at 130 in 1973. This means that there had been a 30 percent increase in consumer prices between 1967 and 1973. In practice, of course, the Bureau of Labor Statistics uses hundreds of items in constructing the Consumer Price Index and not just five.

The selection of 1967 as a base does not mean that there is anything sacred about that year's prices. No one should expect to get back to 1967 prices now. In fact, it would take a catastrophic depression to do that. Inflation is a matter of *rising* prices, not high prices. We can see that there was a 30-percent inflation sometime between 1967 and 1973, but this does not mean we were necessarily in an inflation in 1973. To determine whether we were, we would have had to work out how the value of the market basket was changing during that year.

The Consumer Price Index has a tendency to overstate the amount of inflation. For one thing, the quality of most goods is changing, usually for the better in peacetime. The consumers who bought 1,000 gallons of regular gasoline in 1973 were getting a product comparable to the premium gasoline of a decade earlier. If the index could compare prices for the same octane ratings, therefore, it would show less of a price increase than it did when it compares what was called "regular" gasoline in each year. Similarly, the index includes such items as doctor's office visits and the price of hospital rooms. But what actually matters to the consumer is pneumonia cures. The cost of pneumonia cures has probably gone down since the 1930s, even though the cost of office visits and hospital rooms have gone way up. The reason is much quicker and more complete cures. If the Consumer Price Index could allow for changes in quality it would show less of a tendency to rise over time.

Another reason why the Consumer Price Index exaggerates inflation is that the market basket is fixed in content. If the price of beef rises while the price of pork stays the same, consumers will shift from beef to pork. Yet the official market basket will make no such change. As a result, the Consumer Price Index will rise more than the actual cost of living for a family does.

Altogether, price indexes, like any other measures of the real world, are imperfect indicators of what is happening. Still, they are the best we have.

THE HISTORY OF ECONOMIC FLUCTUATIONS

We have been developing some useful tools: GNP, the unemployment rate, and price indexes. Now we can use these measures to trace the actual fluctuations in output and prices that have occurred in the American economy since the turn of the century.

GROWTH IN THE REAL GNP

Figure 12.2 shows the GNP since 1900, measured in terms of 1971 dollars. This form of diagram may be unfamiliar to some readers. The vertical (GNP) axis is a "ratio scale."[2] Ratio scales are constructed so that equal percentage changes will show up as equal distances. For instance, on the vertical axis it is just as far from 100 to 200 as it is from 200 to 400, or from 500 to 1,000. A constant percentage rate of growth will show up on this diagram as a straight line.

To help make this point clearer, Figure 12.3 plots the GNP again, using the more familiar arithmetic scale. Here the GNP clearly grows at an increasing rate. Fluctuations back in the 1920s, when the GNP was much lower, are hard to read. A billion-dollar change in the GNP was a big thing in 1923, when the whole GNP was only $203 billion. But today the GNP increases that much every few weeks. We are less interested in the absolute changes than we are in the percentages of change. In Figure 12.2 a ten-percent increase or decrease looks the same anyplace on the graph. In Figure 12.3 it is difficult to compare rates of change in distant years.

[2] Technically, Figure 12.2 is plotted on a semilogarithmic scale. That is, distances on one of the two axes (the GNP axis) are proportional to the logarithms of the GNP. But you don't need to know logarithms to use this graph.

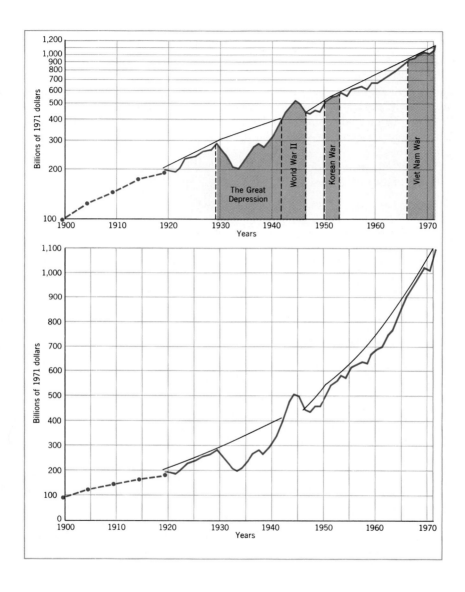

FIGURES 12.2 AND 12.3   Both graphs show our capacity GNP (in dollars of constant purchasing power) since 1900. Peacetime capacity GNP has grown at a steady rate, but we have often dropped below capacity. This fact is made more apparent by the ratio scale of Figure 12.2 than by the standard arithmetic scale of Figure 12.3.

The GNP's of full-employment years have been connected up with straight lines in Figure 12.2. These lines give us estimates of what could have been produced in intervening years if the country had been operating at full employment. Those potential levels of production can be described as **capacity GNP**—the GNP we could have achieved if we had been operating at full capacity. For instance, the GNP in 1937 was as large as it had been in the boom year of 1929. Yet 1937 was a depression year. Some 14.3 percent of the labor force was unemployed. Our labor force had grown between 1929 and 1937, as had our capital stock and technology. We were actually capable of producing a lot more than we did in 1929. The capacity GNP in 1937 is suggested by the straight line that connects 1929 and the next full-employment year, 1941. (Notice that the straight lines in Figure 12.2 show up as curving lines in Figure 12.3.)

We ignore the peaks reached in 1942 to 1945 in drawing these lines. Those were war years, and during World War II we produced well beyond our peacetime capacity. We worked overtime and skipped vacations and employed many people who normally would not have been in the labor force. The straight lines in Figure 12.2 estimate the normal peacetime capacity of the economy.

Capacity real GNP has grown continuously over this century. Over the whole period, it has risen at a rate of about 3.2 percent a year. Our actual GNP has often fallen below capacity, however.

FLUCTUATIONS IN THE GNP

Figure 12.2 does not show fluctuations that occurred before World War I, because only averages for five-year periods are available for that period. That was not an era of completely stable growth, however. There were depressions in 1903, 1907, and 1913. During World War I we operated at and above capacity, but after the war we slipped into a deep depression in 1920.

After the postwar depression ended, in 1922, the country enjoyed a long period of prosperity, interrupted by mild recessions in 1924 and 1927. These declines were small, and most people hardly noticed them. We have had many such minor ups and downs in our history.

THE GREAT DEPRESSION

The boom finally ended in 1929. Output began to slow down early in that year, but at the time the slowdown appeared to be no more than another minor recession. Then, in October, the speculative stock market boom of the late 1920s collapsed. The "market crash" did not by itself cause the Depression, but it made the decline worse. A person who one day owned a share of stock worth $100 found out the next day that it was worth only $50. He was apt to cut back on consumption expenditures accordingly. Businessmen, faced with a less certain future, reduced their investment expenditures at the same time. As a result, the mild recession of 1929 became a major depression in 1930.

By 1931 it seemed that the decline was ending. This is when President Hoover made his famous pronouncement that "prosperity is just around the corner." Then the economy was struck by another blow. An international currency crisis developed. Speculators tried to shift great quantities of money out of countries with shaky currencies. A number of European countries, most notably Germany, stopped converting their currencies except for explicitly approved purposes. Finally, Britain stopped converting its currency at a fixed rate, and the value of the pound was allowed to "float" relative to the dollar. Such events have been fairly common since 1931, but at that time full convertibility at fixed exchange rates seemed only slightly less fundamental to Western institutions than Christianity. Britain had been the keystone of the old international monetary system. When it abandoned the system, the day of disaster seemed to have dawned. Whatever were the chances for recovery before the international monetary crisis, they disappeared during the storm.

In mid-1932 there was another start at recovery, but the economy received yet another shock. There had been many bank failures already, but now they became an epidemic. Each bank failure led worried depositors to try to draw their money out of the next bank. In attempts to meet their depositors' demands the banks refused to renew loans. This action produced crises for millions of businesses. By early 1933, half the banks in the country had closed. In an attempt to stop the epidemic, state governors began calling continuous "bank holidays," so that the banks did not have to honor checks. When Franklin Roosevelt was inaugurated, in March of 1933, practically every bank in the country was closed. The GNP was at only about two thirds of its potential level, and a quarter of the labor force was unemployed.

The economy recovered quite rapidly in the next few years. By 1937 the GNP was back to its 1929 level, though unemployment rates were still very high. There was another decline in 1938, however. We did not get back to really full employment until late 1941, when World War II had been underway in Europe for two years.

THE POSTWAR ECONOMY

The economy ran at full blast during World War II. After the war there was a decline in the GNP because of strikes and retooling for civilian markets. Nevertheless, 1947 and 1948 were boom years. Producers were operating at full capacity in order to meet demands pent up by wartime rationing and shortages.

We had our first postwar recession in 1949, followed by peak prosperity during the Korean War. There were further recessions in 1954, 1958, and 1960. The late 1950s were a period of slow growth. Even at the peak of the recovery from the 1958 recession, 4.9 percent of the labor force was unemployed.

The 1960s were a period of cumulating prosperity. We went for nine years without a downturn, the longest such expansion in the country's history. From 1965 on we were running at full employment.

By 1966 the war in Vietnam had become serious. The Johnson administration, hoping for a quick victory, tried to avoid raising taxes. The result was gradually accelerating inflation. Taxes were finally increased in 1968, yet the inflation went on. By the time the Nixon administration was installed in 1969, there was general agreement that something had to be done. Taxes were raised once more and credit was made much tighter. The result was another recession in 1970, from which the country did not fully recover until 1973. The next year saw another downturn, caused not by inadequate demand but by limited supplies of crucial inputs, especially fuels. This was the first fall in GNP caused by capacity limitations since just after World War II.

INFLATION AND DEFLATION

During this history of fluctuations, prices were changing along with output and employment. Figure 12.4 traces the Consumer Price Index over the years since the turn of the century. We plot it, too, against a ratio scale, because we want to compare rates of change.

The general picture is one of rising prices. Yet there are variations from year to year. There were two periods of significant **deflation,** when the average level of prices fell. These deflations were part of the serious depressions of 1920 and 1929 to 1933. In addition, prices fell slightly in the last years of the 1920s and from 1937 to 1939.

Most other years have been marked by rising prices. There were rapid inflations during World War I, and just before and just after World War II. (Prices were controlled during the period America was in the war.) Prices rose ten percent a year and more during parts of both inflations.

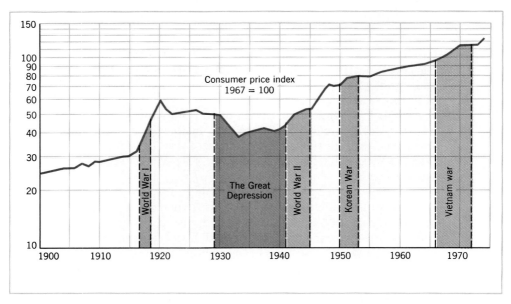

FIGURE 12.4 **Sharp inflation has accompanied each of our wars, and mild inflation has occurred in most periods of peacetime prosperity in this century. Deflation has occurred only in our worst depressions.**

They rose that fast once again in the first months of the Korean War. The peak rate of inflation during the war in Vietnam was a little over six percent a year in late 1969. There was also a major inflation—ten percent a year—caused by worldwide crop failures and the international energy crisis beginning in 1973. It was by far the most severe inflation in this century that was not associated with war.

These inflations were relatively mild compared with many other countries' experiences. For instance, during World War II, prices rose by 1,345 percent in France and 4,735 percent in Italy. In Germany after World War I, and in China after World War II, inflation reached a point at which prices doubled every few days. Such Latin American countries as Brazil and Chile have had inflations of 30 to 50 percent a year over most of the period since World War II. The inflation of 1973 and 1974, and the food and fuel crises that caused it, were also much more severe abroad than in the United States. In 1973 and 1974, prices rose eight percent a year here, against twelve percent in Britain, and eighteen percent in Japan.

Our more common experience has been creeping inflation. The generally prosperous years before World War I were marked by price increases that averaged about 1.3 percent a year. The mid-1920s saw prices rise 1.1

percent a year, though they fell slightly from 1927 to 1929. Even during the recovery from the Great Depression, prices rose 2.6 percent a year although unemployment never fell below 14 percent. Prices rose 1.6 percent a year from the end of the Korean War to 1967, when the Vietnam inflation became serious. In a few years in each period, prices rose as much as three percent. Most European countries experienced more severe inflations than we did in peacetime years since World War II.

Many of these periods of mildly rising prices may not be inflations at all. As we have seen, there have been regular improvements in the quality of goods. In addition, consumers are able to shift toward the goods whose prices rise less. As a result, the actual cost of living does not rise as fast as the Consumer Price Index does. There can be no doubt, however, in the case of the galloping inflations in this century. The inflations associated with the four wars and with the food and fuel crises that began in 1973 really represented rising costs of living, even after we allow for these biases in the statistics.

THE COSTS OF INSTABILITY
DEPRESSION

The periodic depressions in our history have been very costly. Figure 12.5 reproduces a portion of Figure 12.3 in order to give an impression of the cost of the Great Depression. The area marked in color represents the output that we could have had and didn't between 1929 and 1941. The white area represents government expenditure during World War II, from 1942 through 1945. They are of the same order of magnitude. Both sums come to a bit less than $700 billion 1971 dollars. All-out depressions and all-out war rank together as the most expensive economic disasters we can have.

Even a mild recession is costly, however. In the late 1960s we were growing at about $42 billion dollars a year in terms of 1971 dollars. If this rate had been kept up we would have reached a GNP of $1,132 billion in 1971. Instead, because of the recession, we produced only $1,047 billion in that year. In other words, we could have produced—and didn't produce—another $85 billion worth of goods and services in that one year. That figure is considerably more than the whole defense budget for the same year!

This difference is real waste. The man-hours that go unused during a depression are not stored up to be used after the depression is over; they are gone forever. Indeed, this lost output understates the cost of depression. If left unemployed long enough, people lose their skills. Businessmen invest less in plant and equipment during a depression than they do

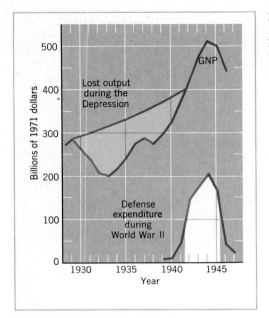

FIGURE 12.5 We lost about as much in output during the Great Depression as we spent on our whole war effort in World War II.

during a boom, so less capital stock accumulates. New techniques are slower to develop during depressions. As a result, we are at a lower level of output when the depression is over than we would have been if we had maintained prosperity throughout the same period. Continuous full employment will produce a more rapid rate of growth than will periodic depressions with only occasional approaches to full employment.

THE COST OF INFLATION

Inflations do not involve real losses the way depressions do. We are usually close to capacity output during an inflation. People may feel cheated because prices go up. But on the average their incomes are rising just as fast.

The main problem with inflation is that it arbitrarily redistributes income and wealth. People with fixed money incomes, such as persons living on interest, rents, or pensions, see the real value of their incomes decline. They can buy fewer goods and services with the same money income as before. The inflation doesn't reduce real GNP, so someone must be gaining what those with fixed incomes lose. The winners are the people who receive the rising prices and pay the fixed costs. These people are the recipients of profits: the corporations and the self-employed. The share of wages and salaries in the national income does not change much one way or another during inflation because wage rates rise almost as fast as prices.

Just the opposite happens during deflations, when prices are falling. Then the earners of fixed incomes, such as interest, rent, and transfer payments, find themselves with increasing real income. Profits, on the other hand, fall off sharply. Deflation is rare in the American economy, however. When it does occur it is usually associated with severe depression, which is a much more serious problem.

Inflation also redistributes wealth. The owners of assets defined in dollars, such as bank accounts, insurance policies, and bonds, find themselves after an inflation with the same dollar values but less in real terms than before. Total national wealth doesn't diminish, however, so again there must be a winner as well as a loser. This time the gainer is the person who was in debt. At the start of the inflation he had a $15,000 house and a $10,000 debt. When it was over he had a house worth $20,000 and a debt of only $10,000. His net assets went up from a third to a half a house. Since most corporations have debts, stockholders have often come out of inflations better off than they were before. People who own real property free of debt, such as real estate or diamonds, are unaffected by inflation. They own exactly the same things at the end of the inflation that they did at the beginning.

What is wrong with arbitrary redistribution of income and wealth? It isn't that people are poorer; on the average they aren't. But some people have gained while others have lost. Many people feel that such redistributions are unfair. Ultimately, of course, that is a value judgment.

To get the full impact of such redistributions you have to look at all-out inflations of a sort Americans have not seen in this century. Consider a frugal middle-class German who carefully provided for his old age and for his family by buying annuities and insurance policies before and during World War I. By 1922, after several years of galloping inflation, those policies weren't worth enough to buy a postage stamp. His entire savings had been wiped out. At the same time, the man down the street who was always in debt and the owners of the great corporations were riding high. Their debts had been effectively cancelled.

After such an experience our frugal German might understandably feel that there was something wrong with the whole system. Hitler's early support came during this period of disastrous inflation. In the late 1920s, after the inflation was over, that support faded. It took the Great Depression for Hitler to reach office. In the last election before he reached power, a majority of the German population voted either for the Nazis or for the Communists and against liberal democracy. The inflation was undoubtedly one reason for their rejection of the existing system.

ANTICIPATED AND UNANTICIPATED INFLATIONS

Our inflations in this century have been far less severe than the German inflation after World War I. Thus, any redistribution of income and wealth that resulted would naturally have been much smaller. In fact, the mild inflations that have accompanied most of our peacetime prosperities probably had no significant effect at all on the distribution of income and wealth.

The creeping inflations were relatively easy to take because most people anticipated them. If inflations are *fully* anticipated, their effect on the distribution of income and wealth will be nil. If everyone is sure that prices will rise three percent a year, then unions that would have settled for a four-percent wage increase with no inflation will insist on seven percent instead. Congress can usually be counted on to make a similar adjustment in social security benefits. Interest rates will rise, too. A rate of interest of eight percent plus an inflation of three percent leaves the depositor or lender just as well off as he would be with interest rates of five percent and no inflation. Owners of bonds or bank accounts with those high interest rates receive enough additional interest to make up for inflation's erosion of their assets. And the debtor gains no more from the reduction of his real debt than he pays in higher interest. Only when inflation is unanticipated does it redistribute income and wealth. After the experience of the last 40 years, it is hard to believe that anyone is surprised or caught unprepared by our typical peacetime inflation. But when the inflation rate swiftly rose from four percent to ten percent a year in 1973 and 1974, many people were caught unprepared.

There seems to be general agreement that we should avoid major depressions and galloping inflations. Most people would undoubtedly prefer to avoid both milder recessions and creeping inflation, too, but here their feelings are less strong. We are sometimes in situations in which we must have a recession to avoid inflation or inflation to keep out of a recession. When these are the choices, people differ about what should be done. The choice between recession and inflation is a value judgment about which the reader will have to make up his own mind.

SUMMARY
GNP is the total output of final goods and services of the country, and the national income is the total payment for factor services. They are two

sides of the same picture. The unemployment rate is the percentage of the labor force that is without work. In the United States, full employment means an unemployment rate of three to four percent. The Consumer Price Index measures the cost of a market basket consisting of the items bought by an average working-class family, expressed as a percentage of its base-year value. When inflation occurs, such an index rises.

The GNP has often fallen below capacity levels. At the bottom of the Great Depression we were operating at two thirds of capacity. Even in recessions, GNP can be tens of billions of dollars below capacity levels. Our normal peacetime experience in this century has been mild inflation punctuated by more severe inflations during each of our wars. The main fault with inflation is the arbitrary redistribution of income and wealth that results. Even this effect is largely avoided if the inflation is anticipated.

STUDY QUESTIONS

1   Would a measure of economic activity that involved adding together consumption and wages and salaries make sense? Why or why not?

2   You take the job mowing my lawn that we discussed back in Chapter 7. I pay you five dollars for it.

   a. Does this five dollars belong in the GNP? In the national income? (The right answer is both. Can you see why?)

   b. Now suppose you had to rent the lawn mower from an equipment rental company for a dollar to do the job. Would my hiring you still contribute five dollars to the GNP? How much would appear in the national income now? (Hint: How does the dollar appear to the man who rents you the lawn mower?)

   c. Now I fire you and mow my lawn myself. What happens to the GNP? To the national income? Has the total output of the country really changed? How about total income?

3   In 1972 the consumer price index was 125, based on 1967. Below are five possible interpretations of the number. They aren't all correct, but I've seen students come up with each of them. Consider each one in turn: Is it a meaningful statement? Is the single consumer price index of 125 sufficient information to justify the statement? If not, what more information would be needed to justify it?

   ☐ Prices were 25% too high in 1972.

   ☐ We were having a 25% inflation in 1972.

   ☐ We were having a 5% per year inflation in 1972.

☐ We were having inflation in 1972.

☐ Sometime between 1967 and 1972 we had a good deal of inflation.

4   In 1969 the GNP was $930 billion. It rose to $977 billion in 1970. That sounds like prosperous growth. But be careful. Real GNP, expressed in 1971 dollars, went from $1,030 billion to $1,025 billion from 1969 to 1970. That sounds more like stability. But be careful again. The unemployment rate was 3.5% in 1969 and 4.9% in 1970. How do all these figures fit together? Specifically, how can GNP rise by $47 billion while real GNP falls by $5 billion? And how can real GNP stay so close to constant while we are going from one of our lowest unemployment rates to quite substantial unemployment? Finally, taking all three numbers together, what kind of year would you say 1970 was?

5   "Nobody gains from inflation." Do you agree? How about depression? Does anyone gain from a depression?

FURTHER READING

Concepts of national income, unemployment rates, and price indexes, and the sources in which they can be found, are described in Ralph Andreano, E. Farber, and S. Reynolds, *The Student Economist's Handbook* (New York: Harper & Row, 1967). Statistics on these and other economic indicators are reported at the backs of the *Economic Reports of the President* prepared each January by the Council of Economic Advisors (Washington: U. S. Government Printing Office). The text of each economic report analyzes recent changes in these variables. Good places to read about the depression are John K. Galbraith, *The Great Crash, 1929*, 3rd ed. (Boston: Houghton Mifflin, 1972) and Lester Chandler, *America's Greatest Depression, 1929–1941* (New York: Harper & Row, 1970).

APPENDIX TO CHAPTER 12
NATIONAL
INCOME
ACCOUNTING

Just 25 years ago, GNP and national income were obscure concepts known only to professional economists and their students. Today they have become familiar parts of the vocabularies of politicians and reporters. The bare-bones discussion of these concepts in the previous chapter should be enough to get you through this book and permit you to understand the politicians and reporters. Yet there is a good deal more to the national income accounting system. This appendix is a quick survey of the whole system.

OUTPUT AND INCOME

GNP is the total value of final goods and services produced in the economy. National income is the value of all factor services used in production. GNP and national income are two sides of the same picture. In fact, in a very simple world they would be exactly the same thing.

Suppose that firms buy only factor services from households and that they sell only final products to households. In other words, assume that there are no sales between firms. Also assume that there is no government. These are essentially the assumptions that underlie the circular flow diagram in Figure 12.6. (For the moment we will also assume that plant and equipment do not depreciate.)

Here is the income statement of one of the firms involved:

INCOME STATEMENT

Output		$1,000
Expenses		
Wages	$800	
Interest	50	
Rents	50	900
Profits		$ 100

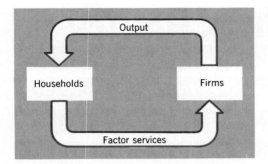

FIGURE 12.6 The circular flow of output and income in a very simple economy.

Its $1,000 of output is its contribution to GNP. Its expenses are all factor payments, which will be part of the national income. The difference between its output and its expenses is profit, which is also factor income. Profits, too, belong in the national income. Each firm's contribution to GNP, therefore, would exactly equal its contribution to national income. This would be true no matter what happened to the value of output or to costs. For instance, suppose its output falls to $800 but that wages, interest and rent stay the same. Then its profit would be

$800 − $900 = −$100

That is, it would have a $100 loss. Its contribution to the national income would be

Wages	$800
Interest	50
Rents	50
Profits	−$100
	$800

That figure is the same as its value of output again.

To arrive at the GNP in this simplified world we could just add up the total outputs of all firms. The national income would be the sum of all factor payments made by all firms. The two would be equal, because profits would just be the difference between the value of all outputs and the value of all the labor, land, and borrowed capital employed.

Of course, the real world is not this simple. Neither are the national income accounts. When the complications of the real world are added, GNP will no longer exactly equal national income. Still, the two measures will be closely related, and they will move together from year to year.

VALUE ADDED

The first complication to tackle is that real firms buy and sell among themselves, and not just with households. If we were to add up the total output of all the firms in the country, we would get a number much greater than the GNP. The reason can be seen in the slightly more complicated circular flow diagram in Figure 12.7. Here the firms are distinguished by industry. The coal firms sell to the steel industry, and steel sells to the auto producers. If we just added up the total sales of coal, steel, and autos, we would be counting the steel twice. Autos are made of steel, so steel is part of the value of the autos produced. Similarly, we would be counting the coal three times.

To get around this problem, the Commerce Department includes in the GNP only the output that is used for final consumption, investment, government purchases, or exports. In the simplified economy shown in Figure 12.7, the only thing counted in the GNP would be the $2,000 of automobile sales.

Counting only goods sold for final use exaggerates the importance of the auto industry, however, while it understates the importance of coal and steel. An alternative that avoids this problem is to measure the value added in production at each level of output. The **value added** by a firm is the value of its output minus what it buys from other firms.

In Figure 12.7 the value added by the coal producer is $500, because it buys nothing from other firms. The value added in steel is $1,000 minus the $500 it had to spend for coal, or $500. Similarly, the value added by the automobile producer is $2,000 − $1,000 = $1,000. The total value added by all three is $500 + $500 + $1,000 = $2,000. That is the total value of the GNP, once more.

FIGURE 12.7   A more complicated circular flow diagram, in which some firms buy from or sell to other firms.

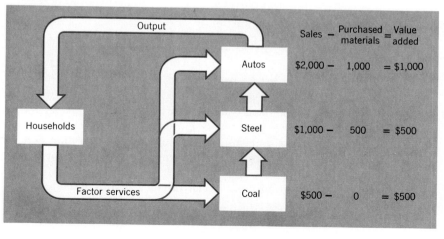

Value added is a useful concept for measuring the economic importance of a particular firm or industry or community. Consider two cities, one with a meat packing plant and one with a cement mill. Both plants make shipments of ten million dollars a year. However, this fact does not necessarily mean that the two towns are equally important economically. If they are like most plants in their industries, the cement plant will have a much higher value added than the meat packer. A typical cement plant that sells ten million dollars worth of cement per year would have a value added of something like $5,600,000. It would yield wages, interest, rents and profits a little under that figure. On the other hand, a typical meat packer with shipments of ten million dollars would have a value added of only $1,500,000 and would employ labor, land, and capital worth no more than that. The reason the cement plant is economically so much more important than the packing plant is that the cement plant buys relatively little from outside (only $4,400,000 in this case). On the other hand, most of what the meat packer ships out was actually produced by farmers and not by the plant ($8,500,000 in this case). Value added is a much better indicator of how important the two firms are than their total output or shipments.

The Bureau of the Census conducts censuses in our major industries about every five years. They include the Census of Agriculture, the Census of Mineral Industries, the Census of Manufactures, the Census of Business (which covers wholesaling, retailing, and many services), the Census of Transportation, and the Census of Governments. Value added is reported directly in the censuses of mining and manufactures. You can look up the economic importance of these industries for particular communities directly. For other sectors of the economy, value added can be estimated from the information given in the censuses. Estimates of the GNP depend heavily on these censuses. The GNP estimate in years between the censuses are based on sample surveys and on various other economic indicators, such as employment, payrolls, and the output of certain goods for each calendar quarter.

NET NATIONAL PRODUCT

The next complication has to do with depreciation, which we have ignored until now. Suppose that the total value added for all the firms in the country were ten billion dollars, while the plant and equipment of the country depreciated one billion dollars each year. If we were to take our whole ten-billion-dollar value added in wine, women, and song, we would find ourselves a billion dollars poorer at the end of the year. Our plant and equipment would have depreciated by that much.

What is the right measure of the national product, then, one that ignores depreciation or one that adjusts for it? The Commerce Department gives us both numbers and lets us make the choice. The GNP is the total output of final goods (that is, the value added in all industries), ignoring depreciation. The **net national product** (NNP) is the GNP minus the depreciation that occurs during the year—what the Commerce Department calls capital consumption allowances. The net national product is the amount that the country can consume year after year without depleting its capital stock.

Depreciation does not necessarily imply replacement. In any one year we could consume more than our net national product. We did this at the bottom of the Great Depression. Again, during World War II, consumption plus government expenditure exceeded the GNP. At the end of these years we had less plant and equipment than when we began. Net national product still moved up and down with GNP, however, since the plants and equipment went right on depreciating even though we didn't replace them. Total depreciation depends on the total value of plant and equipment on hand. It doesn't change much from one year to the next, whether we add to plant and equipment or let them run down. NNP equals GNP minus depreciation in any sort of year. The two measures always move up and down together.

It is useful to distinguish between **gross investment** and **net investment** as well. Part of our investment expenditure each year goes to replace old plant and equipment. (The replacement need not be in the same line of business where the depreciation is occurring. We may replace worn-out buggy whip factories with a new spark plug plant.) Net investment is just gross investment minus depreciation. The net national product is the sum of consumption, *net* investment, government purchases, and exports minus imports.[1]

NATIONAL INCOME

In the very simple economy with which we started, the national product and the national income were equal. Now we have two national products, net and gross. Which one of them is closest in concept to national income? Clearly the answer is net national product. The owners of plant and equipment do not consider depreciation as part of their profits.

Unfortunately, there is yet another complication. When we include government in our picture, we are faced with taxes, and we must decide what to do with them. Should they or should they not be treated as part of factor incomes? Income, social security, and property taxes are no problem. The owners of the factors of production are considered to pay these taxes *after* they receive their

[1] The term used in the Commerce Department's national accounts is "gross or net private domestic investment." The words "private domestic" indicate that government and foreign investments are excluded.

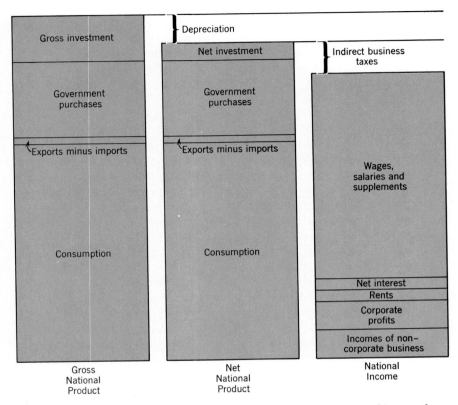

FIGURE 12.8   Gross national product, net national product, and national income: how they are related and what each measure contains.

incomes. In other words, national income is the sum of before-tax incomes paid for factors of production.

Excise and sales taxes do cause a problem, however. A pack of cigarettes that sells for 50¢ should surely go into the GNP at 50¢. Yet half of that amount is an excise tax that no one counts as income. Indirect business taxes (excise and sales taxes) are therefore *excluded* from the national income but *included* in the gross and net national product.

Figure 12.8 summarizes where we have gotten to. Gross national product is the sum of the value added in all industries. In other words, it is the sum of all final goods and services used in consumption, investment, government purchases, and exports minus imports. Net national product is GNP minus depreciation. National income is our total factor payments, or the net national product minus indirect business taxes.

PERSONAL INCOME AND DISPOSABLE INCOME

Not all of our national income is available to the households to spend as they see fit. At the same time, there are some household incomes that are not included in the national income. As a result, national income accountants compute two other measures as well, personal income and disposable income, to show the effects of these additions and subtractions.

Personal income can be thought of as the sum of all individual incomes before personal taxes. To calculate the personal income, starting from the national income, we must first subtract all factor payments that do not go to individuals. We must then add in all transfer payments. The cost of employing labor includes such non-wage payments as the social security tax and contributions to pension funds. These payments must be subtracted from the national income because they do not become a part of personal income. Similarly, corporate profits do not go to individuals directly, though dividends do. Therefore, corporate profits are subtracted from national income, and dividends are added.

Government transfer payments, such as veterans' checks, are available to individuals for consumption. However, they do not represent payments for factor services. They should be included in the personal income, but *not* in national income. Interest paid on the public debt is also treated as a transfer payment. It, too, is included in the personal income but not in the national income. This treatment of government interest payments may seem arbitrary, but there is some justification for it. Suppose the public debt were doubled or tripled. If we were to treat the interest on the debt as a factor payment, then our figure for the national income would go up. Yet we would actually have no more output in the country than before. Whether or not you consider this explanation adequate, you will have to live with the fact that interest on the public debt is considered a transfer payment for accounting purposes. It is certainly part of the incomes of individuals, so it belongs in the personal income.[2]

Finally, the amount of all individual incomes after taxes is **disposable income.** This measure is just personal income minus all personal taxes. The personal income tax and property tax are included in personal taxes. Disposable income is what the individuals in society are left with to spend as they like. What is left of disposable income after consumption is personal saving.

All these different terms are summarized in Figure 12.9. Personal income is national income plus dividends, government transfer payments, and interest on the public debt minus wage supplements and corporate profits. Disposable income is personal income less personal taxes; it is made up of consumption and personal saving.

---

[2] Interest paid by consumers is treated in the same way as interest on the public debt—as a transfer payment rather than as a payment for a factor service.

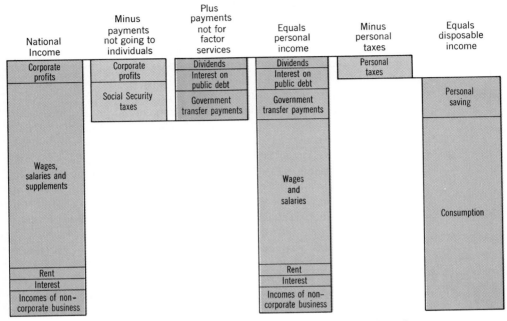

FIGURE 12.9 National income, personal income, and disposable income: how they are related and what each measure contains.

WHAT NATIONAL INCOME CONCEPTS ARE GOOD FOR

The GNP shows the total output of the country. GNP measured in dollars of constant purchasing power is our most commonly used index of economic activity. It shows year-to-year fluctuations in our economic output quite accurately.

If, instead, we are interested in our level of economic welfare and how it is changing, net national product is a better index. We cannot go on using more than our NNP year after year without gradually depleting our capital stock. The net national product is the amount a country has available to use year after year, for whatever purpose it wants.

When we want to know how income is distributed among the various factors of production, national income is the right concept to use. It was used for this purpose in Chapters 7 and 9. GNP or NNP would not be appropriate for this purpose, because they include depreciation or indirect taxes or both, which no one counts as income. Personal income wouldn't be right either, because it excludes some important factor incomes: undistributed corporate profits and social security taxes. Also it includes some things that are not factor incomes, notably transfer payments.

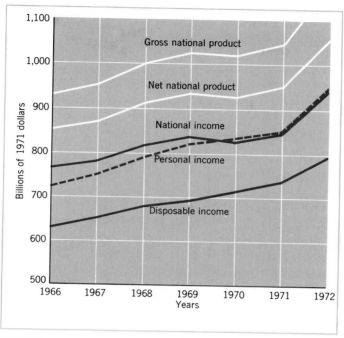

FIGURE 12.10 Gross national product, net national product, and national income always move together. Personal and disposable incomes grow more smoothly, because taxes, transfer payments, and undistributed corporate profits absorb much of the fluctuations in output.

A government official trying to estimate the effects of various income tax rates on government revenue would want to use personal income. Finally, disposable income is the appropriate measure for anyone trying to estimate consumer demand for some commodity, or for consumption goods in general.

An important aspect of the relationship between the various output and income concepts is the way that they change during business fluctuations. Figure 12.10 shows the changes that occurred in these measures between 1966 and 1972, expressed in 1971 dollars. During the expansion from 1966 to 1969, all five measures rose together. When we went into a recession in 1970, our real GNP fell, and net national product and national income fell with it. Personal income continued to rise, however, and disposable income rose even faster.

This experience is typical. Depreciation and indirect business taxes do not change much from year to year, so net national product and national income are bound to move closely with the GNP. Disposable income is well cushioned from short-term fluctuations in the economy, however. When we go into a depression, corporate profits fall, but dividends tend to stay up. Similarly, social security taxes and personal tax collections fall, but transfer payments stay up or even rise (due to such programs as unemployment insurance). As a result, disposable income falls off much less than GNP does. Indeed, it can even rise during a mild recession, as it did in 1969 and 1970. This mechanism keeps the level of consumption up and helps to keep a recession from becoming a more severe depression. In 1929, when the buffers between the GNP and disposable income were much weaker, a drop in output meant an almost equal drop in take-home pay. Consumption could not stay up then as it would today.

STUDY QUESTIONS

1   The numbers below approximate the 1973 values of the items shown, in billions of dollars. Using these numbers, compute the Gross National Product. From that figure derive the Net National Product and the National Income. Then derive Personal Income and Disposable Income from your value for the National Income.

Consumption	$800	Government transfer payments to persons	$110
Wages, salaries, and supplements	785	Government purchases of goods and services	280
Net interest income	50	Interest on the public debt	40
Capital consumption allowances (depreciation)	110	Personal taxes	150
Gross private domestic investment (gross investment)	200	Indirect business taxes	120
Exports	100	Social security taxes	90
Imports	95	Corporate profits	110
Rental income of persons	25	Dividends	30
		Incomes of unincorporated business	85

2   You can check your results in Question 1 by starting from the income side.

First find National Income by adding up total factor payments. Next, derive Net National Product and Gross National Product from your National Income figure. Similarly, you can find Personal Income by adding up total income payments to persons. Then derive Disposable Income from Personal Income. You should get the same answers as you did in Question 1.

13
THE
DETERMINANTS
OF
GNP

What is the cause of economic fluctuations? Why does the GNP fall in some years to levels that involve severe unemployment, and rise in others so fast as to involve us in inflation? In this chapter we will try to work out what determines the level of the GNP.

AGGREGATE DEMAND

At one level, of course, the answer to these questions is very simple. The decision to produce more or less, and therefore to employ more or fewer resources, is made by business. But this answer does not get us very far. Businessmen can hardly be expected to increase their output of their own accord, merely because the country is in a depression. There is no reason for them to decrease it just because inflation threatens. No single firm is large enough to take responsibility by itself for national economic stability. Even General Motors, the largest industrial firm in the world, employs less than one percent of the American labor force.

Firms increase or decrease their output and employment in response to changes in the demand for their products. It follows, therefore, that GNP, employment, and national income all depend on the country's **aggregate demand,** the total demand for all goods and services. Aggregate demand has three major components: consumption, investment, and government purchases.[1] It is worth looking at each of these elements in detail, because the things that determine them differ.

[1] There is one other element of aggregate demand: exports minus imports. We will ignore it at this point, but it will be discussed in Chapter 17. For the present we will assume that the country is a closed economy that neither exports nor imports. In actuality, exports and imports play only a minor role in the American economy.

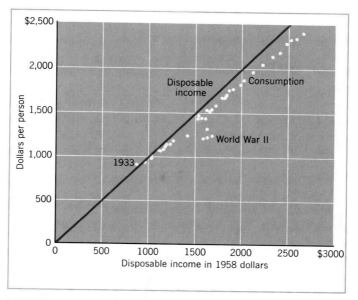

FIGURE 13.1 Over the last several decades, per capita consumption
has been very closely related to per capita disposable income.

CONSUMPTION

By far the largest element of our peacetime aggregate demand is consumption. When we considered the demand for eggs in Chapter 5, we
made a list of variables that were likely to affect it. Now consider the
demand for *all* consumer goods. Why did consumers in 1971 buy $662
billion worth of goods, rather than $600 billion or $700 billion? You
could easily think of some reasons. A good list might include the stock of
durable goods already in the hands of consumers, the amount of money
and other financial assets that they held, and their expectations about
future prices and incomes. However, by far the most important variable
in determining total consumption is income. To keep our analysis man-
ageable, we will focus first on this one variable and assume that all
others are constant. (This is the same sort of thing that we did when we
analyzed the demand for eggs in Chapter 4. Then we worked with the
price of eggs and assumed that all other variables that might affect egg
consumption were constant.)

Figure 13.1 compares per capita consumption expenditures with per
capita disposable income for the years since 1929. Each dot shows the
level of consumption per person and the disposable income per person
for a given year. To make the comparison easier, the chart also includes a

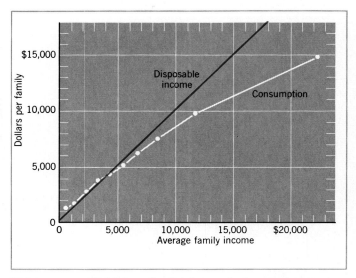

FIGURE 13.2 **The higher a family's income is, the more it consumes.**
However, consumption does not rise as fast as income.

straight line showing disposable income. The amount by which people's
actual consumption differs from their disposable income is indicated by
the position of the points in relation to the diagonal line. Notice that the
higher the disposable income is in any year, the higher is consumption
as well. This relationship holds true over the entire period except for the
obviously unusual years of World War II.

A second piece of evidence about the consumption–income relationship appears in Figure 13.2. It shows the results of a survey, made by the
Bureau of Labor Statistics, of consumption expenditures by families in
1960. The families are grouped by their incomes in that year. The graph
again shows that the higher a family's income was, the more they
consumed.

Neither of these diagrams as it stands, though, can serve as an exact
indication of the relationship between income and consumption. The
other variables—stocks of durable goods, cash, and other assets—all
change as we go from year to year or from poor households to rich ones.
Nevertheless, more complex studies that take these other variables into
account still show consumer spending to be related to income in just
about the way that is pictured in these two diagrams.

One explanation for this pattern is that people try to make the most out
of their lifetime incomes. To accomplish this they tend to even out their

consumption expenditures from high-income to low-income years. When you receive a windfall inheritance you don't spend it all as soon as it comes in. Instead, you spend a little more out of all subsequent incomes than you did before. Similarly, when you lose your job and have an unusually low income for a while, you are apt to keep your spending somewhere close to your usual level. You will save a smaller percentage of your income until things get better. It has been suggested that consumers base their spending decisions on their expected long-term levels, rather than on what they happen to be receiving right now.

Figures 13.1 and 13.2 both compare consumption in particular years with disposable income in those same years. They do not take into consideration people's normal expected incomes. In a depression, most people's disposable incomes are low compared with what they normally expect. Thus, they tend to spend an unusually large percentage of their incomes on consumption and save very little. In fact, in 1933, the worst year covered by Figure 13.1, all Americans taken together spent more on consumption than their *entire* disposable incomes. They drew down their past savings or increased their debts. Conversely, in boom years people save a relatively large percent of their incomes. They increase their accumulated savings or pay off debts in the process.

The same sort of thing shows up in Figure 13.2. Included in the low-income families were many people who were retired or temporarily unemployed. There were also many students. The unemployed and the retired had received higher incomes in most other years than they did in 1960, and the students expected to have higher incomes in later years than they received in 1960. Such people tended to spend more than their 1960 incomes. They either drew on what they had saved earlier or went into debt. To take the extreme case, if you went through the whole year without so much as a penny in income, you would still find some money to spend just to keep alive.

At the same time, many people in the high income brackets in 1960 were earning more than they expected to average over their entire lives. Many of them were people in their most productive years. Such people tend to save a high percentage of their incomes, paying off debts (perhaps incurred when they were unemployed or in school) and building up their savings (to help their children when they get to college or to provide for retirement).

THE CONSUMPTION FUNCTION

Our main goal in this chapter is to find out what determines the level of the GNP. Our next step, therefore, is to work out the relationship be-

GNP (billions)	CONSUMPTION (billions)
$1,200	$900
$900	$700
$600	$500
$300	$300
$0	$100

TABLE 13.1   A consumption function

tween consumption and the GNP rather than disposable income. The main differences between GNP and disposable income are that GNP includes corporate savings (undistributed corporate profits) and taxes of various sorts (excise taxes, corporate taxes, social security taxes, and personal taxes) and excludes government transfer payments (social security benefits, veterans' benefits, and the like). As the GNP rises, so do corporate savings and taxes. At the same time, when the GNP goes up, transfer payments such as unemployment insurance and welfare tend to fall. In general, the result is that disposable income rises with the GNP, but by a smaller amount. Since consumption itself rises by less than disposable income, consumption will certainly rise less than the GNP.

Economists refer to the relationship between GNP and consumption as the **consumption function.**[2] Table 13.1 shows a hypothetical consumption function. That is, it shows the level of consumption that will occur at each indicated level of GNP, if all other things that might affect consumption stay unchanged. Both consumption and GNP are measured in dollars of constant purchasing power. The consumption function from Table 13.1 is plotted as the line marked C in Figure 13.3.

We are particularly interested in the rate at which consumption rises with the GNP, because this rate determines how much total spending will rise or fall when the economy experiences a shock. In economic jargon, this rate is known as the **marginal propensity to consume,** or **mpc** for short. Technically it is equal to the change in consumption divided by the change in GNP, or $\Delta C/\Delta GNP$. (The Greek letter Δ stands for *change.)*

[2] In the complex statistical models that economists use to analyze the real economy and to make predictions for it, the consumption function usually shows the relationship between disposable income and consumption. Other parts of those models determine the relation between GNP and disposable income. We combine the two relationships into one here for the sake of simplicity.

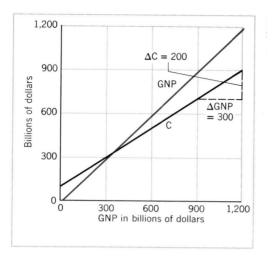

FIGURE 13.3 A consumption function. Consumption rises as GNP does, but not as fast.

In our example, over the range of GNP from $900 to $1,200 billion, the marginal propensity to consume is

$$\frac{\Delta C}{\Delta GNP} = \frac{900 - 700}{1200 - 900} = \frac{200}{300} = 0.667.$$

That is, consumers will spend two thirds of any *extra* GNP on consumption. In the diagram, the mpc shows up as the slope of the consumption curve. The triangle drawn on the consumption curve has the change in GNP as its base. The accompanying change in consumption is its altitude. In the example, a $300-billion increase in GNP leads to a $200-billion increase in consumption. If the marginal propensity to consume were greater, the consumption curve would be steeper.

For simplicity, we have picked a consumption function whose marginal propensity to consume is the same at all levels of the GNP. This would not have to be the case in practice. If national consumption patterns followed those in Figure 13.2, would the mpc rise or fall as the GNP increased? Look the answer up in the footnote.[3]

There is a related concept that is easy to confuse with the marginal propensity to consume. It is the **average propensity to consume.** It is important to keep the two concepts separate. Average propensity to consume is defined as the ratio of *total* consumption to the *total* GNP. In

---

[3] . . . . . .
If it would fall as GNP increased. Rich people seem to consume less out of their *additional* income than poor people do.

our example, at a GNP of 900 the average propensity to consume would be

$$\frac{C}{GNP} = \frac{700}{900} = 0.778.$$

You'll note that the average propensity to consume is quite a bit higher than the marginal propensity to consume, 0.667. The average propensity to consume will generally be greater than the marginal propensity to consume. The reason is that consumers ordinarily spend a larger percentage of their total income on consumption than they *add* to consumption with an increase in their income. Try it for yourself (or for your parents, if you wish). How much of your income do you now consume? If you received another $1,000 per year, how much more would you consume? Unless you are unusual, the percentage of the extra $1,000 that you would consume is less than the percentage of your total income that you consume. At low incomes you are too poor to save. At higher incomes you can save. The saving comes out of the extra income.

The marginal propensity to consume is unlikely to be more than 1.0 or less than zero. If your income goes up by $1,000 a year you will almost certainly increase your consumption, but you are not likely to increase it by more than $1,000. On the other hand, the *average* propensity to consume can easily be more than one, at least for an individual. This is often the case for students and others with temporarily low incomes. According to the Bureau of Labor Statistics survey reported in Figure 13.2, the average propensity to consume was more than one for the average family that earns $4,000 a year or less. Yet the marginal propensity to consume remained less than one, even among those poor families.

SAVING AND TAXES

As we saw in Chapter 12, GNP and national income are two sides of the same picture, except for a couple of accounting quibbles. A substantial part of national income goes into taxes. Anything else that is not consumed is saved in one way or another—either by individuals or by corporations. Saving plus taxes is therefore equal to the difference between GNP and consumption.[4]

[4] For this purpose, transfer payments, where the government pays you instead of you paying the government, are treated as negative taxes. Depreciation can be viewed as a form of (gross) saving. Any profit that corporations receive and do not distribute to their stockholders is saved by the corporation. What is left of the GNP after subtracting "taxes" (taxes minus transfer payments), depreciation, and corporate saving, is disposable income. The part of this last figure that is not consumed is personal saving. This means that the difference between GNP and consumption is "taxes" of all sorts, including negative transfers, plus saving of all sorts, including depreciation, corporate saving, and personal saving.

TABLE 13.2   A saving function

GNP (billions)	CONSUMPTION (billions)	SAVING PLUS TAXES (billions)
$1,200	$900	$300
$900	$700	$200
$600	$500	$100
$300	$300	$0
$0	$100	−$100

Table 13.2 adds another column to our consumption function from Table 13.1. The last column computes the total of saving plus taxes at each level of the GNP by simply subtracting consumption from GNP. The numbers in that column constitute a **saving function.** The function has this name for two reasons: "saving function" is less of a mouthful than "saving-plus-taxes function"; and some of the work on this subject has assumed, for convenience, that there is no government, so taxes are left out. Both the saving and the consumption functions are plotted in Figure 13.4.

The saving function is described in terms very similar to those used for the consumption function. The **marginal propensity to save,** or **mps,** is the ratio of the change in saving plus taxes to a change in the GNP. In this

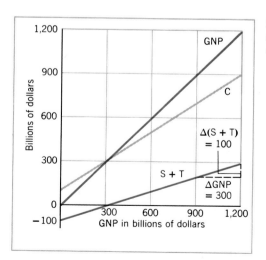

FIGURE 13.4   A saving function. It shows how saving plus taxes change as GNP changes.

example, the marginal propensity to save as GNP goes from $900 to $1,200 billion is

$$\frac{\Delta(S + T)}{\Delta GNP} = \frac{300 - 200}{1200 - 900} = \frac{100}{300} = .333.$$

You may have noticed that the marginal propensity to save is just equal to one minus the mpc. This is always the case. Any change in the GNP that does not go into consumption must go into saving or taxes. That is,

$$\Delta GNP = \Delta C + \Delta(S + T).$$

Now divide both sides of the equation by GNP and you get

$$\frac{\Delta GNP}{\Delta GNP} = \frac{\Delta C}{\Delta GNP} + \frac{\Delta(S + T)}{\Delta GNP},$$

or

$$1 = mpc + mps.$$

Therefore, mps $= 1 - $ mpc. The marginal propensity to save shows up in Figure 13.4 as the slope of the saving-plus-taxes curve.

GOVERNMENT PURCHASES

What determines the level of government purchases of goods and services? Taking one decade with the next, these items undoubtedly rise along with the level of the GNP. But we are interested in year-to-year changes in demand that occur with annual fluctuations in the GNP. A rise or fall in the level of economic activity from one year to the next seems unlikely to affect the level of government purchases at all. The main determinants of government spending in the short run are such things as our military commitments, the number of children of school age, the number of cars expected on the road in the next few years, and the quality of public services we choose to provide. These purchases will be little affected by whether the economy is in a boom or a depression at the moment. It seems reasonable to assume, then, that government purchases will be about the same, regardless of the level of economic activity.

The government purchases function is shown as a horizontal straight line in Figure 13.5. By drawing it this way we do not mean that government spending will not change from one year to the next. Rather, its level is entirely determined by other things. It is independent of the GNP. A

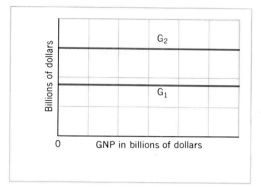

FIGURE 13.5 The level of government purchases is assumed to be
independent of the GNP. It will be a
set number of dollars regardless of
where the GNP is. But government
spending can change for other
reasons, as between G_1 and G_2.

more threatening international situation that increased our military
budgets would shift the whole curve upward, for instance, from G_1 to G_2.
Similarly, a drop in the school-age population that reduced educational
expenditures would shift it downward, as from G_2 to G_1.

INVESTMENT

The remaining element of total demand is investment. There is no doubt
that investment expenditures tend to be higher during a boom than in a
depression. Still, the relationship of investment to GNP is much less
close than that of consumption to GNP. Table 13.3 shows consumption
and investment for two pairs of years in which the real GNP was practically the same. Consumption differed very little between 1929 and 1937,
or between 1956 and 1958. This result is what our stable consumption
function would have led us to expect. On the other hand, investment in
1937 was only three quarters of what it had been in 1929. Investment in
1958 was down to 82 percent of its 1956 level.

In other words, investment is much less closely related to GNP than is
consumption. Investment is influenced strongly by the existing stock of

TABLE 13.3   GNP, consumption, and investment in selected years

YEAR	GNP	CONSUMPTION*	INVESTMENT*
1929	$203.6	$139.6	$40.4
1937	$203.2	$143.1	$29.9
1956	$446.1	$281.4	$74.3
1958	$447.3	$290.1	$60.9

*Figures are billions of 1958 dollars.

TABLE 13.4   Aggregate demand*

IF GNP WERE	PLANNED CONSUMPTION WOULD BE	PLANNED INVESTMENT WOULD BE	PLANNED GOVERNMENT PURCHASES WOULD BE	WHICH ADD UP TO PLANNED AGGREGATE DEMAND OF
$1,200	$900	$150	$100	$1,150
$1,150	$867	$150	$100	$1,117
$1,100	$833	$150	$100	$1,083
$1,050	$800	$150	$100	$1,050
$1,000	$767	$150	$100	$1,017
$950	$733	$150	$100	$983
$900	$700	$150	$100	$950

*Billions of dollars.

old capital goods, by investors' expectations, by technological changes, and by credit conditions. As a result, it can bounce about a great deal with a given GNP. In view of the independent behavior of investment expenditures, we will start out by assuming that they, like government purchases, are entirely determined by factors other than the GNP. This simplification will be removed later.

EQUILIBRIUM GNP

Now we add up consumption, investment, and government purchases and arrive at the **aggregate demand** for our hypothetical year. Table 13.4 shows the arithmetic. The numbers in the last column are simply the sums of consumption, investment, and government purchases in the indicated rows. Similarly, the consumption, investment, and government purchases functions are summed vertically in Figure 13.6 to show aggregate demand.

PLANNED VERSUS ACTUAL EXPENDITURES

The result may be a bit perplexing. In Chapter 12 we saw that GNP was exactly equal to the sum of consumption, investment, and government purchases.[5] Now it turns out that C + I + G is less than the GNP when GNP is $1,200 billion, and more than the GNP when the GNP is $900 billion. How can this be?

[5] Assuming that exports minus imports are zero.

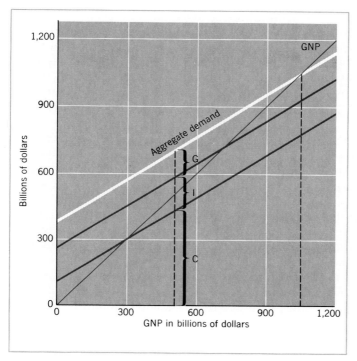

FIGURE 13.6 **Aggregate demand is the sum of consumption, investment, and government purchases. The GNP is in equilibrium when it is just equal to aggregate demand.**

The explanation is that the values of consumption, investment, and government purchases shown in Table 13.4 and Figure 13.6 represent **planned** or **intended expenditures**—what people want to buy—rather than actual expenditures. When business produces $1,200 billion dollars worth of goods, then consumption, investment, and government purchases must come to that amount after the fact. That is the case whether people planned to take that many goods or not. Something must happen to all the goods that are produced. They don't simply evaporate.

What becomes of the unwanted goods when the GNP is $1,200 billion? If the surplus output is in automobiles, the auto companies will find themselves with large inventories of unsold cars. The national income accountants will include these additions to inventory as part of "investment," whether the auto companies and dealers wanted them or not. The same applies to inventories of other storable goods. After all such adjustments, the actual C + I + G will equal the GNP, even if planned expenditures fell far short of it.

Suppose the GNP is $900 billion instead. At this level, consumers, investors, and the government want to buy more goods and services than business is producing. The auto companies will find their inventories unexpectedly depleted. Actual investment, including actual net additions to inventories, are less than were intended. Indeed, existing inventories may not be enough to meet the excess demand. In that case, consumers and investors who want to buy will find themselves on waiting lists. One way or another, the actual purchases will have to be pared down to the $900-billion-worth that was actually produced.

It is clear that planned and actual expenditures need not be the same. Which should we emphasize in our analysis? The natural answer might be that actual expenditures seem concrete, while planned C + I + G is anybody's guess. But that answer is wrong. Planned expenditures are what count in determining output. Suppose that GNP exceeds aggregate demand. In that case it is of little comfort to the auto companies that all the cars they produce will have to go somewhere (many of them into dealers' lots instead of customers' garages). Auto companies will cut back production to a quantity they think people want to buy. Similarly, if GNP is only $900 billion, so that inventories are depleted and order backlogs increase, businessmen will try to expand their output to quantities they estimate can be sold. In general, businessmen respond to the amounts that people *want* to buy, rather than to the quantity they actually succeed in buying.

This argument may still seem perplexing, but we have really been through it before. When we examined the supply and demand for eggs, for instance, we were talking about the *intended* supply and the *intended* demand. At any moment the amount of eggs actually sold exactly equals the amount actually bought. Purchase and sale are two sides of the same transaction. It isn't the levels of actual purchases and sales that determine the price of eggs. It is the amounts that people want to buy and sell. If *intended* demand exceeds *intended* supply, the price will rise, and vice versa. Similarly, it is planned aggregate demand that determines the level of the GNP, not the amounts that are actually taken.

THE DETERMINANTS OF GNP

At last we have the tools to show how the level of economic activity is determined. Suppose that the GNP were $1,200 billion to start with. What would happen if aggregate demand were like the function in Table 13.4 and the curve in Figure 13.6?

At that level of GNP, aggregate demand would be only $1,150 billion, considerably less than total output. Producers, therefore, would find inventories accumulating. Backlogs of orders would unexpectedly fall. Faced with that situation, businessmen would tend to reduce their output. GNP would fall as a result. But even when the GNP reached $1,150 billion, there would still be a gap between GNP and aggregate demand, because consumption would have declined when the GNP did. Consumption is lower with a lower GNP. The GNP would continue to decline until it was just equal to aggregate demand. That would occur at $1,050 billion.

Now try the opposite case, where aggregate demand exceeds the GNP. This would be true if the GNP started off at $900 billion. In that case there would be shortages in most markets. Auto inventories would be depleted, and the building trades and machine tool makers would find their unfilled orders mounting. All these experiences would lead businessmen to expand output. The GNP would tend to rise. But consumption would increase along with GNP, so the economy would expand until it reached $1,050 again.

In this example, $1,050 billion turns out to be what is known as the **equilibrium GNP.** Like other equilibriums in this book, it is a level where there is no tendency to change. If the economy should be away from equilibrium, there will be a tendency to move toward it.

But, as usual, equilibrium does not necessarily mean stability over time. Aggregate demand can change from year to year. Indeed, it normally will change, and equilibrium GNP will change with it. What was equilibrium GNP in 1975 probably won't be in 1978.

The term "equilibrium" does not necessarily mean that the indicated level of the GNP is desirable, either. Suppose that at the GNP of $1,200 billion in our example we were at full employment. In that case, in economic jargon, there would be a **deflationary gap.** That is, the aggregate demand would fall short of the GNP at full employment. The GNP would tend to fall to its equilibrium level of $1,050 billion. As it fell, the country would face a serious depression. By just about any standard the country would be better off at a GNP above the equilibrium.

Alternatively, suppose that the full-employment level of the GNP were $900 billion. In that case there would be an **inflationary gap** between aggregate demand and output. The GNP could not actually rise above $900 billion in dollars of constant purchasing power, because that figure would represent the full capacity of the economy to produce. The resulting shortages on most markets would cause prices and wages to rise. When equilibrium GNP exceeds the full-employment level, we can count on inflation.

Clearly, from a social point of view, the best equilibrium GNP would be one at the full-employment level. Since the full-employment level of the GNP is generally increasing, aggregate demand should ideally be increasing at the same rate.

INVESTMENT AND STABILITY

SAVING AND INVESTMENT

So far we have been looking at the interaction of aggregate demand and GNP. This tale can be retold in terms of saving, taxes, investment, and government purchases. Saving plus taxes constitute all of the GNP that is not used for consumption. Investment plus government purchases join with consumption to determine aggregate demand. The two sums—saving plus taxes and investment plus government purchases —are compared in Figure 13.7. (The saving function was derived in Table 13.2; the levels of investment and government purchases are those used in Table 13.4.)

Now look at what happens at a GNP of $1,200 billion. Saving plus taxes exceed the total of investment plus government purchases. In this situation, the things produced and not consumed will exceed the amounts demanded by the government or investors. In other words, aggregate demand will fall short of total output. The GNP will tend to fall; we will be headed into a depression. People save less and pay less tax when their incomes fall. Therefore, as GNP falls, so do saving plus taxes. The decline will stop only when saving plus taxes have gotten down to the level of investment plus government purchases.

Conversely, if the total of savings plus taxes is less than the sum of investment plus government purchases, aggregate demand must exceed the GNP. GNP must rise. As it does, so do saving and taxes. When saving

FIGURE 13.7 Equilibrium GNP occurs where saving plus taxes just equal investment plus government purchases.

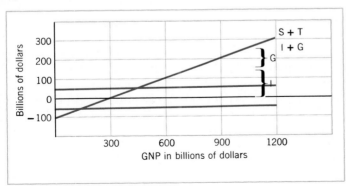

plus taxes just equal investment plus government purchases, there will be no tendency for GNP either to rise or to fall. The GNP will be in equilibrium once more.

As you may have realized, this is really just another way of presenting the aggregate demand analysis. The equivalence of the two methods is shown in Figure 13.8. The white area in the figure is the difference between consumption and GNP. It therefore corresponds to saving plus taxes, because $(S + T) = GNP - C$. The difference between aggregate demand and what is actually consumed is investment plus government purchases. $(I + G)$ is plotted separately in the figure. When $(S + T)$ is larger than $(I + G)$, aggregate demand is less than the GNP. When $(S + T)$ is less than $(I + G)$, aggregate demand is greater than the GNP. And when $(S + T) = (I + G)$, aggregate demand just equals GNP. In that case the GNP is in equilibrium.

This second type of analysis—in terms of saving and investment —does throw new light on the picture. It emphasizes the fact that saving has a depressing effect on the level of economic activity. When Keynes first presented this analysis in the 1930s, it came as a great shock to many people. Here was saving, one of the great virtues of traditional capitalism, now presented as a potential public vice. Thrift was sup- posed to be the way to accumulate capital and promote economic growth. Now we were being told that if we save too much, and nothing else happens, we will have a depression. Of course, if high saving is accompanied by a high rate of investment, it is still consistent with a high GNP. And it *will* result in a more rapid accumulation of capital. The trick is to get the saving decisions made by the general public to match the investment decisions made by businessmen.

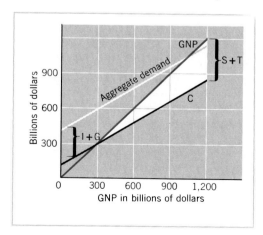

FIGURE 13.8 Equilibrium GNP determined by aggregate demand is the same as equilibrium GNP determined by (S + T) and (I + G).

AN INCREASING INVESTMENT FUNCTION

So far we have assumed that investment is unaffected by the level of the GNP. Now we can relax that assumption. In Figure 13.9, investment is shown rising as the GNP increases. This is undoubtedly a more realistic picture of the world. Businessmen are more likely to find investment profitable when incomes and outputs are high. Equilibrium GNP still occurs at the point where saving plus taxes equal investment plus government purchases. Here, however, the effect of a change in saving plus taxes is different.

Suppose that the public decided to save a larger amount out of each GNP or that tax rates were increased. In either case the result would be a shift in the saving function from $(S_1 + T_1)$ to $(S_2 + T_2)$, as shown in Figure 13.9. If the investment and government purchases functions stayed the same, the result would have to be a fall in the GNP. When the economy reached equilibrium once more, investment would be lower than before, and so would saving plus taxes. In other words, an increase in the rate of saving or taxes would lead to a *fall* in the levels of both saving and investment!

This result may seem paradoxical at first, but it makes reasonable sense. An increase in the saving function means a fall in the consumption function. This change has a depressing effect on the level of economic activity. When the GNP falls, businessmen invest less. Planned expenditures on plant, equipment, and inventories will be lower during a depression than during a boom. The decline will stop only when GNP has fallen far enough that saving plus taxes is brought down to the level of investment plus government purchases again.

This argument does not mean that increased saving is necessarily

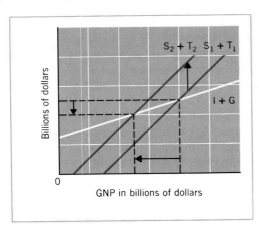

FIGURE 13.9 If investment is higher at higher GNPs, as shown here, then an increase in the saving function will cause a fall in the GNP. Hence, the equilibrium levels of saving and investment will also fall.

undesirable. Suppose that the equilibrium GNP starts out above the full-employment level. The initial situation would then be inflationary. In that case, a higher level of saving plus taxes, by deflating the economy, would bring GNP closer to the optimal level.

A good example arose during World War II. About once every six months the government put on a drive to convince people to buy more bonds. The primary purpose was not to raise money—the government could always get plenty of that; it was endowed by the Constitution with the power to create the stuff. By getting people to join the "bond-a-month plan," in which bonds were purchased automatically from their earnings before they received their paychecks, the government hoped to induce consumers to save a larger proportion of their incomes. The result was not depression. It was a reduced danger of inflation during a period when aggregate demand threatened to exceed capacity GNP.

An even more complex relationship between GNP and investment is included in many analyses. It is presented in the appendix to this chapter.

THE MULTIPLIER

Another implication of this analysis is that any change in the level of government purchases or investment will ultimately lead to a *greater* change in the GNP. To keep things simple, let us go back to the assumption that investment is independent of the level of the GNP. Then consider the effect of a $50-billion increase in investment. Figure 13.10 shows the result. The change in investment raises the total of consumption, investment, and government purchases. However, the equilibrium GNP increases not by $50 billion but by $150 billion. The reason is that the consumption rises when GNP does.

This effect is known as the **multiplier effect.** To see how it works, let us assume that this month's consumption depends on last month's GNP. Everyone is paid at the end of the month, and everyone makes his consumption decisions for the coming month in response to that paycheck. An example is worked out in Table 13.5. In January, GNP was at equilibrium, so there was no tendency for it to change. Then in February, investment (the middle column) increased to a rate of $200 billion a year. Remember that a rise in expenditures means an equal rise in income. The increase in investment showed up as an increase in March paychecks and induced an increase in consumption of

$$\text{mpc} \times \Delta\text{GNP} = \tfrac{2}{3} \times \$50 \text{ billion} = \$33 \text{ billion}.$$

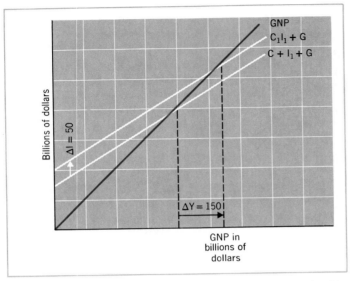

FIGURE 13.10   An increase in investment of $50 billion leads ulti-mately to a rise in the GNP of $150 billion. The reason is the increase in consumption induced by the higher GNP.

In April, the GNP rose by another $33 billion as a result. This growth in the GNP induced a further rise in consumption of $22 billion. Each successive month, the GNP was higher and more consumption was induced, though the steps gradually became smaller. When the process

TABLE 13.5   Effect of the multiplier

MONTH	GNP*	CONSUMPTION*	INVESTMENT*	GOVERNMENT PURCHASES*	AGGREGATE DEMAND*
January	$1,050	$800	$150	$100	$1,050
February	$1,050	$800	$200	$100	$1,100
March	$1,100	$833	$200	$100	$1,133
April	$1,133	$855	$200	$100	$1,155
May	$1,155	$870	$200	$100	$1,170
June	$1,170	$870	$200	$100	$1,180
.	.	.	.	.	.
.	.	.	.	.	.
Ultimately	$1,200	$900	$200	$100	$1,200

*Annual rate in billions of dollars.

finally worked itself out, the GNP had reached $1,200 billion and was in equilibrium once more.

The relationship between the initial change in investment and the ultimate change in GNP is known as the **multiplier.** The value of the multiplier is equal to 1/(1 − mpc). The algebra is worked out in the appendix to this chapter.

To illustrate the use of the multiplier, take the marginal propensity to consume from our example: ⅔. In that case the multiplier would be

$$\frac{1}{1-\frac{2}{3}} = \frac{1}{\frac{1}{3}} = 3.$$

That is, the ultimate rise in the GNP will be three times the initial rise in investment, or 3 × $50 billion = $150 billion.

The principle here is simple. The people who produced the additional investment goods spent two thirds of their additional income on, say, shredded wheat and tires. The shredded wheat and tire makers then spent *their* additional income on other goods. This spending induced yet more consumption by whoever produced what they bought, and on and on. Ultimately, the increased investment plus the *induced* consumption comes to 1/(1−mpc) times the initial change in invest-ment.

The larger the mpc, the greater is the multiplier, as one would expect. The more of any additional income that is consumed, the greater is the ultimate rise in GNP with any given initial rise in investment.

This example was worked out with the initial rise coming from in-vestment. It would have been exactly the same, though, if the initial kick had come from a rise in government purchases or from the amount that people consume with any given GNP instead. And the story can be reversed, as well. A fall in investment or government purchases or in the entire consumption function will lead ultimately to a fall in the GNP equal to 1/(1−mpc) times the initial decline.

This analysis has been intentionally simplified. Investment most likely rises with the GNP, as in Figure 13.9. If so, the ultimate change would be greater than that indicated by our simple model. The rise in GNP itself causes an additional rise in investment. This increased in-vestment must be added to the initial change that set the process moving and to the change in consumption induced by the rise in GNP.

On the other hand, an increasing GNP is likely to carry with it in-creases in interest rates and the price level, and these changes will tend to dampen the expansion. In particular, if the GNP is already at or near full employment, then a rise in investment cannot push the level of economic activity beyond the economy's ability to produce, no matter how high the marginal propensity to consume.

Similarly, if investment falls when the GNP does, a decrease in investment may cause a greater fall in the GNP than the simple multiplier would suggest. But the decline could also be dampened because of the effect of falling interest rates and falling prices. When GNP is falling, however, there is no automatic limit to the possible change in GNP. The full-employment ceiling sets an upper limit on expansion; there is no similar limit to a decline.

Altogether, the multiplier is only an approximation, but the general principle involved is still useful. The story is sometimes misinterpreted, however. During the Great Depression there was much talk of "pump priming." The analogy was to the old fashioned hand pump, which you could sometimes get going by pouring in a little water. The water would complete the seal around the piston and permit the pump to work. This would produce indefinite amounts of water for just a little put in. People who believed in economic pump priming thought that if the government would just start spending going once, it could then go away and let the economy take its course. The GNP was supposed to continue indefinitely at the higher level. In effect, they thought that the multiplier was huge—in the hundreds, perhaps.

That is not the way the system works, however. In our example it took a *continuous* addition to investment or government purchases of $50 billion each year to keep GNP $150 billion higher.

SUMMARY

The level of economic activity is determined by the level of planned or intended aggregate demand. This demand consists of planned or intended consumption, investment, and government expenditures. Consumption rises with the GNP, but not as fast. The rate at which it changes with the GNP is known as the marginal propensity to consume (mpc). Saving plus taxes is the difference between GNP and consumption. The marginal propensity to save is 1−mpc. In the short run, investment and government purchases are much less closely related to the GNP than consumption is. It is convenient, therefore, to treat them as completely independent of the GNP for a first approximation. If planned consumption, investment, and government spending are less than the GNP, there will be a fall in GNP. If they exceed it, the GNP will rise. The GNP will be in equilibrium if it is just equal to aggregate demand.

This analysis implies that saving plus taxes have a deflationary effect. Investment plus government purchases have an offsetting expansionary effect. At equilibrium, saving plus taxes just equals investment plus government purchases. If investment tends to rise with GNP, then an increase in the saving function (a fall in the consumption function) will cause a fall in GNP. The result will be an eventual fall in both saving and investment.

The multiplier shows the ultimate effect on the level of the GNP caused by a change in investment, or government purchases, or the whole consumption function. In general, the GNP will rise or fall by *more* than the initial change in aggregate demand. The reason is that the changing GNP itself leads to changes in consumption. The larger the marginal propensity to consume, the higher the multiplier will be.

STUDY QUESTIONS

1   A family consumes $400 a month out of an income of $500 a month. Can you tell from this information what the family's average propensity to consume is? Can you tell its marginal propensity to consume? What is the highest value its marginal propensity to consume is likely to be? What is the lowest it might be?

2   Work out the effect on equilibrium GNP of:

a. an increase in investment

b. an increase in taxes

c. an increase in saving

d. an increase in the amount we consume out of each dollar of income.

3   "From the point of view of society, the best level of GNP is its equilibrium level." Do you agree?

4   Distinguish between the planned and actual demand for eggs. If planned demand increases, will any more eggs be bought this week? What will happen to the price of eggs?

5   What will happen to the multiplier if the marginal propensity to consume increases? First work out an answer using the formula for the multiplier. Then work out an explanation in words. For instance, how would the numbers in Table 13.5 change if the marginal propensity to consume were greater?

FURTHER READING

The analysis presented in this chapter was developed in a book of revolutionary impact written in the 1930s by John Maynard Keynes, entitled *The General Theory of Employment, Interest, and Money* (New

York: Harcourt Brace Jovanovich, 1936), but it is heavy going for a beginner. Keynes's life and the setting in which he wrote are entertainingly described in Robert L. Heilbroner, *The Worldly Philosophers*, rev. ed. (New York: Simon & Schuster, 1972). A more complete but still popular-level description of Keynes's work appears in Robert Lekachman, *The Age of Keynes* (New York: Random House, 1966). A good place to read further on "Keynesian economics" at an elementary level is Charles L. Schultze, *National Income Analysis*, 3rd ed. (Englewood Cliffs, N.J.: Prentice-Hall, 1971).

APPENDIX TO CHAPTER 13
INDUCED
CONSUMPTION
AND
INVESTMENT

THE MULTIPLIER

The formula for the multiplier given in this chapter, $1/(1-\text{mpc})$, can be worked out using saving and investment functions. The process is shown in Figure 13.11. We have defined the multiplier as the change in GNP per dollar of additional investment. That is, it is $\Delta\text{GNP}/\Delta\text{I}$. For example, in Figure 13.11, a shift in the investment function from $(I_1 + G)$ to $(I_2 + G)$ results ultimately in a rise in economic activity from GNP_1 to GNP_2. By the time GNP is in equilibrium once more, saving plus taxes will have increased by as much as investment. Therefore, the multiplier is also equal to $\Delta\text{GNP}/\Delta(S + T)$. This formula can also be expressed as

$$\frac{1}{\dfrac{\Delta(S+T)}{\Delta\text{GNP}}}$$

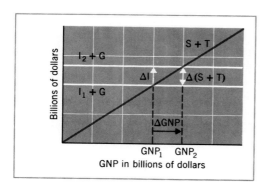

FIGURE 13.11 An increase in investment causes a rise in GNP. This rise in GNP induces a rise in (S + T) equal to the initial rise in investment.

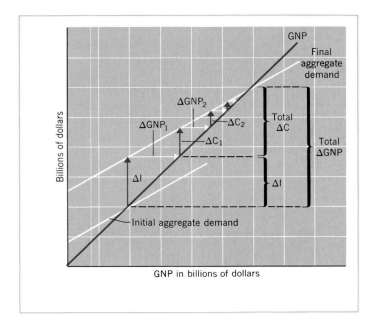

FIGURE 13.12   The multiplier. A rise in GNP due to a change in investment induces a rise in consumption. This increase in consumption leads to another rise in GNP, resulting in yet more consumption, and so forth.

This is the same as 1/(marginal propensity to save). Since mps = 1 − mpc, the multiplier can also be expressed as 1/(1−mpc).

The way in which the multiplier works can be seen graphically in Figure 13.12. The graph shows an enlarged portion of an aggregate demand diagram. An initial increase in investment of ΔI leads to an equal rise in gross national product of ΔGNP_1. This growth in turn results in a rise of consumption of ΔC_1. That increase in consumption gives rise to another increase in economic activity, ΔGNP_2. This rise, in turn, leads to a second rise in consumption, labeled ΔC_2. The process goes on indefinitely; there simply isn't space to label all the increasingly small changes. The process stops only when the equilibrium GNP is reached once more. When that happens, the GNP will have increased by the initial ΔI *plus* the total ΔC.

Those familiar with the algebra of continuous series can derive the multiplier directly from the series of events represented in Figure 13.12. The ultimate rise in the GNP is equal to

$$\begin{aligned}
\Delta\text{GNP} &= \Delta I + \Delta C_1 && + \Delta C_2 && + \cdots \\
&= \Delta I + \text{mpc } \Delta I && + \text{mpc}(\text{mpc} \cdot \Delta I) && + \cdots \\
&= \Delta I + \text{mpc } \Delta I && + \text{mpc}^2 \ \Delta I && + \cdots
\end{aligned}$$

Dividing through by ΔI, the multiplier becomes

$$\frac{\Delta\text{GNP}}{\Delta I} = 1 + \text{mpc} + \text{mpc}^2 + \cdots$$

Multiplying the equation by mpc, we get

$$\frac{\Delta\text{GNP}}{\Delta I} \cdot \text{mpc} = \text{mpc} + \text{mpc}^2 + \text{mpc}^3 + \cdots$$

Subtracting the last equation from the one preceding it, we arrive at

$$\frac{\Delta\text{GNP}}{\Delta I} \cdot (1 - \text{mpc}) = 1$$
$$\frac{\Delta\text{GNP}}{\Delta I} = \frac{1}{1 - \text{mpc}} .$$

This last is the familiar formula for the multiplier.

THE ACCELERATOR

The investment function presented in Chapter 13, where we had investment rising with GNP, is still incomplete. The amount of investment that will be induced by a given level of GNP is apt to depend on how much capital is already in place. In other words, the level of investment depends on how much investment has gone before. A rapid rise in GNP is likely to induce large investments in new capacity to meet the additional demand. Once that new capacity is in place, however, it will take yet a *further* rise in GNP just to keep investment at the previous level. If GNP rises once and then stays at the new high level, investment will eventually fall.

The notion that investment depends on the *rate of change* in GNP, rather than on the level of GNP, is known as the **accelerator principle.** To see how it works, consider the hypothetical shoe factory represented in Table 13.6. Imagine that it takes one shoe machine to produce 50,000 shoes a year. Each machine lasts five years. To start with, the firm is producing a million shoes a year and has been for some time. To maintain this output it needs twenty machines. To keep up its equipment it must replace four of these machines each year.

Now, in year three, the demand for shoes increases from 1,000,000 to 1,100,000. To handle the additional output, the firm needs 24 machines, so this year it has to buy eight machines instead of the usual four. An increase of ten percent in the demand for shoes had led to a doubling in the demand for shoe machines.

TABLE 13.6   The accelerator principle in a shoe factory

YEAR	PRODUCTION (shoes per year)	SHOE MACHINES	ANNUAL INVESTMENT IN NEW MACHINES
1	1,000,000	20	4
2	1,000,000	20	4
3	1,100,000	24	8
4	1,100,000	24	4
5	1,000,000	20	0
6	1,000,000	20	4

In year four, shoe demand stays at the new high level, so 24 machines are needed again. Since the new capacity has already been added in the previous year, the only investment required is the usual four replacement machines. If shoe demand just stays the same, once it reaches the new level investment in new machines will *fall*. It drops back to its old level. In order for investment to stay at eight machines a year, shoe demand would have had to increase again, to about 1,200,000 a year.

Instead, in our example, shoe demand now falls back to the original level of a million pairs a year. The firm now needs only twenty shoe machines again. Investment does not stay at the old level of four, however. Now the factory has 24 machines, and it needs only twenty. When this year's four wear out it simply doesn't replace them. In this case a nine-percent drop in demand—from 1,100,000 to a million—has resulted in a 100-percent fall in investment, from four machines to none.

Finally, in year six, shoe production stays at the lower level. Machine requirements remain at twenty, but now replacements are again needed. There is a *rise* in investment to four machines once more. When consumption stopped falling and stabilized at the lower level, investment *rose*.

Taking all industries together, the accelerator principle holds that investment depends on the rate of growth in aggregate demand. If demand rises rapidly, investment will be high. Then, if demand stabilizes or merely grows at a slower rate, investment will drop.

If nothing else, the rate of growth in GNP is likely to slow down when it reaches the full-employment level. Any further increases in output will be limited by the rate of growth in national economic capacity. Such a slowdown will induce a fall in investment, and hence in aggregate demand. The fall in aggregate demand will mean even lower investment and a more rapid decline in the GNP. However, investment in plant and equipment cannot fall below zero. Realistically, it never reaches even that level. After it reaches its minimum, therefore, the fall in aggregate demand will end. When aggregate demand stabilizes at its lower level, investment will rise again. It will at least reach the level needed to maintain capacity by replacement. But the resulting rise in aggregate demand will induce further increases in investment and more expansion. Moreover, if something comes along to increase aggregate demand once more—such as a war or a major new invention—investment will accelerate the expansion.

The fluctuations in economic activity that are due to induced variations in the rate of investment are difficult to predict. The way investment responds to changes in aggregate demand may vary with the rate of capacity utilization in the economy and with the particular industries affected. Still, one general conclusion can probably be drawn from the accelerator principle. Clearly, when left to its own devices, the level of economic activity would tend to fluctuate. The fluctuations would be centered in the investment demand. For that reason, investment goods industries will tend to have particularly unstable output and employment. These industries include machine tools, construction, and the production of materials used by such industries as steel and cement. Certainly our experience over the century before World War II, when the economy was largely left to its own devices, was one of fairly continuous fluctuations in economic activity, and the instability was generally centered in the investment goods industries.

STUDY QUESTIONS

1   If the marginal propensity to consume is ¾, what is the marginal propensity to save? What is the multiplier? How much will GNP increase as a result of a rise in investment of $10 billion? How much will consumption have risen when the system reaches equilibrium? How much will saving plus taxes have risen by then?

2   Suppose that the number of houses we need depends on the number of families. Then what will happen to the level of house construction if the rate of growth in the population slows down? There actually was a sharp drop in our birth rate in the late 1950s, and the birth rate has stayed low ever since. When would you expect this drop to affect the number of families? What do you think will happen to the house construction industry then?

14 UNEMPLOYMENT AND INFLATION

The analysis presented in the last chapter was developed in the 1930s by John Maynard Keynes. He had been one of the leading contributors to the main line of economic thought, but his new ideas seemed to run counter to many long-established principles of classical economics. A heated debate between the "Keynesians" and the classical economists ensued. The first part of this chapter deals with some of the important points raised by that debate. At the time, the argument was primarily about depressions. Nevertheless, it turns out to be relevant to the more common postwar problem of inflation as well. The second part of this chapter is devoted to the inflation problem.

THE LEVEL OF EQUILIBRIUM GNP

Classical economics said little about aggregate demand or equilibrium GNP. These terms were largely developed by the Keynesians. But it was not their unfamiliar language that sparked the argument. There was little doubt that aggregate demand determined the level of economic activity. The main argument was about where equilibrium income would fall.

SAY'S LAW

Classical economists believed that equilibrium would automatically be at full employment. The Keynesians, on the other hand, believed that it could occur at less than full employment. The original basis for the classical argument was **Say's Law,** named for Jean Baptiste Say, a French economist who wrote during the Napoleonic wars. Say believed that there could never be a "general glut" because "supply creates its own demand." That is, the demand for all goods and services could never fall short of the total amount supplied. Say argued that the whole reason people produce is to get goods and services. If a new producer with an additional load of potatoes enters the market, there is an increase in the total supply of goods—the potatoes—but there would also be an increase in demand for something else by the same amount. After all, our potato producer would want to spend the proceeds on other things. That was the point of his growing and selling the potatoes in the first place. In Say's world, then, any increase in total output automatically carried with it an increase in aggregate demand. It was quite possible, of course, for a surplus of any one product (say shoes) to develop. Consumers might well want other goods instead. However, there could be no surplus of *all* goods and services taken together.

What should we make of this argument? It is true that output carries with it a corresponding income. Remember that factor payments rise when GNP does. As a result, those who do the producing have the wherewithal to buy up the output. But the crucial question is, *will they?* In a world without money, where goods are exchanged through barter, output would carry demand with it automatically. Anything produced would either be used directly or be exchanged for some other good. Decisions to save would necessarily involve decisions to invest in goods by the same amount. A farmer who wanted to save would build a barn or dig a well. Or he could offer potatoes to someone who would do it for him. In a barter economy, Say's Law surely holds.

Of course, we don't live in a barter economy. We are paid in money, not goods. When we save, we often save money *without* buying capital goods. It isn't necessary by definition for individuals' plans to save to equal businesses' plans to invest. The two decisions are now relatively independent.

Say's Law made more sense in the day of the classical economists (the early nineteenth century) than it does now. They did not have a barter economy then, either, but a very large proportion of total output was consumed at home. For self-sufficient farmers, saving and investment *were* the same thing. But specialization has increased greatly since then. Exchanges of goods for money through markets have accounted for a larger and larger part of economic activity. As the economy became more specialized, there was an increasing possibility that planned saving and planned investment might not match. A well-known American economic research organization, the National Bureau of Economic Research, has attempted to trace economic fluctuations over history both in

Europe and in America. In the 1600s and 1700s the bureau did find occasional declines, but they were associated directly with disasters such as bad weather, wars, or disease. The first modern depression that might be blamed on inadequate aggregate demand is dated 1793. We have had such events fairly regularly since then. Business fluctuations due to the changes in aggregate demand arose with the development of our interdependent money economy.

SAVING, INVESTMENT, AND INTEREST

It is still possible to argue for a modern version of Say's Law. Saving decisions and investment decisions are not two sides of the same transaction anymore, but we do have financial markets that bring them together.

In the financial markets, the interest rate serves as a price for money. As interest rates rise, savers receive more for each dollar they set aside. Investors must pay more for each dollar they borrow. Even when people are investing their own money, the higher interest rate still raises the opportunity cost for the funds invested. They could be earning high interest on their money if they weren't putting it into plant and equipment.

The result might be something like Figure 14.1, which relates saving and investment to the interest rate. The saving curve slopes upward and

FIGURE 14.1 Saving and investment as functions of the interest rate. A fall in the interest rate eliminates the deflationary gap.

FIGURE 14.2 Saving and investment as functions of the GNP. A fall in the interest rate leads to a fall in the saving function and an increase in the investment function.

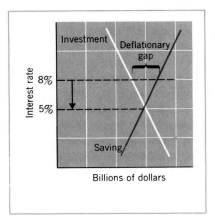

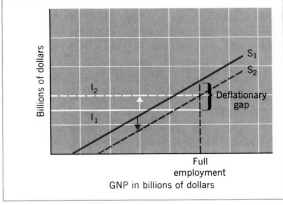

to the right. That is, savers are expected to save more if high interest rates are offered. The investment curve shows less investment expenditure at high interest rates than at low ones, because the high interest rates make investments more costly. At any one time there is a whole array of investment opportunities available to businessmen. Some appear very profitable; they would be undertaken even at very high interest rates. Others appear less profitable; they would be worthwhile only if interest rates were low. As you go down the list of opportunities, the expected yields on the investments get lower. An investment that is likely to yield its owner eight percent would be worthwhile at any interest rate up to eight percent. One that was expected to yield only five percent would be worthwhile only if interest rates were five percent or less, and so forth on down. The lower the interest rate, the more the investment expenditures that can be expected.

Suppose now that the interest rate were at eight percent, as shown in Figure 14.1. In that case, saving would exceed investment. In the Keynesian system, represented by the saving and investment functions in Figure 14.2, this situation would mean a deflationary gap. The GNP would tend to fall.

In the classical world, something else would happen. According to the classical economists, the first response would be for the interest rate to fall. As it did so, saving would decline and investment would increase. When the interest rate reached five percent in Figure 14.1, saving would equal investment. In terms of Figure 14.2, the saving function would decrease, and the investment function would increase, to the broken lines when interest rates fell. When saving came to equal investment at the full-employment level, the threat of depression would be over.

How realistic is this model as a picture of modern capital markets? The Keynesians had their doubts. Many of them questioned the importance of the interest rate in determining the rates of investment and of saving. In many investments, the interest rate is a minor expense. Its influence seems particularly doubtful in the case of high-risk investments such as inventories of finished goods. If there is a good chance that a new investment will yield 50 percent, and also a good chance that it will result in a loss, the investor is not likely to let the difference between five-percent and eight-percent interest rates affect his decision much.

There are some kinds of investments for which credit conditions do make a difference. Interest rates are important in residential housing, for instance. A moderate change in the interest rate can mean a large change in the cost and availability of mortgages. Because of things like housing expenditures, the investment curve in Figure 14.1 undoubtedly does slope downward and to the right. But it may be quite steep, because so many investments are little affected by interest rates.

The response of saving to interest rates is even less certain. You can even imagine situations in which persons might save *less* at a higher interest rate. This would be the case for a person who had a particular saving goal—say, to have $10,000 per child when the children reached college age. The higher the interest rate, the less annual saving would be needed to reach the goal. Another person, especially one who is in debt, might have a stronger incentive to save (and thus to pay off debts faster) at a higher interest rate. At the very least, however, interest rates have little effect on many people's saving. They won't have much effect on people who save for specific purposes, such as college, travel, or retirement. They also won't affect people who merely save because their incomes are higher than they expect over their lifetimes. These people would probably go on saving even if they received no interest on their money at all.

Finally, how far can interest rates fall? Suppose the saving and investment curves looked not like Figure 14.1, but like those in Figure 14.3. Even at an interest rate of zero, the public might be willing to save a lot more than investors were willing to invest. The interest rate could never fall to zero, however. No saver is going to lend at zero interest when he has the safe alternative of holding money. Since there are always costs and risks in lending, the interest rate at which one can borrow will never fall below some positive amount, maybe two or three percent. In a severe depression, investment opportunities could look so bad that planned investment would be far below planned saving, even at these minimum interest rates. If this happened, a fall in the GNP would still bring saving down to the level of investment, but that is little comfort. It would involve the very depression that falling interest rates were supposed to prevent.

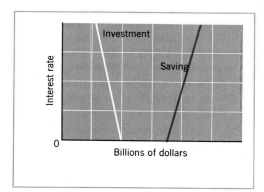

FIGURE 14.3 **If the saving and investment functions looked like this, falling interest rates could not restore equilibrium at full employment.**

Interest rates have been well above their minimum levels over most of the period since World War II. Declining interest rates could conceivably offset the relatively mild sort of recession that we have experienced at times in the last 25 years. Indeed, to some extent they have. In each recession since the Korean War, interest rates fell, and residential construction increased as a result. This induced building activity undoubtedly served to alleviate the declines. However, this interest-rate solution to recessions puts the burden of adjustment on a limited range of industries, especially on construction. The unhappier side of building expansion that occurs during a recession is the contraction that the construction industry has to endure during booms, when interest rates are high. Another problem with this mechanism is that the reaction to easier credit may be quite slow. Falling interest rates may ultimately induce more investment in some lines, but it takes a year or so for easier credit conditions to be reflected in housing expenditures. Many economists are unwilling simply to wait for the credit market to solve the problem for us. They would rather avoid recessions completely.

PRICES AND AGGREGATE DEMAND

Another argument supporting Say's Law emphasizes prices. Classical economists expected the price level to decline if aggregate demand fell below full-employment output. There would be surpluses on most markets, so the prices of most goods would be falling. At lower prices we would buy more. When aggregate demand had increased to the full-employment level of output, prices would stop falling and the depression would be over. This classical picture of the world is illustrated in Figures 14.4 and 14.5. Suppose that full employment output exceeds aggregate demand by the amount shown at P_1 in Figure 14.4. This amount is the familiar deflationary gap, shown in Figure 14.5. This gap would make the price level fall. As a result, people buy more goods. The process stops when price reaches P_2, where demand equals the full-employment output. In terms of the Keynesian diagram, the lower price has resulted in an upward shift in the aggregate demand curve to the dashed line. Once it reaches that level, there is no more reason for GNP to fall. The threat of depression is over.

This is certainly the way the market for any one commodity works. If there is a surplus of eggs, their price will fall until the surplus disappears. But can the same thing work for all goods taken together?

The Keynesian answer is, not nearly so easily. When we looked at the demand for eggs we found two reasons why the quantity sought would be greater at lower prices: the substitution effect and the income effect.

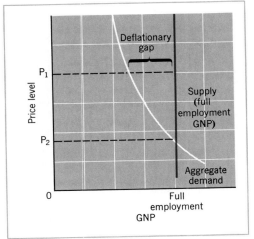

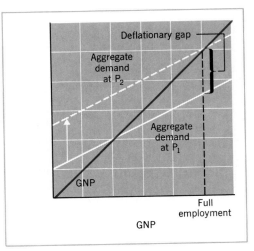

FIGURE 14.4 (left)   Aggregate demand as a function of the price level. A deflationary gap would cause prices to fall until the economy reached full employment.

FIGURE 14.5 (right)   Here the effect of falling price level is to shift the aggregate demand curve upward until the deflationary gap is closed.

Neither of these explanations will work when we are accounting for aggregate demand. When the price of eggs falls, we substitute them for meat and cheese, but if the general price level falls, what can we substitute *all goods* for? Perhaps foreign goods and services. A fall in our own general price level will induce consumers to switch from imports to domestic goods. In addition, foreigners will be induced to buy more of our exports. Both of these developments would indeed increase aggregate demand. However, imports and exports are only a minor part of the United States economy. This sort of substitution cannot be very important. At any rate, depressions tend to be worldwide in scope. The world as a whole would have no substitutes available from which to draw demand as its general price level falls. For the world as a whole, the substitution effect has to be zero.

That leaves us with the income effect. When the price of eggs fell, our money income went farther, so we tended to buy more of most goods —including eggs—as a result. This argument won't work with aggregate demand, either. As we saw in Chapter 12, income and output are two sides of the same coin. If all prices fall, then all money incomes will fall by the same amount. Consumers as a group won't have any more real income. The income effect doesn't apply to aggregate demand, either.

There is still some reason to expect the quantity of all goods taken to be greater at lower average price levels, nonetheless. The money and government bonds held by the public will be worth more in terms of shoes or potatoes when prices are lower. If the general price level were to fall to half its present value, your bank account would be worth twice as much as it is now. If prices reached a third of what they are now, your money would be worth three times as much. Ultimately, at some price level, you would be able to buy a whole city with the change in your pocket. By then you would surely have increased your consumption function. Sooner or later, lower prices can be expected to induce more aggregate demand. The problem is that the price level might have to fall a very long way to get us out of a depression.

There is a certain never-never-land character to this discussion. Do we ever see such big decreases in the general price level in the real world? Only in our worst depressions has the general price level declined appreciably. Any significant decrease in the price level requires a fall in wage rates. For the part of the work force whose wages are set by union contracts, a fall in the wage level could occur only after an enormous struggle. The same applies to jobs where the minimum wage law determines the wage. Even in other sectors of the economy, a decline in wage rates would be likely to be slow. Employers tend to view pay cuts as a last resort. People who are out of work may be willing to take jobs at lower wage rates than they are used to if they are hungry enough, but they will look a long while before they reach that point. Altogether, falling prices and wages are likely to be very slow in coming, even in a serious depression.

Few of us would be willing to wait for the drastic price and wage declines that would be sufficient to solve the problem of a depression automatically. The classical economists' theoretical solution to a depression is more an explanation of why the economy will *not* necessarily run at full employment than a prescription for policy. Our prices and wages just do not move downward that easily today.

A century ago, when the majority of our population was made up of self-employed farmers and artisans, downward price adjustments were easier. The self-employed seem to find it much easier to cut the wage rates that they "paid themselves" than employers do to cut wage rates. During the nineteenth century, depressions were more matters of falling prices and less of unemployment than they are today. When depression struck, farmers went right on producing, but they sold at terribly low prices. This is certainly not an argument for going back to an economy of self-employed artisans and farmers, however. In a world where prices and wages move downward with difficulty, a depression is not likely to solve itself in an acceptable length of time.

Altogether, then, the classical assumption—that there were automatic mechanisms to assure full employment—is open to a lot of question. Hardly anyone today is willing to let a depression just run its course. This change in attitudes is the most important result of the "Keynesian revolution." A generation ago, economic fluctuations were looked upon as acts of God like hurricanes and earthquakes. Perhaps you could find a shelter against them, but you couldn't do anything to prevent them. Today, by contrast, the government of virtually every industrial country in the world sees keeping its economy at or near the full-employment level as a primary obligation. As a result, major depressions of the sort that we saw in the 1930s seem to be things of the past.

INFLATION

Partly because of the general commitment to full employment, inflation has been a much more common problem than depression in the postwar world. As we have seen, the United States experienced major inflations right after World War II, during the Korean and Vietnam wars, and during the food and fuel shortages of 1973 and 1974. It has had milder inflations in most of the intervening years. Many other countries have had more severe inflations than we have.

PRICES ON A RATCHET

The basic cause of inflation has usually been an excess of aggregate demand over GNP at or near full employment. Our typical experience is illustrated in Figure 14.6. It traces out the levels of prices and real GNP that occur as aggregate demand changes. Say the economy starts with substantial unemployment, as at point A. If aggregate demand increases, the main result at first is an increase in output and employment. At this time there is little effect on prices. In the graph, we have moved from point A to point B. As we approach full employment, however, shortages begin to appear in some markets. The shortages lead to some increases in prices. At first, the general price level rises only mildly, and output continues to increase. We go from point B to point C. When aggregate demand reaches the full-employment level, however, shortages appear in most markets. Prices and wages have to rise throughout the economy. Any further increase in aggregate demand now means mainly an increase in prices. There is little, if any, further increase in output and employment. This is the situation between points C and D.

If something now happens to reduce aggregate demand, the real GNP will fall. At first, the resulting increase in unemployment is still accom-

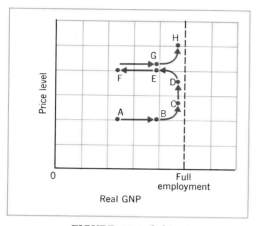

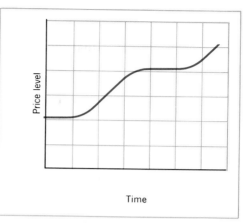

FIGURE 14.6 (left) **Our typical experience has been fairly stable prices when unemployment is high, and rising prices at or near full employment. The general price level almost never falls.**

FIGURE 14.7 (right) As a result of the fluctuations in output and prices shown in Figure 14.6, the general price level tends to grow stepwise over time.

panied by further increases in prices, between points D and E in the figure. This has been our usual experience in the post-World War II period. We will try to work out an explanation later in this chapter. At least, prices have not fallen appreciably with falling aggregate demand. Even a prolonged decrease in aggregate demand results only in stable prices and further unemployment, as between points E and F. Eventually, if aggregate demand rises once more, we tend to repeat the previous experience. Output increases again, and prices rise to yet higher levels, as from points G to H.

Altogether, the general price level seems to be on a "ratchet." (The familiar bumper jack is a ratchet. If set correctly, it will go up when pumped, but it won't go down again.) In a modern industrial economy, many prices and wages just will not go down without a terrible struggle. They will go up quite easily. The result is a price history like that shown in Figure 14.7. Prices may rise rapidly or slowly or not at all, but they hardly ever fall.

THE PHILLIPS CURVE

The problem of inflation is closely tied to the problem of unemployment. The dots in Figure 14.8 show the American unemployment rate and the percentage of price increase for each year since World War II. The curve

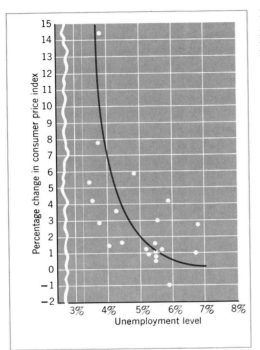

FIGURE 14.8 Historically, the greater the unemployment rate, the lower has been the annual rate of increase in the general price level.

in that figure is an attempt to summarize the apparent relationship between inflation and unemployment. It is known as a **Phillips curve,** named for the English economist who first worked one out from a century of British experience. The Phillips curve is not a theoretical relationship like the demand curve. It is a summary of actual experience.

Some economists take the Phillips curve to imply that we can attain a lower level of unemployment if we are willing to live with a few percent per year of inflation. How much inflation we would be willing to take in return for a one-percent reduction in unemployment is a value judgement about which people can differ. There seems to be a widespread feeling that mild inflation would be a small price to pay for a reduction in the unemployment rate from five to three percent.

THE PATH OF INFLATION

Other economists feel that this interpretation of the Phillips curve may be misleading. To see why, it is necessary to follow the path of inflation in greater detail.

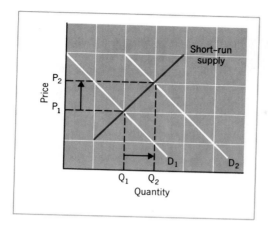

FIGURE 14.9 In individual competitive markets, the first effect of an increase in aggregate demand is likely to be higher prices, but also higher output.

Suppose that the economy has been running along for some time with about four-percent unemployment and little or no inflation. Wage rates have been rising at roughly the same rate as output per man-hour over the country as a whole, so costs of production have neither risen nor fallen very much on the average.

Now something happens to increase aggregate demand. Demand increases in most industries. Figure 14.9 shows what happens in a typical competitive industry, say eggs. Prices rise some, but so do output and employment. The same thing is happening in all industries, so the overall effect is some inflation and lower unemployment. So far things have progressed just as the Phillips curve suggested.

Say this pattern is repeated for a few years, however. Eventually, people will come to expect an annual inflation. Workers will demand larger wage increases to prevent their earnings from being eroded. The prices of materials that our egg producers buy from other firms will rise because of similar cost increases in those industries. As a result of these cost increases, the supply of eggs will shift to the left, as in Figure 14.10. If demand keeps increasing as fast as it did before (also shown in Figure 14.10), prices are likely to rise more rapidly than before. Output may increase, decrease, or stay the same. This development is a lot less like the Phillips curve story. We have a good deal of inflation now with little, if any, increase in output and employment.

Now suppose something happens to decrease demand after the inflation has been going for some time. Workers have all come to expect inflation as a normal condition. As a result, costs will continue to rise. Supply curves continue to shift to the left. This situation is illustrated in Figure 14.11. The decrease in both supply and demand will certainly

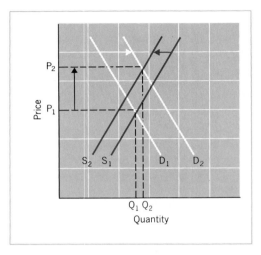

FIGURE 14.10 After inflation has been under way for a time, rising wages and material costs will produce reductions in supply. Now an increase in aggregate demand will mean chiefly rising prices and will have little effect on output and employment.

reduce output and employment, but prices may not fall. In fact, if costs are rising fast enough, we may continue to experience considerable inflation in spite of quite high unemployment. It could take quite a number of years of substantial unemployment to reduce our expectations of inflation. Only then would there be an end to the tendency for costs to rise.

This scenario has been presented in the setting of the competitive egg market. It is at least as plausible in highly concentrated industries, such

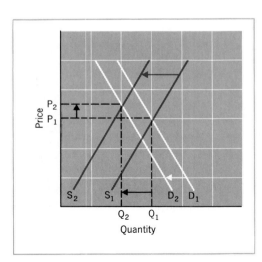

FIGURE 14.11 After a long experience of inflation, it becomes very difficult to stop. Workers and the suppliers of materials continue to expect inflation, so costs continue to rise and supply continues to decrease. Under these circumstances, even a drop in aggregate demand may be accompanied by price increases at first.

as automobiles. Prices in those industries are not set by impersonal market forces, they are set by General Motors or Ford. It does not pay those firms to change their prices every few days, especially if they have to explain each price increase to a congressional committee. They will certainly respond to an increase in demand by trying to increase their output. However, they may not increase price much as long as their costs don't rise. On the other hand, they will definitely find it profitable to raise prices if their production costs go up. They have even been known to do so in the face of declining demand and excess capacity. Concentrated industries have generally raised their prices more slowly than the average when inflations were heating up, but they have sometimes gone on raising prices after the original high demand has passed.

AMERICAN INFLATION EXPERIENCE

The United States has lived through two such cycles since World War II. They are illustrated in Figures 14.12 and 14.13. The former covers the years 1948 through 1961, and the latter, 1960 through 1973. Both figures

FIGURE 14.12 (left) In the early 1950s, we could avoid inflation with a four-percent unemployment rate. At the end of the decade we couldn't escape inflation entirely, even with quite high unemployment.

FIGURE 14.13 (right) In the 1960s we seemed to be able to reduce unemployment by accepting some inflation, but attempts to stop the inflation in the 1970s were unsuccessful, even with quite high unemployment.

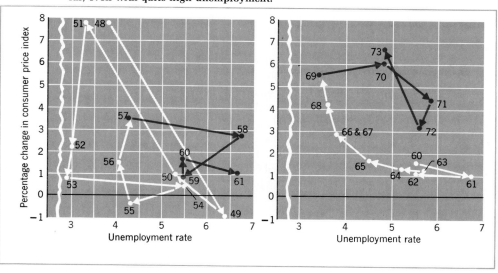

include the appropriate dots from the Phillips curve diagram (Figure 14.8). This time, however, they are labeled, and the path through time is traced. The earlier years of each period are connected by white arrows, the latter years by red ones.

At the start of both periods, substantial drops in unemployment were accomplished with little inflation. Later, prices rose more rapidly, but the declines in unemployment became slimmer. When aggregate demand finally fell (after 1957, and again after 1969), the rate of inflation receded more slowly than it had grown, in spite of fairly serious unemployment.

In 1954, when the main previous peacetime experience was the depressed 1930s, an unemployment rate of five to six percent was likely to mean no inflation at all.[1] However, by the late 1950s, when the public had come to expect full employment and some peacetime inflation, the same unemployment rates meant one- to three-percent-a-year increases. Similarly, unemployment in the five- to six-percent range meant only a one-percent-a-year inflation in the early 1960s. By the early 1970s the same unemployment rates were associated with three- to five-percent increases in price levels. In general, long periods of inflation seem to shift the Phillips curve upward and to the right. Then it takes increasing amounts of inflation to keep unemployment at a low level.

In some other countries the dilemma of inflation in the presence of high unemployment has been worse. Throughout the 1960s, England followed a policy of keeping aggregate demand so high that unemployment was consistently very low. The result was a continuous and accelerating inflation. The public came to accept a quite rapid inflation as natural. By 1971 to 1973, Britain was unable to prevent an eight- to eleven-percent-a-year inflation, even with the highest unemployment rates it had seen since the Great Depression. In some Latin American countries, such as Brazil, rapid inflation has been the continuous experience since World War II. Brazil was not able to reduce its inflation below the twenty-percent-a-year level, even with abnormally high unemployment rates.

One conclusion from all this evidence is apparent. There is a limit to how much a country can reduce unemployment by increasing aggregate demand without increasing the rate of inflation. Beyond that limit, any further reduction in unemployment is likely to be temporary. To reduce

---

[1] In 1954, there had been lots of inflation in the immediate past, but it was all associated with World War II and the Korean War. All our experience had taught us that wartime inflations come to an end. Indeed, there were still some people around who expected the usual great postwar depression at that time.

unemployment permanently, a country would have to make it easier for workers in declining trades to transfer to more promising jobs and make it easier for new members of the labor force to find jobs. That achievement calls for such things as retraining programs for workers with obsolete skills, moving allowances for workers in depressed areas, improved information on where good jobs can be found, and, perhaps, direct government employment in slum areas.

Another conclusion we can draw is that it is harder to stop a fully anticipated inflation than to prevent an unanticipated one. It may take many years of high unemployment rates to convince people that, in the future, prices will rise more slowly than they have expected.

A fully anticipated inflation is less harmful than an unanticipated one of the same intensity. Wage rates, interest rates, and even social security benefits are adjusted to allow for anticipated inflations. Whether a fully anticipated inflation is worth stopping is a value judgement that you must decide for yourself. Bear in mind, though, that the costs of doing so are greater than the cost of preventing an unanticipated inflation, while the benefits of doing so are less. You could quite consistently conclude that we should make major efforts to keep inflation from accelerating and.at the same time that we should not incur much unemployment just to cut the rate of inflation below the level people have come to expect.

PRICE AND WAGE CONTROLS

The dilemma of inflation in the presence of unemployment has led many governments to try to control prices and wages. If the government could prevent inflation directly, we could attain high levels of employment without worrying about the inflationary consequences. The United States has attempted price and wage controls on several occasions.

During World War II we set up an elaborate control system applying to all prices and wages. The program was helped by wartime patriotism and a virtual prohibition on strikes. There can be no doubt that these controls were, at least temporarily, successful. But they involved detailed rules for each industry and a large-scale enforcement organization. Even so, price and wage controls worked imperfectly. When manufacturers couldn't get the price increases they wanted, they often let product quality deteriorate instead. Wage controls were often evaded by means of bogus "promotions." Shortages developed for many goods, forcing them to be rationed. Black markets developed, in which scarce goods were traded at illegal prices. The prices set by the government became less and less appropriate as time passed, but it was difficult to determine what the right prices might be. The changes that did occur tended to reflect the political power of the sellers involved.

The government spent enormous amounts of money on the war, but prices could not rise. The output of domestic consumer goods was, of course, limited. As a result, people earned much more than they could spend. The main effect in the United States was a large accumulation of savings. This money came back to fuel inflation after the controls ended. In Germany during World War II, where controls were in force for a longer time, workers piled up enormous amounts of marks. By the end of the war they didn't really need many more. They often found it more profitable to stay home and tend their gardens than to go to work. The results were massive shortages and wild inefficiency in the years just after the war. Suppressed inflation is distinctly not the same thing as no inflation.

Altogether, wartime price and wage controls worked, but they caused many problems. It is doubtful that we would be willing to accept such complete controls for any length of time in peacetime.

What the government has done in more normal times has been to intervene informally in major price and wage decisions. In the early 1960s the Kennedy administration published a set of "guideposts" that called for wage increases of 3½ percent a year. That limit was roughly proportional to our average annual increase in productivity. Price changes were supposed to reflect changes in costs. The government depended on "voluntary" compliance. In some cases it employed a good deal of pressure, too, using loud publicity, threats of antitrust and procurement actions, sales of materials from its own stockpiles, and liberalization of import restrictions. These pressures were quite effective in industries that were heavily dependent on the government, such as steel and aluminum. But they had little effect on industries in which the government had less clout, such as automobiles and construction.

Inflation was largely eliminated in the early 1960s, but many economists feel that this achievement was due primarily to the low levels of aggregate demand at that time. At least, those same guideposts proved insufficient to stop inflation once aggregate demand got up to full-employment levels again after 1965.

Starting in 1971, the government undertook a series of new experiments in price and wage controls. Prices and wages were frozen for short periods in the fall of 1971 and in the summer of 1973. In 1971, when there was a good deal of unemployment and excess capacity, the freeze worked for a few months. In 1973, however, aggregate demand was higher. Serious shortages of meat and fuel arose almost immediately. Between those two freezes and during late 1973 and early 1974, orders were issued limiting wage increases and requiring that prices rise no more than costs. Enforcement was nothing like that of World War II, however. Agricultural products and prices and wages in small firms were exempt. In 1973, the authorities were forced repeatedly to relax price controls as shortages cropped up in such commodities as chickens, gasoline, fertilizer, and even toilet paper. The controllers seemed unwilling to buck powerful unions that threatened long strikes. Controls were rather similar to the guideposts, in that they depended heavily on voluntary compliance.

In general, the sort of guideposts or controls that we seem willing to accept in peacetime are too weak to actually stop inflation by themselves. They may be able to slow it down, but if they do, it is probably because they serve to reduce our expectations of inflation. Controls won't even change expectations very much if they break down regularly.

Most economists would agree that our main reliance for regulating levels of unemployment and rates of inflation must be on basic controls over aggregate demand. The main weapons for controlling aggregate demand involve controls over the supply of money and credit and over the government budget. These are the subjects of the next two chapters.

SUMMARY

Classical economists believed that equilibrium GNP would automatically be at full-employment levels. This theory depended on the assumption that interest rates and price levels could fall far enough to bring aggregate demand back to full-employment levels. Investment tends to increase and saving may decrease with lower interest rates. Interest rates can fall only so far, however, because savers always have the option of holding cash. Aggregate demand is probably greater, the lower the general level of prices; but in practice, prices and wages do not fall very easily. If interest rates cannot fall below two or three percent, and if it takes a disaster to reduce prices and wages by much, then the "automatic" solution to depression could be very weak and slow to act.

Inflation is a more common problem than large-scale unemployment today. An increase in aggregate demand when the economy is near full employment will usually raise prices, but decreases in aggregate demand merely reduce output and employment; they seldom do much to decrease prices. When a rise in aggregate demand occurs near the full-employment level, the initial effect is an increase in output, with only mild increases in the price level. But an attempt to maintain a low level of unemployment with high aggregate demand will tend to mean greater and greater price increases, as people come to expect further inflation. A fall in aggregate demand after a long period of inflation is likely to mean

both higher unemployment *and* inflation for some period. Fully anticipated inflations are harder to stop than unanticipated ones. At the
same time, they redistribute income and wealth less than unanticipated inflations do.

Full price and wage controls of the sort employed in World War II can
keep prices from rising, but they cause many distortions and inequities.
We seem unwilling to accept that sort of regimentation in normal peacetime. The weaker controls that we have been willing to accept have had a
very uncertain effect. Our main reliance is on controls over the supply of
money and credit and the government budget.

STUDY QUESTIONS

1   What is the effect of a fall in interest rates on investment? Would
your answer be different if the investor were putting up his own money
instead of borrowing it?

2   What would be the effect of a fall in interest rates on the amount you
would save? Would you save more, less, or the same amount? Would
you save anything at all if the interest rate were zero? Would you lend
out any of your savings or buy bonds or mortgages with them if the
interest rate were zero? Explain why the answers to the last two questions may be different.

3   Would you buy less beef if its price were doubled? Why or why not?
Would you buy less of everything if the prices of everything doubled and
if your income were doubled at the same time? Why or why not? Are the
same influences at work when you respond to a rise in the price of beef as
when you respond to a rise in all prices?

4   What do you think the rate of inflation will be next year? On what
did you base your judgment? Would you have made the same prediction
if there had not been any inflation for the past several years? How does
the amount of inflation you anticipate affect the wage you would want
when looking for a long-term job? If everybody anticipated a good deal
of inflation, what does that mean for the supply of labor? For future
prices?

5   In the winter of 1973-1974 there was a quite serious shortage of
gasoline in many cities, but the government maintained control over
gasoline prices. As a result, gasoline was rationed by the willingness of
people to sit in their cars waiting to get to the gas pump. In some cases
the lines could be blocks long and the wait could run into hours. Do you
think that that rationing system was efficient? Was it equitable? One
alternative would have been to issue ration tickets, as was done in World

War II. How could a rationing system be set up so that those who needed their cars for business would get the gasoline they needed? What about those who lived in the suburbs and needed a car to commute? Do you think such a system would have been efficient? Equitable? Finally, the government could simply have let the price of gasoline go up to a level where there was enough to go around. Would that have been more or less efficient? Would it have been more or less equitable?

FURTHER READING

A good analysis of the problems of both unemployment and inflation, plus an extensive discussion of price controls, appears in Abba Lerner, *Flation* (Baltimore: Penguin, 1972). The causes and effects of inflation, including the effects of expectations, are well explained in S. A. Morley, *The Economics of Inflation* (New York: Holt, Rinehart & Winston, 1971). Another book on the subject is Robert Lekachman, *Inflation* (New York: Random House, 1973). Gardner Ackley's *Stemming World Inflation* (Washington, D. C.: Atlantic Institute, 1971) covers the inflation experiences of the world generally since the 1940s. Ackley was the chairman of the Council of Economic Advisors under President Johnson. All four books are available in paperback.

15
MONEY
AND
MONETARY
POLICY

Money plays a crucial role in determining the level of economic activity. This chapter describes the money supply, what determines it, and how it affects the level of economic activity.

THE MONEY SUPPLY

Money is one of the great inventions of mankind. Its main purpose is to facilitate exchange, and hence specialization. Think what life would be like if we did not have money. We would have to make do with barter, the direct exchange of goods and services. To buy a car you might have to ante up a thousand reams of paper or ten thousand nuts and bolts. This would be hard to do if you were a barber and had only haircuts to offer. You would first have to find customers with paper or nuts and bolts to offer you for your haircuts. If you couldn't do that, you would have to take whatever they had to offer and try to exchange it yourself for the necessary items. The whole thing could become so complex that you would very likely wind up not buying the car. In general, nonmoney economies tend to be made up of self-sufficient households that trade little with outsiders. Money is essential to our specialized exchange economy.

WHAT MODERN MONEY IS

Money is commonly defined as anything that is widely accepted as a means of payment. Over most of history it has consisted of particular commodities, usually precious metals. The supply of money depended on the gold and silver miners. Governments could mint coins of convenient sizes, but the overall supply of money depended on the metal supply, which was largely beyond their control.

In the last two centuries, however, the character of money has changed completely. In most countries today the money supply consists mainly of paper and bank deposits that have little or no connection to the precious metals. The supply of money is now easily within the control of the public authorities.

Table 15.1 shows the major components of the American money supply in 1972. The currency items at the top of the table are the familiar types of money that you have in your pocket. The coin is issued by the

TABLE 15.1   The United States money supply (June 1972)

ITEM	BILLIONS OF DOLLARS
Treasury currency	
Coin	7.0
Notes	.6
Federal Reserve Notes	54.6
Total currency held by the public	54.7*
Demand (checking) deposits held by the public	180.1
M₁: Currency and demand deposits held by the public	234.8
Time (savings) deposits at commercial banks	254.2
M₂: Currency, demand and time deposits held by the public	489.0
Deposits at mutual savings banks	87.1
Deposits at savings and loan associations	192.5
M₃: Currency, demand deposits, and savings deposits of all sorts	754.8
Certificates of deposit	35.8
Savings bonds	56.5
Short-term government securities held by the public (less than one year to maturity)	79.5
Total money and near-money	926.6

*Currency in the hands of the public is less than the total of the three listed items because some of the currency is held by banks.

Treasury. So is a little of the paper money, but it mostly falls into the category of collectors' items (such as the United States Notes, or "greenbacks," first issued during the Civil War). Most of the paper money you come across is in the form of Federal Reserve Notes issued by the Federal Reserve banks. These semipublic institutions will be described later in this chapter.

The amount of cash you have in your pocket or under your mattress is probably just a fraction of your money supply. The same is true for almost everyone in economically advanced nations. Coin and paper money account for only a small proportion of our total money supply. **Demand deposits** are much more important. These funds are nothing more than checking deposits; they are called "demand" deposits because the bank stands ready to make payments from such deposits "on demand" any time the bank is open. A bank that holds demand deposits is called a **commercial bank.**

In what sense are demand deposits money? Your check may not always be accepted as a means of payment, because the recipient may doubt that there is enough in your deposit to cover it, but he will always take the check if he has enough time to find out. By far the largest part of total payments made in industrial countries is made by check.

Table 15.1 contains many other things that are very close to currency and demand deposits in most people's eyes. **Time deposits** are savings deposits. They are called time deposits because technically the bank has the right to hold up payment for a month after you ask for it, but in practice they can be converted to cash on demand. Deposits at mutual savings banks and savings and loan associations are similar. **Certificates of deposit** are a special type of savings deposit that can be converted into cash only after a specific period, such as a year. They are close substitutes for money for many purposes. So are federal **savings bonds,** since the owners of these bonds can convert them into specified amounts of cash at any time. The government issues many other bonds that are payable only at a specified future date. When this date is far in the future, the holder is unlikely to consider the bonds as equivalent to money. They have a definite value when they come due in 1990, but they can fluctuate a lot in price this year. On the other hand, government bonds that will mature within the year are almost as good as savings deposits. They can't vary much in price, because owners can always hold them to their maturity within the year and get a definite amount.

The decision of which items from Table 15.1 to include in the money supply is to some extent arbitrary. The assets held by the public lie on a continuum. It ranges all the way from very liquid things (things easily converted into cash), such as demand deposits, to very illiquid things, such as automobiles. You almost certainly do not consider your car as money, but you may well think of your savings deposit that way. The line between money and other things might be drawn at various points. The most common definition of money includes only currency and demand deposits. Either can be used to make payments directly. Both turn over very rapidly in practice. The other items in Table 15.1 must ordinarily be converted into cash before they are spent. In practice they generally stay unspent longer.

The sum of currency and demand deposits is often abbreviated as M_1 in economic discussions. Still, a person with a large savings account is apt to act in much the same way as one with an equally large demand deposit. Some economists, therefore, emphasize M_2, which also includes time deposits at commercial banks. Still others prefer to consider M_3, which includes savings deposits at mutual savings banks and savings and loan associations as well. One could obviously go farther and include the other items in Table 15.1. It does not usually make much difference whether we use M_1 or M_2 or M_3, just as long as we are consistent. All three generally rise and fall together. This chapter will put its main emphasis on M_1 and treat the other items as "near money," things that are almost money.

WHY MONEY HAS VALUE

Most of our money supply consists of promises to pay; the promises are made by banks. But why is money valuable? The first answer is that the banks promise to convert the deposits into currency at any time, but that reply doesn't get us very far. Why is currency valuable? Half a century ago we could have said that it, in turn, was convertible into precious metals. That is no longer true, however. The Federal Reserve banks carry the Federal Reserve notes as debts on their books. The only way they honor these debts in dealing with you and me, though, is to issue new notes in exchange for the old. Of course, you can convert your dollars into coins, but the coins are made of metal worth less than their face value in the marketplace. The Treasury has a large stock of gold (worth about $50 billion at 1974 prices) but neither it nor the Federal Reserve has touched it since 1971. In any event, gold reserves are only a small fraction of our total money supply, and there is every reason to believe that we would go on accepting paper dollars even if there were no gold reserves at all. This has happened in many other countries.

If you read the next dollar bill you receive you will find the words,

"This note is legal tender for all debts, public and private."

This statement means that the government stands ready to accept dollars in payment of taxes. It also means that if you offer a creditor dollars to cover your obligation, he has no further recourse in court. These are comforting provisions, but it seems doubtful that the statement is really very important. Most people don't read their Federal Reserve notes, and a majority of them don't even know what "legal tender" means.

Ultimately, we accept money because we expect other people to accept it. We were born into a society where everyone treats it as valuable, and we accept the convention.[1] This fact is very useful. It makes our economy far more efficient than it otherwise would be.

COMMERCIAL BANKS

The largest part of our money supply is in the form of bank deposits. Some understanding of how banks work is needed to get a clear picture of what governs the supply of money. Table 15.2 shows the assets of a

TABLE 15.2   Balance sheet of a commercial bank (millions of dollars)

ASSETS		LIABILITIES	
Currency and deposits at other banks	$7		
Securities	12	Demand deposits	$18
Loans	27	Time deposits	26
Other assets	2	Owner's equity	4
Total assets	$48	Total liabilities	$48

[1] That explanation may not be very satisfying. After all, where did the convention come from? Undoubtedly, coins originally were valued for the metal they contained, but the values of gold and silver were themselves increased because they were used as money. Only a small part of the world's demand for gold and silver has come from jewelers and dentists. When paper money and bank deposits were first introduced, they undoubtedly were valued because of their convertibility into gold or silver. By the 1920s, however, actual conversion had become miniscule. By 1929 gold coins and silver dollars were only 1.4 percent of the money supply, and most of those were probably lost or in coin collections. By then the main factor that determined people's willingness to hold money was their expectation about what it would buy in goods in the future—in other words, their expectation about future price levels.

typical commercial bank and the claims against those assets.[2] The numbers shown are the averages for all commercial banks in June, 1972, rounded off to the nearest million.

The currency and deposits at other banks are the bank's **reserves,** with which it honors checks and withdrawals. These reserves are always much less than the deposits that the bank has outstanding. Indeed, if its only concern were to meet daily withdrawals, the bank could get by with much smaller reserves than those shown in Table 15.2. In the normal business day about as much is deposited in each bank as is withdrawn from it. A bank could therefore make do with only a tiny fraction of its deposits in cash.

The main reason that banks hold currency and deposits at other banks is to meet their **reserve requirements.** They are obliged by law to hold a specified percentage of their deposits in this form. They could hold more reserves than the minimum required, in which case they would have **excess reserves.** In normal times, however, banks try to keep their reserves near the minimum needed to do business and stay within the law, because these reserves yield no income.

The remaining bank assets are mostly credit instruments: bonds it has bought or loans it has made. The bank's tangible assets, such as its building and equipment, are a tiny percentage of the total.

The main liabilities of the bank are demand and time deposits. To you and me these are assets, the main elements of our money and near-money supply; to the bank they are debts. There is also a small item for owner's equity, the stockholders' claim on the bank.

HOW MONEY IS CREATED

Banks create money. They do so whenever they extend credit. Suppose you go to a bank to finance a new car. Once your banker has determined that you are a good credit risk he will have you sign a note in which you promise to pay the bank, say, $2,000. He will then write into your bank book an additional deposit of $2,000. At that moment, $2,000 of money comes into existence that was not there before. The bank has no less reserves than before, and its other customers' deposits have not changed. The banker has, with a stroke of the pen, brought new money into existence.

---

[2] Technically Table 15.2 is a balance sheet. For a discussion of balance sheets see the Appendix to Chapter 4.

This would be true even if you refused the banker's "funny money" and demanded currency. The banker might have a strange look on his face, but he would give you the cash. Of course you don't borrow money just to keep it in a mattress. You would pay the $2,000 to your auto dealer and he would deposit it in his bank. When the smoke cleared, the auto dealer's bank would have more reserves than before and your bank would have less. The banking system as a whole, though, would have the same reserves. And there would be $2,000 more in total bank deposits than there were before the transaction.

In general, the creation of money is the result of an exchange of IOU's. You give the bank your promise to pay (the note) in return for the bank's promise to pay (the deposit). The bank's promise is generally accepted as a means of payment.

BANK RESERVES AND THE MONEY SUPPLY

This story doesn't mean that banks are in the counterfeiting business. The deposits they create are fully convertible into genuine legal tender whenever they are open for business. Moreover, the amount of money they can create is limited by their reserves and by the reserve requirements.

Any one bank can create no more money than its excess reserves. This was clearly true in the case where you demanded cash. Your banker lost $2,000 in reserves the minute he gave it to you. If he hadn't had at least $2,000 in excess reserves, he would have violated the reserve requirement when he lent you the money.

The same would have been true if he wrote the $2,000 into your bankbook instead. You didn't borrow just to have a big bank account. You planned to spend the money. When you write a $2,000 check to your auto dealer, he deposits it in his bank, which will send it back to your bank for collection. Your bank will honor your check from its own reserves. Once the check has cleared, the situation is the same as before. Your bank will have lost reserves equal to the amount of the loan. Your banker can make loans and create money only up to the amount of his excess reserves.

The reserves didn't disappear when the transaction was completed, however. Your auto dealer's bank received a deposit and additional reserves of $2,000. It has to keep some of those reserves against the new deposit, but it has some new excess reserves as well. For instance, if the reserve requirement were twenty percent, the bank's required reserves would increase by $0.2 \times \$2,000 = \$400$. Setting aside these reserves, it would be left with $1,600 in new excess reserves and new lending power. The bank would be eager to make loans of that amount, since that is how it earns money. And when it does so, the story is repeated. A third bank will receive new deposits and reserves of $1,600. Then *it* will have more lending power in turn, and the process continues.

Figure 15.1 traces several such transactions. We assume that each bank makes loans equal to its new excess reserves as they appear, and that all the new money goes into demand deposits. Each bank in turn sets aside reserves equal to twenty percent of the new deposits it receives. It makes loans and creates more money equal to 80 percent of those new deposits. Already the four banks shown in Figure 15.1 have created money equal to

$2,000 + $1,600 + $1,240 + $992 = $5,832.

In the process, the banks' required reserves went up by

$400 + $360 + $248 = $1,008.

And the process obviously isn't over.

When will it end? When required reserves have increased enough to exhaust the original $2,000 of excess reserves. Since the reserve requirement is assumed to be twenty percent, this means that some bank somewhere will have excess reserves and will be able to make more loans and create more money until the total of all the deposits along the way has risen to a level where the $2,000 will just cover them. This will occur when

$2,000 = 20% × total new deposits.

FIGURE 15.1   A bank having $2,000 in excess reserves can make loans of that amount. They will result in deposits of $2,000, and excess reserves of $1,600, at a second bank. The second bank can then make $1,600 in loans, and so forth.

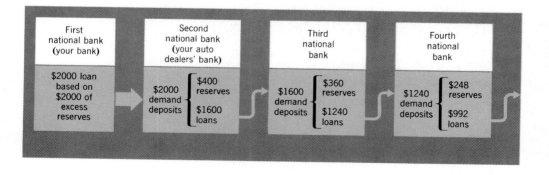

Rearranging this expression,

$$\text{total new deposits} = \frac{\$2{,}000}{0.2} = \$10{,}000.$$

All banks together can create $10,000 in new deposits.

More generally, if all the banks in the country make loans equal to their excess reserves, they can ultimately create money equal to

$$\frac{1}{\text{the reserve requirement}} \times \text{total excess reserves.}$$

Putting it still another way, total demand deposits can increase until the banks' reserves are just enough to cover them. If we assume that there are no time deposits at all, that time will come when

$$\text{total reserves} = \text{the reserve requirement} \times \text{total demand deposits,}$$

or when

$$\text{total demand deposits} = \frac{\text{total reserves}}{\text{the reserve requirement}}.$$

What all these formulas show us is that the money supply of the country is largely governed by the amount of the banks' reserves and by the reserve requirement. Try it out for yourself. How much money could the banks create if they had $5,000,000 in excess reserves with a reserve requirement of twenty percent? Look up the answer in the footnote.[3] Again, how large could total demand deposits be if total reserves were $30,000,000,000 and the reserve requirement is only *ten* percent? Look that answer up in the footnote, too.[4] The process by which banks create money is explained in greater detail in the appendix.

In ordinary times, banks can be counted on to extend as much credit as their reserves and the reserve requirement allow. But the banks don't *have* to make loans when they have excess reserves. If the banks chose simply to hold their excess reserves and make no more loans, the money supply would not expand. This happened during the Great Depression. Businessmen were so pessimistic then that few of them came in to borrow. Many who did were poor credit risks. As a result, the money supply was much smaller than the limit set by the banks' reserves.

[3] .... $30,000,000,000 \times \frac{1}{0.1} = 10 \times \$30,000,000,000 = \$300,000,000,000.$

[4] .... $\$5,000,000 \times \frac{1}{0.2} = 5 \times \$5,000,000 = \$25,000,000.$

THE FEDERAL RESERVE SYSTEM

The money supply depends on the reserve requirements and the reserves of the banks, but who determines these figures? This is the function of the Federal Reserve System, known as the "Fed" for short.

THE STRUCTURE OF THE FEDERAL RESERVE SYSTEM

The **Federal Reserve System** consists of twelve regional banks that serve as America's "central bank." They are considered central banks because they do business with commercial banks rather than with the public. Their main purpose is to control the supply of money and credit rather than to make profits.[5] Most industrial countries have central banks similar to the Fed. Technically, the twelve Federal Reserve Banks are owned by the commercial banks that are members of the system.[6] Actually, the twelve banks follow uniform policies that are determined by a single Board of Governors. The seven members of this board are appointed by the president with the advice and consent of the Senate, in the same way the members of such regulatory commissions as the Interstate Commerce Commission are. Even though it is privately owned, the Fed can be thought of as virtually a public agency. It is a highly independent agency, however. The terms of board members are long (fourteen years), and the system does not depend on congressional appropriations for its support. As a result, neither the President nor Congress has much control over its actions.

The Fed is freer to decide on policy for itself than are most other central banks in the world. This freedom has its advantages. In election years, for instance, if the administration controlled the Fed, it would be tempted to arrange for low interest rates, whether the economy needed them or not. On the other hand, some people feel that the Fed tends to make decisions in the interests of the banks it is supposed to regulate, just as the ICC seems to see things from the point of view of the railroads and truckers, and the CAB, from the point of view of the airlines. Interest rates have persistently risen over the last two decades, and banking has become much more profitable in the process. Actually, the Fed has often

---

[5] Actually the Fed earns a good deal. Out of its profits it meets its expenses and pays a fixed dividend on its stock. Most of the rest of its earnings are turned over to the Treasury.

[6] All national banks are members of the Federal Reserve System. State banks may be members. In 1972, 41 percent of the banks, with 78 percent of the deposits, were members of the system.

TABLE 15.3 Balance sheet for all Federal Reserve Banks (August 31, 1972)

ASSETS	BILLIONS	LIABILITIES	BILLIONS
Gold certificates and related items	$10.7		
Discounts and advances	$1.1	Federal Reserve Notes	$55.1
U.S. Government securities	$71.8	Deposits by commercial banks	$28.2
Other assets	$11.2	Other liabilities	$9.7
		Stockholders' equity	$1.8
Total assets	$94.8	Total liabilities	$94.8

cooperated with various administrations, and not always in a way that would make the economy more stable. If the Fed were stubbornly to follow policies that were drastically different from what Congress and the administration wanted, they would probably change the law to take away the Fed's "independence."

THE ASSETS AND LIABILITIES OF THE FED

Table 15.3 shows the main assets and liabilities of the twelve Federal Reserve Banks taken together. The main assets of the Fed are gold certificates, loans to commercial banks, and government securities. The gold certificates are issued to the Fed on a one-to-one basis for the gold held by the Treasury. The discounts and advances are loans to commercial banks. The securities represent an important part of the public debt.

The main liabilities of the Fed are the Federal Reserve Notes (most of our circulating currency) and the deposits of commercial banks (the major part of those banks' reserves). The other assets and liabilities reflect the important housekeeping operations of the Fed. Most of these other assets and liabilities are checks in the process of collection. The Fed is our main agency for clearing checks written on banks in one place and deposited in other parts of the country.

HOW THE FED CONTROLS MONEY AND CREDIT

By controlling the size of its liabilities the Fed can control the total reserves of the member banks. It also has the power to set reserve requirements for member banks within wide legal limits. These two powers together give it effective control over the whole country's supply of money and credit.

The ability to change reserve requirements is a very powerful tool. Suppose that the reserve requirement were twenty percent and that the banks had reserves of $30 billion in total. This amount would be enough to support $150 billion in demand deposits. If the Fed were to reduce the reserve requirement to nineteen percent, the same $30 billion would now cover $30 billion ÷ 0.19 = 158 billion. In other words, by reducing the reserve requirements by just one percentage point, the Fed could permit the money supply to increase by eight billion dollars, or a little more than five percent. In fact, changes in the reserve requirements are such drastic measures that they are seldom used. When a change is made, it is usually announced well in advance so that the banks can adjust to it.

Generally the Fed controls the money supply by varying the reserves available to the member banks, while leaving reserve requirements constant. The list of Federal Reserve assets and liabilities in Table 15.3 gives some idea of what sort of changes can affect commercial bank reserves. For instance, say the public decides to carry more currency in its pockets. Then the quantity of Federal Reserve Notes outstanding will increase. To meet this demand for cash by the public, the banks will have to draw upon their deposits at the Fed. They will lose reserves in the process. In the Fed's balance sheet, Federal Reserve Notes will increase, and deposits at the Fed will decrease. Such a move to more pocket cash would cause a fall in the total money supply. Each dollar of currency is one dollar of money supply, while a dollar of reserves supports about five dollars of demand deposits.

In fact, shifts to more or less currency occur frequently. The public carries more cash during the long weekends in the summer and during the shopping spree before Christmas. If the Fed didn't intervene, the banks would have to reduce loans and deposits every December. In fact, the Fed systematically changes its other assets and liabilities to prevent this pinch from happening.

The Fed doesn't have any control over the gold certificates it holds, either. If the Treasury should agree to sell gold to you or me or some European central bank, the Fed would find itself with less in assets. If currency in circulation stayed the same, the result would be a drop in commercial bank reserves. We would have a tight money situation (higher interest rates and less plentiful loans) for reasons that had nothing much to do with domestic economic affairs. In practice, the Fed has usually made other changes to prevent changes in the Treasury's gold stock from affecting the American money supply.

THE DISCOUNT RATE

The Fed does have some control over the next item among its assets, its loans to commercial banks. Such loans arise when member banks find themselves temporarily short on reserves and borrow from the Fed to make up their reserve deficiencies.

One of the main purposes of the Fed when it was set up in 1913 was to assure that banks faced with such difficulties would have a place where they could borrow additional reserves. The hope was to prevent waves of bank failures like those that had periodically plagued the country. Yet we succeeded in having another banking crisis during the Great Depression, in spite of the Federal Reserve System. In response to that experience, the Federal Deposit Insurance Corporation (FDIC) was established. It insures bank deposits up to a value of $20,000. Depositors no longer have an incentive to withdraw their funds whenever banks seem shaky. The guarantee seems to have worked; bank failures have become extremely rare. Because of the FDIC, the Fed is no longer our main defense against bank failure, but it still stands ready to lend to the commercial banks when they need to borrow.

While the Fed won't simply refuse to lend, it can make its loans to banks more or less expensive by changing the interest rate it charges. This interest rate is known as the **discount rate.** If the Fed raises it, banks will be discouraged from borrowing, and reserves will be kept down as a result. Lowering the discount rate will have the opposite effect. The discount rate is a relatively weak weapon, however. Total borrowings at the Fed are seldom very large, and banks faced with severe reserve deficiencies are not likely to be deterred from borrowing from the Fed even if the discount rate were very high.

The discount rate may have some psychological effect, however. Any changes in it are announced in the newspapers. The public is likely to read an increase in the discount rate as an indication of tighter credit conditions, and this news may affect business decisions.

OPEN MARKET OPERATIONS

The most important asset of the Fed today is government securities. Here the Fed has all the control it needs. If it wants to expand money and credit it need not wait for borrowers; it can simply go out and buy bonds. The result will be an increase in bank reserves.

Here is the way the process works: When the Fed buys government securities, the seller of the bonds receives a check on the Fed. He deposits this check in his own bank. When the bank collects the check its reserves rise. The overall supply of money and credit can then go on to increase by 1/(reserve requirement) times the amount of the new reserves. Conversely, if the Fed reduces its assets by selling bonds, the buyer will have to pay the Fed with a check on a commercial bank. When the Fed collects the check, the commercial bank will have less reserves, and money and credit will have to fall.

Such purchases and sales of bonds are known as **open market operations.** The Fed trades on the bond markets almost continuously. Some of its huge fund of government securities matures each week, and the Fed must replace those securities if credit contraction is to be avoided. In addition, it buys or sells regularly to offset fluctuations in circulating currency. If it wants to go a little farther and increase the total supply of money and credit, it need only place somewhat larger orders for securities. If it wants to contract credit, it can simply buy fewer bonds than it normally would in a given period.

Open market operations are the best of the Fed's policy weapons. A change in reserve requirements is like a bludgeon which it is unwise to swing very forcefully in the money market. The discount rate is more like a pillow. It can exert some pressure, but its effect on reserves cannot be predicted very accurately. But open market operations are like a surgeon's scalpel. They can be used to change the supply of money and credit quite precisely. By buying or selling particular amounts of bonds the Fed can change bank reserves by any desired amount.

As things usually work, the Fed leaves reserve requirements constant and sets discount rates so that borrowing from the Fed to finance more commercial loans is not particularly profitable. Then it adjusts bank reserves on a day-to-day basis by buying and selling bonds on the open market. Taking the three powers together, the Fed can make the supply of money and credit as large or as small as it wants.[7]

MONETARY POLICY

The Fed does not make loans or buy bonds with the goal of making profits. Its purpose, according to its public statements, is to make the banking system run smoothly and to control aggregate demand and the level of economic activity. The control of bank credit and money with this purpose is known as **monetary policy.** It is our main concern here.

---

[7] The Fed also has some control over particular types of credit. It sets **margin requirements,** which determine the percentage of cash that buyers of stocks and bonds must put up. This power gives the Fed some control over stock market activity. During the Korean War, the Fed also issued regulations controlling the minimum down payments and maximum payoff periods for loans made to finance the purchase of houses, automobiles, and other consumer durables. Unlike reserve requirements, the discount rate, and open market operations, this type of regulation does not control the supply of money and credit generally.

HOW MONETARY POLICY AFFECTS ECONOMIC ACTIVITY

Suppose the Fed decides to reduce the money supply. The Fed will sell bonds on the open market. Banks will find themselves with less reserves and as a result will have to reduce their loans and securities. With the supply of credit reduced, interest rates will rise. The increase in interest charges will discourage investment. Aggregate demand will be reduced as a result, since investment is part of aggregate demand. Similarly, if the Fed buys bonds, the supply of money and credit will be increased, interest rates will fall, investment will be encouraged, aggregate demand will rise, and equilibrium GNP will increase.

Along with the changes in credit go changes in the money supply. Some economists believe that the money supply has an effect on aggregate demand in and of itself. Certainly over the long pull, taking one decade with the next, the ratio of the GNP to the money supply is fairly stable. This ratio is known as the **velocity** of money. If the money supply increases, we can be fairly sure that sooner or later the GNP will increase about proportionately. We are much more interested in short-run fluctuations in the GNP, however. On a month-to-month or year-to-year basis the velocity of money can fluctuate a good deal. How much difference the money supply by itself makes on a short-run basis is a matter of controversy among economists. However, there is little doubt that tight money and credit will slow things down or that easy money and credit will work to expand economic activity.

Monetary policy is probably more effective in slowing down a boom than in bringing about an expansion. The Fed can reduce the lending power of the banks directly. Interest rates will rise almost at once, and investment in such sectors as housing will respond within a year. If its goal is to expand economic activity, however, the Fed may be less effective. Interest rates will fall when the Fed buys bonds, and this change will increase bank lending power. But still, the Fed can't require businessmen to use the additional credit. Loans could respond quite slowly to easier credit conditions. This is especially likely in a depression, when investment prospects are bleak and the interest rate is near its minimum.

MONETARY POLICY IN THE GREAT DEPRESSION

We know what the Fed should do in dealing with a depression or an inflation, but will it do the right things? Unfortunately, the most hopeful answer we can give is, "perhaps." At many points in its history, the Fed has seemed to make the wrong moves.

One of the most striking cases occurred during the descent into the

Great Depression. The decline of economic activity was already underway before the Wall Street crash. During 1929, when the decline was
beginning, the Fed followed a very tight money policy, paying more
attention to the spectacular stock market boom than to the general level
of economic activity. Immediately after the October stock market crash,
however, it reduced its discount rate and started buying bonds.
Throughout 1930 and early 1931 it followed the expansionary policies
that seemed appropriate in a declining economy.

Then came the international financial crises. Foreign countries installed controls over international payments and devalued their currencies.
Depositors became worried about the safety of their banks and began to
withdraw their deposits in large amounts. Bank borrowings from the
Fed rose. But instead of continuing its easy money policy to damp down
the crisis, the Fed responded by *raising* the discount rate, while keeping
its holdings of government bonds almost constant. What in heaven's
name did it think it was doing running a tight money policy in the midst
of a depression? The rather lame answer is that it feared that low interest
rates would lead to a flow of funds out of the United States and force us to
devalue the dollar. But the net effect was surely to make an already bad
depression much worse and to accelerate the weakening conditions of
the banks. During 1932 the banking crisis eased up, but when it recurred
at the start of 1933, up went the discount rate again!

Altogether, the Fed probably helped to slow down the decline during
1930 and 1931, but it distinctly made things worse from 1931 through
1933, when the country was in more desperate economic condition than
ever before or since. The lesson drawn by most observers from this
episode is that the Fed cannot effectively pursue two policy goals at
once. Maintaining domestic stability called for easy money. Keeping the
dollar convertible at the old exchange rate seemed to require tight
money. The Fed had to choose. Almost all the Monday-morning
quarterbacks have concluded that the Fed chose the wrong goal.

From the bottom of the Depression in 1933 until World War II the Fed
was generally helpless. It bought bonds until interest rates had fallen too
close to their minimum levels. In addition, gold poured into the country;
bank reserves soared. From 1933 until 1942 the country's commercial
banks held large excess reserves, but credit expanded very little. The Fed
could make credit available, but it couldn't make businessmen use it.[8]
Many economists interpret this experience to mean that monetary policy

---

[8] The Fed did not expand as much as it might have, and at one point, in 1936, it actually
raised reserve requirements to sop up some of the excess reserves. The banks still had
unused lending power, so the effect on interest rates was minimal. But some observers still
feel that this action played a role in bringing the second depression that started in 1937. As
we shall see in Chapter 16, there are other possible explanations for that depression.

can do little to get a country out of a deep depression. Easily available credit at very low interest rates (for those with acceptable credit ratings) just wasn't enough to induce the investments needed for full employment. Not when business prospects looked as bleak as they did in the 1930s.

MONETARY POLICY AND WARTIME INFLATION

The Fed wasn't any more effective in dealing with the serious inflations of World War II and the Korean War. This time the problem was the public debt. The government borrowed heavily to finance World War II. Tight money would have made the cost of that borrowing much greater. For a decade, therefore, the Fed followed a policy of standing ready to buy any government bonds that no one else wanted. This policy guaranteed that the interest rates on the bonds would not rise. But it also meant that the commercial banks could get all the reserves they wanted; they had only to sell bonds. The Fed would buy them if nobody else did, and bank reserves would rise accordingly. As a result, the money supply more than doubled during the 1940s. Inflation proceeded apace while the Fed stood by.

Again the Fed had let another purpose displace its goal of maintaining economic stability. We cannot keep interest rates stable if our purpose is to prevent inflation and depression.

POSTWAR MONETARY POLICY

The Fed's commitment to guarantee the market for government bonds ended in 1952. Since then the Fed has at least had the power to do something about the level of economic activity. Yet its life was still not easy.

For one thing, monetary policy sometimes requires the sort of foresight that is not usually given to mortals. Suppose an economic decline begins. Unemployment rises and industrial production declines. It takes at least a month for the statisticians to record the change, and even then it isn't clear whether there is a recession in the making or only a temporary aberration in the statistics. It takes three or four months of consistent decline in the figures for them to be convincing. Then the Fed must decide to act, and that may take a little longer. Even after it does move, it will be half a year or more before investment begins to respond. The investment projects that the Fed does induce will then go on for some time. Peak employment on those projects may not be reached for another year or two. Altogether, the response to a decline that begins now is apt to reach its peak a year and a half or two years later. By that time the situation may be completely changed. If the Fed could see two years into the future it might often take quite different actions from those that it actually undertakes.

The problem has sometimes been complicated by dilemmas about which stability goals should be pursued. In the late 1950s the country experienced a mild inflation despite quite substantial unemployment. Should the Fed have tightened up to check the inflation or should it have expanded credit to reduce unemployment? Throughout 1957 it maintained a tight money policy. In 1958 we had our most severe postwar recession. The Fed responded to it with conventional expansionary policy and we recovered quite rapidly. There was still a good deal of inflation, however, so a year later the Fed returned to its tight money policy, even though the unemployment rate was still 5.5 percent. By 1960 we were in yet another recession. Many things contributed to these declines, but the Fed's obsession with inflation played an important part.

In the early 1960s life was comparatively easy for the Fed. Inflation was slight and unemployment was high. All signs pointed to an expansionary policy, which the Fed followed for five years.

The war in Vietnam made life at the Fed difficult once more. By 1966 we were back at full employment, and government spending was rising rapidly with no corresponding tax increases. An inflation problem was in sight. The Fed stepped into the breach. It stopped the expansion of money and credit almost completely. In the face of rapidly increasing demand for credit, this action resulted in what came to be known as the "credit crunch." Interest rates rose to the highest levels in four decades. Mortgage money seemed to evaporate. The number of residential units on which construction was started fell by 41 percent in nine months. Total investment declined. It began to look as if the Fed were engineering another recession. By the end of 1966 the complaints became intense. The Fed let up. It expanded credit enough during 1967 to fully compensate for the restrictions of 1966. Investment turned around by mid-1967, and the country was back on its path to inflation. Within two years the Fed was clamping down again. Interest rates broke records that had stood since the Civil War. The building trades had another catastrophe. This time the Fed, assisted by tax increases, really did produce a recession.

The Fed struck again after the feed and fuel crises of 1973 had created another inflation in the mid-1970s. This time interest rates set all-time records, and construction collapsed for the third time in a decade.

Altogether, the Fed bounced back and forth from extremely tight money in 1966 to easy money in 1967 and 1968, to tighter money in 1969, to easy money in 1970 to 1972, to extremely tight money in 1974. It came within an ace of causing a recession in 1967 and it really did cause recessions in 1969 and 1974, with some help from the Treasury. In the easy-money years it did a good deal to help inflation along.

One clear implication of the experience of the late 1960s was that monetary policy really can pack a wallop during a boom. After the helplessness of the Fed in the 1930s and 1940s, many economists had come to doubt the power of monetary policy, but few doubt it now.

Another, not too surprising lesson of the 1960s is that anti-inflationary monetary policy is not very popular. From the point of view of the businessman, the Fed gets out its big wet blanket just as the party really gets interesting. There are marvelous investment opportunities right out there, but the bankers will not let us at them.

Tight monetary policy is especially unpopular among builders. Their business went through wild gyrations because of the alternating monetary policies. The basic cause of the inflation was excess demand, in which government spending had led the way. We had to cut back aggregate demand somewhere in order to offset the effect of the government's increases. By using monetary policy we put the largest burden on the builders. Many economists wonder whether periodic drastic booms and depressions in the construction industry are the best way to stabilize the economy.

AN AUTOMATIC MONETARY POLICY?

After this series of flip-flops by the Federal Reserve over the last quarter century, a number of economists have come to feel that **discretionary monetary policy,** which involves conscious decisions to expand or contract money or credit, is more likely to cause instability than to offset it. Imperfect foresight, conflicting goals, and mistakes about the amounts of monetary medicine prescribed seemed to produce unnecessary fluctuations. Some economists have argued that we would be better off if the Fed would simply increase bank reserves at a constant rate roughly proportional to the growth in the real GNP, come hell or high water. If a recession developed, credit would automatically become easier because of reduced demand for credit. If inflation became a problem, interest rates would rise of their own accord. This mechanism would surely have been better than what the Fed actually did during the descent into the Great Depression and during the inflations of World War II and the Korean War. It might well have yielded better results than the unpredictable shifts in policy we experienced later.

Other economists, however, are reluctant to give up one of our main tools for controlling economic activity. They tend to emphasize better and faster economic statistics and efforts to improve our knowledge of the effects of monetary policy instead.

To some extent, the different opinions on this subject reflect differences in basic philosophy. The advocates of stable monetary growth are often people who oppose government intervention in the economy generally. Supporters of a revised but still active monetary policy tend to feel that a planned economy can perform more smoothly than uncontrolled private enterprise.

SUMMARY

Money makes possible efficient exchange and economic specialization. Most of our present money supply consists of obligations of banks: Federal Reserve Notes and commercial bank demand deposits. Money is created whenever the banks extend credit. Any one bank can extend credit, and thus create money, by the amount of its excess reserves. All banks taken together can create money equal to 1/(reserve requirement) times their excess reserves.

The overall supply of credit and money is controlled by the Federal Reserve System, twelve regional banks whose policies are determined by a federally appointed Board of Governors. The main weapons of the Fed are its controls over reserve requirements, discount rates, and open market operations. In practice, its main reliance is on open market operations. When it buys bonds, member bank reserves are increased, and the supply of money and credit can rise. When it sells bonds, the effect is to contract money and credit. An easy-money policy results in low interest rates and readily available credit and therefore serves to increase investment and aggregate demand. Tight money discourages investment and thus reduces aggregate demand.

The monetary policies pursued in practice have not always contributed to economic stability, particularly during the Great Depression and wartime inflations. Since 1952 the Fed has clearly had control over the supply of money and credit, and it has been able to affect the level of economic activity. Its policy actions have often seemed erratic, though. Some economists feel that monetary performance has been so bad that we would do better to switch to a simple policy of stable monetary growth and let the remaining fluctuations in the economy take care of themselves.

STUDY QUESTIONS

1   Bankers often object that they are not creating money, that they are just lending out what is deposited with them. Why does it look that way to individual bankers? How could you convince a banker with such a point of view that banks really do create money?

2   What open market operations would have the same effect on bank reserves as a rise in the reserve requirement? As a fall in the discount rate? As a large increase in the amount of pocket currency carried by the public?

3   What happens when the Fed buys bonds on the open market? How does the transaction affect bank reserves? How does it affect interest rates? How does it affect the supply of credit? How does it affect the money supply?

4   Suppose the Fed simply kept the reserve requirement and its holdings of government bonds constant for the next few years. What would happen to bank reserves? To currency in circulation? To the overall supply of money? To the supply of credit? To interest rates? To the level of economic activity? To the unemployment rate?

5   In the fall of 1973, our supplies of petroleum were cut unexpectedly as a result of an embargo by the Arab oil-producing states. As a result, output and employment fell in many American industries. At the same time, prices were soaring, partly because of the oil shortage and partly because of a shortage of feed grains that occurred at the same time. What sort of monetary policy should the Fed have pursued under such circumstances? Could easy money have solved the unemployment problem caused by the fuel shortages?

FURTHER READING

For more on how banks operate, the reader may want to look at Paul S. Nadler's *Commercial Banking in the Economy,* rev. ed. (New York: Random House, 1973). A good place to read up on the Federal Reserve System and its policies is *The Federal Reserve System: Purposes and Functions;* it is available free from the Board of Governors of the Federal Reserve System, Washington, D.C. Lawrence Ritter and William Silber, *Money,* 2nd rev. ed. (New York: Basic Books, 1973) and James Duesenberry, *Money and Credit: Impact and Control,* 3rd ed. (Englewood Cliffs, N.J.: Prentice-Hall, 1972) are good elementary surveys of money, monetary institutions, and monetary policy. A running commentary on monetary policy in the late 1960s and early 1970s by an articulate advocate of stable monetary growth appears in Milton Friedman, *An Economist's Protest* (Glen Ridge, N.J.: Horton, 1972), Chapter 3. This is a collection of articles that Friedman wrote for *Newsweek* magazine. They are always entertaining, but they present a special point of view.

APPENDIX TO CHAPTER 15
THE
MULTIPLE
CREATION
OF
MONEY

This appendix contains an alternative explanation of the way banks create money. The results are the same as those in the chapter, but the method used is more conventional.

THE EFFECT OF A LOAN ON A BANK'S BALANCE SHEET

Let us look at a bank's balance sheet again. We are mainly interested in its reserves, its securities and loans outstanding, and its demand deposits. Hence we will simplify the picture by assuming that the other items in the bank's balance sheet are zero. Now let's trace through the effect of a loan on the position of "The First National Bank." Here is the bank's balance sheet at the start of business:

ASSETS		LIABILITIES	
Reserves	$3,000,000	Demand Deposits	$10,000,000
Loans and Securities	7,000,000		

Assume that the reserve requirement is twenty percent. Then this bank would be required to have reserves of $0.2 \times \$10,000,000$, or $2,000,000. Since at the start of business its actual reserves are $3,000,000, the bank has excess reserves of $1,000,000. That million dollars isn't earning anything for the bank, so the bank will want either to increase its loans or to buy more securities.

Now let it make a $1,000,000 loan. The new balance sheet looks like this:

ASSETS | | LIABILITIES |
---|---|---|---
Reserves | $3,000,000 | Demand Deposits | $11,000,000
Loans and Securities | 8,000,000 | |

The bank's loans and deposits go up by a million dollars each. For the moment the bank still has excess reserves, but this situation won't last long, because the borrower can be expected to spend his new deposit. Soon the First National Bank will have to honor $1,000,000 in checks. The checks will generally be payable to people doing business at other banks. (We'll assume here that all of them are.) The balance sheet of this bank after those payments are made looks like this:

ASSETS | | LIABILITIES |
---|---|---|---
Reserves | $2,000,000 | Demand Deposits | $10,000,000
Loans and Securities | 8,000,000 | |

The demand deposits are $1,000,000 lower after the borrower writes his checks. The reserves are reduced by the same amount when the checks come through. Thereafter the bank has just enough reserves to cover its deposits. It cannot make any more loans. In general, individual banks can safely create money only by the amount of their excess reserves.

The excess reserves that we started with have not entirely disappeared, however. Checks were drawn on the First National. The banks in which those checks were deposited received additional reserves in the process. Suppose, for simplicity, that the entire million dollars in checks goes to the Second National Bank. Here is the situation at Second National just before the checks come in:

ASSETS | | LIABILITIES |
---|---|---|---
Reserves | $2,000,000 | Demand Deposits | $10,000,000
Loans and Securities | 8,000,000 | |

The bank has just enough reserves to cover its deposits. Then the million dollars are deposited and collected from First National:

ASSETS | | LIABILITIES |
---|---|---|---
Reserves | $3,000,000 | Demand Deposits | $11,000,000
Loans and Securities | 8,000,000 | |

The Second National Bank now has $1,000,000 more in deposits, and also in reserves. However, it needs only $200,000 in reserves to cover those extra deposits. It therefore has $800,000 in excess reserves.

If the Second National also tries to keep its earning assets as large as possible, it will increase its loans and securities by $800,000. Suppose, for variety's sake, that it has no new lending opportunities. Let's say it buys bonds worth this amount instead. It will pay for these bonds with an officer's check drawn on itself. When the seller of the bonds deposits this check, he will have a deposit of $800,000, and no other depositor will have any less. In short, more money will have been created. The Second National Bank will have to honor the check when it comes through. Its balance sheet after that transaction looks like this:

ASSETS		LIABILITIES	
Reserves	$2,200,000	Demand Deposits	$11,000,000
Loans and Securities	8,800,000		

The Third National Bank that received the check will have additional deposits and reserves of $800,000. Since it needs only $160,000 in reserves to cover the new deposit, it will now have excess reserves of $640,000. It can make loans or buy securities of that amount.

Obviously the process can go further. Each successive bank receives deposits and reserves equal to the loans made or securities bought by the previous bank. It needs only twenty percent of the additional deposits to meet its reserve requirements, so it can extend credit and create money equal to up to 80 percent of the additional deposits received. This process can go on as long as there are excess reserves in any bank in the system.

ALL BANKS TOGETHER

To see where the process ends, let us work out the position of all the banks taken together. Say the whole banking system has a balance sheet like this:

ASSETS OF ALL BANKS		LIABILITIES OF ALL BANKS	
Reserves	$201,000,000	Demand Deposits	$1,000,000,000
Loans and Securities	799,000,000		

All banks together are shown as having $201 million in reserves against deposits of one billion dollars to start with. Their required reserves would be twenty percent of one billion, or $200 million. In other words, just as in the example of the individual bank, the banks as a whole are shown as having a million dollars in excess reserves. Those banks that have the excess reserves will have an incentive to make loans or buy securities. As they extend credit, their deposits will increase, and their required reserves will rise accordingly. Unlike any one bank, however, the banking system as a whole does *not* lose reserves when loans are made or securities are bought. Checks drawn on one of the banks are deposited at other banks, so the total of *all banks'* reserves stays the same. Credit can therefore increase until the $201,000,000 reserves are just twenty percent of total deposits. This point is reached when deposits reach $1,005,000,000:

ASSETS OF ALL BANKS		LIABILITIES OF ALL BANKS	
Reserves	$201,000,000	Demand Deposits	$1,005,000,000
Loans and Securities	804,000,000		

The million dollars in excess reserves permitted an increase in credit and deposits of five million dollars.

The result is precisely the same one we reached in Chapter 15. The reserve requirement determines how much credit expansion is possible with a given amount of excess reserves. The general rule is that

initial excess reserves = reserve requirement × potential increase in deposits.

Turning this equation around, the relationship becomes:

$$\text{potential increase in deposits} = \frac{\text{initial excess reserves}}{\text{reserve requirement}}.$$

In other words, the banks can extend new credit and create new deposits by an amount equal to 1/(reserve requirement) times their excess reserves. In this example the potential increase in deposits was:

$$\frac{1}{0.2} \times \$1,000,000 = 5 \times \$1,000,000 = \$5,000,000.$$

Alternatively, you can look at the total resources of the banks to find how many deposits they can support. Here the rule is:

total reserves = the reserve requirement × total potential deposits

or

$$\text{total potential deposits} = \frac{1}{\text{reserve requirement}} \times \text{total reserves}.$$

In our example, the total potential deposits come to

$$\frac{1}{0.2} \times 201,000,000 = 1,005,000,000.$$

Since the banks started off with a billion dollars in deposits, this rule means that they can create five million dollars in additional deposits.

DESTROYING MONEY

The process works in reverse, too. Suppose someone withdraws $1,000 in cash and puts it in a mattress. His bank loses $1,000 in deposits and reserves. But its required reserves fall by only $200. As a result, it will have a reserve deficiency of $800. To make up the deficiency, the bank must either sell $800 of bonds or accept an $800 loan repayment without making any new loans.

Either way, some bank somewhere will lose deposits and reserves of $800 when one of its customers buys the bonds or withdraws money to pay off the loan. Its own required reserves will fall by only $160. Now it will have to sell $640 of bonds or reduce its loans by that amount. You can probably tell where this story is headed. By how much will the money supply ultimately fall? Look up the answer in the footnote.[9]

SOME QUALIFICATIONS

This story and the one in Chapter 15 were both highly simplified, though they covered the essentials. For one thing, as was pointed out in the chapter, banks don't *have* to extend more credit when they have excess reserves. Our story tells only the *maximum* amount of money they can create. They might create a lot less. When it comes to destroying money, the same qualifications would apply if the banks have excess reserves. If they don't, however, they *must* reduce their deposits by 1/(reserve requirement) times the reduction of their reserves.

These examples assumed that all the money created went into demand deposits. If some of it went into cash, then the banks would lose reserves, and the maximum increase in the money supply with a given amount of excess reserves would be less. Some of the money might go into time deposits instead. This would also reduce the ultimate increase in M_1 (currency and demand deposits), since banks are required to hold reserves against time as well as demand deposits. On the other hand, M_2 (currency, demand, and time deposits) could increase more, because the reserve requirement against time deposits is lower than that for demand deposits.

Finally, the picture of one bank making a loan and all the proceeds winding up in another bank is unrealistic. In practice the proceeds will spread through the whole banking system. Some of them are apt to wind up in the bank making the loan. As a result, when there are excess reserves in the country, most banks will have excess reserves. Even if a bank makes loans equal to its excess reserves on Monday it is apt to find itself with new excess reserves on Tuesday. It and the other banks can all go on making loans and creating new deposits until the whole banking system's excess reserves are exhausted.

STUDY QUESTIONS

1   A bank has $10,000,000 in deposits, $3,000,000 in reserves, and $7,000,000

---

[9] Deposits will fall by $5,000. However, the $1,000 in the mattress is part of the money supply, too, so the total money supply falls by only $4,000.

in loans and investments. The reserve requirement is ten percent rather than the twenty percent used in the examples in this appendix. How much more credit can the bank extend? Show that it creates money when it makes the loans or buys the bonds involved.

2   When business begins, the bank in the question above is the only bank in the whole banking system with excess reserves. How much credit can the banking system as a whole extend, given those excess reserves and a ten percent reserve requirement? You should get a number a good deal higher than you did in the answer to question 1. Explain how the two answers are consistent.

3   The Fed wants to prevent the extension of credit that would occur in this situation. Should it buy or sell bonds on the open market? What value of bonds should it buy or sell?

16 FISCAL POLICY

The government collects almost a third of the GNP in taxes, spends 22 percent of it on goods and services, and distributes transfer payments worth about ten percent of it. Such a large chunk of our economy seems bound to be important in determining whether we face prosperity, inflation, or depression. The particular taxes collected and the expenditures made were the subject of Chapter 10. The manipulation of the government's overall budget to affect the level of economic activity is known as **fiscal policy.** It is the subject of this chapter.

THE ELEMENTS OF FISCAL POLICY

ALTERNATIVE ROUTES TO AN INCREASED GNP

Suppose the government's goal is to raise the level of the GNP by, say, $30 billion. Several alternative fiscal policy moves are possible. The government might do any of the following things:

☐ Increase its expenditures

☐ Cut taxes

☐ Increase transfer payments

or, as we shall see,

☐ Increase government expenditures and taxes simultaneously.

The effects of these four alternative policies are worked out in Table 16.1. Each of them deserves some explanation.

Government purchases of goods and services are part of aggregate demand itself. Any increase in government purchases, therefore, should affect the level of economic activity the same way that an increase in investment did in Chapter 13. If the marginal propensity to consume is

TABLE 16.1   Four ways to raise GNP by $30 billion*

FISCAL POLICY ACTION	(1) AMOUNT OF CHANGE IN THE BUDGET DEFICIT	(2) INITIAL CHANGE IN CONSUMPTION DUE TO CHANGING TAXES OR TRANSFER PAYMENTS	(3) CHANGE IN CONSUMPTION DUE TO THE MULTIPLIER EFFECT	(4) NET CHANGE IN GNP
Increase government purchases	+$10	—	+$20	+$30
Reduce taxes	+$15	+$10	+$20	+$30
Increase government transfer payments	+$15	+$10	+$20	+$30
Increase both government purchases and taxes:				
Purchases	+$30	—	+$60	+$90
Taxes	−$30	−$20	−$40	−$60
Net change in GNP				+$30

*Assuming a marginal propensity to consume of 2/3. All numbers are billions of dollars.

two thirds, so that the multiplier is three, then a $30-billion increase in GNP can be accomplished by a $10-billion increase in government purchases—provided, of course, that tax rates and transfer programs do not change. For this purpose it makes no difference whether the government spends its money on bombs or highways or red sticky tape. Producers of the goods and services bought by the government will spend two thirds of the proceeds on extra consumer goods. That spending will induce yet more consumption. The process will finally work itself out with consumption increased by $20 billion, government purchases by $10 billion, and GNP by $30 billion.

A tax reduction with government spending held constant will increase aggregate demand indirectly. A tax reduction works through its effect on disposable income. With lower taxes, the public's take-home pay will be increased. The amount of consumption to be expected with each level of the GNP will increase as a result. The tax reduction necessary to bring about a $30-billion increase in GNP is greater than the rise in government spending needed to accomplish the same result, however. The reason is that some of the tax reduction will go into saving. The initial upward shift in consumption due to the tax cut will be equal to the marginal propensity to consume times the change in tax. Equilibrium income will ultimately increase by the multiplier times that initial increase in consumption. For instance, to bring about a rise in GNP of $30 billion, we must cut taxes enough to induce an initial change in consumption of $10 billion. Since the marginal propensity to consume is two thirds, we need a tax cut of $15 billion. The initial change in consumption will then be

$\frac{2}{3} \times \$15$ billion $= \$10$ billion.

This increased consumption will lead ultimately to a rise in the GNP of

$3 \times \$10$ billion $= \$30$ billion

because of the multiplier.

It may make a difference whose taxes are cut. A tax cut for the poor may induce a larger initial change in consumption than an equal tax cut for the rich. Similarly, a tax increase aimed at checking inflation will have more effect on consumption if it falls on those with high marginal propensities to consume, presumably the poor again.

Transfer payments can be treated as negative taxes: the government pays us instead of our paying the government. An increase in transfer payments, like a cut in taxes, would make households better off at each level of the GNP. It can be expected to lead to an increase in consumption as a result. Again, to bring about a $30-billion increase in GNP, we would need an increase in transfer payments of $15 billion, since a third of the increase would go into saving. Of course, if transfer payments go to people with particularly high marginal propensities to consume, the initial change in consumption may be more than two thirds of the increase in transfers. In that case, less than a $15-billion increase in transfers would be needed.

Equal increases in government purchases and taxes will also raise the GNP. This is true because all of the government purchases are part of aggregate demand, but some of the increased taxes come out of saving. For every dollar of additional expenditures, equilibrium GNP rises by three dollars. For every dollar of additional taxes, equilibrium GNP falls by two. A dollar more of both government purchases and taxes will then have a net expansionary effect of $3 - \$2 = \$1$ on the GNP. This reasoning implies that the government could attain a $30-billion increase in GNP by raising both expenditures and taxes by $30 billion.

The calculations in Table 16.1 ignore any effect that fiscal policy might have on investment. Tax cuts often increase the net returns that business receives on its plant and equipment. They might be expected to increase investment accordingly. Government purchases, on the other hand, have uncertain effects on investment. If the government spending improves services to business (for instance, by building better roads) it may encourage investment. But if the government expenditures are in competition with business (for instance, public power projects) it may work the other way. Taking the effect of fiscal policy on investment into account, a cut in taxes is likely to increase GNP more than is indicated by our simple analysis based only on consumption effects. At the same time, an equal increase in government purchases and taxes may be less expansionary than indicated.

The policy changes outlined in Table 16.1 were all oriented toward increasing the GNP. They were the sorts of things that the government might do in order to prevent a depression. If, instead, we are faced with a problem of inflation, these policy actions would be reversed. To check inflation the government would have to reduce its purchases, increase taxes, reduce transfer payments, or reduce purchases and taxes equally. The increase in taxes or cut in transfers needed to reduce equilibrium GNP by $30 billion would be greater than the reduction in government purchases needed to accomplish the same thing. And the cut in expenditures plus taxes needed to reduce aggregate demand that much would be greater yet.

CHOOSING AMONG FISCAL POLICY WEAPONS

Altogether, we have found four alternative routes to increasing the GNP. Which is preferable? The answer depends on individual value judgments. If you worry about big government, you might advocate lower taxes. This policy would leave public spending the same and let the private sector expand. On the other hand, if you feel that public services are slighted in our economy, you might favor a simultaneous increase in both government expenditures and taxes.

As a practical matter, it is usually easier to change taxes than to change government purchases or transfer payments in response to fluctuations in economic activity. Most government spending is part of long-term programs that are apt to go on for decades. The public power program, begun in the 1930s, and the interstate highway program, begun in the 1950s, are still generating government expenditures today. In general, public expenditures are hard to turn off, once started. This is even more true in the case of transfer programs. An increase in old age pensions might be suitably expansionary during a recession, but imagine the howls if we tried to reduce them again the next time inflation threatened.

Unlike government spending, tax rates *can* be increased or decreased from one year to the next. Because of the greater flexibility of taxes, many observers—including some who feel that government spending is too low—tend to favor tax changes as fiscal policy moves. Particular expenditure and transfer programs would then be adopted or rejected on their own merits. Taxes would be adjusted to whatever levels are needed to assure full employment without inflation.

PROBLEMS OF FISCAL POLICY

THE PUBLIC DEBT

Fiscal policy in time of inflation calls for increases in taxes or decreases in government purchases and transfers. It is likely to involve a government **surplus**—that is, a reduction in the public debt. Such a policy sounds plausible to most people, though it may not be easy to do politically. In time of depression, however, fiscal policy requires lower taxes or more government spending. These policies are likely to bring on government **deficits**—increases in the public debt. Many people worry about these deficits. How can we go on borrowing money year after year without going broke? Aren't we just shifting the burden of present problems to future generations? The individual who regularly lives beyond his income, borrowing more each year, seems bound to face a day of reckoning. Eventually he must either cut back and pay off his debts or face bankruptcy. Doesn't the same reasoning apply to the public debt?

In general, the answer is no. The basic reason is that the public debt and private debt are quite different in concept. In the case of a private debt, the borrower owes someone else. He can run out of the means of payment and face all the embarrassment that that can entail. By contrast, in the case of the public debt, the people of the United States owe the people of the United States. The government may owe $300 billion, but the citizens of the country own bonds worth $300 billion. For the country as a whole the two cancel out.

There is no possibility of bankruptcy on a domestically-held public debt. The government has promised to pay dollars, of which it has, literally, an infinite supply. When it runs short it is always capable of printing more. In fact, informed investors consistently treat government bonds as subject to no risk of default at all. That is the reason why government bonds always yield lower interest rates on the market than do private bonds with similar maturity dates. Even the bonds of the defeated German and Japanese governments continued to yield interest and sell at reasonable prices after the war.

Many people picture the public debt as something that must be repaid someday. Certainly individual government bonds must be paid off when they reach maturity. Normally, though, this is done with more borrowing. The only reason to run a surplus, thereby paying off some of the debt, would be to reduce aggregate demand when inflation threatens. But if inflation is not currently a problem it would actually be economically harmful for the government to pay off its debt. Such a policy would impose depression on the country.

In refinancing its debt, the government is following the same policy that most large corporate borrowers do. American Telephone and Telegraph and the electric utilities have regularly refinanced their debts. Unlike the federal government, they do not have unlimited borrowing power, but they still take advantage of the borrowing power they do have. Their debts have regularly increased as the firms themselves have grown.

The "burden on future generations" is also largely a phantom. We cannot shift the opportunity cost of what the government buys now to the future by borrowing. If the government is to spend more now, and we are at full employment, then we *must* give up other goods and services *now*. We simply have no choice, regardless of whether or not the government borrows to finance the extra spending. There is no way we can use future goods and services to provide for present government needs.

Similarly, if we pay off part of the government debt, and if we remain at full employment, we won't have any more or less goods and services in the country than if the debt were to stay high. The largest part of the public debt was incurred during World War II, when federal deficits were equal to about a fifth of the GNP. These deficits didn't transfer the burden of the war to the postwar generation. People had to go without cars in 1943—not in 1975—so that the army could have tanks in 1943.[1] Similarly, if we ever pay off the public debt, we won't have a higher standard of living as a result. The government would owe less, but the public would own less in bonds by the same amount. The real wealth and the total output of the country would be just as high whether the debt was large or small.

If the public debt were owed to foreigners, however, the situation would be different. In that case, we *could* run out of the means of payment. The federal government has an infinite supply of dollars, but not of French francs or German marks. When we borrow abroad instead of from ourselves we *do* receive more goods and services as a result. When we pay off a foreign debt we do have to give up some of our GNP to the rest of the world. Foreign debt means about the same thing to the

[1] There is one way in which some of the cost of World War II was shifted to people after the war. Investment expenditures were much lower in those years than they probably would have been without the war. The nation's capital stock was smaller after the war as a result. However, this would have been the case whether the war was financed with taxes or with borrowing.

country that a private debt does to the individual. A domestically-held public debt does not.

State and local governments generally borrow from "foreigners" in the sense that most of their debt is placed with lenders who are residents of other places. Moreover, state and local governments can't create money. As a result, the state and local governments do face definite limits on how much they can borrow. It is quite possible for them to run out of the means of payment. Their credit ratings will deteriorate if their debts get too large relative to their tax bases. For the most part, state and local expenditures are closely tied to their revenues. The federal government has no such limitation.

The federal government may want to maintain a balanced budget or run a surplus in some period, but it shouldn't do so because of any concern about its credit rating. That won't be affected. The only reason it ever needs to do so is to keep the equilibrium GNP from rising above the full-employment level—in other words, to prevent inflation. In other times, when the equilibrium GNP is well below the full-employment level, the expansionary effect of a deficit would be welcome.

THE REAL BURDENS OF THE DEBT

This long argument doesn't mean that there is no burden at all to the public debt, however. The larger the debt, the more the government will have to collect in taxes if we are to avoid inflation. These higher taxes are not net losses to the economy; we collect the money and pay it back to domestic bondholders. But a large debt and the accompanying high taxes *do* mean a redistribution of income from taxpayers to bondholders. If bonds were owned by the rich and taxes were paid by the poor, a large public debt would tend to increase inequality. In fact, though, federal bonds and federal tax obligations are distributed similarly enough so that income distribution is largely unaffected.[2] In any case, redistribution of income is an equity question. The people who bought bonds during World War II gave up consumption then to do so. Those who did not buy bonds benefited from lower taxes at the time because the other people bought bonds. We collect taxes now to pay interest to the people

[2] More than half of the publicly-held debt is owned by banks, insurance companies, and savings and loan associations. The income on these bonds can be distributed among the general public approximately in proportion to deposits and insurance policies held. Only a third of the public debt is held by individuals. The largest part of this amount is in savings bonds, traditionally a middle-class asset. Since federal taxes are mildly progressive, the bulk of the taxes are paid by the middle class. At the same time, the bulk of the interest on the public debt is received by the middle class.

who hold those bonds. You can judge for yourself whether it is equitable to do so.

Another burden of the public debt is that taxes themselves are costly. Even if the government just collects the money from the public and turns around and pays it to the same people as interest, the efforts of the Internal Revenue Service to collect the extra taxes—and of the taxpayers to avoid them—will use up resources. Moreover, the higher taxes will distort incentives. They will leave the economy less efficient than it would be with a lower debt and less taxes.

Finally, a large debt may have an inflationary effect. The public feels richer because of all the bonds it owns. It may consume more out of income as a result. An increase in aggregate demand is fine as long as our problem is unemployment. But in boom times, an increase in demand makes inflation more common and harder to control. Fiscal and monetary policy have to be more restrictive than they would be with a lower debt, and investment is discouraged as a result.

It is important here to distinguish between the expansionary effects of a *debt* and of a *deficit*. The expansionary effect of a deficit is the whole point to fiscal policy in time of recession. It is welcome. In years when inflation rather than unemployment is the problem, good fiscal policy would require a surplus, not a deficit. But the debt will be with us even when the recession is over. A large debt will make subsequent booms more intense and harder to control.

THE SIZE OF THE FEDERAL DEBT

The distributive, incentive, and inflationary effects of the debt should be put in perspective. Net interest on the public debt is only seven percent of the federal expenditures and one percent of state and local expenditures. The two together are less than two percent of the GNP. In practice, taxes collected to cover this interest cannot have very serious distributional and incentive effects.

The total Federal debt is about $425 billion. A quarter of this debt is held by government agencies, however, and another $70 billion is in the hands of the Federal Reserve Banks. That leaves about $250 billion in the hands of the public. The federal debt is less than a quarter of one year's GNP today.

Figure 16.1 shows the public debt as a percentage of the GNP over the last three decades. It grew rapidly during World War II, but it has declined almost continuously since then. This decline has been due to growth in the GNP, rather than to any repayment of the debt. The federal budget has shown a deficit in a majority of years since then. The debt is

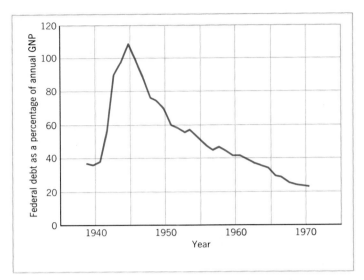

FIGURE 16.1   **The federal debt rose rapidly during World War II.
Since then it has steadily fallen as a percentage of our GNP. This
decline is due primarily to growth in GNP.**

higher than ever, yet it has steadily *declined* as a percentage of the GNP.
Any burden that results from the debt has declined accordingly.

In fact, the government can run a deficit on the order of $15 billion a
year indefinitely and still leave the ratio of the debt to the GNP stable or
declining. About $5 billion a year of this deficit will be taken by the
Federal Reserve Banks if they continue to expand the money supply as
they have in recent years. The remaining $10-billion increase would
represent about a four-percent increase in the debt in the hands of the
public. This is roughly equal to the average rate of growth of the GNP. In
fact, the federal deficit has seldom been as great at $15 billion a year. As a
result, the debt has usually grown by less than the GNP.

In general, the burdens of the debt are vastly exaggerated in most
public discussions. Moreover, such burdens as the debt does impose on
us are of declining importance, due to the growth in the GNP. The
deficits that fiscal policy may call for are seldom large enough to increase the debt as a percentage of the GNP.

THE TIMING OF FISCAL POLICY

The picture of fiscal policy given so far makes it look easier than it really is. In Chapter 15 we saw that monetary policy required a year or two of foresight to assure us of making the right moves. The lags in fiscal policy are worse. Just as at the Fed, it will take several months for the fiscal authorities to recognize an incipient inflation or recession. Once the problem has been identified, the government must decide what to do about it. That decision can be quite fast at the Fed, but it is apt to take months or years when we try the fiscal policy route. The reason is that any change in tax rates or in appropriations must be made by Congress. The debate over whose taxes are to be changed or which expenditures are to be increased or decreased is likely to be long. The tax cut proposed by President Kennedy in August 1962 was finally passed in February 1964. The tax increases proposed by many economists in 1966 were recommended by President Johnson in August 1967 and passed by Congress in June 1968.

Expenditure changes are just as slow. The administrative work on the fiscal 1975 budget began at the start of 1973. The budget message reached Congress in January 1974, and Congress voted most of the appropriation bills during the summer and fall of 1974. These authorizations became effective on July 1, 1974 (the "New Year's Day" of fiscal 1975).[3]

Once Congress has acted, the new policies will take some time to have an effect. A tax change may affect income tax withholding rates almost immediately, but its full effect on disposable income won't be known until the returns are in next April. And any resulting changes in consumption come only after disposable income has changed. If fiscal policy takes the form of a change in expenditures, rather than in taxes, the impact is likely to show up even later. Construction of a new highway authorized in 1976 is likely to start in 1977 and reach a peak several years later. The full impact of fiscal policy moves planned in 1975 and enacted in 1976 is apt to reach its peak in 1978 or 1979.

Our machinery for changing taxes and expenditures is much too slow to allow for quick responses to unforeseen developments in the economy. The lags in fiscal policy are greater even than those in monetary policy. Fiscal policy is not a very suitable tool for "fine tuning" the economy.

That fact doesn't mean that fiscal policy should be ignored. Indeed, it

---

[3] The president does have some short-term control over the rate at which previously authorized expenditures are made. Without going to Congress, he can slow down work on government construction in one period and speed it up in another. Such changes don't require congressional action, so they can be made much faster than changes that require new appropriations or new tax laws.

cannot be. The government does, in fact, make large expenditures and collect lots of taxes. These activities inevitably have a heavy impact on the economy. If government were to ignore the economic effects of its budget it would be apt to *generate* depressions and inflations of its own making. The government can adjust taxes and expenditures to yield an aggregate demand near full-employment levels, taking one year with the next. On the other hand, it probably cannot be very effective in offsetting short-run fluctuations in aggregate demand.

BUILT-IN STABILIZERS

To some extent the federal budget serves to damp down economic fluctuations automatically. Tax *receipts* rise and fall with GNP if tax *rates* are held constant. When we have a recession, personal and corporate incomes fall, and personal and corporate tax payments fall accordingly. Indeed, with progressive taxes such as the personal income tax, the government's take falls off proportionately faster than incomes do. In addition, such government transfer payments as unemployment insurance and welfare are likely to rise in time of recession. Then, if government purchases are simply left unchanged, the budget will automatically show a growing deficit as GNP declines.

The opposite happens when the GNP rises. Tax receipts increase,

FIGURE 16.2 As a result of built-in stabilizers such as the progressive income tax and unemployment insurance, fluctuations in the GNP are damped automatically by the federal budget.

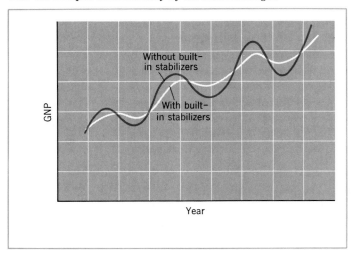

transfer payments fall, and the deficit is reduced or the surplus increased.

The result is illustrated in Figure 16.2. With no government, the economy might show fluctuations like those indicated by the red line. With a big government that keeps its tax *rates* and transfer programs fixed, the fluctuations will be reduced to those shown by the white lines. Because they respond to fluctuations in the GNP in this way, taxes and transfer payments are known as **built-in stabilizers.** Because of them, disposable income fluctuates much less than GNP today. Consumption is more stable as a result.

The fluctuations are not completely eliminated by the built-in stabilizers, however. Many economists believe that the government should use *discretionary fiscal policy* to supplement the automatic tendency for the budget to offset inflation and depression. That is, they want the government to change expenditures or tax rates to eliminate economic fluctuations altogether. Others are skeptical about discretionary fiscal policy. They fear that the long lags involved are apt to mean that the government will have a *de*stabilizing effect instead. Many of the people who oppose discretionary fiscal policy and emphasize automatic stabilizers are persons who object to government intervention in the economy generally.

Built-in stabilizers are apt to mean deficits in time of recession or surpluses in time of boom. Governments are sometimes tempted to adjust tax rates to eliminate the deficits or surpluses. If they do, they will make economic fluctuations more severe than they need to be.

State and local governments are particularly likely to respond to deficits or surpluses in this way. On the deficit side, they have little alternative. Their borrowing power is limited, so if a recession reduces their receipts, they must either cut spending or find new taxes. Most of the states, for instance, raised taxes as we descended into the Great Depression. State and local governments are also inclined to raise expenditures or settle for lower tax rates in boom times. For instance, most states cut taxes when World War II increased their revenues. These moves were just the *wrong* things to do from a fiscal policy point of view. The increased state taxes of the 1930s made the Depression worse, and the reduced state tax rates during World War II increased inflationary pressures.

State and local governments are unlikely to take their effects on economic activity into account. Inflations and depressions are national problems. No one of the fifty states could gain enough from any stabilization it could accomplish to be willing to run a large surplus in time of inflation, or a deficit in time of depression.

Fiscal policy must be the responsibility of the national government for two reasons: because it can take a national view, and because it has unlimited borrowing power. If the federal government is to have a stabilizing effect, it must adjust its taxes and expenditures to what is needed to stabilize the GNP. It should accept any surpluses and deficits that result.

THE FULL-EMPLOYMENT SURPLUS

It is not easy to judge the economic effect of the federal budget by just looking at federal revenues and expenditures for the current year. Revenues may be low, and transfer payments high, because of a recession; the situation may be reversed because of a boom. To make budgets more nearly comparable from year to year, therefore, economists try to estimate what the surplus or deficit would be at full employment. Federal tax receipts rise by about twenty cents for every dollar increase in the GNP if tax rates are left unchanged. Economists can also estimate the effects of the level of economic activity on such transfer programs as unemployment insurance and welfare payments. Taking all of these factors into account, they can estimate what the budget surplus would be at full employment.

Figure 16.3 illustrates how such estimates work. The two diagonal lines show the surpluses that would hold with various levels of employment. With budget A there would be a surplus of ten billion

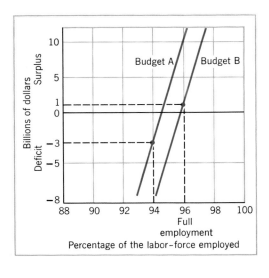

FIGURE 16.3   **If budget A is used in a recession year, and budget B in a full-employment year, budget A may show an actual deficit while budget B shows an actual surplus. Yet budget A is clearly less expansionary than budget B.**

dollars at the 96-percent employment level (four-percent unemployment), which corresponds roughly to full employment in the United States. The same budget would yield a deficit of three billion dollars if the employment rate were 94 percent (unemployment at six percent). With budget B, the full-employment surplus would be lower, at one billion dollars. If the employment rate were 94 percent, though, there would be a realized deficit of eight billion dollars. Budget A is clearly less expansionary than budget B. If budgets A and B were in effect under the same conditions (perhaps in two identical but separate countries), budget B would lead to higher levels of employment than would budget A.

Suppose that budget A were in operation in a depressed year, when the employment rate was 94 percent, but that budget B were in effect at a time when the economy was at full employment. The dots in Figure 16.3 show the actual government budget balances for those two years. Budget A, in the depressed year, yields a deficit of three billion dollars. Budget B, in a full-employment year, yields a surplus of a billion dollars. These two figures alone would suggest that budget A is more expansionary, but it clearly is not. The actual surplus or deficit is a poor indicator of the economic effect of the budget, because it depends on the state of the economy. The full-employment surplus or deficit is a better basis on which to compare budgets.

Figure 16.4 compares the estimated full-employment surplus and the actual surplus in the late 1950s and the 1960s. The federal budget had a continuous full-employment surplus from 1955 through 1965, although the actual budget was often in deficit because of unemployment. In the 1960s, the full-employment surplus was gradually reduced. After 1965 there was a full-employment deficit, except in 1969. This meant that in the inflationary period of the late 1960s the federal budget was considerably more expansionary in effect than it was during the depressed period of the late 1950s and early 1960s.

FISCAL POLICY IN PRACTICE

We have a fair idea of how the budget can be used to maintain economic stability, but we have not always followed the rules of good fiscal policy.

THE GREAT DEPRESSION

The 1930s are often pointed to as a period when fiscal policy did not work. Actually, the fiscal policy of that period was seldom very expansionary. In fact, it often served to make the Depression worse.

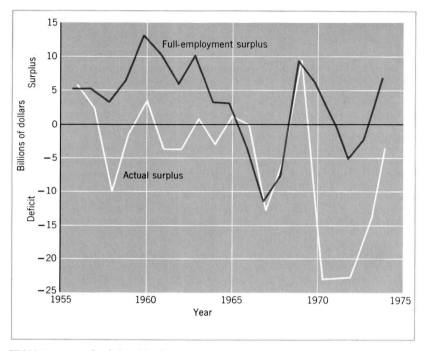

FIGURE 16.4   The federal budget often showed an actual deficit in the late 1950s and early 1960s, but it had a large full-employment surplus throughout the period. It was much less expansionary then than in the late 1960s.

As we descended into the Depression, the government found itself faced with increasing deficits, as might be expected. The states dealt with this problem by introducing new taxes, mainly the then-new sales tax. These extra taxes provided the states with enough revenues to meet most of their obligations, but, of course, the new taxes also acted to depress the economy further.[4]

The federal government could have just sat back and let the deficit accumulate. If it had done so, the automatic stabilizers in its budget would have slowed down the decline. Instead it tried to reduce its growing deficit. In 1931—in the middle of the financial crisis —President Hoover called for drastic cuts in federal spending and tax increases that almost doubled full-employment federal revenues. He said the tax increases were needed to preserve "the unimpaired credit of

---

[4] State and local finance was important in those days. Total state and local expenditures were twice as great as federal expenditures during the 1930s.

the federal government." Amazingly, Congress passed the requested legislation in 1932, at the bottom of the Depression. More than half of the tax increase was in the form of excise taxes, since revenue from these sources held up even when economic activity declined. Congress was intentionally reducing the automatic stabilizers in the budget. Wrongheaded fiscal policy was contributing to the Depression at the same time that the Fed was clamping down. Why did the President and Congress behave this way? The politicians were not stupid, but most of them probably did think of the Federal debt in the same terms as personal or state debt. (A century or so earlier they would have been right. When money was created by gold and silver miners the government *could* run out of the means of payment. It can't now.)[5]

Despite these efforts, the federal government continued to run a large actual deficit. This deficit was entirely due to the Depression, however. At full-employment, the budget would have been in substantial surplus.

In 1932, Franklin D. Roosevelt campaigned on a platform of economy in government. But once the New Deal was installed in office, it changed its tune and raised federal spending. Yet the high tax rates were retained and actually increased. As a result, the budget could have only a mildly expansionary effect. Actual deficits averaged 2.8 percent of the GNP between 1933 and 1940. These deficits were weak medicine for the country's worst depression. The Eisenhower administration ran a deficit of 2.3 percent of the GNP in 1958, and the Nixon administration ran one of 2.2 percent of the GNP in 1971—both during far milder recessions. The deficits that did occur in the 1930s were due to built-in flexibility in the presence of massive unemployment. The federal budget was in full-employment surplus in every depression year except 1936.

The most drastic rise in taxes occurred in 1937, when the introduction of social security brought a whole new tax onto the scene. In that year the *actual* budget was almost balanced, and the full-employment surplus reached a new peak, even though the unemployment rate was still 14 percent. By the end of 1937 we were in a second depression.[6]

---

[5] Actually, 70 years earlier, the government was printing up money (the famous "greenbacks") to pay for the Civil War. But this practice was still looked upon as an emergency measure. After the war the government made major sacrifices to restore the dollar's old relationship to gold. During the 1920s the British did essentially the same thing with all the paper pounds they had issued during World War I. In 1932, most congressmen, presidents and prime ministers were still thinking about money and debt the way the Stuart kings had. Charles II really could not create money and really did have a limit on what he could borrow. The same was not true for Herbert Hoover in 1932, but most people did not know it. Now we all do.

[6] The Fed had reduced the banks' excess reserves drastically, by raising reserve requirements, in 1936. Banks still had some excess reserves, and interest rates stayed low, but some observers feel that this action also helped to bring about the second depression.

Some people looking at the whole decade of deficits have come to the conclusion that deficit finance in time of depression was no solution. But actually, by postwar standards, fiscal policy was quite restrictive throughout the depression period. It made the initial depression much worse than it needed to be, it probably brought on the second depression in 1937 and 1938, and it provided little expansionary pressure in other years.

WAR AND INFLATION

Deficit finance finally did end the Depression when World War II came. During the war, government expenditures were increased until they reached almost half of the GNP. Deficits were increased to a peak of 21 percent of the GNP. The expansionary effect of these budgets was unmistakable.

The economic effect of heavy wartime spending and large deficits was to create severe inflationary pressures. Perhaps this kind of policy was the only way to win the war. If the government had instead collected half the GNP in taxes we might have had much less incentive to produce. Still, fiscal policy could hardly be thought of as having had a stabilizing effect in these years.

Inflation was contained during the war by price controls. After the war's end, though, we went on a spending spree with the unused dollars we had accumulated as a result of the wartime deficits. The result was one of our most severe inflations. In the early postwar years, government spending was cut drastically, and the budget showed a large surplus. The postwar inflation ended within three years.

The Korean War brought another sharp inflation. Taxes were raised almost as soon as the war began. The Korean War is our only important war to date in which the government ran a surplus. The inflation was virtually over within a year.

FISCAL POLICY SINCE KOREA

In the years since the Korean War, fiscal policy has had a mixed record. Taxes were cut during the recessions of 1954 and 1958, and these actions probably helped in the subsequent recoveries. In general the federal budget was not very expansive during the late 1950s, however. As Figure 16.4 shows, there was a large full-employment surplus from 1955 until well into the 1960s, though the actual budget showed a deficit in many of these years. The full-employment surplus reached a peak in

1959. The actual budget, too, was in surplus in that year, despite an unemployment rate of 5.5 percent. Many economists feel that the recession of 1960 was due to this tight fiscal policy and the simultaneous tight monetary policy.

During the early 1960s the country was considerably below full-employment and prices were stable, so a policy of expansion seemed indicated. Corporate taxes were cut in 1963, personal income taxes were cut in 1964, and many excise taxes were eliminated in 1965. The full-employment surplus was gradually pared down. The economy responded beautifully. With plenty of lead time, with unequivocal economic goals, and with the cooperation of the Fed, fiscal policy proved to be very effective in these years.

The war in Vietnam ended this interlude. Government spending rose sharply in 1966 and 1967, but no new taxes were introduced. The result was a $12-billion actual and full-employment deficit in 1967 despite a growing inflation. This was when the Fed created a "credit crunch" while trying to check the inflation single-handedly. Finally, a ten-percent surcharge was added to all personal and corporate income taxes in 1968, and the Fed let up.

In 1969, with inflation an increasingly serious problem, the government cut its spending and raised taxes further. The budget swung into a $7-billion surplus. This surplus, combined with very tight money, brought a recession in 1970. After the recession was well established, taxes were reduced once more and the lid on expenditures was removed. By 1972 the actual budget deficit was $23 billion, the full-employment deficit was $7 billion, and recovery was underway.

Inflation accelerated with the international feed and fuel crises of 1973 and 1974. Once more, the federal budget became less expansionary. Both Presidents Nixon and Ford tried to check federal spending. At the same time, the inflation drove personal and corporate income tax payments up sharply. As a result, by the fall of 1974, the actual budget was nearly balanced. Since the unemployment rate was 5.5 percent by then, there was a full-employment surplus. The combination of a tightening budget and drastically tight money led to increasing unemployment, but the worldwide inflation continued.

Altogether, fiscal policy was wrong in the early Depression, timid during the recovery from the Depression, and oriented toward waging war rather than limiting inflation during World War II. Fiscal policy has been less consistently perverse since World War II, but it has still sometimes worked to create recessions (as in the late 1950s) or inflations (as in 1966–1967).

WAR AND PROSPERITY

An aspect of this story that distresses many people is that war seems to bring prosperity. It does generally bring full employment, though part of the reason is that we draw off a good part of the work force into the armed forces. The prosperity involved doesn't necessarily mean higher standards of living, either, since much of our output goes to the Pentagon (the "regretables" of Chapter 12). In 1944 we were producing almost a third more than we had in 1941, but consumption per person had not increased at all. The reason was that the government was taking almost half the GNP for the war. During the Korean War and the war in Vietnam our standards of living did rise, but they could have risen even more if less of the GNP had gone into defense.

It is sometimes suggested that we would have a hard time avoiding depressions without wars. It seems altogether possible that the Great Depression would have lasted longer if World War II had not come along. (In this writer's opinion, it would take an unretrievable cynic to believe that the reason for entering *that* war was to end the Depression!) The war began only three years after Keynes published his theory. We still had only the sketchiest ideas of how to use fiscal and monetary policies to maintain full employment then.

In any case, this experience certainly does *not* mean that full employment requires heavy defense expenditure today. Germany and Japan have maintained highly admired prosperities for two decades now. Yet Germany puts only 3.3 percent of its GNP into defense, and Japan, only 0.8 percent (as of 1970). Indeed, one reason for their remarkable economic growth has been that they have *not* had to put eight to ten percent of their GNPs into defense as the Americans and Russians did. They could put those resources into investment instead. With what we know now, we should be able to avoid another great depression. We should also have the means of getting out of any recessions we should stumble into—even if peace breaks out and the Pentagon becomes an old soldiers' home.

FISCAL POLICY, MONETARY POLICY, AND STABILITY

Both monetary policy and fiscal policy are in operation all the time. The effect of one depends on what is happening to the other. A full-employment deficit may have a more or less expansive effect on economic activity, depending on what the Fed is doing. Similarly, the GNP that is attained with a tight or an easy money policy depends on the condition of the budget. A complete picture of the effects of policy can be reached only by considering the two policies together.

THE MONETARY EFFECTS OF FISCAL POLICY

What the Treasury does affects money and credit conditions directly. If the government runs a deficit during a recession the effect may be more or less expansionary, depending on where it gets its money. If it borrows from the general public it will bid against private borrowers for funds. Interest rates will therefore be higher than they would be if the government avoided a deficit. As a result, the expansionary effect of fiscal policy will be offset to some extent by reduced private investment.

On the other hand, if the government borrows from the Federal Reserve Banks, interest rates will be reduced. Such transactions amount to open market purchases by the Fed. Not only will the government get its money without bidding it away from private investors, but the banks will have increased lending power as well. Private investment will be encouraged and will reinforce the effect of the deficit. Clearly, by a judicious combination of borrowing from the public and from the Fed, the treasury can have any effect it wants on credit conditions.

Similarly, if the government were trying to damp down economic activity with a budget surplus it could reduce interest rates by retiring privately-held debt, or it could raise them by retiring bonds held by the Federal Reserve Banks. Retiring privately-held bonds would reduce the demand for credit and make interest rates lower. Retiring bonds at the Fed, on the other hand, would have a more restrictive effect on economic activity. Commercial bank reserves would fall and interest rates would rise.

COORDINATING FISCAL AND MONETARY POLICY

What these possibilities mean in practice is that monetary and fiscal policy must be coordinated to have the desired effects. The Fed decides how many government bonds it will hold. If it opts for a tight money policy and buys few bonds, we may have to maintain a full-employment deficit to attain full-employment without inflation. If it buys more bonds, so that the supply of money and credit increases rapidly, we may be able to maintain full employment without inflation with a full-employment surplus.

The makeup of the GNP will be different in the two situations, however. A combination of budget surpluses and easy credit will mean less consumption and more investment than a combination of budget deficits and tight credit. People who put a high value on economic growth, and therefore on the rapid accumulation of capital, tend to favor the combination of budget surpluses and easy credit.

Over the years since World War II, the general trend has been in the other direction. Interest rates have fluctuated from year to year, but the overall trend has been distinctly upward. Rising interest rates discourage investment, especially in such areas as housing. At the same time, we have reduced federal taxes several times and have increased government spending persistently. As a result of the particular combination of monetary and fiscal policy we have chosen, we have probably increased the share of the GNP that goes into consumption and government purchases. This means we have probably cut investment's share.

THE EFFECTIVENESS OF FISCAL AND MONETARY POLICY

Economists differ on the question of which is more effective: fiscal policy or monetary policy. After the long period of monetary passiveness from 1933 through 1952, many economists came to the conclusion that monetary policy could accomplish little, especially in depressions. But today, after twenty years of more active monetary policy, most experts are convinced that the Fed can be effective, especially in boom times. By now, in fact, a school of **monetarists** has arisen. These economists put their main emphasis on monetary policy. Indeed, some of them feel that fiscal policy is irrelevant, except to the extent that it affects the money supply. They look to monetary explanations for all economic fluctuations.

The majority of economists today believe that both fiscal and monetary policy matter. Though fiscal policy and monetary policy have usually had similar goals, there have been enough divergences to suggest the effectiveness of both types of policy. For instance, the inflations after World War II and during the Korean War seem clearly to have been checked by fiscal policy. At that time the Fed was pegging interest rates to stabilize the cost of the public debt; it applied no checks on the supply of money and credit at all. On the other hand, the inflation of the late 1960s was postponed for a year by the 1967 "credit crunch" engineered by the Fed, even though the Treasury was following a policy well designed to create inflation.

In the more common situation, American monetary and fiscal policy have pointed in the same direction. The economy has almost always gone in the direction indicated. While there is still room for argument about how much difference monetary and fiscal policy make individually, there can be little doubt that the two together do work.

This conclusion is possibly the most important result of modern economics. We need no longer simply accept inflation and depression as acts of God. Probably we cannot avoid mild fluctuations due to unforeseen events or fiscal or monetary gaffs, but we need no longer be battered by the kind of severe fluctuations that marked our history in the nineteenth and early twentieth centuries.

SUMMARY

Fiscal policy works by varying government purchases, taxes, and transfer payments, or government purchases and taxes together. A dollar of increased government purchases will raise the GNP more than a dollar tax cut will, because some of the tax reduction will go into saving. It follows that an equal increase in government purchases and taxes will have an expansionary effect.

Fiscal policy may involve deficits, especially in time of recession. But the burden of the increased debt that results is easy to exaggerate. Unlike personal debts, a domestically held public debt carries no risk of bankruptcy nor any transfer from one period to another. A large public debt may produce problems because of the higher taxes that result. These problems are minor in present-day America, however, because the public debt is a small and declining percentage of the GNP.

The long lags in introducing fiscal policy changes make it an even poorer instrument for dealing with short-run fluctuations in the economy than monetary policy is. Long-term fiscal policy decisions are essential, though, if the huge government budget is not to have destabilizing effects. Economists evaluate the impact of fiscal policy in terms of the full-employment, rather than the actual, surplus or deficit.

Fiscal policy has often been off the mark. It probably intensified the decline into the Great Depression, it did little to bring about recovery from that depression, and it was the major cause of the inflation following World War II. Even in the postwar years it has been right only part of the time.

Fiscal policy and monetary policy play complementary roles in affecting economic activity. A tight monetary policy implies a smaller full-employment surplus (or a larger full-employment deficit) than an easy money policy, if we are to maintain full employment without inflation. In the period since World War II the trend has been toward tighter monetary policy and more expansive fiscal policy. Economists differ on the effectiveness of monetary and fiscal policy individually, but there can be little doubt that the two together can control the level of economic activity.

STUDY QUESTIONS

1   Compare the effects on the GNP of a $10-billion cut in taxes and of a

$10-billion increase in government purchases. Which move would increase the GNP more? Why? Which would you prefer if an expansionary fiscal policy was needed? There is a large element of value judgment here, so no one can call your answer to the last question wrong. Work out why you prefer one fiscal policy weapon over the other.

2   "Reliance on deficit finance in government raises a fundamental ethical issue. It is a sign of the moral deterioration of our times that governments throughout the Western world have been ready to jeopardize national solvency and to impose huge burdens on the yet unborn to finance the popular extravagances of the day." Do you agree?

3   Why don't states concern themselves about fiscal policy? Do the expenditure and tax policies of states affect the level of economic activity? Should the states worry about the effects of their budgets on economic activity?

4   How was it possible for the full employment surplus to increase while the federal budget was actually yielding a mounting deficit in the early 1930s? Do you think fiscal policy had anything to do with the divergence between the actual and the full employment surplus or deficit?

5   Over most of our history, down to the 1950s, the government ran large deficits during wars and tried to pay off the public debt gradually in the intervening periods of peace. Over most of the period no one thought in terms of fiscal policy. But a fiscal policy was being pursued, nevertheless. What effect would you expect this policy to have had on the level of unemployment and/or the rate of inflation?

6   In the fall and winter of 1973-1974, we faced both rapidly rising prices and a reduction in output and employment as a result of the Arab oil embargo. You were asked about appropriate monetary policy at the end of Chapter 15. Now, what fiscal policy do you feel would have been appropriate under the circumstances? Could a generally expansionary policy have increased output and employment without accelerating inflation—given that our ability to produce was limited by the oil embargo? Yet the increased unemployment was real enough. Is there anything that fiscal policy could have done to deal with that problem without intensifying the inflation?

FURTHER READING

A good summary of present knowledge on fiscal policy appears in Joseph Pechman, *Federal Tax Policy,* rev. ed. (New York: Norton, 1971),

Chapter 1. Two useful commentaries on fiscal and monetary policy appear in Walter Heller, *New Dimensions in Political Economy* (Cambridge, Mass.: Harvard U. Press, 1966) and Arthur Okun, *The Political Economy of Prosperity* (New York: Norton, 1970). Heller was chairman of the President's Council of Economic Advisers in the early 1960s, and Okun was a member of that body in the late 1960s. The different views on the role and effectiveness of monetary and fiscal policy are well expressed in Milton Friedman and Walter Heller, *Monetary versus Fiscal Policy* (New York: Norton, 1969). Recent economic developments and proposed fiscal and monetary policy moves are described in the *Economic Report of the President,* a very valuable report prepared by the Council of Economic Advisors and sent to Congress every January.

UNIT SIX
THE
INTERNATIONAL
ECONOMY

17
THE
BALANCE
OF
PAYMENTS

So far this book has largely ignored international economic affairs. No country exists in a vacuum, however. What happens abroad affects us, and what we do affects the rest of the world. In this chapter we look at how we pay for our imports and how such payments affect our domestic economy. Chapter 18 deals with international trade and the public policies designed to control it. Chapter 19 makes some comparisons among major world economies.

THE MEANS OF INTERNATIONAL PAYMENTS

HOW TO BUY A BRITISH BOOK

Suppose I want to buy a book from Britain. How do I pay for it? The first answer is very easy. I simply write a check. That answer just shifts the problem to the English bookseller, however. He receives a check for dollars and wants pounds. How can he make the conversion? He probably has an easy solution to the problem, too. He deposits the check in his bank, which gives him pounds for my dollars at the current exchange rate.

That explanation still doesn't settle the matter, however. The bank can't go on taking dollars and paying pounds indefinitely. It, in turn, must find a way to change my dollars into pounds if it is to stay out of trouble. In most cases the solution will present itself to the bank in the normal course of business. It will probably have customers who are

TABLE 17.1 United States balance of payments* (1970)

U.S. PAYMENTS ABROAD		U.S. RECEIPTS FROM ABROAD		BALANCE	
Merchandise Imports	$39.9	Merchandise Exports	$42.0	Balance of Trade	$2.1
U.S. Military Expenditures Abroad	4.9	Military Sales Abroad	1.9		
U.S. Travel Abroad	4.0	Foreign Travel in U.S.	2.5		
U.S. Transport on Foreign Carriers	4.0	Foreign Transport on U.S. Carriers	3.6		
Payment of Income on Foreign Investments in the U.S.	5.1	Income on U.S. Investments Abroad	11.4		
Other Services Purchased from Foreigners	1.4	Other Services Sold to Foreigners	2.1		
U.S. Gifts and Grants Abroad	3.1				
Total Goods, Services and Grants	$62.4		$62.9	Balance of Payments on Current Account	−$0.5
U.S. Investments Abroad	8.5	Foreign Investments in the U.S.	−1.8		
Total	$70.9	Total	$61.1	Balance of Payments	−$9.8

*Figures are billions of dollars.

trying to make payments to the United States in pounds. The bank can just accept those pounds and pay out the dollars that it gets from people like my bookseller. If it should turn out that the attempts to change dollars into pounds exceed the payments in the other direction, so that the bank's dollar balances pile up, it can usually exchange dollars for pounds at other banks that have the opposite problem.

Ultimately, most payments from America to England are settled by Englishmen making similar payments to the United States. In the final analysis, my book purchase is completed as a result of some Englishman buying American machinery or wheat.

THE BALANCE OF PAYMENTS

Since a country's payments to the rest of the world are financed primarily by its receipts from the rest of the world, it is useful to compare the totals of those payments and receipts. Table 17.1 makes that comparison for the United States in 1970. This set of accounts is known as the **balance of payments.** Transactions that give rise to foreign payments by the United States are listed in the left-hand column. The other column shows receipts from the rest of the world.

The most important items in most countries' balances of payments are imports (payments) and exports (receipts). The difference between the two is known as the **balance of trade.** A country that exports more than it imports is said to have a "favorable" balance of trade—though it is not always clear what is "favorable" about sending more goods to the rest of the world than are received in return. The United States had a "favorable" balance of trade in 1970 and for 82 years before that, but in 1971 and 1972 our imports exceeded our exports.

The next several items in the balance of payments are services purchased from, or sold to, foreigners. When an American tourist buys a dinner in Paris or an American exporter makes a shipment on a British vessel, they make payments abroad just as I did when I bought the book. Similarly, a foreigner who flies on an American airline has the same effect on the balance of payments as a foreigner who buys American machinery.

Some of the service items are less obvious. One important item among America's payments is the goods and services purchased by the American armed forces overseas. One of our most important receipts from other countries is the interest and profits earned on American-owned stocks, bonds, oil wells, and factories in other countries. In effect, Americans are selling the services of these investments to foreigners.

American gifts to foreigners, most notably foreign aid, have the same effect as imports on the balance of payments. Foreign aid involves Americans making payments to the rest of the world, just as if we were buying something. It is true that foreign aid permits the receiving country to import goods from the United States. When those goods move, they will show up as American exports in the "Receipts" column of Table 17.1. But the grant itself involves payments, just as imports do.

Let's take the balance of trade, then, and add in figures for services and foreign aid. On the one side we have American imports of goods and services and American grants to the rest of the world. On the other side are American exports of goods and services and foreign grants to the United States. The difference between the two totals is known as the **balance of payments on current account.** This figure is a more meaningful statistic than the balance of trade, because a country can pay for its imports by selling services abroad just as well as by supplying goods. The American balance of payments on current account was just about even in 1970. We paid out more on current account than we received in 1971 and 1972.

American investments abroad have the same effect on the balance of payments as American imports do. In effect, when we invest abroad we are importing stocks, bonds, and the deeds to oil wells and factories. Similarly, when the rest of the world invests in the United States, the result is a receipt in the American balance of payments. In 1970 net foreign investment in the United States was negative, meaning that foreigners were selling off more American assets than they were acquiring.

The grand total of all American imports of goods and services, all American grants abroad, and all American investments abroad provides dollars to the rest of the world. With these dollars the rest of the world buys goods and services from the United States or makes gifts or investments in the United States. The difference between the two totals is the overall balance of payments. If a country's payments abroad exceed its receipts from abroad, it has a balance of payments **deficit.** If receipts exceed payments, the country has a balance of payments **surplus.** The United States has had a balance of payments deficit almost continuously for two decades.

When the United States runs a deficit, someone abroad winds up with more dollars than before. If he doesn't want them, he will exchange them at his central bank. Until August 1971, foreign central banks could, in turn, exchange their dollars for gold at the Federal Reserve. About a quarter of the $9.8-billion 1970 deficit shown in Table 17.1 was covered in this way. The remaining $7.6 billion took the form of increased dollar balances in foreign central banks. Since August 1971, however, the Fed and the Treasury have refused to convert dollars into gold. Now the only means by which the American balance of payments deficit can be covered is for foreign central banks to take more dollars.

BALANCE OF PAYMENTS PROBLEMS

What is wrong with a balance of payments deficit? The answer is probably nothing, so long as the rest of the world is willing to pile up dollars. We can supply dollars in any quantity that other countries may want to take, at virtually no cost to ourselves. And we get real goods and services and real foreign investment properties in return.

The rub comes when the rest of the world decides it doesn't want any more dollars. When that happens, some sort of adjustment will have to occur if we are to continue to buy and invest abroad. The United States was able to run deficits throughout most of the 1950s and 1960s without much difficulty, because the rest of the world thought of dollars as valuable assets and was ready to take quite a lot of them.

By the early 1970s, however, so many dollars had accumulated abroad that our trading partners became skeptical about taking yet more bits of green paper for the goods and services they sent us. At that point we had to find some way to adjust. The problem disappeared for a while when the value of our agricultural exports skyrocketed in 1973, but it returned in 1974 when the value of our oil imports rose even more. The world feed and fuel crises produced even more serious balance of payments problems for many other countries. Nations that have to import most of their feed grains and oil were hard hit.

The crunch comes much sooner for countries that are economically less important than the United States. We and the other countries of the world just don't need a lot of pounds, lire, pesos, or escudos. This means that most countries must find some way to eliminate any balance of payments deficit that persists for just a few years. Even the United States must get rid of a deficit sooner or later.

BALANCE OF PAYMENTS ADJUSTMENT

There are several alternative ways of dealing with a deficit. Which one is best depends on the circumstances.

THE SUPPLY AND DEMAND FOR DOLLARS

To analyze these possible adjustments, it is useful to think of the American balance of payments as the supply and demand for dollars in international markets. American payments to the rest of the world represent the supply of dollars. When an American imports goods or services or invests abroad he supplies dollars to the rest of the world. Similarly, U.S. balance of payments receipts are the demand for dollars by the rest of the world. The exchange rate between dollars and deutsche marks is the price of dollars in terms of that currency. Of course, there are other currencies in the world besides dollars and marks. There are as many dollar exchange rates as there are foreign currencies. But fortunately, these various exchange rates are consistent. In other words, the value of the dollar in terms of pounds is equal to its value in terms of marks times the value of the mark in terms of pounds. The price of the dollar in terms of marks will serve to represent its price in terms of any other foreign currency.

Figure 17.1 shows the demand and supply of dollars, using the mark exchange rate as the price. The demand for dollars slopes downward and to the right like most demand curves. The reason is that the value of the dollar determines the price of American goods to foreigners. If the value of the dollar is reduced, American goods will be cheaper abroad, and foreigners will be induced to buy more of them. Similarly, the supply of dollars slopes upward and to the right. A fall in the exchange rate makes foreign currencies more expensive to Americans. At a lower exchange rate foreign goods will be more expensive, and imports will be discouraged.

Until recently, most of the countries of the world have had pegged

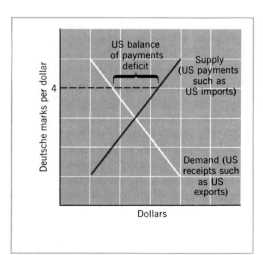

FIGURE 17.1 The supply of dollars on money markets results from U.S. payments abroad; the demand arises from foreign payments to us. If the exchange rate were pegged at four marks per dollar, as in this example, the United States would have a balance of payments deficit.

exchange rates. That is, the authorities have acted to keep exchange rates fixed. In Figure 17.1 the exchange rate is pegged at four marks per dollar. At this rate the United States has a balance of payments deficit, because the supply of dollars is greater than the demand. Keeping the exchange rate at four requires government intervention similar to the price support program in agriculture. In other words, someone must buy up the dollars that no one else wants or the price will fall. To cover such deficits the countries of the world maintain **reserves** of gold and foreign currencies. They use these reserves to buy any surplus of their own currency. The U.S. dollar is the main currency used for such transactions at present. When the United States runs a deficit it pays out either gold or dollars. Since August 1971 the United States has refused to pay out gold, however, so the only way that the dollar could be pegged since then has been for other countries to buy dollars. The central banks in the countries with surpluses, such as Germany and Japan, did this consistently from 1971 until mid-1973.

If the exchange rate were two marks per dollar instead of four, as in Figure 17.2, the United States would have a balance of payments surplus. Demand would be greater than supply. To keep the exchange rate pegged in that case, the United States would have to buy the surplus foreign currencies, or the rest of the world would have to pay out dollars. Instead of supporting prices, the authorities would be acting to keep the price of dollars down.

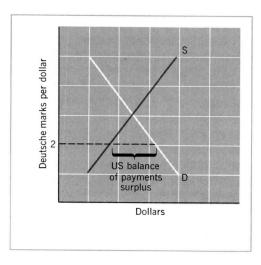

FIGURE 17.2   If the exchange rate were pegged at two marks to the dollar, the United States would have a balance of payments surplus.

SHORT-RUN DEFICITS AND INTERNATIONAL RESERVES

If the cause of a balance of payments deficit is something temporary, such as a strike or a crop failure, the best solution is for the deficit country to pay out reserves or for the surplus countries to buy up the surplus currency. It seems foolish to make long-run adjustments to deal with short-term problems.

One reason for the periodic international payments crises that have plagued the world since World War II has been a shortage of international reserves. The amount of gold in the world is limited by what the miners can produce. Gold supplies did not grow nearly as rapidly as international trade from the end of World War II until 1971.[1] The supply of dollars abroad is not limited in the same sense, but it does depend on the American balance of payments. In the 1940s and early 1950s, when the United States had a balance of payments surplus, the rest of the world's reserves were very short. But from the mid-1950s on we ran continuous deficits, and the dollar reserves of the rest of the world increased rapidly. Indeed, the rest of the world's need for reserves was a major reason for our deficits. Dollars were among our most attractive exports. Today, after two decades of American deficits, the supply of dollars abroad is ample, However, the elimination of the American deficit would slow down the growth of reserves abroad once more.

In an attempt to make the supply of international reserves less dependent on the quirks of gold and the American balance of payments, the major trading countries of the world have created a new form of reserves known as **special drawing rights** (SDRs, for short). In effect, SDRs are an international currency created each year by the International Monetary Fund. The Fund is an international agency to which all the major trading countries belong. The member countries have agreed to accept SDRs in settlement of balance of payments deficits. This agreement makes SDRs as good as gold. In fact, they are often described as "paper gold." Each year the Fund creates an agreed-upon amount of SDRs and assigns them to individual countries according to a predetermined formula. In this way the world supply of reserves can increase with the volume of world trade, just as bank reserves within a country are increased along with domestic economic activity. The first SDRs were created in 1969, and so far they account for only a small part of world reserves. If the system continues, however, they may eventually offer a rational and important way of expanding international reserves.

---

[1] The *value* of gold in the world *can* grow rapidly, though, if its price changes. This has happened in the years since 1971.

THE GOLD STANDARD

The right way to handle a short-term balance of payments deficit may be to pay out reserves—whether in gold, dollars, or SDRs. But this process cannot go on forever. What does a country do if it has a long-term deficit?

There is one system under which balance of payments deficits can actually solve themselves. This is what happened repeatedly under the system that prevailed down to World War I and again in the late 1920s. It is known as the **gold standard.** For almost a century, most of the major trading countries of the world promised to convert their currencies freely into gold at fixed exchange rates. This policy meant that international payments could be made freely at virtually fixed exchange rates. Bankers who wanted to convert dollars into pounds could exchange their dollars for gold at a fixed price, ship the gold to Britain, and convert it there into pounds at the fixed exchange rate observed by the Bank of England. Since there was no limit on the amounts of gold that could be bought or sold at those fixed rates, international payments were completely free. Actually, international gold shipments were small compared with total trade, but the possibility of shipping gold assured that international exchange rates could not fluctuate much.

Over most of the gold standard period no one worried much about the balance of payments. A country's payments and receipts seemed to balance automatically. How did the system work?

The basic explanation is that the balance of payments affected the domestic level of economic activity. This, in turn, brought about adjustments in the balance of payments. Suppose, for instance, that a country began to import more or to export less, thereby developing a deficit. The deficit had a depressing effect on the deficit country's economy, because exports are part of the aggregate demand for the country's goods and services, while imports are not. An increase in imports or a decrease in exports, therefore, meant a fall in the demand for domestic goods and services. This drop in demand led to lower incomes and employment. As incomes fell, so did demand for all goods, including imports.

Say the imbalance occurred between the United States and Germany. The situation is illustrated in Figure 17.3. The supply of dollars—the deficit currency—was shifted from S_1 to S_2. Sometimes the fall in incomes brought with it a fall in the price level. If that happened, domestic goods would be cheaper when compared with foreign goods, further discouraging imports and encouraging exports. In Figure 17.3 the effect of lower American prices shows up as a shift in the demand for dollars from D_1 to D_2 and a further shift in supply, from S_2 to S_3.

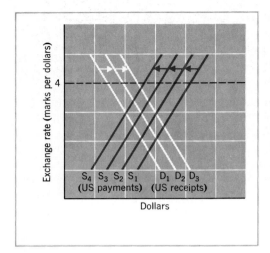

FIGURE 17.3 How a U.S. deficit was corrected under the gold standard. Lower incomes and prices in the United States would reduce imports and, therefore, the supply of dollars (to S_2 or S_3). The lower prices would also encourage exports and increase the demand for dollars (to D_2). Rising incomes and prices in the surplus countries would further reduce the supply of, and increase the demand for, dollars (to S_4 and D_3).

The process was assisted by opposite changes in other countries. If we were paying out more than we received, some other countries must have been receiving more than they paid out. The surplus countries, where exports rose or imports fell, found their incomes rising. Their citizens bought more of all goods, including imports. Moreover, if their prices rose with the boom, their goods became less attractive compared with the deficit country's goods. Their imports rose while their exports fell. As their balance of payments surpluses disappeared, so did our country's deficit. These changes are represented in the figure by further shifts in the demand and supply for dollars, to D_3 and S_4.

If the automatic adjustment didn't do the job completely, the monetary authorities could complete it by contracting the supply of money and credit in the United States while expanding them in the surplus countries. They tended to take these steps because the central bank of the deficit country was losing reserves, while the central bank of the surplus countries gained reserves. In fact, these policies were thought of as proper functions of central banks at the time. Monetary policy in the nineteenth century was oriented toward correcting balance of payments deficits and surpluses, rather than toward maintaining domestic economic stability.

Figure 17.4 summarizes the whole process. A balance of payments problem was solved by a depression in the deficit country and a boom in the surplus country.

This story may seem a little abstract but is surely correct. Though we have gone off the gold standard, precisely the same process still works within our own country in trade between the various states. Interstate trade involves the same sort of free inter-regional payments at fixed exchange rates. (Only the states use U.S. dollars instead of gold.) Suppose that peace breaks out, for instance, and we stop buying defense goods. California is a major producer of weaponry, so it will see its exports to the rest of the country fall. It will have, in effect, a balance of payments deficit. For the time being, Californians may go on importing from the rest of the country, paying for their imports with their "reserves"—their accumulated dollar balances. When those reserves become too thin, they will have to cut back on all goods purchased, including imports. Perhaps, ultimately, California wage rates will fall. At least they will rise less rapidly than wages in other parts of the country. When that happens, California products will become cheaper. California imports will fall further, and California exports of non-defense goods will increase. Altogether, we won't even notice California's balance of payments deficit. What we *will* see is a California depression.

PROBLEMS WITH THE GOLD STANDARD

The automatic gold standard solution to balance of payments problems is not very satisfactory to many people today. Many modern countries have rebelled at the idea of having a depression just to avoid a balance of payments deficit. Another value judgement is involved here. Most people probably feel that it would be better to avoid a deficit if everything else were the same. But most of us also feel that domestic prosperity without inflation is a good thing. What if the choice is between a deficit with domestic full employment or a depression with international payments and receipts in balance? The reader must make his own decision about this issue. Most countries that have been faced with the choice in

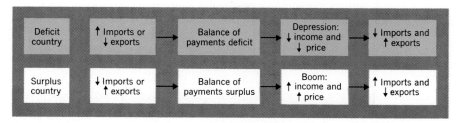

FIGURE 17.4 **Automatic adjustments in the balance of payments under the gold standard involved depression in the deficit countries and economic expansion in the surplus countries.**

the last few decades have opted for domestic stability. They have tried to find other ways to deal with their balance of payments problems.

There has apparently been a major change in values in this respect in recent generations. The United States was faced with the same choice twice in the nineteenth century, and both times it voted for correcting the balance of payments deficit while maintaining fixed exchange rates, even though this policy meant domestic depression. The first time was at the end of the Civil War, when the United States had an inflated economy in an uninflated world. During the war it had issued paper money ("greenbacks") that was not convertible into gold. After the war the question arose whether the country should "resume specie payments," meaning whether it should go back to converting dollars into gold at the prewar exchange rate. To do so required American prices to fall to levels in line with those of the rest of the world. The country was divided on the issue, but it finally decided to go back on the gold standard at the old exchange rate, even though this move involved the worst depression in decades.

A similar question arose in the 1890s. The world was having a depression. At the same time, the price of silver was falling compared with the price of gold. A powerful American political group advocated that the dollar be made convertible into silver at a fixed dollar price so that its international value would decline. By taking that course we could avoid the world depression. The issue was debated heatedly but when Grandpa went to the polls in 1896 he voted for McKinley and thus for gold and deflation.

Britain faced a similar problem in the 1920s. During World War I it had experienced more inflation than the United States had. To go back on gold at the prewar exchange rate Britain would have had to deflate its domestic economy, just as America did after the Civil War. After some debate, the British did so anyway. The result was that Britain experienced almost continuous depression throughout the late 1920s. By the time Britain finally abandoned gold in 1931, "gold standard" had become a dirty word. The country has been resolved ever since not to accept domestic unemployment to attain balance of payments equilibrium. Most other countries have come to agree with Britain on this point.

One reason why we tend to vote differently from Grandpa on the issue of domestic versus international stability is that the setting has changed. In the nineteenth century, when a majority of our people were self-employed farmers and artisans, a depression primarily meant falling prices. Declining prices could be painful, but once they had fallen far enough the problem was solved. Exports were encouraged, and imports discouraged, by the lower prices. The deficit was permanently eliminated. But in a modern industrial economy, few people are şelf-employed. Most people work for wages, which are hard to cut. As a result, a modern depression mainly means reduced output and employment. Prices seldom fall very much. As a result, a modern industrial country that tried to correct a balance of payments deficit using the old gold standard medicine would be faced with a long period of a depressed GNP. If the authorities ever let up, the deficit would be likely to recur. It is not surprising that modern states find such solutions unappetizing.

Grandpa got something for his devotion to gold. By insisting that the value of the dollar in terms of gold remain fixed, he assured that the money supply could not expand without limits. This "monetary responsibility" prevented large-scale inflations.

DEVALUATION

If we are unwilling to run a depression to get rid of a balance of payments deficit, what alternative is there? One possibility is to **devalue** the deficit country's currency—that is, to reduce its exchange rate relative to other currencies.

The effect of devaluation is shown in Figure 17.5. Instead of depressing its domestic economy, the United States reduces the value of the dollar from four marks per dollar to three marks per dollar. American goods are now cheaper abroad, so exports are encouraged. Foreign goods are now more expensive at home, so imports are discouraged. At an exchange rate of three marks per dollar the demand for and supply of dollars are in equilibrium in Figure 17.5

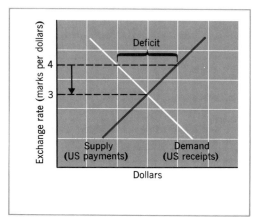

FIGURE 17.5 By devaluing the dollar, the United States may eliminate a deficit in its balance of payments.

For devaluation to work, of course, the rest of the world must go along with it. A drop in the value of the dollar in terms of marks is equivalent to a rise in the value of the mark in terms of the dollar. The United States can't just announce that the dollar will now be worth less. If the Germans continue to convert dollars into marks at the old exchange rate there just won't be any devaluation. If a smaller country adjusts the value of its currency, the rest of the world will generally accept the change. However, the United States is just too important to the rest of the world for it to be able to devalue its currency unilaterally.

Even if the value of the dollar does fall, devaluation won't do any good if it is offset by inflation. A ten-percent fall in the exchange rate coupled with a ten-percent increase in prices will leave exports and imports no more or less attractive than before. Some Latin American countries, such as Chile and Brazil, have devaluations and inflations almost continuously, but their balances of payments stay about the same.

Inflation is likely to accompany devaluation unless something is done to avoid it. The increase in exports and decrease in imports brought on by devaluation create an increase in domestic aggregate demand. This rise in demand will have the same effect on prices as an increase in investment or government purchases. Devaluation automatically increases the domestic prices of imported goods. The prices of export goods are also likely to rise, because of increased demand. For devaluation to work, the authorities must act to keep aggregate demand from rising enough to push up prices generally.

Governments sometimes find devaluation to be difficult politically. The public often seems to consider the value of its currency a matter of pride. People look upon a decline in the value of their currency as a reason for national embarrassment. Many countries have paid dearly in terms of domestic unemployment or restricted trade in order to keep the values of their currencies too high. It is not particularly clear that a country actually gains much prestige by having an overvalued currency. Yet the general public certainly seems to see a fall in the international value of its currency as a Bad Thing.

DEVALUATION VERSUS DEFLATION

Altogether, devaluation can work if the rest of the world agrees to it and if it is not offset by inflation. Whether it is the best solution to a balance of payments deficit depends on domestic circumstances.

If a deficit country is running an inflation, it can improve both its domestic and its international situation by using tighter fiscal and monetary policy. Devaluation is likely to make the problem of inflation worse.

On the other hand, if the deficit country has serious domestic unemployment, then tightening up to improve the balance of payments would make the domestic situation worse. Devaluation would both improve the balance of payments and cut domestic unemployment.

Probably most economists today feel that monetary and fiscal policy should be used to keep the country as near as possible to full employment without inflation. Then, if it turns out that the country runs a continuing balance of payments deficit, it should adjust by changing its exchange rate.

CONTROLS ON TRADE AND PAYMENTS

A third way for a country to adjust its balance of payments is to control its foreign payments directly. A deficit country would simply prevent payments abroad in excess of its receipts from abroad. It could use tariffs, import quotas, or direct controls over foreign payments. In terms of Figure 17.6, the supply of the deficit country's currency would be forced back from S_1 to S_2.

Many deficit countries have attempted to solve their balance of payments problems in this way. In the years just after World War II, most of the countries of Europe had elaborate systems of "exchange

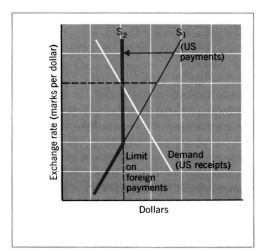

FIGURE 17.6 Direct controls on payments to foreigners, such as tariffs, import quotas, or exchange controls, may eliminate a balance of payments deficit by forcing supply down to the level of demand.

controls." Their authorities attempted to ration their scarce foreign currencies among competing uses. The result was a great deal of interference with international trade and finance. Importers were often prevented from buying from low-cost sources or from importing at all. Competition among importers was limited, because they each received fixed quotas of foreign currencies. They could make high profits on anything they did bring into the country. Travelers had limits on the amounts of money they could take abroad, and they could have their purses and wallets searched on entering or leaving the country. In the worst of circumstances, even the mails had to be censored to prevent illegal foreign payments. Almost everyone who lived through the experience is convinced that it should be avoided.

The major trading countries of the world have abandoned such exchange controls today, but less drastic controls over trade and payments are still used by countries with balance of payments deficits. American bank loans abroad were controlled by the Fed from 1965 through 1973. Foreign investments by American corporations were regulated from 1968 through 1973. Ordinary trade restrictions, such as tariffs and import quotas, are often proposed or defended as means of improving the balance of payments.

Such controls may reduce balance of payments deficits, but they reduce the amount of trade and foreign investment as well. Controls prevent us from buying from the lowest-cost sources and from making the most profitable investments. It will be argued in Chapter 18 that such restrictions on trade and investment make the world poorer.

Controls may not even do much for the balance of payments. A common response to regulation has been the development of ingenious evasions. For instance, the American controls on foreign loans and investments led American corporations to borrow funds abroad. In the last decade a large market developed in "Eurodollars." That term refers to dollars owned in Europe. They can be used without any of the restrictions that affect American-owned dollars. Similarly, many American banks set up branches abroad. These branches borrowed and reloaned funds there, thereby avoiding the Fed's controls over American-based loans. It seems doubtful whether controls cut back American foreign loans and investments at all. The American investment and loan controls ended in January 1974.

Direct controls on foreign payments won't do any good if the rest of the world retaliates with controls of its own. If the United States installs new tariffs or import quotas, the effect may be for other countries to put in tariffs and quotas of their own. Then the demand for dollars will shift downward along with the supply. The balance of payments problem may not be solved, in spite of the controls. This is precisely what happened in the 1930s. Many countries that were running deficits imposed controls on foreign purchases. But the countries whose exports were affected responded with controls of their own. The net effect was that the level of international trade was forced lower and lower, but the balance of payments problems persisted. It would have been much better if the surplus countries (mainly the United States then) had lowered their barriers to trade instead.

Altogether, most economists reject direct controls in favor of other methods for adjusting the balance of payments. They prefer the use of domestic fiscal and monetary policy, or of changing the exchange rates among currencies. That way the world can have the advantages of both a high level of international trade and investment and of balance of payments equilibrium.

THE INTERNATIONAL MONETARY SYSTEM TODAY

From World War II to 1971, most of the major trading countries maintained pegged exchange rates. They used their international reserves to offset short-run deficits. Long-run deficits were adjusted by means of deflation or occasional devaluations, depending on which strategy best suited their domestic situations. This system worked tolerably well. International trade and investment grew dramatically, and the nations of the world became much less isolated economically. Yet there were difficulties.

SPECULATION AND THE POSITION OF THE DOLLAR

One problem was the development of large balances of foreign currencies that can move quickly from one country to another. Businessmen naturally tried to minimize their holdings of any currency that they thought might be devalued. This was easy to do. For instance, the United States was making payments of about six billion dollars a month to the rest of the world in the early 1970s. If traders and companies with foreign operations just held up their payments abroad or postponed their receipts from abroad for a week they had $1.5 billion less in U.S. money and $1.5 billion more in foreign currencies. Firms had strong incentives to reduce their balances in a deficit country because of the possibility of devaluation. If the country did devalue, they could replace their balances after devaluation at better exchange rates. For instance, a ten-percent devaluation meant that they could replace their balances at ten cents less per dollar than before devaluation. If no devaluation occurred, they lost nothing. After the crisis blew over they simply replaced their balances in the troubled country at the former exchange rate. Speculative flows were so great in the late 1960s and early 1970s that deficit countries faced the prospect of losing *all* their reserves in a matter of days in some cases. Public officials often saved their strongest language for the speculators on the international currency exchanges. Actually, most of the speculation was done by ordinary businessmen in the course of ordinary international business.

Another problem with the pegged exchange rate system was the position of the dollar. Another country faced with a deficit could solve its problem by devaluing, but as long as exchange rates were pegged in terms of the dollar, the United States could not. It could reduce the value of the dollar in terms of gold, but if it did so the rest of the world would follow suit. The only way it could reduce the value of the dollar relative to the mark was to get the others to agree to the change. In general, this meant that the United States could adjust its balance of payments in only two ways: by changing domestic incomes and prices, or by instituting direct controls. The United States had a balance of payments deficit from the middle 1950s on. We did, in fact, restrict our domestic economy—at least partly with an eye to the balance of payments—in the late 1950s. We imposed various direct controls during the 1960s. Still, we had to pay out half of our gold reserves in that period. In addition, foreign central banks piled up dollars. By 1971 they had 37 billion of them. Yet the deficit continued.

Various efforts were made to shore up the system of pegged exchange rates as these strains became more severe. The creation of SDRs in 1969 was one such effort. Finally, in 1971 the United States announced that it would no longer convert dollars into gold. Thereafter, the value of the dollar depended on what foreign central banks were willing to pay for it. For a few months this value fluctuated. Then a stopgap agreement was made to peg the exchange rates at new levels with the dollar devalued slightly in terms of the French franc and the British pound, and more substantially relative to the Japanese yen and the German mark. But this agreement still left foreign central banks guaranteeing the value of the dollar. During 1972, foreign central banks accumulated another fourteen billion dollars.

This situation was quite satisfactory from the point of view of the United States so long as it lasted. It meant that we could buy real goods and services and make real investments abroad and give up nothing but dollars in return. It was unsatisfactory for the rest of the world, however. In early 1973 the central banks of surplus countries stopped buying every dollar that came their way, and the value of the dollar was allowed to fall further.

The world feed and fuel crises in 1973 and 1974 resulted in a series of severe shocks to the balances of payments of many countries. The United States experienced its first balance of payments surplus in years during 1973, and the dollar rose relative to most other currencies. When the balance of payments turned back into deficit in 1974, the value of the dollar fell once more. However, the value of the pound and the yen fell even further. None of these changes in exchange rates was very large in view of the huge changes that were taking place in balances of payments. Most exchange rates fluctuated by less than ten percent in the two years.

FLOATING EXCHANGE RATES

In late 1971, and after March 1973, the value of the dollar was allowed to "float." That is, its exchange rate was determined by supply and demand. When the United States had a deficit, demand for the dollar was low relative to supply, and the exchange rate fell. Similarly, when we had a surplus, the value of its currency rose. Both changes tend to move the balance of payments toward equilibrium.

Floating exchange rates were not completely new. The value of the Canadian dollar was left to the marketplace from 1950 to 1962, and again in the years after 1970. The Germans let the value of the mark float upward during 1971, when the alternative was for them to buy a flood of dollars at the fixed exchange rate. By 1974 most exchange rates were floating. None of these experiences resulted in drastic instability.

One problem with floating exchange rates is that they fluctuate from day to day. This instability introduces additional risk into international trade, because an exporter doesn't know how much he will receive in terms of his own currency when he contracts to sell goods abroad.[2]

---

[2] There is a way around this problem. There is a market for "future exchange." An exporter to Britain who wants to avoid risk can sell a promise to deliver pounds on the date that he expects payment. Then if the pound goes down in value he will lose money on his export but will make it back when he buys pounds at the lower exchange rate to honor his promise. If the pound goes up in value he will make something extra on his export but will lose the same amount in covering his promise to deliver pounds. Either way he will avoid the risk of changing exchange rates. Businessmen who deal with commodities such as wheat or soybeans, whose prices fluctuate unpredictably, have used future contracts to "hedge" against price fluctuations in this way for many years.

One way to prevent day-to-day instability in floating exchange rates is for the monetary authorities to buy and sell foreign currencies as needed to offset short-run changes in demand and supply. The pound was allowed to float during the 1930s. However, an exchange equalization account was established that used British reserves to prevent unwanted fluctuations in the exchange rate. Similarly, when the Canadian dollar was floating, the Canadians intervened in the foreign exchange market to keep exchange rates stable in the short run. Many countries followed such policies in 1973 and 1974.

This solution is a compromise between pegged and freely floating exchange rates. Exchange rates move little from day to day, but they can move up and down if underlying balance of payments conditions call for it. The main defect in this approach is that the authorities may be tempted to effectively peg their exchange rates, even when they shouldn't. Some advocates of floating exchange rates have opposed the use of exchange equalization accounts for this reason.

One advantage of floating exchange rates is that they discourage speculation. With pegged exchange rates, a firm that dumps a weak currency can't lose. The value of that currency can go down, but it is almost certain not to go up. The worst that can happen to the speculator is that he will move out of and back into the troubled currency with no gain. With floating exchange rates, however, there is a good possibility that the rate will move in either direction. In that case, the speculator has some chance of losing if he dumps currency. He may have to buy it back at a higher rate rather than a lower one. For instance, those who got out of dollars in the spring of 1973 had to buy them back at five- to ten-percent *higher* values after the world feed and fuel crisis erupted that summer and fall.

Some of our experience with floating exchange rates has been less satisfactory than the recent floats of the mark, the pound, and the Canadian and American dollars. In the early 1920s, most European currencies were floating. In some cases exchange rates fell drastically. These declines were usually associated with extreme domestic inflations. The countries that lived through that experience have generally opposed a return to floating exchange rates. For them, fixed exchange rates are a device to prevent irresponsible monetary policy, just as it was for Grandpa.

The general floating of exchange rates that occurred during 1973 and 1974 did not contribute seriously to instability. Most countries experienced inflation at that time, but the changes in the international values of their currencies contributed only mildly to the problem. Going by past experience, we would almost certainly have seen a series of payments crises if exchange rates *had* been pegged. Still, if inflation rates continue to differ greatly from country to country, falling exchange rates could fuel inflation in some countries in the future.

WIDE EXCHANGE BANDS AND CREEPING EXCHANGE RATES

One compromise between pegged and floating exchange rates is to let the dollar and other currencies fluctuate freely within a limited range. For instance, for a while in 1972, exchange rates of major currencies were allowed to rise and fall as much as 2¼ percent from official rates. Some observers advocated that these bands be widened further, perhaps up to ten percent. This loosening would prevent extreme fluctuations, but it would allow exchange rate changes to adjust for small disequilibriums automatically.

By itself, such an arrangement would not solve serious balance of payments problems. Some economists have therefore added the suggestion that the official rate be allowed to move gradually. For instance, the official rate might be set at its average level over the previous five years. The actual exchange rate would then be allowed to fluctuate within a range of, say, ten percent above and below the official rate. If this were the case, the currency of a country that had a long-term deficit in 1978 would be near the lower limit. As a result, the official value of the currency would be lower in 1979, when the 1978 rates were included in the five-year average. The official rate would continue to drift downward year by year as long as the deficit continued. Similarly, a surplus country would see the value of its currency gradually increase. This situation is illustrated in Figure 17.7. Over the long pull, exchange rates would tend to move to levels that kept all countries' international payments equal to their receipts.

SUMMARY

The total foreign payments of a country include its imports of goods and services, its gifts to other countries, and the investments it makes abroad. These payments provide currency that can be used by the rest of the world to buy that country's exports of goods and services, to make gifts to that country, and to make investments in that country. The difference between total payments and total receipts constitutes the balance of payments. If payments exceed receipts, the country has a deficit. If receipts exceed payments, it has a surplus. Short-term balance of payments deficits are covered by payments

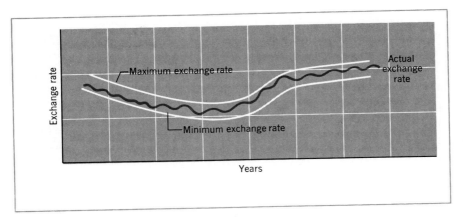

FIGURE 17.7 One compromise between pegged exchange rates and floating exchange rates would be to let the rate fluctuate between limits that are adjusted according to recent exchange-rate levels.

from reserves of gold, dollars, or special drawing rights. All foreign settlements with the United States since 1971 have been in dollars.

Long-run deficits in the balance of payments can be adjusted in three ways: (1) The deficit country can deflate its economy while surplus countries expand. This happened automatically under the gold standard, but most countries today are unwilling to sacrifice domestic stability to adjust their balances of payments. Deflation may still be the best solution for a country faced with both domestic inflation and a deficit. (2) The deficit country can devalue its currency relative to those of surplus countries. This method requires international agreement and the avoidance of inflation by the devaluing country. It is appropriate if deflation would involve unemployment in the deficit country. (3) The deficit country can restrict payments abroad by direct controls over payments or by tariffs and import quotas. This method involves extensive government regulation, and it reduces the amount of international trade and investment. Most economists would oppose it on these grounds.

One proposal for reforming the international payments system is to let exchange rates float—that is, to let them be determined by supply and demand on international markets. This system would automatically solve payments imbalances and would discourage speculation, but continuously fluctuating exchange rates might discourage trade. The world backed into a floating exchange rate system in 1973 because neither deficit nor surplus countries were willing to support the values of deficit currencies. A possible alternative is to let exchange rates fluctuate freely within specified bands and to let these bands gradually change. This system would prevent extreme fluctuations in exchange rates, while allowing gradual adjustments in balances of payments.

STUDY QUESTIONS

1 What is the effect of each of the following changes on the American balance of payments?

   a. European teen-agers develop a taste for genuine American blue jeans and will not be satisfied with cheap (or even expensive) European imitations.

   b. Pan American Airlines has a strike, so many international travelers switch to non-U.S. airlines.

   c. An American company that has been exploring for gold in Guatemala strikes it rich and makes lots of profits.

   d. An Arab government buys 10,000 shares of General Motors stock.

2 What would be the effect of a rise in the international value of the dollar on the U.S. balance of payments? Why? Why would a country intentionally increase the value of its currency? Why would the value of its currency go up if it were letting its currency float?

3 Describe how the gold standard worked. Would you favor such a system today? Why or why not?

4 What difference does the American balance of payments make to you, personally? Are you hurt if the country has a balance of payments deficit? If the dollar goes down in value relative to other currencies? If the government imposes new controls over imports and foreign payments? If the government runs tight monetary and fiscal policies aimed at maintaining the value of the dollar? From your own selfish point of view, what balance of payments policy seems most attractive?

5 When the oil exporting countries quadrupled the royalties they demanded on oil exports, it was plain that the balance of payments of various countries was going to change. What do you think happened to the balance of payments of oil producers like Iran and Saudi Arabia? Of countries with few domestic sources of energy, such as Japan, India and Italy? Of the United States, which had near, though not complete, self-sufficiency in energy? Some observers thought that the balances of payments of the more stable countries might wind up in surplus because the oil exporting governments would invest much of their new wealth in those countries. Can you see how this would work out?

FURTHER READING

There are several good books on the balance of payments and international monetary policy. They cover all of the issues discussed in this chapter, generally more thoroughly than they are discussed here. They include Benjamin J. Cohen, *Balance of Payments Policy* (Baltimore: Penguin, 1970); Delbert Snider, *International Monetary Relations* (New York: Random House, 1966); and William M. Clarke and George Pulay, *The World's Money* (New York: Praeger, 1971). The last book is particularly interesting, because it includes a selection of comments from the press on international monetary events over the last few years. All three are in paperback.

18 INTERNATIONAL TRADE AND INVESTMENT

Almost every session of Congress is presented with some proposal to limit imports by means of higher tariffs or import quotas. In recent years, as international investment has become more important, there has been a series of proposals to control it also. This chapter examines the case for and against restrictions on international trade and investment.

THE GAINS FROM TRADE

Foreign trade has been a prime subject of debate in the United States since our beginnings as a nation. Advocates of protection have pointed to the threat of cheap foreign labor and to the needs of national defense. Opponents have argued for freer trade as a means of keeping the world interdependent and peaceful, or of helping low-income countries develop. Both the opponents and the advocates of trade restriction often seem to believe that we give up something when we permit more imports.

COMPARATIVE ADVANTAGE

In fact, a basic principle of economics holds that trade makes the world as a whole, and each of the trading countries in it, richer, not poorer.

COUNTRY	GALLONS OF WINE PER MAN-YEAR	POUNDS OF COFFEE PER MAN-YEAR
France	3,000	5,000
Brazil	1,000	20,000

TABLE 18.1 Outputs per man-year in hypothetical wine and coffee industries

The point is most easily made if we use a set of simplifying assumptions. First, assume that there are only two countries and that they produce only two goods. Let the outputs per man-year in the two countries and industries be those shown in Table 18.1, regardless of how much is produced. In this example the French are more productive than the Brazilians in wine but less productive in coffee (they have to grow it in hothouses). In economic jargon, France has an absolute advantage in wine, and Brazil has one in coffee. It is pretty clear that the world will produce more of both goods if the French produce the wine and the Brazilians, the coffee. Absolute advantage is the basis for a good deal of our trade, especially with tropical countries. They are clearly more productive than we are in things like coffee and bananas.

The largest part of our trade is with advanced industrial countries, however. In this type of trade the example in Table 18.2 is more likely to apply. In this case America has an absolute advantage in both products. The particular numbers in this table came out of the blue, but realistic studies do show that American productivity is greater than those of other countries in practically all manufacturing industries.

Both countries in Table 18.2 can still gain from specialization and trade, even where one has an absolute advantage in both goods. All that is necessary is that productivity ratios differ among the trading countries. In this example the Americans are three times as productive as the British in automobiles but only half again as productive

TABLE 18.2 Outputs per man-year in hypothetical automobile and bicycle industries

COUNTRY	AUTOMOBILES PER MAN-YEAR	BICYCLES PER MAN-YEAR
America	3	30
Britain	1	20

in bikes. America is said to have a **comparative advantage** in automobiles, where its absolute advantage is greatest. Britain has a comparative advantage in bicycles, where its absolute disadvantage is least.

TRADE AND EFFICIENCY

To see that there is still a gain from trade under these circumstances, assume that labor is the only cost and that both industries are competitive in both countries. If there were no trade, then the American prices of automobiles and bicycles would settle to a level where one auto was worth ten bikes. If cars sold for $2,000, bicycles would cost $200. Similarly, without trade, an auto would be worth twenty bikes in Britain.

Now let the barriers to trade be removed and assume that there are no transport costs. The American and British economies become, in effect, a single market. One feature of a competitive market is that a single price must prevail throughout. If different prices should temporarily appear, traders can be counted on to buy and sell in such a way as to bring prices quickly back into equality. For instance, suppose that at some moment the price of wheat were $3.00 in Chicago and $3.10 in Kansas City, after allowing for transport costs between the two cities. Traders can buy Chicago wheat and simultaneously sell the same amount of Kansas City wheat. They will make ten cents on every bushel traded. The purchases in Chicago will push prices up there, and the sales in Kansas City will reduce prices there. The difference in price will quickly disappear. Such transactions are referred to as **arbitrage.** They go on all the time. In fact, a price difference as great as ten cents a bushel for wheat could never develop between Chicago and Kansas City. Even tiny differences will disappear almost immediately on such well-organized markets as the grain exchanges. As a result of arbitrage, all traders on a well organized competitive market can be assured of buying or selling at the same price.

Now to return to our example. Before trade, one automobile sold for as much as ten bikes in America and for as much as twenty in Britain. With no restrictions on trade, we can count on it that automobiles will be shipped from America to Britain, where they are worth more in terms of bikes. At the same time, bicycles will be shipped from Britain to America, where they yield more in terms of automobiles. When things settle down, the prices in the two countries will have to be the same. The world price ratio may be anywhere from 1A = 10B to 1A = 20B. Most likely it will fall somewhere between those limits, say at 1A = 15B.

At that price, the British will find it unprofitable to produce automobiles. Their auto producers need twenty times as many workers to produce a car as their bicycle makers need to produce a bike. However, the auto makers get only the price of fifteen bikes for their efforts. For the same sort of reasons, the Americans will find it unprofitable to produce bicycles. In the long run, each country will specialize in the commodity in which it has a comparative advantage.

The result of this specialization is an increase in productivity in both countries. For instance,

Without trade two American workers might produce:	3 automobiles + 30 bicycles
With trade they would specialize in automobiles and produce:	6 automobiles
They can keep three automobiles and trade the rest for bikes at the world price of fifteen bikes per automobile. This will yield:	3 automobiles + 45 bicycles

As a result, Americans receive more goods for each man-year of labor if there is trade than if there isn't. The most efficient way for Americans to acquire bicycles is to produce cars and trade them for bicycles. The amount of the gain from trade in this example, fifteen extra bicycles for every two workers employed, depends on the particular combination of autos and bikes that the Americans choose to consume. There will be some gain from trade with *any* combination, however, as long as the Americans want any bicycles at all.

It is important to realize that this gain was not made at the expense of the British. They gain, too:

Without trade two British workers might produce:	1 automobile + 20 bicycles
With trade they would specialize in bicycles and produce:	40 bicycles
They can trade fifteen of these bikes for an automobile and have:	1 automobile + 25 bicycles

In other words, British labor is also more productive if there is specialization and trade. Britain would gain from trade at the international price if it consumed any automobiles at all.

CHANGING THE NUMBERS

These results clearly depended on the numbers chosen. With other numbers, the gains will be different. For instance, if the international price ratio settled at 1A = 10B, the Americans would gain nothing from trade. (They wouldn't lose anything, either.) The British would gain even more in this case than they did in our first example. On the other hand, if the international price ratio fell at 1A = 20B, the Americans would receive all the gains from trade, while the British would get none.

Could the example be set up so that neither country gained from trade? Yes. It would require changing the basic productivities to something like those in Table 18.3. In this case, American labor is exactly twice as productive as British labor in both industries. The price ratios without trade are 1A = 10B in both countries. Neither country has a comparative advantage in either good. And neither country could gain from trade, so no trade would occur. The gains from trade arise because of international differences in productivity ratios. The greater those differences, the greater the gains will be.

In the real world there are many countries with very different resource bases and a vast number of commodities. This variety makes it virtually certain that all countries will gain from trade. It is inconceivable that the ratios of output per man-year could be the same for all countries. Similarly, no one country could conceivably have ratios among its domestic productivities that were exactly the same as the international price ratios for every good traded.

FOREIGN TRADE WITH MONEY

In the real world, automobiles are bought with money rather than bartered for bicycles. Our analysis can easily be worked out in money terms, however. Suppose a man-year of labor cost $6,000 in the United States and £1,000 in Britain. Then, using the productiv-

TABLE 18.3 Hypothetical outputs where there is no gain from trade

COUNTRY	AUTOMOBILES PER MAN-YEAR	BICYCLES PER MAN-YEAR
America	2	20
Britain	1	10

ities in Table 18.1, automobiles would cost $2,000 to produce in America and £1,000 in Britain. Bikes would cost $200 to produce in America and £50 in Britain. At any exchange rate between £1 = $2 and £1 = $4, American automobiles would be cheaper than British cars. At the same time, British bicycles would be cheaper than American bikes.

At a higher exchange rate, say £1 = $5, both automobiles and bicycles would be cheaper in America. The pound would be over-valued. Britain would have a balance of payments deficit as a result. As we saw in the last chapter, Britain could adjust this deficit by re-ducing the value of the pound relative to the dollar. Alternatively, it could reduce its wage rate and price level. It would have to reduce the value of the pound at least to £1 = $4 or reduce its wage rate at least to £800 a year in order to sell bikes in America. Conversely, if the exchange rate were very low, say £1 = $1.50, both goods would be cheaper in Britain. In that case the Americans would have to de-value or deflate. Otherwise they wouldn't have enough exports to pay for their imports. Ultimately, with free trade, either wage rates or exchange rates must adjust to levels at which both countries can ex-port.

IT PAYS TO SPECIALIZE

There is still an air of unreality about this whole discussion, because we have made so many simplifying assumptions. In the real world there are many commodities and many countries. Labor is not the only cost of production. Transport costs are important. And not all of a country's resources are equally adaptable to the production of every possible good. It is possible to work through this same analysis with all the unrealistic assumptions removed, but if we did so, this chapter would be much longer.

In a more complex and more realistic analysis, countries would no longer specialize in one good each. Some specialized resources would be used to produce goods for which the country is at a com-parative disadvantage. Britain would still produce some beef, and America would still produce some oil, even though foreigners can produce these goods more cheaply than the average British acre of land or the average American oil pool. Some goods that have high transport costs wouldn't be traded at all. We wouldn't import hair-cuts even if they were much cheaper abroad.

Rather than work out the whole analysis with all the realistic complications included, it seems preferable to show that you knew it all along. All that this whole argument about comparative advantage shows is that it pays to specialize. An individual can produce more, and therefore earn more, if he specializes in the thing he is best at and trades for other goods and services. Imagine a good lawyer who is also the best typist in town. He can type twice as fast as his secretary. Should he fire her and type his own mail? Probably not. Maybe he can earn $25 an hour practicing law, while she costs $3 per hour. Then every hour he would spend typing would save him six dollars in secretarial costs. But it would have an opportunity cost of $25 in legal fees that he had to give up. He would do better to specialize in law, where he has a comparative advantage.

Just as it pays individuals to specialize, so is it profitable for regions to produce the things in which they have the greatest comparative advantage. California land will yield more bushels of wheat per acre than Kansas land does. However, it yields far more prunes or grapes per acre. We're all better off with California specializing in prunes and grapes, and Kansas in wheat, than if both states tried to produce each of these items for itself. To carry the point farther, imagine what would happen if a single *county* tried to be self-sufficient in everything. Its standard of living would be reduced to minimal levels, if it could survive at all.

These examples are not as far-fetched as they seem at first glance. The average American state has a gross state product of over twenty billion dollars. That figure is as great as the GNPs of substantial countries such as Denmark or Chile. California is bigger economically than any nation except the Soviet Union, Germany, Britain, France, Japan, and perhaps mainland China. There are a hundred American counties that are larger economically than Syria, Tunisia, Ecuador, or twenty other countries. Yet many nations that are as small as American states—and some nations in a class with American counties—do, in fact, pursue protectionist policies designed to make themselves as nearly self-sufficient as possible.

The United States is, in effect, the largest free-trade area in the world. We benefit greatly from the economies that result. The European Economic Community or "Common Market" is an attempt to do the same thing for Europe. It was formed in 1957 by Belgium, France, Germany, Italy, Luxemburg, and the Netherlands. In 1972 it expanded to include Britain, Ireland, Denmark, Switzerland, and Austria. The Common Market is designed to eliminate all restrictions on trade among the countries involved, and thus to create a free-trade area somewhat comparable to, though still economically smaller than, the United States.

THE ECONOMIES OF SCALE AND COMPETITION

Trade offers other advantages besides simple gains from comparative advantage. One is in the economies of scale. The United States is large enough to accommodate at least several plants of the most efficient scale in almost every industry. Usually we can support many. But even countries as large as Germany, Britain, and France often have room for only one or two efficient producers of products such as chemicals, automobiles, aircraft, electric motors, generators, and computers if they must depend on home markets. In some industries, no country other than the United States is large enough to support even one efficient producer by itself.

In all of these cases, an efficient firm that was limited to the domestic market would be a near-monopolist. With international trade, however, an aircraft plant can supply world markets, not just the domestic ones. It can thus attain scales that could not be realized with domestic demand alone. With international trade, there is room for competition among the auto producers of various countries, even though each country by itself could support only one or two automobile companies. Even in the United States, international trade has been a major source of competition in a number of our industries that are domestically oligopolistic, such as automobiles and steel. Of course, these opportunities for economies of scale and competition are much greater for the many small countries of the world than they are for a nation the size of the United States.

TRADE RESTRICTIONS

In spite of the strong case that can be made for trade, no country in the world follows a completely free trade policy. All countries impose some restrictions on trade. We will look at the kind of restrictions that are in effect and at some of the arguments for them.

TARIFFS

The most common restrictions on trade are tariffs and import quotas. **Tariffs** are taxes on imported goods. They have the effect of raising the domestic price of imports, and therefore of discouraging them. The tariff makes up the difference between the domestic and the foreign price of an imported good. The government captures that difference on any imports that do come in.

In most cases, however, the main gainer is not the government but the domestic producer of the goods involved. He receives, in effect, a hidden subsidy from domestic consumers. Industries that would have to compete with imports at world prices receive hidden subsidies equal to the difference between the domestic price and the international price that would prevail if there were no tariff. Consumers pay these subsidies in the form of higher prices. The total tariff revenue collected in the United States is only two billion dollars a year. However, the hidden subsidies to the industries that compete with imports are many times that amount. The average American tariff is twelve percent, and rates are often much higher than that on goods in which the foreign competition is intense. To some extent, tariffs act to depress foreign prices by decreasing demand for foreign goods. But their main effect is to increase domestic prices. Since the total output of our import-competing industries is in the hundreds of billions of dollars, the total hidden subsidy must be in the tens of billions.

IMPORT QUOTAS

An **import quota** specifies the quantity that can be imported of some particular product. The quota reduces supplies of that product on the domestic market. As a result, the price is generally higher at home than abroad. In the case of a quota, though, the government does not collect the difference between the foreign and the domestic price. Instead, the traders who import the product reap substantial profits on the goods they are allowed to bring in. As a result, there is a long line of people eager for the right to import the goods on which quotas have been applied. The government must usually develop an elaborate system for allocating the valuable import privileges among domestic importers or foreign exporters.

As with tariffs, however, the main beneficiaries of import quotas are not the importer or the government but the protected industries. It has been estimated that oil import quotas alone cost the American people about seven billion dollars a year before they were suspended in May 1973. Much of that subsidy went into high-cost oil production that wouldn't have been undertaken with free trade. However, some of it resulted in high oil industry profits and wages, and in high prices for oil leases.

It is theoretically possible to set up tariffs that have precisely the same effects on trade as quotas. However, in general, most economists feel that quotas are the more restrictive device. With a tariff, if foreign prices fall, the domestic price will fall by the same amount (if the tariff is low enough to let any goods into the country at all). With quotas, however, a fall in the foreign prices will have no effect on domestic supplies. It therefore will not affect domestic prices. For instance, the American price of oil rose throughout the 1950s and early 1960s, while world oil prices were falling. No more oil came into this country, however, because of the American oil import quotas. The only domestic effect of the falling foreign price was to make the right to import oil more profitable.

THE HISTORY OF AMERICAN IMPORT CONTROLS

The United States has had a long history of high tariffs. During the nineteenth century our tariffs were up and down, but after the Civil War they were mostly up. For most of the time from the Civil War until 1929, they averaged between 40 and 50 percent of foreign prices on dutiable items. They reached a peak of over 60 percent in the early 1930s.

Since 1934 our tariffs have fallen. That was the year of the original Trade Agreements Act. The law has since been extended and revised many times. Under that act, we have repeatedly reduced particular tariffs in return for tariff reductions by foreign countries on American exports. At the same time, inflation was reducing our tariffs more. Many tariffs collect fixed dollar amounts per gallon or per pound of an import. As the prices of imports rose during and after World War II, such duties became smaller and smaller percentages of the import price. In earlier periods of world inflation, the United States reacted by raising the duties. This time it did not. As a result, we changed from a high-tariff into a low-tariff country. Since 1950, American tariffs have averaged twelve percent or less of the foreign value of dutiable goods. The change represented a revolution in United States foreign trade policy.

Tariffs have not gone up again. However, we have imposed new restrictions on foreign trade in response to more severe international competition. These restrictions have been in the form of quotas, such as those on oil, steel, textiles, and meat. In some industries, such as steel, we have induced foreign suppliers to control their exports to the United States, rather than controlling our own imports directly. This way foreign exporters, rather than domestic importers, got the difference between the foreign and domestic prices. The effect on trade was the same, however. The quotas we have installed in recent years are at least as restrictive on trade as higher tariffs would be. However, they seem to be politically easier to introduce.

THE CASE FOR TRADE RESTRICTIONS

It is clear enough why firms and unions in protected industries favor trade restrictions. Tariffs and quotas give them hidden subsidies. But is there any reason why you and I should support them?

There are lots of arguments, and the people seeking protection will be happy to tell you about them. Some of them are pure hokum. Others are reasonable points if properly understood. You should always keep the principle of comparative advantage in mind, however, when considering them. In general, the world is poorer as a result of trade restrictions. The question is whether the purported benefits are worth the cost.

CHEAP FOREIGN LABOR

One old chestnut has to do with low wages abroad. It holds that Americans cannot compete with foreign "pauper labor." There is obviously something wrong with this argument, though, since we export just about as much as we import. Our export industries face competition from the same lower wages abroad, yet they compete quite effectively. Certainly wages in the aircraft and computer industries, where we export, are not depressed by their low-wage foreign competition.

The explanation is that our productivity is much greater than those of other countries. Low wages abroad reflect low output per man-hour. In industries where American productivity exceeds that of the rest of the world by a large ratio we can compete quite successfully. In those where American productivity exceeds that in other countries by only a small amount, the United States has a comparative disadvantage. With free trade we wouldn't be in such industries at all—and we would be richer for it.

A major reason for the low wages and productivity abroad is that most foreign workers have much less land and capital to work with than we do. Our plentiful land and capital and our extensive education and research give us a comparative advantage in such fields as agriculture, aircraft, computers, drugs, and machinery. At the same time, we have a disadvantage in industries that require lots of unskilled labor and little land and capital. Textiles, apparel, shoes, and radios are such industries.

The rest of the world might just as reasonably complain about "cheap American land and capital" as we do about "cheap foreign labor." Indeed, the countries of Europe do protect their farmers against cheap American land. That is precisely what they accomplish when they impose barriers against the importation of American farm products.

Nations differ in the abundance and quality of their factors of production. These differences, and the differences in costs that result, are the main reason for international trade. The greater these differences, the greater the gains from trade will be. It is sometimes suggested, however, that tariffs should be imposed that would merely equalize the foreign and domestic costs of production. What could be fairer? Actually, if the countries of the world were to impose restrictions great enough to eliminate all cost advantages of foreign suppliers, they would eliminate most of the reason for trade in the process. We could grow bananas in the United States in hothouses, if only a tariff were imposed that would equalize our costs with those of Nicaragua—maybe five dollars a pound. Everyone can see that this policy would be inefficient. Yet this sort of tariff, on a smaller scale, is often proposed. Our 35-percent tariff on woolen textiles, for instance, raises the cost of imported woolens to the domestic level. This tariff is different from our banana tariff only in the size of the duty required. It still serves to take resources out of our efficient export industries and divert them to our inefficient import-competing industries.

KEEPING THE MONEY AT HOME

A second argument for trade restrictions concerns the incomes earned in protected industries. If I buy a suit from a Hong Kong tailor, I get the suit, but someone in Hong Kong gets the money. But if I buy it at home, Americans get both the goods and the money. Import restrictions obviously raise incomes in import-competing industries. Isn't the country better off as a result?

The answer is no. The American suit-maker is better off, of course. However, American consumers pay more than is necessary for the goods purchased. In addition, our opportunities to export are reduced because there are fewer dollars abroad. What the protected industry gains comes out of the pockets of American consumers and exporters. Indeed, since trade restrictions reduce our overall productivity, the losses of consumers and exporters are *greater* than the gains of those protected.

MILITARY SELF-SUFFICIENCY

Many industries seeking protection have argued that they should be protected in peacetime because they are essential in time of war. They argue that the higher costs we pay now due to protection are worth it in terms of military strength.

This argument has been accepted by many economists in the past. Yet it needs a good deal of qualification. Certainly, many of the industries that have made this argument have little military importance. If you're interested you can hear all about how essential the textile, shoe, and even the cloth glove industries are for military purposes. In fact, the United States seems to have a natural comparative advantage in a large number of militarily essential industries. We don't need tariffs to be strong in aircraft, computers, atomic energy, and heavy machinery.

In the case of exhausting resources, such as oil, the argument for protection is questionable even if the industry does seem essential. It is true that by imposing trade restrictions now we will have more oil wells. We will thus be able to produce more oil at home in the near future. But at the same time we will exhaust our domestic, reserves sooner. If the need for self-sufficiency comes next year we will be stronger. If it comes three decades from now, we are likely to be weaker because of the restrictions.

Many economists doubt that military self-sufficiency makes any sense today, anyway. In the 48-hour, all-out war that the defense people have planned for us, it can make little difference whether or not we have a domestic oil or steel industry. And in a limited war, like Korea or Vietnam, we would probably be able to continue to trade with most of the world. It seems particularly likely that we could still get supplies from our near neighbors, such as Canada, Mexico, and the Caribbean nations. Yet our restrictions on trade are generally just as strict for these countries as for any other.

There probably is something to the military self-sufficiency argument. When the Arabs turned off their oil spigot during the fourth Arab–Israeli War in 1973 we were the only major industrial country with almost enough oil. However, we had paid something like seven billion dollars a year more than we had to for a decade and a half to get that way. And we had exhausted our domestic reserves faster than we had to in the process. It would have been cheaper to have stockpiled oil than to have maintained quotas on oil from 1957 to 1973.

After the Arab oil embargo, President Nixon proposed an all-out program to make the United States completely self-sufficient in energy. Part of the program was to be an intense research effort to develop alternative energy sources. This project may prove useful, though much of the money will probably be misdirected, as has happened in other all-out research efforts. Most important, complete self-sufficiency is likely to be very costly in terms of fuel prices and environment. The goal is probably not worth the costs. If we can meet a substantial part of our energy needs at home—say 75 percent—we will be able to weather any future oil embargo with only minor difficulties. It probably isn't worth tens of billions of dollars to avoid relatively mild and short-term dislocations of the sort we experienced in 1973 and 1974. A goal of 75-percent self-sufficiency would be much less costly to attain than one of 100-percent self-sufficiency.

REVENUE

One argument for the tariff (but certainly not for quotas) is that the tariff yields revenue for the government. This argument isn't a terribly good one in advanced countries. The reason is that the tariff has all the disadvantages of excise taxes: it distorts consumption decisions and makes us poorer in the process.

The revenue argument is relevant in less developed countries, however. An import duty is one of the easiest taxes to collect. Income and sales taxes require more elaborate accounting systems than many low-income countries possess. All you need for a tariff is a few bureaucrats in each port.

In the nineteenth century, tariffs were the main source of federal revenue. At one point in the 1830s, so much money was collected in duties that the federal debt was paid off and federal funds were distributed to the states! Tariffs are a minor source of revenue in the United States today, however. They account for only 1.3 percent of all federal revenues. We don't really use tariffs for revenue. If we did, we would put duties on things that cannot be produced at home, such as coffee and bananas. Instead we levy them on shoes and textiles.

INFANT INDUSTRIES AND ECONOMIC DEVELOPMENT

Another argument for restricting trade deals with "infant industries." Again, it makes some sense in less developed countries but little in an advanced country like the United States. Suppose a new industry can't compete with foreign sources right now, but that after a few years of protection it can be expected to be efficient. This might happen because of economies of scale, the creation of a skilled work force, the development of advanced technology, and so forth. Once the infant is grown, no more protection will be needed. The world will be richer if the initially protected industry turns out to be the low-cost source in the long run.

The high tariffs of nineteenth-century America could often be defended on infant industry grounds. Protection undoubtedly accelerated the growth of industries that could not compete with superior English sources at first. Many of them ultimately became world leaders. The United States is the last country in which to apply the infant industry argument today, however. Our industry is highly developed, and some of our main comparative advantages are associated with new technology.

Even in less developed countries, the infant industry argument can be a trap. Not all industries that seek protection can be expected to do well after a period of protection. If a country does protect an unpromising infant, it will find itself saddled with a weak, high-cost grown-up that must have permanent protection in order to survive. A nice example is the *first* American protective tariff, on woolen textiles. The American woolen industry that resulted was always a high-cost producer. And it is still dependent on one of our highest tariffs—two centuries later.

Many of the low-income countries of the world have erected high barriers to imports in the post-World War II period. They have done so in an attempt to industrialize. The results have been small, high-cost, often monopolistic industries that supply only local needs.

The low-income countries often seem to feel that the cost of such protection is worth it. With free trade their economies would be largely dependent on a few raw-material exports: rubber or tin or coffee or sugar. Dependence on one or two crops may mean instability. The country is exposed to all the unpredictable fluctuations of world commodity markets. Therefore, such countries often prefer to diversify by protecting other industries, even if the costs are increased in the process.

Finally, some countries feel that industry is valuable in and of itself. A nation with the bulk of its resources in agriculture and traditional handicrafts may have little opportunity to invest or to acquire modern skills. Protection could create a relatively modern sector of industrial entrepreneurs and skilled workmen. It could induce additions to capital stock that would not occur with free trade. Even if the industries created by protection are inefficient, they could help to get the country out of its ancient rut. This argument is controversial, however. General industrial protection has been accompanied by rapid economic growth in some countries, such as Mexico. But other conditions for growth were also present there. Similar protection in other countries has just saddled the economy with inefficient, hothouse industries, as in the Philippines and Argentina. And one of the stars in the economic development race has turned out to be Hong Kong, which pursues an almost completely free trade policy. Their only trade restrictions are export quotas on textiles and apparel, measures that *we* insisted on! Whether or not protection for economic development makes sense in low-income countries, it is clearly irrelevant in twentieth-century America.

INCOME DISTRIBUTION

Trade restrictions affect the distribution of income. A general return to intense protectionism in the United States would shift demand to industries that require lots of low-skilled labor, such as textiles, shoes, and radios. At the same time, it would shift demand away from our export industries. These are generally industries such as wheat, computers, and aircraft, which require lots of land, capital, and advanced technology. As a result of the shift in demand, wages for semiskilled labor would tend to rise. But the returns on land, capital, and advanced technology would be lower.

Some people may be willing to sacrifice the gains from trade in order to attain such a redistribution of income. But if that is our goal, there are other ways to achieve it. The better solution might be to take the larger GNP that goes with freer trade and redivide it. There are many tools to use: the income tax, the negative income tax, and the other instruments discussed in Chapter 7.

In much of the rest of the world, trade restrictions redistribute income *away from* labor. When Europe and Japan protect their farmers against agricultural imports, they are raising the return to land at the expense of their food consumers. By protecting small manufacturing industries, low-income countries raise the incomes of persons who invest or work in those industries. But they reduce the incomes of their export industries. In many low-income countries this policy means that trade restrictions lower the incomes of their peasants—already the poorest people in the world!

TRADE RESTRICTIONS TO INCREASE EMPLOYMENT

Any one country that is faced with a domestic depression can pump up demand for its own goods by imposing new trade restrictions. The restrictions reduce imports and shift that demand to domestic goods.

The reduction in trade brings a loss in efficiency, but the increase in employment and income may be worth it.

Other countries can play the same game, however. In fact, they are quite likely to do so. They will have less demand for their own domestic goods as a result of the first country's restrictions on its imports. A small nation might be able to get away with trade restrictions to increase employment, but a huge country like the United States would surely face retaliation. Certainly the world as a whole cannot solve the problem of unemployment this way. What one country does gain comes at the expense of another. Most economists prefer fiscal and monetary policy as a means of maintaining full employment.

If the domestic problem is inflation rather than unemployment, just the opposite strategy would apply. Imports reduce aggregate demand for domestic goods. They put competitive limits on price increases.

TRADE RESTRICTIONS AND INTERNATIONAL PRICES

A country can sometimes use trade restrictions to affect the terms on which it trades with the rest of the world. By reducing its imports it can force down the prices of the things it does buy. As a result, it will have to give up less in export goods for each unit of imports purchased.

Just as when trade restrictions are used to increase domestic employment, however, other countries can play the same game. When they all impose tariffs to improve the terms on which they trade, it is doubtful that any will win much. Total trade and world income will be reduced, and one country's trade restrictions are likely to be offset by another. The net effect of such a "trade war" is apt to be that we are all poorer.

BALANCE OF PAYMENTS RESTRICTIONS

As mentioned in Chapter 17, many countries have imposed restrictions on trade to improve their balances of payments. Again, this policy can work if the rest of the world goes along with it. It is likely to fail, however, if the other countries impose restrictions of their own. Even when trade restrictions do improve the balance of payments, they do so at the expense of international trade. The world is worse off as a result. Changes in exchange rates or in domestic prices and wages can adjust the balance of payments without reducing the overall level of world trade.

MULTINATIONAL DECISIONS ON TRADE RESTRICTIONS

Altogether, there are many arguments for protection. Some make no real sense, such as the "cheap foreign labor" or "keep the money at home" arguments. Several arguments make some sense for less developed countries, but not for advanced ones like the United States. This is true of the revenue, infant industry, and diversification arguments. Finally, some arguments make sense even in advanced countries acting individually. This is true of the full-employment, terms of trade, and balance of payments arguments. Any one country can gain by trade restrictions in these cases. However, the world as a whole loses. Indeed, if everyone restricts trade for these reasons, most countries are likely to lose.

The possibility that any one country can gain by restricting trade implies that there is a strong case for multinational negotiations to reduce barriers to trade. In the postwar world, the major trading countries have held periodic conferences under the General Agreement on Tariffs and Trade (GATT), at which they have negotiated mutual tariff reductions. As a result, the limits on world trade have been kept down. This achievement is in great contrast to what happened in the two decades following World War I. GATT has never done much about non-tariff barriers to trade, however. This is one reason for the flowering of import quotas in recent years. In principle we could negotiate for their removal also, but so far we haven't done so.

PRESSURE GROUPS AND EXTERNALITIES

There is a general case for free trade, at least in advanced industrial countries. Yet there is continuous pressure for protection of one sort or another. Trade restrictions such as the American import quotas on meat, steel, and textiles, once installed, are terribly hard to remove. Why do we behave in such a perverse way?

One reason is our political system. Consider our tariff on garlic—yes, we have one! It hurts you and me by raising the price of garlic. However, the hurt isn't very great. Maybe I pay ten cents a year more for what I eat than I would without the garlic tariff. At that rate it would not be worth the stamp I put on my envelope for me to write my Congressman about it. It also reduces the demand for our export goods slightly—maybe a hundredth of a percent. Few exporters are going to get very exercised about that.

But now look at the group that gains from the garlic tariff. It's a dozen or two garlic farmers in California. The tariff is worth tens of thousands of dollars apiece to them. For them it pays to pull all the strings they can to keep the tariff. They'll try to get it raised if possible. Their congressman will vote for all sorts of other bills in return for the support of other congressmen and of the President on the garlic tariff issue. Who do you think is going to win the argument over this garlic tariff?

Garlic is a very minor product, but the pressures we have seen are typical. Relatively few people stand to gain from any one tariff, but those gains can be enormous. By contrast, the losses are greater, but they are spread over a vast number of people. As a result, the pressure for protection is always high.

The oil import quotas that existed from 1957 to 1973 cost the average consumer $35 a year. That loss *might* have been worth writing your congressman about, but it was still rather low on most people's priority lists. Not for the oil industry, though. They got seven *billion* dollars a year from it. As a result, they were willing to devote millions of dollars in political contributions and propaganda to keep the quotas intact. The quotas were finally suspended in 1973, but only after the world price of oil had risen to domestic levels.

Government has a tendency to pursue policies that help one minority a lot while hurting each member of the majority a little, even when the total gain is less than the total loss. This tendency is not limited to trade restrictions. We have seen it in the success of TV station owners in restricting cable television. It also explains the ability of the airlines to get fare increases to "solve" their problem of excess capacity. It is a factor in the amazing ability of a limited number of sportsmen to stop a general movement for gun control.

These are all cases of externalities. The benefits are real and large for the limited numbers who receive them. But those people do not bear the costs of government policies to any great extent. The costs fall on you and me. Usually these costs are well enough hidden, and cost you and me so little, that we don't spend much effort to counter them. We give other issues much higher priorities. Often, the issues that are high-priority to us turn out to be the same sort of special policies—only this time designed to benefit you and me.[1] The result is a great pile of

---

[1] I once had a friend who spent about two hours a week in a deep rage over the size of the federal budget. But in some of his quieter moments, he and a few fishermen friends organized a campaign for a government program to eradicate lampreys in the Great Lakes. Lampreys are eel-like creatures that attach themselves to fish, ruining the fish for fishermen. Probably not one American in a thousand cares at all about them, and a few might even like them (they are considered a delicacy in parts of Europe). Still, my friend got his program. He never saw any inconsistency between his views on the budget and his feeling on the lampreys. Perhaps there wasn't any. What the government spent on other things besides lampreys helped *other* people at *his* expense.

special-interest legislation. Each part of it helps someone, but a very large portion of it makes the country as a whole poorer, not richer. Any one of these policies cuts into your income mildly. All of them together take a sizable chunk of what you earn.

ADJUSTMENT ASSISTANCE AND FREER TRADE

Once trade restrictions have been installed for a while, they become especially hard to remove. It can even be argued that society has a moral obligation to help the people in the protected industries. The workers who learned those skills, and the businessmen who invested in those industries, were simply responding to existing public policy. If we now take the tariffs and quotas away, they will suffer serious loss. The rest of us, however, would gain more than they would lose from the removal of trade restrictions. A case can be made that we, the winners, should compensate those harmed. Questions of morality aside, it may be politically impossible to eliminate trade restrictions unless some compensation is made.

At present, under the Trade Agreements Act, the government can grant adjustment assistance in the forms of special unemployment insurance, retraining allowances, and industrial loans to businesses harmed by import competition. This provision has been little used, however. Many economists feel that such assistance should be much more readily available. It not only helps those who would be hurt by the removal of restrictions, but it also yields a more efficient world when the adjustment is done. If, instead, we help them by preserving trade restrictions, we simply maintain the old, inefficient situation.

INTERNATIONAL INVESTMENT

The basic reason for international trade is the fact that countries differ in their supplies of the various factors of production. If land, labor, capital, and various types of knowledge moved freely from country to country, there would be much less reason for trade in goods. Of course, land cannot move, short of conquest. Migration of labor does occur, but there are many barriers to it. In particular, high-wage countries have tended to restrict immigration, at least partly to keep wages high.

There are also limits on international investment. Sometimes these limits are imposed by the investing country and sometimes by the host country. In the years since World War II the flow of international investment has become very large and controversial. In 1969, American private investors owned property abroad valued at $110 billion.

Like trade, international investment makes the world's output greater.

In fact, operations owned by foreigners are usually at a disadvantage compared with native businesses. They face regulations, tax officials, and unions on terms that are commonly less advantageous than those for local businesses. Hence, only investments that yield exceptionally large amounts abroad are worthwhile. In this situation, investments made abroad surely yield more output abroad than they can at home. As a result, the world produces more with foreign investment than if the same funds are invested domestically.

The world is richer if capital is invested where it yields the highest return. But what about the investing country? Investment at home would increase labor productivity. Investment abroad increases productivity in other countries. It raises their ability to compete with domestic producers. Indeed, a substantial part of American foreign investment is devoted to plants that provide the American market with such goods as radios and television sets. Does the United States gain from such investments? Generally, the answer is yes. Radios and television sets cost us less, and we have a higher return on our capital, than if the investments were made at home.

While it is true that investment abroad raises the income from capital, it also makes domestic labor incomes lower than they would be if the investments were made at home. As in the case of trade, though, we can have our cake and eat it too. We can accept the higher GNP that accrues with international investment and then use income tax or other policies to redistribute income.

What about the host countries where the foreign investment occurs? They also gain, in the sense that they receive additional capital beyond what was available domestically. Their labor is more productive as a result. In addition, a large percentage of international investment today carries with it the technical expertise of the investing firms. As a result, international investment results in the spread of advanced techniques. It promotes more rapid world economic growth than would otherwise occur.

Host countries sometimes feel that foreign investors in extractive industries, such as oil and copper, are given access to their natural resources on unfair terms. Fairness is difficult to judge. Sometimes the investing firms are too few to bid actively for the right to invest. Sometimes the host country governments are too weak or their officials too corrupt to take full advantage of their resources. A more competitive industry might indeed offer a different division of income. Yet there can be little doubt that, even on the existing terms, the host countries have higher GNPs than they would if international investments were prevented. Moreover, the host countries' share of total income from such investments has risen rapidly in the years since World War II. Before the war, for instance, Middle Eastern oil concessions gave the host countries royalties equal to about twelve percent of their profits. In the 1950s and 1960s royalties and taxes were well over 50 percent of the profits actually earned, and in the early 1970s they became almost astronomical.

Host countries are sometimes very concerned about the control of their industries by foreign corporations. There have been cases in which foreign firms have intervened in local politics or have followed policies different from those that domestically-owned companies might pursue. ITT, one of the largest conglomerates, offered a million dollars to the Central Intelligence Agency around 1970 as part of a proposal to prevent the election of a Marxist, Salvador Allende, as president of Chile. (The CIA says it turned the offer down.) For years American companies in Canada did not trade with mainland China, although the Canadians did not prohibit such trade.

The extent of such conflicts is easy to exaggerate, however. Foreign companies often serve as political whipping boys in the host countries. The issue often comes down to a value judgement about the effect of foreign ownership on national prestige. Only the host countries can make that judgement. Countries that decide to prohibit (or nationalize) foreign-owned business may pay a lot for their policies. They are likely to wind up with less capital and a more backward technology.

SUMMARY

There is a general case for international trade and investment. With trade, each country will tend to specialize in the industries in which it has the greatest comparative advantage. It will trade for other goods it needs. Both it and the rest of the world will be able to produce more as a result. The gains from specialization and trade are further enhanced by economies of scale and increased competition.

Tariffs and import quotas both raise the domestic prices of imports. In the case of tariffs, the government takes the difference between the foreign and the domestic price. With quotas, licensed importers get the difference. In either case, the main gains go to the protected industries in the form of high domestic prices. American tariffs have been drastically reduced since 1934, but new trade restrictions in the form of import quotas have offset this trend in some important instances.

Many of the arguments for trade restrictions are spurious. A few are plausible in less developed countries but hardly in the United States. Others make some sense for each country taken individually but just make the world as a whole poorer when applied by all countries. There is a strong case for multinational negotiations on tariffs and quotas.

The country as a whole loses more from restrictions than the protected industries gain. But protected industries have a large stake in trade restrictions and are likely to lobby hard for them. A good case can be made for assisting labor and capital already committed to protected industries. But if this assistance takes the form of continuing restrictions, we merely preserve an inefficient situation. If it consists of aiding labor and capital to transfer to other industries, we can assist people who are now dependent on trade restrictions and still attain a more efficient economy.

International investment shifts capital to countries where it yields the greatest returns. It often carries advanced techniques with it. The world as a whole, and both the investing and host countries, are more productive as a result. The effect on income distribution in the investing countries, and fear of foreign political control in host countries, may result in limits on international investment. These restrictions are likely to be costly, however, in terms of economic advantages foregone.

STUDY QUESTIONS

1   In the comparative advantage example in Table 18.2, why can't the world price settle at 1A = 5B? Or at 1A = 25B? Why won't America gain from trade if the world price is 1A = 20B?

2   Who gains from an import quota such as the one we had on oil from 1957 to 1973, under which the right to import was assigned to particular American-based individuals and firms? Who gains when we get foreign countries to impose export quotas on the goods that they ship to the United States, as is the case with steel? (The Japanese and Belgians and Germans decide who may ship what steel to us, but we negotiated the total amounts those countries could export.) Are the two cases different?

3   The steel industry makes several arguments for the present quota system. It claims that it should be protected because its wage rates are much higher than those in Japan, because the Japanese have more modern mills and less stringent environmental controls, because without protection the industry will be unable to adopt advanced technology, and because steel is essential for national defense. Do you believe that these arguments justify quotas controlling the importation of steel? Examine each of them in turn.

4   Most economists in the non-Communist world probably believe that

trade restrictions reduce efficiency, and therefore the incomes of most of the world. Moreover, this belief has probably been shared by a large majority of economists for at least the last century and a half. Yet, in spite of this near consensus, virtually every country in the world protects some local producers against foreign competition. Most countries that have had control over their own trade policies have done so over the whole last century and more. Even in the last few decades, when economists have had remarkable influence in other areas, tariffs have been hard to cut, and import quotas have often replaced them. Why do you think this happened?

5   The government of a small oil-producing country in the Persian Gulf has annual revenues of $5 billion and current expenditure needs of about two percent of that amount. Now it decides to put a year's revenue into buying a controlling interest in United States Steel. This corporation is the leading American steel producer, with about a fifth of our steel market; it ranks eleventh among U.S. industrial corporations in assets. Do you approve of the purchase? Why or why not? Should the U.S. government intervene? U.S. firms have taken over the leading firms in many industries in Europe and Canada. Have the Europeans and Canadians been hurt? Can you see why they sometimes get uncomfortable when the takeovers occur?

FURTHER READING
There are several good and brief books on international trade and investment. Jan Pen, *A Primer on International Trade* (New York: Random House, 1967) is the simplest of them. James Ingram, *International Economic Problems,* 2nd ed. (New York: John Wiley, 1970) is a little more advanced but still easily within the reach of beginners. It covers the subject matter of Chapter 17 as well as this one. The same is true of Peter Kenen and Raymond Lubitz, *International Economics,* 3rd ed. (Englewood Cliffs, N.J.: Prentice-Hall, 1971). It contains a good chapter on the history of international trade policies here and abroad.

19
AMERICA
AND
THE
WORLD

This book has covered many subjects: economic growth, efficiency, income distribution, the environment, unemployment, and inflation. This chapter will try to evaluate the American economy in terms of all these considerations. Perfection is not attainable in this world (even if we could agree on what constituted perfection), so this chapter will try to give you a basis for judging how well we are doing by comparing the United States with other countries. You can draw your own conclusions about how the American economy measures up, using your own value judgements. Many of the comparisons will be in the form of numerical tables. The numbers are *not* there to be memorized. Just look them over for their main messages.

THE THREE ECONOMIC WORLDS

The countries of the world can be classified into three major groups: the industrial private enterprise countries; the Communist countries; and the "Third World," where peasant and handicraft enterprises still make up a large part of the economy. Table 19.1 shows estimates of the populations, GNPs, and GNPs per person for these three groups and for a few of the leading countries in each group.

SOME QUALIFICATIONS

The classifications in Table 19.1 are mildly arbitrary in places. There are

TABLE 19.1   Population and GNPs of the world in 1970[1]

COUNTRY	POPULATION (MILLIONS)	GNP (BILLIONS OF DOLLARS)	GNP PER CAPITA (DOLLARS)
United States	205	$974	$4,756
West Germany	59	186	3,027
France	51	147	2,906
United Kingdom	56	121	2,172
Other non-Communist Europe	158	327	2,070
Japan	103	197	1,904
Canada, Australia, New Zealand, and South Africa	57	136	2,386
All industrial, private enterprise countries	689	$2,088	$3,030
USSR	243	$525	$2,160
Eastern Europe	123	150*	1,200*
China	800	120	150
North Korea, North Vietnam, Cuba	43	7*	150*
All Communist countries	1,209	$800	$663
Brazil	95	$ 35	$364
Other Latin America	175	105	617
Ethiopia	25	2	78
Other Black Africa	229	35*	150*
Iran	29	10	355
Other Middle East and North Africa	166	50*	286*
India	537	53	96
Indonesia	121	8	66
Other South and East Asia	337	77*	229*
All Third World countries	1,714	375	219
Total	3,612	$3,263	$903

* Notes: Eastern Europe GNP based on 1967 estimates assuming 5 percent per year growth thereafter. North Korea, North Vietnam, and Cuba based on populations and $150 per year GNP per capita. Other Black Africa based on average GNP per capita for six countries and total population. Other Middle East and North Africa based on average GNP per capita for seven countries and total population. Other South and East Asia based on average GNP per capita for seven countries and total population.

still substantial peasant sections in some of the countries counted as industrial, mainly in the Mediterranean parts of Europe and the black parts of South Africa. At the same time, a few of the countries usually counted as "Third World" are largely modern industrial states (Israel, Hong Kong, Singapore, Kuwait, Argentina, Chile, and Uruguay). Moreover, a minority of the populations of many Third World countries live modern lives in industrial, market-oriented parts of their economies. The modern industrial minority is quite large in such countries as Mexico, Brazil, and Taiwan. And a very large proportion of the GNP in the oil-producing countries comes from their modern sectors, even though most of their populations still live typical Third World lives.

The distinction between the private enterprise and the Communist countries is also blurred. Private agriculture is important in some Eastern European countries, and something resembling private enterprise has become the rule in much of Yugoslavian industry, where the workers own and control most businesses. Even in Russia there is a quite large unofficial private enterprise sector. The output from private plots on the collective farms is sold on officially recognized markets. Theoretically this private trade is just the sale of surplus output, but actually it represents a large part of Soviet agricultural production. Substantial amounts of it are shipped hundreds of miles to the cities. In addition, essentially private repair services, beauty shops, and tourist accommodations are often provided by workers trying to supplement their skimpy official wages with second jobs.

At the same time, the public utilities are government-owned in the majority of non-Communist countries. Various parts of manufacturing and mining are government-owned in many European countries. This is true of coal in Britain, France, and Italy; steel in Britain; much of automobiles and oil in France; and a large part of heavy industry in Italy.

In spite of these quibbles, the main distinctions made in Table 19.1 are correct. The industrial private enterprise countries contain about a fifth of the world's population. Most of these people lead economic lives that an American would find quite familiar. The Communist countries contain about a third of the world's population, and most of those people have a very different economic life from yours. That leaves the Third World, with a little less than half of world population. Life in Hong Kong or Buenos Aires or for those employed in modern industrial jobs in Mexico City would also be familiar to an American, but the bulk of the Third World—maybe two fifths of the world's population—is living in almost another century.

OUTPUT AND INCOME

The GNP per person figures in Table 19.1 are only rough indicators of the standards of living available. For one thing, GNP is expressed in dollars using 1971 exchange rates. As the value of the dollar floats up and down, the international comparisons change. For example, when the dollar reached its lowest value in 1973, GNP per person was a little higher in Germany and Sweden than in the United States. More seriously, international comparisons among very different economies are quite shaky. Services and locally produced foods and handicrafts are often unbelievably cheap in Third World countries. A GNP per person of $96 in India is very low compared with $4,756 in the United States, but the Indian standard of living is certainly greater than two percent of ours.

The comparisons with the Communist countries are even less certain. The GNPs of Russia, China, and Eastern Europe are based on estimates made by Westerners. These estimates don't come out of the blue. They are derived from some concrete data on the outputs of wheat, steel, electric power, and so forth. Still, there's lots of guesswork. The estimates are least certain in the case of China, where the concrete numbers are fewest. We don't even have a very clear idea of how many Chinese there are. Estimates of China's 1970 population ranged from 760 million to 820 million. If the high estimate was right, then the people who made the lower estimate were misplacing somewhat more than the entire population of France or Germany! Even when the estimates are based on solid numbers, there is quite a lot of disagreement about Communist GNPs, because their mixes of products and relative prices for various goods and services differ so greatly from those in Western countries. The figures for the Communist countries in Table 19.1 fall near the middle of the range of estimates that Western specialists take seriously, but they should be interpreted only as broad orders of magnitude.

Altogether, small differences in Table 19.1 shouldn't be taken very seriously, but the big differences are meaningful. *The differences are very big.* The industrial private enterprise countries, with a fifth of the world's population, produce about two thirds of its output. The Communist countries produce about a quarter of world output. And the Third World, with almost half of the world's population, accounts for something like only a tenth of gross world output. If we could exclude the islands of modernity, the peasant and handicraft parts of the Third World might produce a twentieth of the total.

GNP AND NATIONAL POWER

A nation's total GNP tells you something about its international political power. The nations with the biggest GNPs are also the great powers. And their relative ranking in international influence is pretty close to their ranking in GNP. This correspondence isn't new. Britain was the richest country in the world in the nineteenth century, when it was the dominant power. The rise of Germany and the United States coincided with the growth of their economies to the level of the British. And Russia became the leading power in Europe only when its economy surpassed that of any other single European country after World War II. On a smaller scale, Israel, with about a tenth of the population of Egypt but about the same GNP, is a major power in the Middle East.

GNP per person tells you more about the economic life of a country than total GNP. By and large, high standards of living go with high GNPs per person. That figure now exceeds $2,000 in most of the industrial private enterprise countries and in the Soviet Union. In Eastern Europe and Israel, Argentina, and Venezuela, it falls in the neighborhood of $1,000. Most of the people in these countries have access to adequate food, shelter, and medical care (though the peasant parts of Venezuela and South Africa are exceptions, and Americans might not consider the shelter available in the Communist countries adequate). China and most of the rest of the Third World have GNPs in the few-hundred-dollar-per-person range or less. The majority of that two thirds of the world lives in what we would consider desperate poverty.

STANDARDS OF LIVING

GNP per person is not the same thing as the average standard of living for several reasons. For one thing, the amounts of the GNP available for consumption differ greatly from country to country. In addition, such considerations as the amount of leisure, the quality of goods, the range of personal choice, and many intangible elements in the quality of life all contribute to how well the residents of a country live.

HOW THE GNP IS USED

Table 19.2 shows how a number of countries use their GNPs. The United States and the USSR put a good deal more of their GNPs into defense than most major countries do. The same is undoubtedly true of China, though even the usually uncertain Western estimates aren't available here. Other countries, faced with direct military threats, spend more on defense. Israel used 26.5 percent of its GNP this way, and Egypt used 19.6 percent, in 1970. The part of the GNP that goes for defense can't

TABLE 19.2   The uses made of the GNP in selected countries, 1970

| | PERCENTAGE OF THE GNP USED FOR: | | | | |
COUNTRY	DEFENSE	OTHER GOVERNMENT PURCHASES	GROSS DOMESTIC INVESTMENT	PRIVATE CONSUMPTION	EXPORTS MINUS IMPORTS
United States	7.8%	14.7%	14.0%	63.2%	−0.2%
Germany	3.3	12.6	28.6	53.8	1.8
France	4.0	8.3	29.1	58.1	0.3
United Kingdom	4.9	12.9	18.9	61.5	−0.8
Japan	0.8	7.4	39.5	51.2	1.3
USSR (1969)	10.1	9.5	29.5	50.9	n.a.[1]
Brazil	11.6		16.5	71.8	0.0
Ethiopia	9.9		12.4	79.4	−1.3
Iran	7.1	8.8	18.9	59.2	n.a.[1]
India	3.4	5.3	16.2	75.6	−0.4
Indonesia	2.3	6.6	13.8	81.8	−3.1

[1] Not available.

contribute to the standard of living, at least in the way most people think of it.

Output that goes into investment is not available for current consumption, either, though it may result in higher consumption in the future. The United States spends relatively little of its GNP this way. Germany, France, and Russia put twice as much of their GNPs into capital formation as we do, and Japan, almost three times as much. These high investment rates probably made sense when Europe and Japan were recovering from World War II. However, one wonders whether such heavy sacrifices for the future are worth it today for countries whose levels of output per person are already very high. Investment rates in the Third World are closer to those of the United States. Those countries have a desperate need for capital, but there is only so much that they can wring from their poor populations.

The percentage of GNP left over for consumption is higher in the United States than in most other industrial private enterprise countries. Our standards of living are higher, relative to GNP per person, as a result. Consumers get even a smaller percentage of the total in the Communist countries, where *both* defense and investment receive very high priorities. The low-income Third World countries generally use higher percentages of their output for consumption than we do. One reason is that their populations need a great deal of total output just to survive. Another is that a large part of their output is accounted for by self-sufficient farmers. It is very difficult to divert that kind of output to government use or industrial investment. Iran can do it because much of its large oil income goes to the government and can be funnelled off at that point. Brazil and India can divert as much as we do to investment because they both have substantial urban, industrial sectors. Ethiopia and Indonesia, with larger peasant sectors, don't accomplish even that.

PUBLIC SERVICES

The non-defense expenditures of government are a form of consumption, and they do contribute to the standard of living. They appear as "Other Government Purchases" in Table 19.2.

These expenditures are remarkably high in the United States. The most important reason is that we spend more of our resources on education than most private enterprise countries do. The first column of Table 19.3 compares the percentage of the GNP devoted to public education. This figure is higher for the United States than for any other country on the list. In fact, the *only* countries that use more of their GNP for public education than we do are Israel, Canada, and Finland.

TABLE 19.3   Public education, health expenditures, and health for selected countries

COUNTRY	PUBLIC EXPENDITURES AS A PERCENTAGE OF THE GNP FOR:			PERSONS PER DOCTOR (1970)	PERSONS PER HOSPITAL BED (1970)	INFANT MORTALITY (PER 1,000 BIRTHS) (1970)
	EDUCA-TION (1969)	HEALTH CARE (1969)	SOCIAL SECURITY (1965–66)			
United States	5.7%	1.4%	7.2%	645	127	19.8
France	4.0%	n.a.	15.6%	747	139	15.1
Germany	3.2%	n.a.	17.4%	561	87	23.6
United Kingdom	5.2%	4.0%	12.6%	787	110	18.3
Japan	3.5%	n.a.	6.0%	390	173	13.1
USSR	5.6%	3.2%		421	91	24.4
China	about 3% (1960)	n.a.		about 5,000 (1972)	n.a.	n.a.
Brazil	about 3%	0.2%		1,953	247	n.a.
Ethiopia	about 2%	0.7%		73,797	2,984	n.a.
Iran	2.9%	0.8%		3,145	761	n.a.
India	2.4% (1966)	0.7%		4,795	1,571	139 (1951–61)
Indonesia	about 1%	0.1%		27,655	1,452	n.a.

The Soviet Union puts about as much into education as we do. Indeed, education has been one of its greatest accomplishments. The majority of Russians were illiterate at the time of the Russian Revolution (1917). Today illiteracy has virtually disappeared, and there are more scientists and engineers in Russia than in any other country. The Chinese have not released data on educational expenditures since 1960. Visitors to China report that the country is making a major effort in primary education and in technical secondary education but that the availability of higher education has declined sharply since 1960.

Most of the Third World puts much less into education than the industrial countries. As a result, the majority of the population in Ethiopia, India, and Indonesia still cannot read.

Table 19.3 also shows public health expenditures and social security payments as percentages of GNP. Public health funds are not reported separately by the United Nations for a number of advanced countries. Large parts of their health programs are imbedded in their social security systems. Both programs are small in the United States. In most of the industrial world and all of the Communist world, health care is provided by the state. In the United States this is true only for some of the aged, the poor, and veterans. The Third World spends far less for health care, public or private. For most of the population of those countries, modern health care is simply not available.

The low level of public health expenditures in the United States does not mean that health care is poor in this country. The fourth and fifth columns of Table 19.3 show numbers of persons per doctor and per hospital bed. The total supply of health care in the United States is similar to that of the other industrial countries covered by the table (though Germany, Japan, and Russia have fewer persons per doctor). At its best, American medical treatment is superior to any other in the world. But it is much less evenly distributed than health care in much of Europe and Japan. As a result, we compare unfavorably with much of the rest of the industrial world in our general health statistics. For instance, our infant mortality rates (shown in the last column of Table 19.3) are higher than those of France, Britain, and Japan and eleven other countries not shown in the table.

Statistics on Chinese health care expenditures are very old and unreliable. However, visitors report that health care is remarkably good compared with what is available in most Third World countries. This fact shows up in China's death statistics. The leading causes of death in the 1930s and 1940s were infectious and parasitic diseases and malnutrition (read: starvation). Today they are cancer, stroke, and heart disease, at least in the large cities. This means that far fewer Chinese now die as children or young adults. Chinese health conditions are apparently superior to those in much of the Third World. This transformation was accomplished by the training of hundreds of thousands of "barefoot doctors" and midwives, what we would call paramedics.

The low level of American *public* expenditure on health does mean that several percent of our *private* consumption expenditures go for medical services that would be provided by the state in other industrial countries.

The United States has a mixed record on public expenditures other than education and health. We have a more complete and better-quality highway network than any other major country, even though our population is much more dispersed than those of Japan and Western Europe. We also have a unique set of national parks and national forests. At the same time, our public housing programs are tiny compared with those of some European countries. Partly *because of* our heavy expenditure on freeways and our limited expenditure on public housing, our central cities have deteriorated more rapidly than those in most industrial countries. Be careful, though. Some of what we consider slums might seem merely "quaint" in Europe or Japan.

LEISURE

Leisure is part of your standard of living along with the things that you buy or that the government buys for you. Table 19.4 provides some basis for judging the availability of leisure in selected countries. Americans work slightly fewer hours per year than industrial workers do in most

TABLE 19.4   Standard industrial working time in selected countries, 1971

COUNTRY	WORKING WEEK	ANNUAL PAID VACATIONS	PAID PUBLIC HOLIDAYS	CALCULATED STANDARD HOURS WORKED PER YEAR
United States	40	2–4 weeks	12	1,824–1,904
France	44¾	4 weeks	8–10	2,068–2,084
Germany	40–43	15–18 days	10–13	1,832–2,036
United Kingdom	40	2–3 weeks	5–6	1,912–1,960
Japan	42–48	6 days	10	2,056–2,368
USSR (1967)	40	12 days	8	1,944
China (urban)	48	—[1]	6–7	2,440–2,448

[1] Automatic paid vacations are not available, but leave with pay is often granted for education or for husbands and wives living in different locations.

other countries listed, but the difference is usually small. Moreover, paid holidays and vacations are required by law in some countries (France and Russia) but are the result of collective bargaining or employers' decisions in the United States. Not everyone gets them.

Americans do start work later in life, on the average, so we have more leisure over our lifetimes—if you count going to school as leisure. Major household appliances are also a good deal more widespread in the United States than they are in other industrial countries. Housewives probably have more leisure here than elsewhere as a result.

Data on leisure are not available for most of the Third World. The figures wouldn't be comparable in any case. Peasants often have a lot of unwanted leisure imposed on them by the climate. In most of the Third World, urban working hours apply to only a minority.

QUALITY AND CHOICE

The quality of goods and services available to consumers in various countries does not lend itself to numerical comparisons. In the case of easily shipped products, the countries with low trade barriers have access to most of the products available on world markets. Goods and services sold on local markets can differ in quality, however. Frenchmen have access to better restaurants than most Americans do. At the same time, their telephone service is notoriously bad compared with ours. Just how such things add up depends on how much value you give to good restaurants, to good telephone service, and to the quality of other goods and services sold on a local basis in the two countries. In general, the inhabitants of private enterprise industrial countries with low barriers to foreign trade have access to a broad range of goods and services. They can commonly expect domestic or international competition to assure them of the quality they want.

In the Communist countries the consumer has much less choice. Products such as shoes, apparel, and processed foods are often of a quality that would not be saleable on competitive Western markets; sometimes they aren't even saleable there. One reason is that the suppliers are often monopolists. Another is that they are pressed by stringent output quotas. Style receives little weight in Communist countries. On the other hand, many, though not all, products are of remarkable durability. As a result, consumer goods often last longer. The common statement of visitors is that the people of Eastern Europe and Russia receive adequate food, clothing, and medical care, but that life seems drab for most of them.

Freedom of choice is a major element in the quality of life. In most industrial private enterprise and Third World countries there are few limitations on the jobs one may pursue or the things one may choose to buy. Eastern Europeans and Russians are also generally free to take whatever work they can find and to buy whatever they can find, but what they actually can find is determined by the government. The choices available are generally much more limited than ours and often do not reflect demand very closely. Choice is even more limited in China. The main foods and apparel are still rationed. Jobs are often assigned, and voluntary migration between jobs or localities is difficult because of government control over rationing and housing.

THE QUALITY OF LIFE

Many elements of the social and physical environment affect the quality of life. Table 19.5 compares some measurable aspects of the environment. The first two columns have to do with space. Americans live in a relatively uncrowded part of the world and have larger dwellings, larger yards, and more open field and forest per person than do inhabitants of most industrial countries. I once visited the home of a managing director of a major Japanese corporation. He had a chauffeur-driven car and

TABLE 19.5   Some indicators of the quality of life in various countries

COUNTRY	PERSONS PER SQUARE MILE	PERSONS PER ROOM OF OCCUPIED HOUSING	BOOKS PUBLISHED IN 1970	TELEVISION CHANNELS IN THE FIFTH CITY OF THE COUNTRY[1]
United States	57	0.9	79,530	4
France	242	0.9	22,935	3
Germany	624	0.7	45,369	2
United Kingdom	593	0.7	33,441	3
Japan	728	1.0	31,249	6
USSR	29	1.3	78,899	2
China	205	n.a.	n.a.	1
Brazil	29	1.1	6,392	3
Ethiopia	52	2.7	5,595	0
Iran	47	2.3	1,381	1
India	426	2.6	14,145	0
Indonesia	211	n.a.	1,381	0

[1] In most countries the largest city has more TV channels than others. At the same time, small cities and rural areas often have little or no access to TV. The fifth city is chosen as approximately typical. The fifth cities of Ethiopia, India, and Indonesia have no TV, but the leading cities do. Addis Ababa, New Delhi, and Djakarta have one channel each.

owned extremely valuable art. Yet his yard consisted of an exquisite garden smaller than my bedroom. And his house would have looked cramped to an American auto worker. Space is not quite as limited in Europe as in Japan, but few people in the European cities have as much space as the average American surburbanite does.

Housing space is always in short supply in the Communist countries. One reason is that rents are unbelievably low. Another is that housing has quite a low priority: after defense, investment, education, and health. The shortage is worse in China. On the average, Chinese urban dwellers have a housing area per person just slightly larger than a double bed. Almost all Chinese housing would be substandard in the United States. The Chinese must share not only bathrooms but also kitchens.

Some Third World countries have plenty of open space. But the urban parts of the Third World contain some of the worst slums anywhere. The possibility of getting into the modern, industrial sector has attracted large numbers of people out of the desperate peasant life. They live by the hundreds of thousands in shacks or mud huts around the edges of São Paolo, Mexico City, Calcutta, Djakarta, Cairo, and many other Third World cities. We will refer to these suburban slums as *barrios,* a Spanish word meaning "neighborhood." It is a common term for these slums in Latin America. In the *barrios,* unemployment rates are terribly high, living standards are pitiable, sanitation is rudimentary, and water is often poisonous. The *barrios* are a common source of social unrest in the countries that contain them.

KNOWING WHAT'S GOING ON

The third and fourth columns of Table 19.5 give some indication of the inhabitants' access to information in various major countries. The number of books published depends on the size of the reading population. The United States and Russia far surpass all other countries in this respect. Russian books are closely censored, while there are hardly any limits on what an American publisher can print. Since Americans can read books published in a half a dozen other English-speaking countries as well, we have access to more books in our own language than do any other people in the world. Your counterpart in most of the world would have spent a large part of his education learning two or three or four foreign languages in order to get access to what you can reach with the language you learned as a baby.

Radio and television are another major source of information. The fourth column of Table 19.5 shows the number of television channels available in the fifth city of each listed country. In most countries, the largest one or two cities have considerably more channels than most other cities do. At the same time, small towns and rural areas have fewer channels than normal.

Only Japan has more channels in the "typical" city than the United States. However, the variety available to us may be less than that in some Western European countries. In Britain and Germany, several different groups control several hours each on prime-time TV. Cable and communications satellites are capable of delivering many more channels than are available in any country today.

Regardless of how our TV stacks up with that of Western Europe or Japan, we all have far more access to broadcast variety than most people in the Communist countries or the Third World. The Communist nations offer only publicly controlled TV and radio. I once spent several days in Czechoslovakia. In each hotel room there was a radio with only one switch—on or off. On the street or in a restaurant you didn't have even that choice. At lunch or supper time you could count on a loudspeaker presenting news, marches, and classical music, whether you wanted them or not.

Except in a few of the largest cities, the people of the Third World have little access to TV. In view of the low level of literacy in many of these countries, radio and TV could be of great value in bringing them into the twentieth century. The technology is available to broadcast a dozen channels or more to every country in the world via satellite.

CRIME

A part of life that has received growing attention in the West in recent years is crime. It appears to be on the increase almost everywhere. Crime statistics are notoriously unreliable, though. What constitutes a crime differs from country to country. A majority of crimes are never reported to the police. And, to make matters worse, the police in different countries have very different success in detecting crimes and varying incentives for reporting them. Table 19.6 shows the reported rates of homicide per 100,000 population in selected countries. Unlike other crime statistics, these numbers are based on public health records concerning causes of death, rather than on police records. There is still probably a good deal of under-reporting, especially in the Third World. Data are not available for many of the Communist or Third World countries that we have been following in this chapter, so other countries from the same areas have been substituted.

COUNTRY	RATE
United States (1971)	11.2
France (1970)	2.5
Germany (1970)	2.6
United Kingdom (1971)	3.2
Japan (1971)	2.5
Hungary (1971)	2.8
Poland (1971)	4.3
Mexico (1970)	46.7
Chile (1968)	23.1
Kenya (1971)	11.4
Sri Lanka (Ceylon) (1968)	2.2
Singapore (1971)	5.5

TABLE 19.6   Homicides per 100,000 population in selected countries[1]

[1] Death from "external causes" other than accidents and suicide. Disease, malnutrition, and old age are internal causes. Deaths due to infanticide and manslaughter are included, however.

The United States has a higher reported homicide rate than any other private enterprise industrial country or Communist country for which we have data. One reason is our remarkably lax gun control. Murder is typically a crime of passion. When Americans have fights with their friends or families, they often have guns nearby with which they can express their views more forcefully. Most Europeans don't. They must make do with fists and rolling pins.

Many Third World countries, especially in Latin America, have homicide rates higher than ours, however. It has been estimated that the probability of being murdered in Mexico City is greater than was the probability of dying due to bombs in London during World War II! Third World statistics are more likely than ours to under-report homicides. Third World police and public health officials often have incomplete information about what is going on in the villages and *barrios*.

Our murderous record in Table 19.6 is all the more surprising in view of the general belief of criminologists that crimes of violence tend to be low in economically advanced countries. The specialty of the industrial countries is crime against property, not crime against persons. Theft tends to rise with economic progress, while violence tends to decline. One reason is that peasants live in villages where everyone knows everyone else, while we live in cities where we are unknown to most of the people we meet. This anonymity makes theft easier. It doesn't help in most murders, however, since we are usually murdering family or friends. In some Third World countries violence is a part of the culture, but this is seldom the case in the advanced countries. Another reason for the advanced countries' preponderance in theft is that we have more things to be stolen. Comparable international statistics on theft are not available, but it seems likely that the United States holds some sort of record there, as well.

Finally, white-collar crime is primarily the province of the industrial private enterprise countries. That's where most of the world's large-scale embezzlers, swindlers, and fraudulent stock manipulators operate. It takes big money and complex accounting systems for them to make off with much money. And the biggest property crimes of all depend largely on corporate organizations and the stock market. The officers of the Equity Funding Insurance Company wrote $50 millions worth of bogus insurance policies and sold them to other insurance companies before they were caught. The company's security holders lost a quarter of a billion dollars in assets when the fraud was discovered and the firm went bankrupt. Thefts on that scale probably wouldn't be possible anywhere else in the world, simply because other countries wouldn't have such large lumps of money lying around to steal.

Large-scale, corporate crime is generally impossible in the Communist countries, because private property there is so limited. You do run into cases in the Soviet press of managers selling government property for personal gain, but the take is small compared with Equity Funding's $50 million. And the Soviets have shot quite a few of the convicted offenders. Managers of Soviet enterprises do break the rules outrageously in hoarding labor and capital, in delivering shoddy goods, or in misrepresenting their outputs. But these acts work to the benefit of their government-owned firms. What would count as illegal for a private American firm appears as normal bureaucratic behavior there.

The Third World economies just don't present opportunities for large-scale white-collar crime. Such crimes as bribery and tax evasion seem to be almost universal in some Third World countries, however.

Altogether, we have more violent crime than any other industrial country. We probably have close to a world record in theft. And we almost surely have larger-scale white-collar crime than anyone else.

THE ENVIRONMENT

One more element of the quality of our lives is the physical environment in which we live. This chapter was supposed to have included a table showing sulfur dioxide and hydrocarbon intensities in a dozen leading cities around the world. It turned out that the data were simply not available, even though environmental issues have reached the front pages throughout the industrial world in the last decade. The best we can do is an impressionistic sketch.

Air quality deteriorated from the Industrial Revolution through the 1930s over the whole of the industrial world. In the years just after World War II, the problems were dramatized by a few disasters, such as those in Donora, Pennsylvania, in 1948 and London in 1952, when many people died as a result of high sulfur dioxide concentrations. At the time, London probably had the most polluted environment in the world. There has been a serious effort to clean up the air throughout the industrial countries since then. Britain may still suffer from a high level of pollution, but there seems to be general agreement that it wins the prize for the most *improved* environment today. Tokyo probably has the most polluted atmosphere in the world today. Some American cities that were enshrouded in soot a generation ago, such as Pittsburgh, have substantially improved their environments in the same way that London did. At the same time, however, we have created Los Angeles smog. Altogether, the best that can be said of our big-city environments is that some other big cities in the world are as bad or worse.

You might expect that the Communist countries could avoid environmental problems because industry is owned and controlled by the state. Central decision-makers should be able to take externalities into account. But in fact, environmental problems in Russia seem to be similar to those in the West. No consideration seems to have been given to air quality at all until after World War II. The first air monitoring station in Moscow was set up in 1945, and they did not become widespread until the 1950s. They showed that sulfur dioxide levels in the industrial and eastern parts of Moscow were "almost lethal." During the 1950s and early 1960s, major efforts were made to reduce pollution. By 1964, sulfur dioxide levels were reduced by two thirds, to about the level found in Philadelphia.

The Russians have kept the number of private automobiles very low while emphasizing mass transit, so one might expect their level of hydrocarbons to be low. In fact, the long lives of Russian autos (because it's so hard to get replacements), the poor quality of Russian gasoline and diesel fuel, and the lack of any auto pollution controls result in three or four times as much pollution per vehicle in the Soviet Union as in the United States. Altogether, the Russians have roughly the same sort of problem that we have. One of the ironies of recent years has been that the

United States has become an important exporter of pollution control equipment to Russia.

The Third World's record is mixed. Its low use of energy means relatively low levels of emissions, but very little is done to control what pollution does arise. In much of the Third World this lack of control makes little difference. Where geographic conditions are right, however, the effect can be deadly. Mexico City, in a mountain valley, has some of the worst smog in the world. In addition, much of the Third World suffers from age-old environmental problems that we have largely conquered: bad sanitation and disease. The cost in terms of early deaths and disease is worse than the costs of pollution yet realized in any Western city.

THE DISTRIBUTION OF INCOME

So far we have been concerned about the average or overall quality of life in various countries. But a high average standard of living in a country may just mean frustration for the country's poorest inhabitants. The degree of inequality is an important element of the quality of life.

IN THE DEVELOPED COUNTRIES

Table 19.7 shows the shares of the poorest twenty percent and the richest five percent of all families in personal income before tax in selected countries. By these standards, the United States has one of the most equal income distributions in the non-Communist world. This statement requires a good deal of qualification, however.

First, the distributions in Table 19.7 refer to incomes before the personal income tax. After-tax incomes may be more equally distributed if income taxes are large and progressive. The third column of Table 19.5 shows personal income taxes as a percentage of national income. In most of the countries shown, the income tax is much too low to have any important effect on the distribution of income. Only in the United States, Sweden, and Britain does the tax amount to much. In these countries, the effect of the tax depends on how progressive it is. In general, the taxes in Scandinavia and Britain are somewhat more progressive than ours. A study based on the early 1950s concluded that after-tax incomes were mildly more equal in Scandinavia than in the United States. So were those in Israel and the Netherlands, both of which have high progressive income taxes. In Britain and Japan, income distribution after tax was similar to that in the United States. Distribution was less equal in most of

TABLE 19.7 **The distribution of income in selected countries**

COUNTRY	SHARE OF THE POOREST 20% OF FAMILIES IN PERSONAL INCOME	SHARE OF THE RICHEST 5% OF FAMILIES IN PERSONAL INCOME	PERSONAL INCOME TAX AS A PERCENTAGE OF NATIONAL INCOME
United States (1969)	5.6%	14.7%	10%
France (1962)	1.9	25.0	5[1]
Germany (1964)	5.3	33.7	8[1]
United Kingdom (1970)	6.0	15.0	12
Sweden (1963)	4.4	17.6	10
Japan (1962)	4.7	20.0	2
Hungary (1962)	9.1	12.3	2[2]
Poland (1965)	9.2	12.1	4[2]
Brazil (1960)	3.5	38.4	3
Nigeria (1959)	7.0	38.4	1
Iraq (1956)	2.0	34.0	2
India (1965)	6.6	25.0	1
Philippines (1961)	3.6	30.0	2

[1] Direct taxes on households and on property and entrepreneurial incomes.

[2] Direct taxes on households.

the other countries studied. Even after taxes, then, the United States has one of the most equally distributed incomes of the non-Communist world.

Another qualification has to do with government services. In much of the rest of the industrial world, medical and higher education expenses are provided by the government free or at nominal prices. This is true for many of the poor in the United States as well. The American government *does not* pick up similar expenses for the middle-class people of working ages, however, while the Scandinavian and British governments do. As a result, the figures in Table 19.7 probably overstate the share of the top five percent in Scandinavia and Britain relative to the United States.

Altogether, standards of living may be moderately more equal in Scandinavia, Britain, and Israel than they are in the United States. However, standards of living are probably more nearly equal in America than anywhere else in the non-Communist world. The high degree of equality in the United States is particularly striking because we have a much less homogeneous population than many other countries do. There is no group in Scandinavia and only a small one in Britain to correspond to our blacks, Chicanos, and Indians.

INCOME DISTRIBUTION IN THE COMMUNIST COUNTRIES

As usual, comparisons are much harder to make when we come to the Communist countries. Income distribution data are shown for Poland and Hungary in Table 19.7 because no such information is directly available for Russia and China. We do have official wage rate data for certain types of jobs in Russia, and they seem similar in relative levels to those for Poland and Hungary.

All of the income distribution data from the Communist countries refer to income from work and from money transfer payments. Property income is excluded. In most cases it is not important. The effect of eliminating property income is to make incomes more equally distributed there than in any place in the West. Our distribution of income from work is similar to theirs, but we have property incomes as well.

Again there are serious qualifications. Like the Swedes and Britons, the Poles and Hungarians have access to virtually free medical care. They also have what amounts to an automatic scholarship, including a living allowance, at the university (if they can get in). Moreover, their rents are ridiculously low. Basic housing is almost free (again, if they can get it). So are basic foods. At the same time, some "luxuries" (shoes!) are very expensive; others (opera or ballet tickets) are very cheap. And a fair part of income is earned in unofficial, after-hours jobs and doesn't get into the statistics.

The low income share of the elite does not tell the whole story there, either. Traditionally the elite has had access to better housing and better goods than the rest of the population does. Moreover, they control large enterprises, even if they don't own them. Soviet managers have as much power as their Western counterparts do, even though they don't own the properties they manage.

As usual, our data are worse for China. The most we can do there is interpret the qualitative statements of visitors and emigrés. Money incomes seem to have only a mild connection with the standards of living for urban Chinese. Basic foods and clothing are rationed. Housing is both extremely cheap and terribly scarce. Medical care, education, and most forms of entertainment are virtually free. And nobody has a car in China. The result is an apparently quite uniform standard of living in the Chinese cities. Living standards often appear to be lower in rural areas, but the government prevents excessive migration to the cities by its control over jobs, housing, and food. And, of course, managers still have power, prestige, and prerogatives, even though their money incomes are close to those of the ordinary workers.

In general, the Communist countries have probably attained more equality in physical standards of living than most of the West has. This achievement has not eliminated the social differences among managers and professionals on the one hand and industrial and farm workers on the other. And it is not at all clear that the child of an official has a greater head start in the West than his counterpart does in the Communist countries. Those countries may have no more equality of opportunity than we do.

INCOME DISTRIBUTION IN THE THIRD WORLD

Income distribution data are not available for a number of the Third World countries that we have been following through this chapter. Hence, in Table 19.7, Nigeria has been substituted for Ethiopia, Iraq for Iran, and the Philippines for Indonesia. Note that in the poorest countries (Nigeria and India), the poor have a remarkably high share of total income. Without it, they would surely starve.

In most of the Third World countries, the richest five percent have an exceptionally large share of total income. This inequality is natural in countries that are in the process of industrialization. They generally still have large peasant populations, which continue to earn the minimal livelihoods that have been their lot over all of history. At the same time, those who get into the modern, industrial sector of their economies can generally earn livable incomes. In the non-Communist Third World countries, some people in the modern sector will get rich, even by Western standards. Then there are the former peasants in the barrios, who are either unemployed or working in low-paying personal service jobs. They are waiting for opportunities to break into the modern world. The contrast between the successful members of the modern sector and the rest seems bound to create unrest.

Perhaps, if they can hold out for two or three generations, these countries can attain the sort of increasing equality that the most advanced industrial countries have. But it's hard for people with limited lives to wait. A shift to the Communist pattern is likely to produce greater equality in incomes. It certainly will yield greater equality of wealth: no one owns much of anything. But, going by past experience, it will also mean a great loss of personal freedom and a large-scale diversion of output from consumption into defense and capital formation.

ECONOMIC PROGRESS AND STABILITY

The prospects for further improvements depend on economic growth. Countries with stagnant economies can change, but it is a painful thing

TABLE 19.8   Rates of growth of selected countries, 1960–1970

COUNTRY	AVERAGE ANNUAL PERCENTAGE RATE OF GROWTH IN:		
	REAL GNP (1960–1970)	REAL GNP PER PERSON (1960–1970)	POPULATION (1963–1970)
United States	4.0%	2.7%	1.1%
France	5.8	4.7	0.9
Germany	4.9	3.8	1.0
United Kingdom	2.9	2.3	0.5
Japan	10.6	10.1	1.1
Russia	5.0	4.0	1.1
China	2.9	1.1	1.9
Brazil	6.5	3.7	2.8
Ethiopia	4.4	2.4	2.3
Iran	8.7	5.8	3.0
India	4.0	1.9	2.6
Indonesia	3.5	1.1	2.8

to accomplish. Without growth, efforts to clean up the environment or to improve the distribution of income require that somebody take a lower real income. With growth, such policies require only that some people's incomes increase more slowly than the economy as a whole.

OUTPUT GROWTH

Almost all the economies of the world are growing. Table 19.8 shows growth rates during the 1960s in the leading countries. The overall rate of growth in GNP was similar in all three groups of countries. The industrial private enterprise countries as a whole and the Third World as a whole both averaged about a five-percent-per-year increase in GNP in the 1960s. So did Russia.

China's slower growth was due mainly to the disruptions that occurred during the "Great Leap Forward" of 1958–1961 and the "Cultural Revolution" of 1967–1969. The "Great Leap Forward" was a drastic attempt to decentralize by shifting to village industry. It resulted in a drop in the GNP by about a quarter. The Chinese GNP had barely recovered from that fiasco when the "Cultural Revolution" occurred. This revolt against bureaucracy and a growing intellectual elite resulted in another decline in both farm and industrial output. The decline was reversed only in 1970. In the years when they were not having some sort of revolution the Chinese were progressing quite rapidly. Because of the uproars, however, China was one of the slowest growing economies in the world, along with Britain, Uruguay, Ghana, and Burma.

The different growth rates in the world today are closely associated with the different rates of investment that we saw in Table 19.2. The countries that invested large parts of their GNPs also grew the fastest. This fact does not necessarily mean that investment, by itself, will produce rapid growth. Investment occurs when technical change, new resources, or population growth make investment profitable. It is the combination of these changes *and* investment that leads to economic growth.

The United States grew faster than Britain or China but more slowly than the average during the 1960s. Moreover, our growth rate is exaggerated because we started the 1960s in a recession. Some of our "growth" in that period was merely the use of formerly unemployed resources.

On the other hand, there are plausible reasons why the most advanced country in the world might grow more slowly than countries that started at lower levels of GNP per person. For one thing, the less developed countries are in large part adapting techniques and organizations that have already been developed in the more advanced countries. The United States must attain most of its further growth through techniques that are yet to be developed. In addition, much of the rest of the world still has a lot of people in low-productivity peasant and handicraft occupations and can gain rapid growth by shifting them to modern sectors. We have hardly any peasants left in the United States. Neither does Britain or Germany. But France and Japan still have some people in that category, and Russia has quite a few. Finally, a five-percent increase in a GNP per person of $5,000 (as in the United States) might plausibly be harder to attain than a five-percent increase starting at $2,000 (as in Russia) or at $100 (as in India). The first is $250 per person per year. The second is only $100, and the last is only five dollars per person per year. We attain a growth of five dollars per person every week.

Over the long pull of the whole past century, the United States' GNP per person has grown at about 2.0 percent a year, which puts it in a class with Japan and Sweden, and ahead of all the other countries for which we have data. This growth rate and the high levels at which we started account for our high output per person today. The slower growth of the European countries (from 1.2 percent in Britain to 1.8 percent in Germany) is partly explained by the disastrous setbacks they suffered in two world wars. The long-term Japanese growth record is all the more impressive because they *did* experience the second of those two disasters, with a vengeance. If economic growth is still a goal, the United States has a good long-term record, though Japan is growing faster. But our record is only mediocre in the years since World War II.

POPULATION GROWTH

There is a darker side to this worldwide picture of economic growth. One aspect of it shows up in the last column of Table 19.8. It is one of the saddest stories of our world. Population is growing at the fastest rate in history in the Third World today. In the 1960s the GNPs of most Third World countries grew so rapidly that they were able to attain some increase in GNP per person in spite of their population explosions. But that was the decade of the "green revolution" and a period of relative political stability in most of the world. In spite of Vietnam, it was one of the most peaceful decades the world has ever seen. Many question whether such luck can continue. Certainly, sustained increases in standards of living in these mostly poor countries depend crucially on checking their rapid population growth. It is hard to believe that many of them can permanently join the modern world if they do not.

Population growth is not a serious problem in the industrial private enterprise countries, nor is it in Eastern Europe or Russia. China, still a largely rural country, has a rapidly growing population, but its government has adopted an active birth control policy with apparently substantial success. Birth rates in Peking and Shanghai are among the lowest in the world. Rural birth rates seem still to be high by Western standards, but they apparently fell sharply in the late 1960s. The national population goal is a birth rate of fifteen per thousand. If the Chinese can attain it, their birth rates will be as low as any in Europe and close to the level required for zero population growth.

ENVIRONMENTAL DECAY

In the industrial private enterprise countries and in Russia and Eastern Europe, the bulk of economic growth goes into higher output per person. The problem there is increasingly the cost of growth in terms of externalities: congestion, pollution, and ugliness.

Japan, while growing spectacularly, has enshrouded itself in some of the worst smog in the world. From the rapid growth of the Japanese GNP in the 1960s we should subtract a substantial price for the drastic deterioration of her beautiful environment. At the same time, Britain's slow growth in the 1960s is partially offset by the fact that during the same decade the brown London fog disappeared and people in the Midlands could see clear, blue sky once more.

STABILITY

The rate of economic growth is intimately associated with economic stability. At least in the West, periods of slow economic growth are almost always times of widespread unemployment. At the same time, attempts to grow faster than the available resources and technology can permit have consistently ended in inflation. Table 19.9 compares unemployment rates and rates of inflation in two recent periods for some of the countries we have been following in this chapter.

THE COMMUNIST WORLD

The Communist countries are conspicuous omissions from both tables. The reason is that data are not available for either variable for those countries. Unemployment is a minor problem in those countries, however. The usual situation is a labor shortage. Students of the Communist countries often report that labor is hoarded, and effectively wasted, by managers concerned with meeting their output quotas. In addition, there are undoubtedly large pockets of misplaced workers, especially in agriculture. But workers who want work and can't find it are rare in the Communist countries.

There is a good reason why. Government officials determine the levels of investment and government purchases directly, and they have

TABLE 19.9   Unemployment and inflation in selected countries

COUNTRY	UNEMPLOYMENT RATE (Adjusted to U.S. concepts)		AVERAGE ANNUAL RATE OF INCREASE IN PRICES[1]	
	1969	1971	1960–1970	1967–1972
United States	3.5%	5.9%	2.5%	3.7%
France	2.1	2.7	4.0	4.8
Germany	0.8	0.7	3.2	4.4
United Kingdom	3.7	5.3	3.6	5.2
Japan	1.1	1.3	4.4	3.8
Brazil	n.a.		37.6	17.5
Ethiopia	n.a.		2.0	1.4
Iran	n.a.		1.1	3.0
India	n.a.		5.5	3.6
Indonesia	n.a.		114.0[2]	25.3

[1] Gross national product deflators.

[2] 1965–70.

enough control over consumer incomes to determine the level of consumption as well. If the bureaucrats make the correct judgements, they should be able to assure full employment. Actually, the Communist countries have been so hell-bent for growth that their main problem has been to scale down government purchases, investment, and consumption to levels that are feasible.

They have experienced some inflation, but it is well hidden. The prices of all goods and services bought and sold in official transactions are fixed. The problems that appear as inflation in the West turn up in the Communist countries as shortages—of housing, raw materials, and many other things. There has been a mild inflation of official prices, and visitors report considerable inflation in the unofficial private markets of Eastern Europe and Russia. Undoubtedly, these problems would be more severe without the all-embracing controls of the Communist world.

INSTABILITY IN THE WEST

Unemployment and inflation have been regular events in the industrial private enterprise countries over the last century or more. In the postwar years, unemployment has been much less severe than it was before World War II, but it still cannot be ignored. Different countries have made different tradeoffs between the two problems.

The United States has almost always had more unemployment and less inflation than the other private enterprise, industrial countries. This was clearly the case during the boom of 1969 and the recession of 1971. Indeed, for the whole of the 1960s, our unemployment rates were higher than those of any of the countries compared (except that Britain had unemployment rates similar to ours in 1967–1969). Part of the reason for the low unemployment rates in Europe was that many of the temporary jobs were filled by Spaniards, Algerians, Yugoslavs, and Turks. A recession in Germany or France meant that fewer of these people could migrate and more were left on the farms of Southern Europe. Not many Frenchmen or Germans lost their jobs. No such explanation is possible in Japan, but there the *nenkyo* system prevails, in which the large firms retain anyone they hire as part of their permanent staffs regardless of economic conditions. Ordinary factory workers get "tenure" in large Japanese corporations. In addition to all this, the United States has greater interregional and interindustry mobility than do most of the other countries in Table 19.9. This mobility almost necessarily means a higher level of unemployment during periods of prosperity. Many of our unemployed are people who have quit one job and are looking for another.

Yet in spite of all these quibbles, you can't come away from Table 19.9 without the feeling that America has put a higher value on stable prices, and a lower value on full employment, than have most of the other economically advanced countries.

UNEMPLOYMENT AND INFLATION IN THE THIRD WORLD

Both problems, unemployment and inflation, are more severe in the Third World. We don't have comparable unemployment figures there, but they are undoubtedly high. The *barrios* are filled with unemployed people or people working at unproductive jobs who are waiting for a chance at the good life in the modern sectors of their economies. The high unemployment rates in the Third World are seldom due to depression. They are a by-product of economic growth.

Inflation is also a common, though not inevitable, part of life in the Third World. Argentina, Chile, and Uruguay are in the same category as Brazil and Indonesia, shown in Table 19.9. The extreme inflations in some Third World countries arise basically from the limited ability of their governments to collect taxes. Their investment and government service goals greatly exceed what they can collect from their people. They turn to their central banks for the rest. After many years of this sort of policy, the people of Brazil have come to expect galloping inflation. They sell and buy goods or take jobs on the assumption that prices will rise twenty percent or so in the next year. The result is that ending an inflation becomes very costly. A country with a twenty-year record of inflation finds it almost impossible to stop.

PUTTING IT ALL TOGETHER

How does it all come out? America has one of the highest per capita levels of GNP, and almost certainly the highest consumption per person, in the world. We also have slightly more leisure than most of the rest of the world, and a good deal more space and access to education and information. We have as wide a range of choices and as much freedom as anyone. Our good fortune is quite equally distributed, except perhaps in the area of health care.

On the other hand, our central cities are deteriorating faster than most, we have dirtier air and water than much of the industrial world, and we have achieved one of the highest crime rates. Our economic growth is relatively slow today, though over the whole past century we have done as well as anyone on that score (largely because the great wars were fought elsewhere). We have less inflation, but more unemployment, than most industrial countries do, though some of the Third World's big cities outdo us in both.

You must decide for yourself how these comparisons add up. It all depends on your personal values. We probably do have one advantage over much of the world, however. We *can* improve in most of the areas where we have not performed well. The United States can and probably will clean up its air, water, and cities in your lifetime. And we can and probably will attain more general access to good health care. We might be able to grow faster, too, if we really want to, though that goal seems to be less and less popular.

It does not seem possible for the countries of Western Europe or Japan to provide their people with more space. They could improve their educational opportunities, but their access to information seems bound to be more limited than ours so long as they speak a dozen different languages. The Communist countries can, and probably will, give their people more choice as consumers and workers. But they are not likely to attain the personal freedom available in the West, short of a revolution.

It is hardest to be optimistic about the Third World. Some countries, such as Mexico, Iran, and Malaysia, have a good chance of getting on the industrial gravy train. The oil-producing countries and perhaps some of the others with reserves of scarce natural resources may be able to turn their temporary luck into permanent physical and human capital. And China may be able to attain steady growth while limiting its population if it can avoid the revolutions that have stopped its growth periodically in the past. If China does so, it will be by means of a degree of regimentation that few in the West would accept. But for about a third of the world, the prospects must seem dim even to the most optimistic of people. If there really is a desperate crisis waiting for us in the next few decades, the Third World is its most likely setting.

STUDY QUESTIONS

1   Rank the great powers in order of what you estimate to be their influence in international decisions. Now rank them by their total GNPs. How do your two rankings compare? (Mine are almost identical.) Why should they be similar?

2   What are the *barrios* discussed in this chapter? Who lives in them? What are the income levels, unemployment rates, and living conditions

like there? Why do so many people move into the *barrios*? Would those people be better off if they were prevented from moving into the *barrios*?

3 In some respects the comparisons in this chapter are unfair. Different countries have differing endowments to begin with. For instance, no matter what policies the Europeans and Japanese adopt, they cannot possibly provide for the amounts of space per person available in the United States. How do you think the United States stacks up in view of what it has to work with? Evaluate U.S. performance in terms of its potential in each of the following areas:

□ medical care

□ inequality

□ education

□ unemployment

□ inflation

4 A decade and a half ago, Americans were very concerned about the rapid rate of economic growth in the Soviet Union compared with that in the United States. How do you feel about that now? Does the moderately faster growth of the USSR concern you? What about the much faster growth of Japan? What about the disappointing growth of India?

5 Where would you prefer to live today if you had your present skills and knowledge and complete freedom to choose? (You may assume that you are fluent in the language of whatever country you choose.) Where do you think you would prefer to live in 1990?

FURTHER READING
Good descriptions of several major economies appear in Clair Wilcox, et al., *Economies of the World Today*, 2nd ed. (New York: Harcourt Brace Jovanovich, 1966). It contains chapters on Russia, Britain, China, India, and Nigeria. For a slightly more analytical approach, see Gregory Grossman, *Economic Systems* (Englewood Cliffs, N.J.: Prentice-Hall, 1966). It contains a brief discussion of planning in several Western European countries and chapters on Russia and Yugoslavia.

A good place to read further on the Western European countries is Moisei M. Postan, *An Economic History of Western Europe, 1945–1964* (London: Methuen, 1967). William Moskoff has compiled a fascinating collection of articles on the whole range of economic policy from the various industrial private enterprise economies, entitled *Comparative National Economic Policies* (Lexington, Mass.: Heath, 1973). Angus

Maddison, *Economic Growth in Japan and the USSR* (New York: Norton, 1969) not only offers a good discussion of the two economies in its title, but also contains many international comparisons of the sort used in this chapter. Perhaps the best brief paperback reading on Russia is Robert W. Campbell's *Soviet-Type Economies: The Performance and Evolution* 3rd ed. (Boston: Houghton Mifflin, 1974). On China, see Walter Galenson and N. R. Chen, *The Chinese Economy Under Communism* (Chicago: Aldine, 1969). Angus Maddison has done another fine job of summarizing the growth experience of many Third World countries in his *Economic Progress and Policy in Developing Countries* (New York: Norton, 1971). There are many other books on the developing countries. A good one is Jagdish Bhagwati, *The Economics of Underdeveloped Countries* (New York: McGraw-Hill, 1966). For a non-quantitative, well-written, and fairly angry approach, see Barbara Ward, *The Rich Nations and the Poor Nations* (New York: Norton, 1962).

GLOSSARY

accelerator principle: the notion that the level of investment depends on the rate of change in GNP rather than on the level of GNP. It implies that if GNP is stable, investment will drop. This almost assures that an uncontrolled economy will be unstable.

AFL–CIO: a federation of unions—not a union itself—which attempts to represent organized labor before the public and to settle jurisdictional disputes among its member unions.

aggregate demand: total planned or intended expenditures; the sum of consumption, investment, and government purchases.

alternative product function: a function that shows the alternative combinations of products that a country could have, given its endowment of factors of production and its technology.

antitrust law: the body of American law that has been used to preserve competition and prevent monopoly in the unregulated portion of the economy; the most important antitrust rules today are the prohibitions of collusion and anticompetitive mergers.

arbitrage: taking advantage of price differences within a market by buying at the low price and selling at the high price. As a result of arbitrage, price differences for the same good cannot persist on well-organized competitive markets.

arbitration: a situation in which parties to a dispute agree to accept the decision of a neutral third party; It is often used to settle grievances under union contracts but seldom used to determine major contract provisions.

asset: something of value. In a balance sheet an asset is something owned by the firm.

average propensity to consume: the proportion of GNP used in consumption. It is equal to the total consumption divided by total GNP.

balance of payments: the total receipts a country gets from the rest of the world minus the total payments it makes to the rest of the world.

balance of payments on current account: total exports of good and services plus gifts from abroad, minus total imports of goods and services and our grants and gifts to foreigners.

balance of trade: total exports minus total imports.

balance sheet: an accounting statement showing the assets, liabilities, and equity of a firm at a specified date.

bank: a business institution whose main function is to accept deposits and to extend credit through the making of loans and the purchase of securities.

bank reserves: a bank's cash and deposits at other banks. In the case of members of the Federal Reserve System, the deposits must be at Federal Reserve banks.

barrios: districts housing extremely low-income persons that exist in and around many cities in the Third World. Many of the inhabitants are former peasants hoping for a chance in the modern, industrial world.

barter: the exchange of goods for other goods rather than for money.

bond: a long-term debt instrument of a corporation or a government. It ordinarily involves a legally enforceable promise to pay a specified amount of interest and to pay off a specified principal at maturity.

built-in stabilizers: elements of the federal budget that automatically dampen fluctuations in the level of economic activity. For instance, given tax rates, government tax receipts will rise during a boom and decline during a slump. As a result, disposable income and consumption fluctuate less than GNP.

capacity GNP: the approximate maximum peacetime GNP attainable, given our population, capital stock, resources, technology, and economic organization. We run at or near capacity in years of full employment.

capital: (1) as a factor of production, all man-made productive resources, including buildings, machinery, inventories, but not stocks, bonds, mortgages, or money. (2) in the balance sheet, owners' equity.

capital formation: the process of saving and investment by which the man-made resources of the economy are increased.

capital gain: an increase in the value of an asset. If you buy a stock at $100 and it goes up in value to $150, you have a capital gain of $50.

capitalized value: the present value of a constant income expected to continue indefinitely into the future. It is equal to the expected annual income divided by the going rate of return.

cartel: an agreement to prevent competition. The term is commonly applied to government-enforced agreements.

central bank: a banker's bank that holds commercial bank reserve deposits, extends credit to commercial banks, and controls the supply of money and credit. The Federal Reserve System serves as the American central bank.

certificate of deposit: a deposit at a commercial bank that can be converted into cash only after a specified period, such as a year.

closed shop: situation in which an employer can employ only union members.

The union has the power to determine who gets the job and how many workers there will be in the field overall. Made illegal by the Taft–Hartley Act, though some apprenticeship and hiring-hall arrangements have the same effect.

cobweb theorem: the theory of a competitive market in which output takes a long time to produce, and producers, when they first make output decisions, assume that the prices then prevailing will continue to apply. As a result, they produce alternately too much and too little; output and prices may fluctuate indefinitely.

collusion: secret illegal agreements. In antitrust, collusion refers to agreements to fix prices, rig bids, allocate customers, or in some other way to restrain competition.

command economy: an economy in which the main economic decisions are made by central authorities.

commercial bank: a bank that holds demand deposits (checking deposits).

Common Market: see *European Economic Community.*

common stock: a generalized share in the ownership of a corporation, which carries voting rights and the right to participate in dividends distributed, though normally the corporation has no obligation to pay common dividends.

comparative advantage: a situation in which one person or country is relatively more productive in one occupation or industry than in others, or where a person or country is at a smaller disadvantage in one occupation or industry than in others. If country A does twice as well as country B in making X but three times as well in making Y, A has a comparative advantage in Y, and B has a comparative advantage in X.

concentration ratio: the percentage of total sales in an industry accounted for by a certain number of leading firms. In the United States it is usually based on the top four or top eight firms.

conglomerate: a firm that does business in many different and unrelated industries.

Consumer Price Index: a widely used price index produced by the Bureau of Labor Statistics, which shows the value of the goods making up the annual budget of an urban working-class family. If the same goods in the same amount that cost $5,000 in 1967 came to $8,000 in 1975, then the consumer price index for 1975 would be $8,000 as a percentage of $5,000, or 160.

consumption: the use of goods and services to satisfy current human wants.

consumption function: the relationship between GNP and consumption.

corporation: a form of business which is legally different from its owners (the stockholders). Its owners usually have limited liability; they can lose no more than what they invest in the firm. The corporation can have unlimited life because it does not depend on any particular stockholders for its existence.

cost: the amount given up for the inputs used in production. It includes the opportunity costs of resources owned by the producer. See *opportunity cost.*

Cost–benefit analysis: an attempt to estimate the total costs and total benefits to society of individual elements of public programs. It is applied to public expenditure programs in an attempt to determine their optimal size.

craft union: a union made up of workers with a particular skill regardless of where they work, such as the carpenters or airline pilots.

currency: (1) money in the form of coin or bills; (2) on international exchanges, the money of a particular country.

curve: a relationship between two variables expressed as a line on a graph. It may or may not be a straight line.

debt: a legally binding promise to pay.

deflation: a situation in which the average level of prices falls. In this century it has occurred only in severe depressions.

deflationary gap: the difference between GNP and aggregate demand at full employment if aggregate demand falls short of GNP at that level.

demand: the amounts of a commodity that people are ready and willing to buy.

demand deposits: checking deposits. They are payable on demand any time the bank is open and can be freely transferred to other persons.

depletion allowance: an amount that mining and oil companies are allowed to subtract from their receipts to compensate them for mineral reserves used up through production.

depreciation: the decline in the value of capital due to its wearing out or becoming obsolete. Although the building or equipment may be useful until it is scrapped, accountants usually write off some of its value each year during its lifetime rather than writing it all off when it is scrapped.

depression: a situation in which GNP falls far below its peacetime capacity level. Associated with large-scale unemployment.

devaluation: reducing the value of a nation's currency on international exchange markets.

diminishing returns: an economic principle that holds that if some inputs are held fixed and another input is increased, we will ultimately reach the point where output per unit of variable input declines. The same principle also implies that after some point, the marginal product must decline.

discount rate: (1) the going rate of return used in calculating the present value of an income-earning asset. (2) the interest rate charged by the Federal Reserve System when it makes discounts and advances (loans to commercial banks).

discounted value: same as present value.

discretionary fiscal policy: changing the federal budget to affect the level of economic activity. An alternative is to determine government purchases and transfer programs on their merits, set taxes that will yield full employment without inflation in an average year, and rely on built-in stablizers to damp booms and depressions automatically.

discretionary monetary policy: a monetary policy under which conscious decisions are taken to expand or contract credit as economic conditions seem to warrant—as opposed to an automatic monetary policy, in which the money supply is increased at a constant rate roughly proportional to the rate of growth in full-employment GNP

disposable income: the amount of income that persons have to spend on consumption or to save. It is equal to personal income minus personal taxes.

dividends: payments by corporations to their common and preferred stockholders. They are usually paid out of profits but often do not include all profits.

easy money policy: a situation in which the Federal Reserve board allows the supply of money and credit to grow rapidly compared with the GNP. It is usually accompanied by low interest rates.

economies of scale: the tendency in most industries for cost per unit to be lower for larger-scale firms, out to a point. In most industries there is a *minimum efficient scale* beyond which there is no further tendency for costs to fall as firms become larger.

elastic demand: a demand function such that the percentage change in quantity is greater than the percentage change in price. With such a demand curve, a fall in price will lead to a more than proportional increase in quantity; therefore, the total receipts of sellers increase.

elasticity of demand: the percentage change in quantity sought by buyers with a given percentage change in price, or

$$\frac{\Delta Q}{Q} \Big/ \frac{\Delta P}{P}$$

entrepreneur: the person who undertakes a business enterprise; the ultimate decision maker, who takes any profit or loss that results.

entry: the appearance of new firms in an industry other than by merger. It is the means by which long-run equilibrium conditions are assured in pure competition.

equilibrium: a state in which forces are in balance so that there is no tendency for the situation to change.

equilibrium GNP: the level of GNP where aggregate demand just equals GNP.

equilibrium price: in a purely competitive market, a price at which the quantity demanded and the quantity supplied are the same, so that there is no tendency for the price to change.

equilibrium quantity: in a purely competitive market, the quantity that corresponds to the equilibrium price in both the demand and supply functions.

equity: (1) fairness. (2) in accounting, the value of the firm to its owners; sometimes referred to as "net worth" or "capital." It equals assets minus liabilities.

European Economic Community (EEC): the Common Market, a group of European countries that have adopted common tariff policies towards the rest of the world and free trade among themselves. Originally (1957) they were Belgium, France, West Germany, Italy, Luxembourg, and the Netherlands. Expanded in 1972 to include Great Britain, Ireland, Denmark, Switzerland, and Austria.

excess reserves: a bank's cash and deposits at other banks in excess of what it must have to meet the reserve requirement.

exchange controls: direct government controls over payments abroad and receipts from abroad. Such controls were common in the first decade after World War II.

excise tax: a tax on a particular good, such as cigarettes. Although the manufacturer pays the tax to the government, its cost is shifted to the consumers, at least in the long run.

export: sale of a nation's goods to customers in foreign countries.

external benefits: benefits from an economic activity (either production or consumption) that accrue to someone other than those making the economic decisions; for instance, the reduced danger of my house burning down if you have fire protection.

external costs: costs from an economic activity (either production or consumption) that fall on others besides those making the economic decisions; for instance, the dirtying of laundry by industrial soot.

externality: a cost or benefit, arising from an economic decision, that falls on someone else besides the decision maker. Externalities will usually be ignored in economic decisions unless the government intervenes.

extractive industries: industries devoted to extracting products from nature, such as agriculture, forestry, fishing, and mining.

factor markets: the markets on which the services of factors of production are bought and sold.

factors of production: real productive resources; often divided into land, labor, and capital.

fallacy of composition: the belief, often mistaken, that what is true of each individual must be true of the group.

featherbedding: the practice of requiring employers to retain unneeded workers or preventing them from adopting labor-saving devices and techniques. It is most common in skilled craft unions, especially where they face declining markets.

Fed: nickname for the Federal Reserve System.

Federal Deposit Insurance Corporation (FDIC): a federal agency that insures bank deposits up to $20,000 each against losses due to bank failure.

Federal Reserve System: a semipublic agency that controls the supply of money and credit. It consists of twelve regional bankers' banks that hold the reserve deposits of member banks, extend credit to them, and clear checks between cities. The system is governed by the Federal Reserve Board, appointed by the President.

firm: a group of productive facilities under common ownership and control. It may consist of one plant or many. Firms buy factor services, use them in production, and sell the resulting goods and services.

fiscal policy: control of the government budget with the purpose of regulating the level of economic activity.

flow concept: a quantity that can be measured only over a period of time, such as income, consumption, or profits.

free rider: a person who benefits from a public good but does not pay for it. The term originated in trade unions, where it referred to persons who benefited from union successes but refused to join.

free trade: a policy of imposing no restrictions on imports and exports.

full employment: a situation in which unemployment rates are near their normal peacetime minimum (about four percent in the United States but lower in most other advanced countries).

function: a relationship between two or more variables. May be expressed as a schedule, a curve, or an equation.

futures contract: an agreement by which the seller promises to deliver a specified amount of an item at a future date indicated in the contract.

General Agreement on Tariffs and Trade (GATT): an international system under which the major non-Communist trading countries have negotiated many multilateral agreements reducing trade restrictions since World War II.

ghetto: originally, the section of old European cities were Jews were required to live. More commonly today, the area where blacks or other minorities live.

GNP: gross national product.

gold standard: the international payments system that prevailed in the late nineteenth and early twentieth centuries, whereby the major trading countries fixed the values of their currencies in terms of gold and stood ready to buy or sell indefinite amounts of gold at those fixed rates. It meant free international payments at fixed exchange rates.

goods: products; often included in the phrase "goods and services," which refers to the output of society.

grant-in-aid: a transfer payment from one level of government to another, such as federal grants to state and local governments or state grants to local governments.

gross investment: total expenditures for plant, equipment, and additions to inventory.

gross national product: the total output of final goods and services in the nation as a whole. Equal to the sum of consumption, investment, government purchases, and exports minus imports. Also equals the total value added at all plants in the country. Also equals national income plus indirect business taxes plus depreciation.

holding company: a corporation whose main assets are the stocks of other corporations.

horizontal equity: fairness in the taxation of persons with the same income.

household: a group of people who consume jointly. This generally implies that most of the incomes they earn are pooled. Households own most of the factors of production either directly, as in the case of labor, or indirectly, in that households own firms.

human capital: the education, health, skills and experience that make a human being more productive. It is the result of investments in such things as education, health care, and on-the-job training.

import: a good brought into the country from abroad.

import quotas: regulations that specify the maximum quantity of a good that can be imported.

income effect: the effect of a change in real income, due to a price change, on the quantity purchased. A fall in the price of a product makes you a little richer and you will probably buy more of all products, including that one.

industry: all the plants that produce a certain product.

industrial union: a union made up of workers of a particular industry regardless of their specific skills; e.g., auto workers, steel workers, or coal miners.

inelastic demand: a demand function such that a change in price will lead to a less-than-proportional change in the quantity bought. If demand is inelastic, a fall in price will lead to a fall in the total receipts of sellers.

inflation: generally rising prices. Not all prices must rise for us to have an inflation, but the average price level must rise.

inflationary gap: the difference between GNP and aggregate demand at full employment if aggregate demand exceeds GNP at that level.

in-kind transfers: programs in which the government gives goods or services rather than money; they include medicare, medicaid, food stamps, and public housing.

interest rate: (1) a fixed charge of so many percent per year on any kind of debt (bonds, loans, mortgages) or on deposits (saving deposits, savings and loan association shares, etc.). (2) more generally, the going rate of return used in discounting future incomes of income-earning assets, or in determining the rate of investment.

International Monetary Fund (IMF): an international organization of which all major non-Communist countries are members. Its purpose is to facilitate international payments settlements and to increase international reserves.

international reserves: a nation's holdings of foreign currencies and gold with which it can support the value of its currency.

inventory: the stock of materials on hand or in process, or of finished goods on hand; part of the capital stock.

investment: (1) the use of goods and services to add to the capital stock; includes new buildings and equipment and additions to inventories but excludes new stocks, bonds, and mortgages. (2) in bank balance sheets, the securities (bonds) owned by the bank.

labor: as a factor of production, all human effort available for use in production, including self-employed as well as paid workers and white-collar as well as blue.

labor force: the number of people working or actively seeking work.

laissez faire: ("less-ay fair") a policy whereby the government enforces contracts and prevents fraud and violence but leaves economic decisions to individuals.

land: as a factor of production, all natural resources, including fertility of the soil, location, minerals, original forests, climate, harbors, and water.

liability: a debt, a legally binding obligation.

limited liability: an essential characteristic of most corporations, it means that the stockholders are not liable for the debts of the corporation. In most corporations, stockholders cannot lose any more than what they paid for the stock.

liquid asset: cash or something easily convertible into cash on short notice.

liquidity: ability to meet current obligations as they arise. It depends on holdings of cash or assets that can quickly be turned into cash, as compared with obligations that can come due in the near future.

long run: a period so long that factors of production can enter or leave an industry, firms can enter or leave, and new plant scales can be adopted, in response to changes in demand.

Lorenz curve: a curve showing the percentage of total income or wealth going to cumulatively richer percentages of all families. That is, it shows the percentage of all income or wealth for the poorest 20 percent, the poorest 40 percent, etc. The more bowed the curve, the greater the inequality.

macroeconomics: the study of the overall level of economic activity and its determinants; such issues as inflation, unemployment, and their control.

marginal: pertaining to an infinitely small change.

marginal product: the change in output that goes with a small change in one input, all other inputs being held constant.

marginal propensity to consume (mpc): the rate at which consumption changes when GNP changes. It is equal to the change in consumption induced by a change in GNP, divided by that change in GNP.

marginal propensity to save (mps): the rate of change in saving plus taxes with a change in GNP. It is equal to the change in saving plus taxes induced by a change in GNP, divided by that change in GNP. It is also equal to $1 - \text{mpc}$.

marginal revenue: the addition to a seller's receipts due to selling one more unit. In the case of monopoly, marginal revenue will be less than price because of the downward-sloping demand curve faced by the monopolist.

margin requirements: the Federal Reserve System's rules governing the percentage of the value of stocks and bonds that their owners must put up. They limit the amounts that stock- or bondholders can borrow to carry those securities.

market: the place where sellers compete for a common group of customers and within which prices are determined. Markets may be local (as in residential housing) or worldwide (as in coffee).

mercantilism: the economic system of the states of Western Europe in early modern times. It involved central regulation of the national economy with the goal of increasing national power.

merger: the combination of two or more business firms into a single firm.

microeconomics: the study of firms, households, and individual factor and product markets; in other words, the study of the individual elements of the economy.

minimum efficient scale: the smallest size at which a firm can attain minimum possible cost per unit. In most industries, costs per unit fall as size increases until the minimum efficient scale is reached. Firms larger than minimum efficient scale do not have any systematic cost advantage over firms of minimum efficient scale.

minimum wage law: a law prohibiting wage rates below a specified level in covered industries.

money: anything generally accepted as a means of payment.

money supply: usually defined as currency plus demand deposits (M_1). Sometimes also includes time deposits at commercial banks (M_2) and, less commonly, also deposits at mutual savings banks and savings and loan associations (M_3).

monetarist: an economist who believes that fluctuations in the quantity of money are the primary causes of economic fluctuations. Monetarists tend to doubt the effectiveness of fiscal policy except where it affects the money supply.

monetary policy: the control of the supply of money and credit with the purpose of controlling the level of economic activity.

monopoly: the situation in which there is only one seller in a market (see *pure monopoly*). The term is often used loosely wherever large firms appear to have control over prices, even when there is more than one.

monopsony: the situation in which there is only one buyer in the market.

multiplier: the ratio of the change in equilibrium GNP to the initial change in investment, government purchases, or consumption that caused it. The multiplier is equal to $1/1-\text{mpc} = 1/\text{mps}$.

multiplier effect: the ultimate effect of a change in investment or government purchases on the equilibrium level of GNP. An initial increase of a dollar will lead to more than a dollar increase in equilibrium GNP because of the induced increase in consumption as GNP rises.

national income: the total of all payments for factors used in production. It equals gross national product minus depreciation and minus indirect taxes.

negative income tax: a proposal under which the government would make payments to those with incomes below a specified level, making up part of the difference between earned incomes and that level.

net investment: gross investment minus depreciation; the amount the nation's capital stock increases during a year. Net investment can be negative if our spending on new plant, equipment, and inventories is less than depreciation.

net national product: gross national product minus depreciation. It is the amount we could consume year after year without depleting our stock of capital.

normative economics: statements about what is desirable or undesirable in economic life; they consist of value judgments and therefore are not subject to proofs by logic or empirical study.

oligopoly: the situation in which a few firms dominate a market.

open market operations: purchase or sale of government securities by the Federal Reserve Banks with the goal of expanding or contracting the supply of money and credit.

opportunity cost: the cost of a resource in terms of what is given up by using it. Its opportunity cost is equal to what it would be worth in its best alternative employment.

partnership: two or more persons in business together. Each partner has unlimited liability for the obligations of the firm. The firm has limited life, because it must be reorganized whenever a partner dies or withdraws.

personal income: total of all income payments to persons before personal taxes. Equal to national income minus corporate profits and social security taxes, but plus dividends, government transfer payments, and interest on the public debt.

Phillips curve: the realtionship observed over history between the unemployment rate and the rate of increase in the price level. In general, rates of inflation have been less, the greater the rate of unemployment.

physiocrats: a group of eighteenth-century French thinkers who promoted a policy of laissez faire. Adam Smith was strongly influenced by them.

plant: the productive facilities at a particular location owned by a particular firm; most produce only one or a few products, but some produce many different goods. In a broad sense a plant may be an office, a farm, a store, a mine, a factory, or a railroad.

positive economics: the body of statements about what the economic world is like. These statements can be proven right or wrong by logic or by empirical tests.

preferred stock: a form of corporate stock in which the stockholder is promised a certain dividend before any dividend is paid on common stock. If the firm should be dissolved, the preferred stockholder has a specified claim on the firm's equity before the common stockholders get anything. Preferred stock is commonly "cumulative preferred," meaning that any back dividends must be paid on preferred before a dividend can be paid on common; nevertheless, a corporation is not bankrupt merely because it cannot pay preferred dividends.

present value: the amount you would pay now for an asset that is expected to yield a given stream of future income in order to earn the same return you can earn elsewhere. For an asset expected to yield a constant income per year indefinitely into the future, the present value is equal to the expected annual income divided by the going rate of return.

price index: a measure of average price level. It ordinarily shows the value of a fixed market basket of goods in one year expressed as a percentage of the value of the same market basket of goods in a base year.

primary industries: extractive industries, those devoted to extracting products from nature, such as agriculture, forestry, fishing, and mining.

product: a good or commodity, part of the output of society.

productivity: output per unit of input; commonly output per man-hour.

profit: receipts of a firm in excess of its costs. As used by economists, profit does not include the opportunity cost of the capital put up by the owners of the firm—that is a cost. In the accounting statement of a firm, however, opportunity cost will be included in profit.

progressive tax: a tax that collects a higher percentage of income as taxes, the higher the taxpayer's income. Incomes are more equally distributed after a progressive tax than before.

proportional tax: a tax that collects the same percentage of incomes from each income class. Incomes are distributed as equally after a proportional tax as before.

proprietorship: one person in business. The law makes no distinction between that person and his business. As a result, the proprietor is liable for the obligations of the firm up to the full extent of his property.

proxy: a document with which a stockholder can assign his voting right to someone else in a stockholder's election.

public good: a good or service that anyone can enjoy without diminishing anyone else's enjoyment of it, and that it is impossible to exclude anyone from enjoying.

pure competition: a situation in which buyers and sellers are so many and so small that no one of them can affect the price. For each buyer and each seller the price will be the same regardless of how much he buys or sells.

pure monopoly: a situation in which there is only one seller in the market and no possibility of entry.

real GNP: GNP measured in dollars of constant purchasing power; it corresponds to the total physical output of the economy.

real income: income measured in dollars of constant purchasing power. If your money income stays the same, but the average level of prices rises, your real income (standard of living) falls.

recession: a mild depression; it usually means some fall in real GNP, and unemployment rates of five to seven percent.

regressive tax: a tax that collects a smaller percentage of one's income in taxes, the higher one's income. Incomes are less equally distributed after a regressive tax than before.

regulation: government control of business. In the utilities, transportation, and communications, government agencies usually control prices, service, and entry.

reserve requirement: the reserves that a bank is obliged to hold, usually expressed as a percentage of deposits.

reserves: see *bank reserves* and *international reserves.*

revenue sharing: an arrangement whereby the federal government makes transfers to state and local governments with few, if any, limits on their use. The idea is to take advantage of the superior tax-raising power of the federal government while preserving state and local incentives to keep costs low.

right-to-work laws: laws prohibiting both the union shop and the closed shop.

sales tax: a tax of a certain percentage of retail sales. When applied to all goods but not to professional services, it is a regressive tax; when food is exempt it is roughly proportional.

saving: refraining from spending income on consumption; producing without consuming.

saving function: the relationship between GNP and saving plus taxes.

savings: the accumulated result of past saving; they may take the form of cash, deposits, securities, or real capital (buildings, equipment, and inventories).

Say's law: the belief that there would always be enough aggregate demand to assure full employment. An increase in society's resources would automatically be accompanied by an equal increase in aggregate demand.

secondary industries: industries devoted to processing raw materials and fabricating goods; manufacturing and construction.

securities: stocks and bonds.

short run: a period so short that inputs are committed to their present employment. In the short run, a rise in demand must be met by the equipment and skills already available.

solvency: the ability of a firm to meet its debts.

special drawing rights (SDRs): an international currency that the major trading nations have agreed to accept in settlement of balance of payments deficits. They are created each year by the International Monetary Fund and assigned to various countries according to a predetermined formula.

stock: the ownership of a corporation divided into shares which give the owners an interest in its assets and, usually, voting power.

stock concept: a quantity that can be measured accurately only at an instant in time, such as assets, liabilities, the population, or the public debt.

suppressed inflation: a situation in which aggregate demand exceeds GNP at full employment, but price and wage increases are prevented by government controls. The results are shortages, black markets, and, if taken far enough, the elimination of incentives to work for money.

tariff: a tax on imports of a particular good.

tertiary industries: industries devoted to exchange, such as transportation, wholesaling, and retailing.

theory: a body of thought which derives the logical implications from a set of assumptions. It is the usual source of hypotheses empirically tested by scientists.

Third World: the countries that have neither Communist nor highly industrialized private enterprise economies. Most have majorities that are still peasants or artisans.

tight money policy: the case in which the Fed keeps the supply of money and credit growing slowly compared with the growth in GNP. Usually accompanied by high interest rates.

time deposits: savings deposits at commercial banks.

trade union: an organization of workers in particular industries or having particular skills; usually organized to win better wages and working conditions for its members.

transfer payment: a payment for which no good or service is given in return. Government transfer payments, such as welfare or veterans' benefits, are a large part of the government budget and serve to redistribute income.

unemployment rate: the number of people seeking work expressed as a percentage of the labor force.

union shop: a situation in which an employer can hire anyone he wants, but new employees must join the union within a specified period.

urban renewal: a federal program which helps local governments to acquire large blocks of deteriorating property and resell it, redevelop it, or put it to public use.

value added: short for "value added in production," the value of the output of a plant minus the cost of goods and services received from other plants.

value judgment: a view about the desirability of a situation: whether something is good or bad. Value judgments cannot be proven right or wrong by logic or empirical test.

value of the marginal product: marginal product times the price of the product. What one more unit of input adds to the receipts of a competitive firm.

velocity of money: the ratio of GNP to the money supply.

vertical equity: fairness in the taxation of persons with different incomes.

welfare programs: direct payments of cash to the poor, under such programs as aid to dependent children, old age assistance, and state and local general assistance.

Index

Page references in boldface denote page containing illustrations.